MARX

Studies in Phenomenology and Existential Philosophy

MARX

A PHILOSOPHY OF
HUMAN REALITY

Michel Henry

TRANSLATED BY
Kathleen McLaughlin

Indiana University Press
Bloomington

Manufactured in the United States of America

Library of Congress Cataloging in Publication Data

Henry, Michel, 1922–
  Marx: a philosophy of human reality.

  (Studies in phenomenology and existential philosophy)
  Abridged translation of the two-volume work: Paris:
Gallimard, c1976.
  Includes index.
  1. Marx, Karl, 1818–1883.   2. Marxian economics.
I. Title.   II. Series.
HX39.5.H46132   1983   335.4'092'4   83-48067
ISBN 0-253-33680-5
1 2 3 4 5 87 86 85 84 83

CONTENTS

Foreword   vii

Translator's Note   xiii

Introduction: The Theory of Marx's Texts   1

1. The Critique of Political Essence: The 1843 Manuscript   17

2. The Humanism of the Young Marx   54

3. The Reduction of Totalities   86

4. The Determination of Reality   118

5. The Place of Ideology   160

6. The Transcendental Genesis of the Economy   190

7. The Reality of Economic Reality   224

8. The Radical Reduction of Capital to Subjectivity: $c = 0$ 265

Conclusion: Socialism   287

Notes   307

Foreword

This outstanding book, one of the first major studies of Marx's entire position, is notable for its unified reading, within the scope of a single theory, of the early philosophical and later predominantly economic aspects, in terms of an underlying concept of human being. More precisely, the considerable merit of this illuminating work is that it represents one of the few large-scale endeavors to demonstrate in detail, beyond mere assertion, that Marx is indeed fundamentally concerned with human being, in fact, with the real conditions of human individuality.

Michel Henry, a Frenchman, is Professor of Philosophy at the Université Paul Valéry in Montpellier, France. His competence, like Sartre's, is both literary and philosophical. He is the author of three novels: *Le jeune officier* (1954), *L'amour les yeux fermés* (1976), and *Le fils du roi* (1981). The second novel was awarded the Prix Renaudot, one of the major French literary awards in a country where good writing is taken very seriously. As a philosopher, Henry has written a series of articles and two other books, and his own work has been the subject of a book-length study.[1] *L'essence de la manifestation* (Paris: Presses universitaires de France, 1963), translated as *The Essence of Manifestation*, is a work of original philosophical thought. *Philosophie et Phénoménologie du Corps: Essai sur l'ontologie biranienne* (Paris: Presses universitaires de France, 1965), translated as *Philosophy and Phenomenology of the Body* (The Hague: Nijhoff, 1975), is a study of the thought of the early nineteenth-century philosopher and psychologist, Maine de Biran. The fact that the later-published study was in fact Henry's initial philosophical work provides an important indication of the continuity in the development of his own thought. The study of Maine de Biran deals with the theme of the body and of subjectivity in general, a perspective that Henry further develops in his essay on manifestation. Accordingly, his study of Marx represents a continuation of Henry's earlier interest in subjectivity, as here applied to the problem of social activity, especially as concerns forms of economic life.

Henry's treatment of Marx displays some unusual features. One such feature, which should be mentioned immediately, is the extraordinary richness of detail in which Henry elaborates his interpretation. The reason for the detailed nature of Henry's discussion is primarily methodological. The specific form of textual interpretation he employs is the so-called *lecture de textes*, literally, "the reading of the texts." This approach, uncommon in Anglo-Saxon scholarship but prevalent in continental circles, especially in France, can be described as an

immanent form of interpretation dependent for its development on close attention to indications present in the writings under study. Although interpretation
of this kind is not in itself specifically phenomenological, it does have obvious
affinities with the recent developments in hermeneutical theory as well as with
certain aspects of psychoanalysis, both of which are, of course, strongly interrelated in recent French structuralism and poststructuralism. But although the
general technique is widely applied in other areas, Henry's use of it here is
unusual in that, despite frequent claims to the contrary, close textual study of
Marx's writings is more the exception than the rule. More often than not, the
appearance of such study has been substituted for the real thing, most notably
perhaps in Althusser's quasi-structuralist reading of Marx. Althusser's well-
known antihumanism can be briefly described as a politically motivated response, on the philosophical plane, to the different forms of liberalization which
followed Stalin's death and his later denunciation by Khrushchev. In fact,
although not often named, a reaction against Althusser's antihumanist reading,
as well as a rejection of the latter's Stalinist penchant, is clearly apparent in
Henry's study. As a result, even if this is not Henry's primary purpose, his
essay is closely related to the efforts by Schaff and others to show that Althusser's supposedly strict textual reading of Marx's position is in fact largely
fanciful.

Henry begins his discussion with an intelligent inquiry into the conditions of
the interpretation of Marx's writings, a problem all too often treated parentheti-
cally or passed over in silence, although it is crucial for the comprehension of
the writings for several reasons, including their close relation to political doctrine. Here we can isolate three main themes. Marxism, to begin with, is
polemically defined by Henry as the series of misunderstandings concerning
Marx's position. This claim, for which he does not explicitly argue, is, to say the
least, controversial. It can, however, be supported by the historical accident of
the tardy publication of such important Marxian texts as the *Paris Manuscripts*
and the *Grundrisse*. In the context of the Marx debate, this fact means that a
number of Marx's major writings were unavailable to those who early on claimed
to speak in his name and whose views subsequently exercised a decisive influence on the shape of Marxism. Nevertheless, Marxists, including Engels,
Lenin, and others, have never hesitated to invoke Marx's authority as the
justification for their own views. In recent years, however, there has been
increasing emphasis in the discussion, for instance by Kołakowski, on important areas of disagreement between Marx on the one hand and various Marxists
on the other. The inference which follows is that Marx's views should be
interpreted solely in terms of his own texts, not through the eyes of his self-
appointed political heirs. In stressing the difference between Marx's view and
Marxism in this controversial manner, Henry helps to remove, and if not to
remove at least to reduce, a tremendous obstacle to the grasp of Marx's thought.

Second, Henry insists, Marx's theory is primarily a philosophical position.
This assertion, for which Henry argues only indirectly in the course of his

interpretation, is, of course, highly charged in the context of Marx scholarship, especially from the Marxist perspective, as a moment's reflection will show. Since Engels, there has been a widespread emphasis on the alleged discontinuity between philosophy, which is often assimilated to mere ideology in a manner not found in Marx's writings, and Marxism, which is held either to be a science, as in the views of Engels, Lenin, and Althusser, or at least to be nonphilosophical in character, as in the writings of Lukács and Korsch. Against this background, Henry's emphatic claim that Marx's position is philosophy, a view which has been heard with increasing frequency in the recent discussion, represents a denial of the adequacy of treating Marx's views as other than philosophical. And this claim further affects the evaluation of the Marxian position, which, to the extent that it is philosophy, as Henry and others insist, must be judged in terms of the preceding philosophical tradition, from which it differs in degree but not in kind, and which can hence no longer merely be ignored, as has mainly been the case in the Marx discussion.

The first and second theses, although important, function in Henry's interpretation in prolegomenal fashion, namely as conditions necessary to the elaboration of the overall argument. Henry's basic point is expressed in his third thesis, to whose demonstration the book as a whole is devoted, to wit, that Marx's fundamental insight concerns a theory of praxis. The suggestion itself is not novel, since it is one of the oldest themes in Marx scholarship, present at least since the end of the nineteenth century.[2] But although the importance of praxis for Marx's position has often been noted, or perhaps for that very reason, most commentators are content merely to invoke this term without further endeavor to attach a precise meaning to it. Precise discussions of praxis in general are few indeed.[3] Nor does this concept, surprisingly enough, seem to have been studied in detail very often in the Marx literature.[4] It is accordingly a major merit of Henry's work that, if it does not definitively complete the inquiry into the concept of praxis in Marx's thought, it carries our comprehension of this aspect of the position much farther than has previously been possible, and it does so often in new and interesting ways.

How does Henry understand Marx's concept of praxis? In broadest terms, Henry suggests that from the philosophical angle of vision Marx's contribution is to substitute for the traditional view of the individual as defined by its consciousness a conception of the real person as producer and consumer located in a social world. In his view of praxis, in other words, Marx proposes a view of human being in terms of the activity of the person in the social context. This view is, according to Henry, highly unlike that presented more often in the modern philosophical tradition in theories either uninterested in or incapable of grasping the concrete social context or the person's role in it.

This point is important, both for Marx studies and for philosophy in general. Henry's analysis of the Marxian concept of human being gains in interest when seen against the backdrop provided by the debate concerning it in the recent literature. In this debate, the most diverse claims have been made, such as that

Marx's view of the individual is the focus of his position (Fromm), that a view of individuality is absent and must be supplied lest the position "collapse" (Sartre), that the concept of human being present in the early, philosophical writings is absent in the later, mature, scientific thought (Althusser), and that Marx's interest is not in the individual at all but in the class (Sève). In this confusing and often confused, but significant, region of the Marx discussion, Henry's contribution is distinguished by the unusually detailed nature of his endeavor to demonstrate, in a manner far surpassing mere assertion and counterclaim, the nature and function of the concept of human being in Marx's thought.

Had Henry done no more, he would already have done a great deal. This is so even if the insistence on the importance of the concept of human being for Marx's position, or variants of this point, has been urged with increasing frequency in recent years, although not, to be sure, in such detail. But he goes further, to make a general philosophical claim on behalf of Marx's position, a claim which does not ignore, but precisely takes into account, the philosophical tradition. For Henry makes us aware of the sense in which Marx's view of human being can be regarded as a rethinking of the concept of subjectivity in a basically anti-Cartesian direction. More precisely, in terms of his concept of the person Marx opposes the abstract view of human being as reduced to an intellectual capacity, stressed by Descartes and others, including Kant.

This assessment of Marx's philosophical contribution is, in the context of the Marx discussion, doubly interesting, as concerns the general grasp of the relation between Marx's position and philosophy in general and as concerns the specific nature of Marx's supposed contribution. From the former perspective, Henry's assessment is interesting in that, rather than presenting Marx's position as an alternative to philosophy as such, a suggestion which is often but almost always vaguely made, Marx's view is presented as a valid alternative to one major form of philosophy. Perhaps even more significant in view of the usual depiction of Marxism as an economically oriented analysis of social reality oriented toward revolution is Henry's description of the philosophical nature of Marx's theory. For we have here a powerful, indeed formidable, effort to establish the startling claim that Marx's position is, in the final analysis, a metaphysics of the individual.

Finally, a word should be said about the form in which Henry's interpretation of Marx's thought is presented here. This new version of Henry's study, whose publication in 1976 aroused much discussion in French scholarly circles, has been largely rewritten and greatly shortened by the author especially for this translation. The result, made available in English by Kathleen McLaughlin's extremely faithful but equally supple translation, conserves the power and freshness of the French original in what is doubtless a conceptually more rigorous form of Henry's novel reading of Marx's entire position in terms of the concept of human individuality.

NOTES

1. See Gabrielle Dufour-Kowalska, *Michel Henry. Un Philosophe de la vie et de la praxis* (Paris: Vrin), 1980. For other studies of Henry's thought, see ibid., pp. 254–55.

2. See, for instance, B. Croce's early study, *La filosofia di Marx* (Florence: Sansoni), 1974; first published in 1899.

3. The obvious exception is Nicholas Lobkowicz's excellent study, *Theory and Practice: History of a Concept from Aristotle to Marx* (Notre Dame and London: University of Notre Dame Press), 1967. See also Kurt Röttges, *Kritik und Praxis: zur Geschichte des Kritikbegriffs von Kant bis Marx* (Berlin: de Gruyter), 1975.

4. Other than Henry's book, perhaps the most complete recent contribution to our understanding of Marx's view of praxis is found in Klaus Hartmann's book, although it is not directly focussed on this aspect of Marx's view, *Die Marx'sche Theorie* (Berlin: de Gruyter), 1970.

TOM ROCKMORE

Translator's Note

A brief analysis of some of the difficulties encountered in this translation may help to provide an orientation for the reader as he or she begins Michel Henry's *Marx*.

(1) Along with problems of a general nature related to translating a philosophical work coming out of a tradition quite distinct from that of English-language philosophy, it becomes apparent early in this text that the French terminology is itself as if superimposed on an underlying current of German philosophy. In the present work reference is frequently made in particular to Hegel, to Husserl, and to Heidegger, as is not uncommon in contemporary French philosophy. The author's broad familiarity with these philosophers allows him to incorporate their thought into the discussion, assuming on the part of the reader some knowledge of their work and of the implications of their terminology when applied to the philosophical problems treated in this book. So that, while at times these philosophers become the explicit object of the discussion (this is the case, in particular, for Hegel), in many other instances they provide the implicit backdrop against which the author's own arguments are formulated and developed. The latter case is more characteristic of references to Husserlian and Heideggerian terminology. For example, in coining the term *"historial"* to contrast with *"histoire,"* reference is made to the Heideggerian meditation on history and to the collusion there between the terms *Geschichte*, *Geschehen*, *Geschick*; for Henry, then, *"historial"* is an internal history as opposed to the external science of history, an essential history, which also involves the notion of destiny. Husserl's phenomenology underlies a great deal of the discussion, and readers familiar with Husserlian terminology will find that it is at once borrowed and transformed by Henry in this work. Notions such as eidetic analysis, the role of evidence, intuition, and the constitution of the object, and the overwhelming preoccupation with revealing the ground of true experience assume at once a specific reference to Husserl and, in the context of Henry's study of Marx, an implicit critique of the idealist elements retained in his phenomenology.

Of course, notes and parenthetical remarks are insufficient to establish the full context within which the author is working. Nevertheless, as an aid to the reader, terms appearing in the text which, in French, are obvious references to German counterparts will be accompanied by a short explanatory note and, when necessary, by the original German term.

(2) The second series of difficulties concerns Marx's texts themselves. The

major problem here is the discrepancy between the "standard" translations of Marx in English and in French. Often the differences are minor and do not affect the overall import of the passages that are quoted. At times, however, the divergences are so great as to change the point of the text cited by Henry, and in these cases the translation has been checked against the original and, when the author has deemed necessary, the text has been modified. Any such modification has been indicated in the corresponding note. Most often, the German expression in question has been added, either directly in the text or, if some explanation is required, in a note.

The following editions of Marx's major works are referred to in the text:

Early Writings, trans. Rodney Livingstone and Gregor Benton (New York: Vintage Books), 1975. This volume includes, among other texts, *Critique of Hegel's Doctrine of the State* (1843); *A Contribution to the Critique of Hegel's Philosophy of Right. Introduction* (1843–44); *Economic and Philosophical Manuscripts* (1844).

Surveys from Exile (New York: Vintage Books), 1974. This volume includes, among other texts, *The Class Struggles in France: 1848–1850*, trans. Paul Jackson; *The Eighteenth Brumaire of Louis Bonaparte*, trans. Ben Fowkes.

The Revolutions of 1848 (New York: Vintage Books), 1974, including *Manifesto of the Communist Party*, trans. Samuel Moore.

The Poverty of Philosophy (New York: International Publishers), 1963.

A Contribution to the Critique of Political Economy, trans. S. W. Ryazanskaya, ed. Maurice Dobbs (New York: International Publishers), 1970.

Marx and Engels, *The Holy Family*, trans. Richard Dixon and Clemens Dutt (Moscow: Progress Publishers), 1975.

Marx and Engels, *The German Ideology* (Moscow: Progress Publishers), 1976 (3rd ed.).

Capital, trans. Samuel Moore and Edward Aveling, vols. 1, 2, 3 (New York: International Publishers), 1967.

Grundrisse, trans. Martin Nicolaus (New York: Vintage Books), 1973.

In quoting from these translations, American spelling has been retained throughout.

(3) In general, whenever an English translation of works quoted by Henry exists, reference has been made to this edition. In the absence of an English translation for other texts cited, I have translated the passage. In keeping with the French text, references to *The Critique of Hegel's Doctrine of the State* also include page references to the German text, Marx, Engels, *Werke* (Berlin, 1961), vol. I.

I should like to thank Michel Henry, who, in the course of preparing the text for the English-language edition, went over the work with me in great detail with regard to matters of terminology and, more generally, with respect to his reading of Marx, of Hegel, and of Feuerbach. I also want to thank Tom Rockmore for his careful reading of my translation. His comments and suggestions contributed a great deal to the readability and consistency of the final version.

In striving to respect the specific nature of this work, its philosophical viewpoint and its literary character, and at the same time to make it a book that can be read and appreciated by an English-language audience, I am, of course, alone responsible for any and all shortcomings that may appear.

Kathleen Blamey McLaughlin

MARX

Introduction

THE THEORY OF MARX'S TEXTS

No philosopher has had more influence than Marx; none has been more misunderstood. The reasons why Marx's philosophical thought has remained plunged in almost total darkness up to the present day are numerous, and yet they are all related to Marxism and in a certain way are inseparable from it. Marxism is the interrelated set of misinterpretations that have been given concerning Marx. This situation—the gradual divergence, which becomes decisive at an early stage, between, on the one hand, Marx's own thought and, on the other, the required set of theoretical and practical postulates which constitute what can be called Marxism or Marxisms—did not come about by accident. Certainly, Marxism claims to speak in the name of Marx. What characterizes it, however, is that, since it is directed essentially toward political action and its attendant problems, Marxism has retained of the original work only what might stimulate this action and, in the urgency of a given situation, make it more effective. Theory, of course, has not been entirely neglected, since it becomes a force once it has penetrated the masses, but it is precisely this very theory, itself a more or less lengthy résumé in the service of "revolutionary praxis," which is substituted for the philosophical content under the pretext that it displays what is "essential" therein. In the preface to the second German edition of the *Communist Manifesto*, written in the spring of 1883, after Marx's death, Engels declares, ". . . the fundamental proposition, which forms its nucleus, belongs to Marx. That proposition is: that in every historical epoch the prevailing mode of economic production and exchange, and the social organization necessarily following from it, form the basis upon which is built up, and from which alone can be explained, the political and intellectual history of that epoch; that consequently the whole history of mankind (since the dissolution of primitive tribal society, holding land in common ownership) has been a history of class struggles, contests between exploiting and exploited, ruling and oppressed classes; that the history of these class struggles forms a series of evolutions in which, nowadays, a stage has been reached where the exploited and oppressed class—the proletariat—cannot attain its emancipation from the sway of the exploiting and ruling class—the bourgeoisie—without, at the same time, and once and for all, emancipating society at large from all exploitation, oppression, class distinction and class struggles."[1]

1

What is remarkable about this passage, and others like it, is not only that Marx's "fundamental proposition" is reduced here to an overly simplistic, if not fallacious, formulation but also that this summary, which claims to contain what is essential and what will, in fact, become one of the dogmas of revolutionary Marxism, is made on the basis of a *political text*. Now, *the political texts* (it would be better to say the historico-political texts)—*The Communist Manifesto, The Eighteenth Brumaire of Louis Bonaparte, The Class Struggles in France, The Civil War in France*, etc.—*do not contain their principle of intelligibility in themselves*, the concepts they develop are not the basic concepts, and their basis is neither expressed in these texts nor even indicated therein. To consider only Engels' above-cited summary, it must be admitted that this text muddles everything completely. "Economic production" is not for Marx real production and cannot, as such, constitute "the basis upon which . . . political and intellectual history [are built]." Despite the restrictive brackets placed around Marx's teaching, the reflections on history which are supposed to form the logical sequel to the text tend to make one believe that the *being* of history is constituted by class struggle, so that the classes themselves would be at once the driving force and the "explanation" of history. What is passed over in silence in this external summary is the *origin* of the classes, the fact that, far from constituting a principle on the level of being or of knowledge, they are themselves founded on and refer to a productive principle *(naturans)*, and one of the accomplishments of Marx's philosophy was precisely to bring this relationship to light. The now classical interpretation of history as "the history of class struggle" is not just an overly general approximation; it is purely and simply mistaken if, as we shall show, in Marx the concept of class is foreign to the "fundamental" theory of history. The concepts which enter into the political texts have, therefore, only a limited significance, relative to the function they serve in these texts. Philosophically, they refer to their own proper theory, formulated explicitly by Marx. We shall term philosophical those texts that contain this ultimate theory and that define it. Marx himself indicates the outer bounds of the significance attaching to the political writings when, in reference to his participation in the first Geneva Congress, he writes to Kugelmann on November 9, 1866: "I neither was able nor did I want to go, but I wrote the program for the London delegates. *I purposely limited it* to points that would meet with immediate agreement and would allow a concerted action on the part of the workers, points that reply directly to the needs of class struggle and to the organization of the workers into classes, and that stimulate them to do so."[2]

Let us add that the political texts are addressed to a wide public and that here Marx once again returns to being a writer: Hegelian rhetoric flourishes once more, all the more freely as these texts were hastily written. This is notably the case for *The Eighteenth Brumaire of Louis Bonaparte*, written for an American newspaper. Here we find more than simply the writer's tics of Hegels's most brilliant student, and yet these *are* Hegelian concepts which then make their reappearance. And this not without reason. Indeed, insofar as what is at issue is history—and not the theory of history—what matters are social formations. And the concepts used to formulate them—which have in every instance as their object a general reality, its structural formation, its distinctions and internal oppositions—belong philosophically to an ontology of the universal to which they secretly refer. It is on this basis that the strange analogy which appears between the political writings and the early writings is founded. In this way one can explain the fact that after the decline of scientific positivism a certain type of Marxism was able to envisage basing itself conjointly on both sets of writings. From Hegel to Marxism the genealogy is then only too blindingly obvious; in each we find the same primacy of the universal, of the general, of the political or social essence, of the dialectic, of negation and revolution, of the internal movement—of being or of society—itself understood as a unique essence at work at the heart of all things.

With regard to the divorce intervening between Marx and Marxism, there is a deeper reason than the primacy accorded to the historical texts or to political action and which, although purely accidental, will prove to be decisive: it is the extraordinary fact that *Marxism was constituted and defined in the absence of any reference to Marx's philosophical thought and in total ignorance of it*. Plekhanov, Lenin, Stalin and so many others had no knowledge of the 1844 *Economic and Philosophical Manuscripts*, nor in particular of *The German Ideology*, which were not published until 1932, that is to say at a time when "dialectical materialism" had already been presented as a finished doctrine. Let us go even further: Engels, who signed, we might say, *The German Ideology* with Marx, remains in fact totally unrelated to the fundamental philosophical content which unfolds in this explosive text. To be convinced of this one has only to compare the original with the summary Engels gives of it after Marx's death in his *Ludwig Feuerbach and the End of Classical German Philosophy*: the two texts have nothing in common. On the one hand, Engels' summary includes extremely serious historical errors, since he reverses the order of Feuerbach's and of Stirner's influence on Marx, which alone is sufficient to render unintelligible the internal development of Marx's thought during these critical years. Further, we see how in place of the brilliant and decisive intuitions of *The German Ideology*, which overturn the concept of being as it has dominated Western thought since ancient Greece and unsettle the philosophical horizon within which this thought has always moved, Engels substitutes an exasperatingly dull, banal discourse, which, at the very most, marks a return to the immediate and superficial past, to the materialism of Feuerbach and to that of the eighteenth century. And yet even this materialism, just as the idealism which is naïvely opposed to it, is presented in such an external form that any possible philosophical sense is lost. Here we find statements like the following: "Thus the question of the relation of thinking to being, the relation of the spirit to nature [is] the paramount question of the whole of philosophy. . . . The answers which the philosophers gave to this question split them into two great camps. Those who asserted the primacy of spirit to nature . . . comprised the camp of idealism. The others, who regarded nature as primary, belong to the various schools of materialism."[3] These lines would not be worth citing—in any event, there is no statement corresponding to them either in *The German Ideology* or in Marx's entire corpus—if they had not been quoted by Lenin in his article on Marxism, where they are followed by assertions of this sort: "After 1844–45—this was the period when his ideas were being formed—Marx was a materialist and, more particularly, an adept of Feuerbach whose weaknesses later appeared to Marx to reside solely in the lack of rigor and in the insufficient scope of his materialism. The 'epoch-making' worldwide historical importance of Feuerbach stemmed precisely, according to Marx, from his break with Hegel's idealism and from the affirmation of materialism. . . ."[4] Far from extending Feuerbach's materialism, *The German Ideology* in 1845 rejects the basic concept of this materialism in the very act by which it opens up the new dimension that Marx henceforth specifies as the domain of reality and, at the same time, of all the problems that will constitute the exclusive theme of his reflection.

The immense philosophical blank left for almost half a century at the heart of Marx's work has had numerous theoretical consequences. Not only was materialism, which the problematic of *The German Ideology* had placed outside its reach, to provide the title under which the entire work was henceforth to be classified, but as it was still necessary to distinguish this materialism from that of Feuerbach—Engels had published his "Theses on Feuerbach" at the same time as his *Ludwig Feuerbach*—it was decided that Marx's materialism was opposed to the earlier materialism in that it was "dialectical." In this way a second absurdity was added to the first: the dialectic—the concept of action as it is defined within the ontological presuppositions of Hegelianism—is just what *The German Ideology* and the "Theses on Feuerbach," which are intelligible only in relation to the former work, had rejected along with materialism; in both cases, this was due to the actualization of a single fundamental intuition, that of praxis. By presenting itself as "dialectical materialism" Marxism claimed to be constructed out of the union of the two elements which found in *The German Ideology* the principle of their decomposition. A union such as this could only be a "synthesis": each element, secretly undermined by Marx's critique, referred to the other. Marxist materialism, and it is in this that it differs "fundamentally" from the others, is "dialectical"; Marxist dialectic, and it is in this that it differs "fundamentally" from that of Hegel, is "materialist." The two absurdities are not just added onto one another; each calls upon the other to save it. But is this synthesis possible? The question posed by idealist philosophers—for example, Gentile in Italy—whether materialism is compatible with the dialectic, and vice versa, dominates the intellectual debate in the USSR for over a quarter of a century. This question is of doubtful interest if materialism and the dialectic are equally alien to Marx's thought. What is more, placing the basic concepts of "dialectical materialism" out of reach in this way must be understood to carry with it the force of a thematic exclusion inasmuch as the intelligibility of praxis is to be acquired only by way of a radical critique of the dialectic and inasmuch as materialism, in *Capital*, is to reveal itself to be incompatible with the presuppositions which found the economic analysis and make it possible.

The absence of Marx's philosophy during the entire period when Marxist doctrine was being formed had another, no less disastrous, consequence, namely the belief that Marx had come to toll philosophy's death knell. The theme of the death of philosophy, borrowed from Feuerbach, has in Marx only a very limited significance and is aimed solely at Hegel. But when all substantive philosophical content seemed to have disappeared from his work, of which only the political and economic texts were known, since the philosophical works were then as yet unpublished, strange misunderstandings arose and were perpetuated. The break Marx made with regard to Western philosophy was held to consist precisely in this farewell to philosophy, and this in the name of political action on the one hand—this is how the ninth Thesis on Feuerbach is hastily interpreted—and in the name of science, especially of economics and of sociology, on the other hand. This affirmation is a constant in Marxist authors, in Marcuse for example. "The transition from Hegel to Marx is, in all respects, a transition to an essentially different order of truth, not to be interpreted in terms of philosophy. We shall see that all the philosophical concepts of Marxian theory are social and economic categories, whereas Hegel's social and economic categories are all philosophical concepts. Even Marx's early writings are not philosophical. They express the negation of philosophy, though they still do so in philosophical language."[5] Mandel, taking up in his turn this unexamined presupposition of Marxism, declares that Marx's starting point is not the "concept of alienated labor" but "the practical ascertainment of working class poverty," that his thought will "henceforth be rigorously socio-economic" even if "philosophical scoria" subsist within it, and that, finally, it is to be interpreted as a transition to action: "its conclusion is in no sense a philosophical solution. . . . The call to revolutionary action—to be carried out by the proletariat—has already been substituted for the abnegation of a 'philosophy of labor'."[6]

Far from belonging to conceptual analysis, these insipid declarations are but the result of the sorry history of Marxism at the end of the nineteenth and in the twentieth century. Here again, Engels' responsibility is overwhelming. Although he was the one who contributed to directing Marx's attention to the condition of the workers and to all the related problems, and who, after Marx's death, accomplished such a precise and remarkable task in classifying and publishing the economic manuscripts out of which he carved what we now call books two and three of *Capital*, Engels himself was not a philosopher. His correspondence, as Riazanov notes, "reveals to us that he retained a keen interest in the study of coloring agents (which is explained by the fact that Engels ran a textile business) as well as in chemistry, physics and the natural sciences in general, which had been his strong subjects even in high-school. In

Manchester, with his friend Karl Schorlemmer, a well-known chemist, he continued to study the natural sciences. When he moved to London, he gave himself over to this work with great zeal."[7] In this way is explained the strange essay on "phlogistic" chemistry which Engels decided to place right in the middle of his preface to book two of *Capital*. Or again, we might mention the addition to the above-cited preface to the second German edition of the *Manifesto*, an addition which had already appeared in the preface to the English edition: "This proposition [regarding the class struggle which reaches the point where it is about to liberate all of society] . . . , in my opinion, is destined to do for history what Darwin's theory has done for biology. . . ."[8]

Considerations such as these, which appear to be only incidental, contain the premises of the subsequent evolution of Marxism. Not only do we see the dawning of the decisive role played by Darwinism, with which Marxism will strive to agree, as is shown, for example, in this text by Enrico Ferri: "What is this famous 'class struggle' which Marx revealed as the positive key to human history if not the Darwinian law of the 'struggle for life' transferred from individuals to collectivities?"[9] More than the emergence of a science or of particular scientific theories, however, what is remarkable in Engels' indications (as in the subjects and titles of some of his manuscripts: "Dialectic and Natural Sciences," "Mathematics and Natural Sciences," etc.) is the fact that the very knowledge that Marx had come to establish was not only in agreement with the positive results of the various sciences but itself constituted in reality one science among others and was, precisely for this reason, "scientific" knowledge. The theory of history in Marx's sense is comparable to biology, and the progress it achieves with the development of the concept of class struggle is comparable to and is actually compared with the progress made by Darwin in the natural sciences. What is signified by this substitution of scientific knowledge for philosophical knowledge and, in the instance with which we are concerned, for Marx's philosophy is not, in the absence of the philosophical texts, simply unknown and ignored, it is denied.

This collapse of Marx's thought into pseudo-scientific positivism affects this thought internally in its substantive content when it is no longer limited to establishing a comparison or an analogy with the existing sciences but concerns the specific object of its investigation, material production and the social forms related to it. To the extent that these forms are involved, Marxism, as science, designates nothing other than a sociology and, of course, a—or rather *the*—"scientific sociology." Durkheim was simply looking at Marxism through the lenses of his own presuppositions and making it his own when he wrote in December 1897 in his review of Antonio Labriola's *Essais sur la conception matérialiste de l'histoire* for *La Revue philosophique:* "We find fruitful the idea that social life is to be explained not through the conception that those who participate in it may have of it but through the deep causes which escape conscious reflection, and we think that these causes are to be sought primarily in the manner in which the associated individuals are grouped together." To the extent that it includes material and, as it is called, "economic" production, Marxism is precisely only an economic theory, a "scientific" and rigorous one through its contrast with the conceptions of the English school, which remained ideological. In this way, Marcuse's thesis, according to which "the concepts of Marxist theory are social and economic categories," is verified. Thus *Capital* is reduced to a treatise on economics. In this way, Marx's thought as such is lost, since, far from being able to be confused with one or—mysteriously—several factitious sciences, it constitutes, inasmuch as it is philosophy, a foundational theory: the theory of the foundations of history—and not just a simple historical science; the foundational theory of social formations—and not just simple sociology; the theory of the transcendental foundation and the internal possibility of the market economy and of economics in general—and not simply one economic doctrine among others, destined, as they are, to represent only the relative truth of a transitory phase in scientific development.

With the appearance in 1932 of Marx's philosophical texts, and in particular of *The German Ideology*, which contained the theory of history and of social forms along with the premises of a transcendental theory of the economy, the ideological situation created by the existence of Marxism in the form of a completed doctrine was the following: *in light of the postulates required by dialectical materialism, it was impossible to grasp the content of the philosophical texts, but it was also impossible not to perceive that this content had, precisely, nothing to do with established Marxism.* At the very moment when Riazanov discovered the manuscript of *The German Ideology* in the archives of the German Social-Democratic Party, it became immediately evident that Marxist ideology obscured Marx's philosophical thought. On the one hand, Riazanov understood the decisive importance of the discovery he had just made, since the link that was missing between the early writings, which conformed at least in appearance to Feuerbachian humanism, and the works of maturity was at last reestablished and a new reading of Marx was now possible. This was no longer a superficial reading which confronted, from an external position, the various texts and the concepts they conveyed but a philosophical reading which grasped the movement of the thought from inside and identified with it and with its development. On the other hand, and in a striking manner, Riazanov showed us that the ideology, of which he was the high priest before then becoming its victim, prevented him from understanding a single word of the explosive manuscript he had before him. He believed that he found in *The German Ideology* the confirmation of the summary Engels gave of it in *Ludwig Feuerbach and the End of Classical German Philosophy* and, in the same stroke, he reduced Marx's philosophical thought to the dismantling it underwent at the hand of the Marxism of the period 1930–40, that is, to a purely formal dialectics, the content of which was constituted by the various positive sciences.

> Up to now the period which is called real humanism and the period of Marx's and Engels' revolutionary communism have lacked any connection, any intermediary

link. Now, not only in their own intellectual evolution but in that of the entire German ideology, the transition from Hegel, by way of Feuerbach, to Marx and Engels, has remained entirely incomprehensible, unexplained and unknown. Besides, from this period on, Marx and Engels abandoned, so to speak, philosophy in general. In the manuscript in question we find indications confirming that Marx and Engels had already developed their doctrine, which corresponds to the formulations Engels provided of it later. Of philosophy, there remains only the dialectic and the formal logic. All the rest comes under the dominion of the various individual sciences.[10]

Whereas in Riazanov the Marxist ideology placed in contact with Marx's philosophical texts continued naïvely to accept their content—or what seemed to be their content—an analysis of this content soon made apparent the irreducibility of the latter to the former. This is the start of a long story, the tragicomic story in which the incompatibility of Marx's philosophical thought with Marxism is at once revealed and hidden, in which the latter does away with the former. As to the comic passages in this story, let us cite as examples the remarks made by Lucien Goldmann which were inspired by the publication date of *The German Ideology*. This is explained, according to our author, by the fact that, in the eyes of Engels, who was knowledgeable in such matters, this text was of no interest whatsoever: "thus Engels, at a time when he no longer had any problem having a text published, considered that *The German Ideology* offered no major interest for publication." Such is the opinion of Goldmann as well, for whom Marx's text presents "a considerable interest to all those who want to follow the genesis of the thought of the two founders of scientific socialism, but a lesser interest to those who would seek theoretical and scientific truths therein." And this is so because "the polemic directed at Stirner occupies a disproportionate place since it alone comprises . . . more than half of the work." "These polemics," Goldmann continues, "are completely outdated today" and for this reason constitute just "a dull text."[11] The ignorance of the decisive role of *The German Ideology*, and in particular of the Stirner polemic, which explains not only Marx's explicit renouncement of Feuerbach's materialism but also the definition of the real individual in opposition to the ideological concept of the individual found in Stirner as in classical philosophy in general—the ignorance of this role in an author who claims to be a follower of Marx, demonstrates at once the opaqueness of the ideological veil cast by Marxism over Marx's basic texts and the secret attempt to minimize the importance of these texts, when they are not simply dismissed.

The elimination of Marx's philosophical thought in favor of the dogmatic theses of dialectical materialism as it had been constituted and defined over almost half a century in ignorance of this thought is the explicit project of Louis Althusser and the avowed aim of his investigation. Since the philosophical writings do exist, this existence is to be dealt with as a mere matter of fact, as an historical phenomenon whose principle of intelligibility is situated outside of itself, since this principle is deemed to reside in the set of postulates required by dialectical materialism. ". . . we cannot say absolutely that *'Marx's youth is part of Marxism'* unless we mean by this that, like all historical phenomena, the evolution of this young bourgeois intellectual can be illuminated by the application of the principles of historical materialism."[12] Not only are the philosophical writings nothing but the writings of "youth," those of a young German bourgeois, but the possibility that they could provide an explanation for the later work and constitute the genesis of this work is categorically excluded. Rejected on the level of the given and considered as an ideology, the philosophical work is no longer a source of enlightenment but a dead letter, opaque, capable of receiving its light only from elsewhere. Between what enlightens and what is enlightened the break is radical indeed and such that, on the one side, we find only ideological concepts and, on the other, the set of scientific concepts which constitute the "theory." The ideological concepts are unusable; their only possible use consists in providing an object for the application of Marxist theory. Marx's philosophy is sent to the chopping block in order to give the knife of dialectical materialist critique the opportunity to put its blade to work. If the 1844 *Economic and Philosophical Manuscripts* form a "privileged object," this is because they "provid[e] the Marxist theory of ideology with an excellent opportunity to exercise and test its method."[13]

Between what the philosophical manuscripts say, between their explicit immanent meaning and their "genuine" sense, the sense conferred upon them by Marxist theory and which is apparent only in terms of this theory, the split is so great that we are actually dealing with two different discourses, one of which is false and the other true. If, for example, we want to understand the evolution of Marx's thought during the course of the tremendous theoretical labor by means of which, rejecting successively both Hegel and Feuerbach, both idealism and materialism, this thought attains its own identity through a development which is precisely that of its successive intuitions, a development which is the very movement of this thought, which it experiences, of which it is conscious and which it recognizes as such, this self-consciousness reached by Marx is here simply not what is to be taken into account or even taken seriously. Marx's thought is considered no proof of itself, it provides no criterion, it is no judge, but instead it is judged, submitted to the criterion of an alien thought.

Of course, the quotation in which Marx himself attests to and locates this break ("we resolved . . . to settle accounts with our erstwhile philosophical conscience") in 1845 at the level of *The German Ideology*, [cannot] . . . be treated . . . as a proof of the existence of the break and a definition of its location. The examination of the status of this declaration called for a theory and a method—the *Marxist theoretical concepts* in which the reality of theoretical formations in general (philosophical ideologies and science) can be considered must be applied to Marx himself.[14]

The way in which the question of the evolution of Marx's thought is to be treated is therefore only a particular case of the manner in which the entire work is to be explained:

> . . . that all this critical effort, the absolute precondition of any interpretation, in itself presupposes activating a minimum of provisional Marxist theoretical concepts bearing on the nature of theoretical formations and their history; that the precondition of a reading of Marx is a Marxist theory of the differential nature of theoretical formations and their history, that is, a theory of epistemological history, which is Marxist philosophy itself; that this operation in itself constitutes an indispensable circle in which the application of Marxist theory to Marx himself appears to be the absolute precondition of an understanding of Marx and at the same time as the precondition even of the constitution and development of Marxist philosophy, so much is clear.[15]

Too clear: "A theory which enables us to see clearly in Marx . . . is in fact simply Marxist philosophy itself."[16] The methodological prescription of this "critical" reading of Marx then finds its precise formulation: "Let us return to Lenin and thence to Marx."[17] The so-called rereading thus does no more than to repeat what Marxism has always done. A thought of genius is to be measured by the yardstick of an elementary catechism.

We shall discover little by little the false notions to which this sort of "method" inexorably leads. Let us note straightaway a rather important discrepancy concerning this split. Although it is claimed that it is up to Marxism and not to Marx's own thought to determine where the mutations occur, it is nevertheless insinuated that Marx himself could not have failed to recognize the "ideological" character of his philosophical writings and that it is for this reason that he decided not to publish them. This assertion is made twice concerning the *Economic and Philosophical Manuscripts*[18] and extended surreptitiously to include *The German Ideology,* as if the awareness attained by Marx in this work had as its conclusion the very rejection of the work itself, its abandonment without regret to the gnawing criticism of the mice. Due to the confusion surrounding the "split," *The German Ideology is no longer the principle of the liquidation of the earlier consciousness but its object, and so is itself liquidated*. An interpretation such as this is not only abusive, it is categorically denied by Marx himself, when in 1859, with the distance of the intervening years, he makes the irrevocable judgment in the preface to the *Critique of Political Economy* by which the radical critique of German thought as well as the clear awareness of its results are attributed to *The German Ideology*, whose failure to be published is explicitly attributed to its rejection by the publisher: "When in the spring of 1845, he [Engels] too came to live in Brussels, we decided to set forth together our conception as opposed to the ideological one of German philosophy, in fact to settle accounts with our former philosophical conscience. The intention was carried out in the form of a critique of post-Hegelian philosophy. The manuscript, two large octavo volumes, had long ago reached the publishers in Westphalia *when we were informed that owing to changed circumstances it could not be printed.* We abandoned the manuscript to the gnawing criticism of the mice all the more willingly *since we had achieved our main purpose—self-clarification.*"[19]

Even more serious are the errors that appear in the evaluation of the transcendental history of the concepts developed in the "early writings"; by this we mean the theoretical order of their foundation, their emergence, their elaboration, their rectification, their erasure, and, finally, their replacement by adequate concepts. With respect to the most important contribution of the philosophical writings, namely the radical critique of Hegel, this is held to be worthless because it remains Feuerbachian, whereas one has only to read the 1843 manuscript, *Critique of Hegel's Doctrine of the State,* to see that this critique, which is absolutely new and original and which remains unequalled in the entire philosophical literature of the nineteenth and twentieth centuries (if we omit Kierkegaard), is autonomous. The Feuerbachian themes appear only at the end of the text in question, as a borrowed element foreign to its content and as a solution brought in from outside to a problem which Marx himself had not yet resolved. The 1844 *Economic and Philosophical Manuscripts* are condemned wholesale, although the third manuscript contains an implicit questioning of the first two, and although the synthesis of Hegel and of Feuerbach in the first texts, which is indicative of a stroke of genius consisting in the clear perception of their identity—of the identity of materialism and idealism—determines the critique of Hegel in the third manuscript as a critique which, precisely, can no longer be strictly Feuerbachian and which already implies the rejection of Feuerbach as the inevitable consequence of the rejection of Hegel, thus prefiguring the decisive reversal to be performed in the *Theses on Feuerbach.* The sense of this reversal, by which the philosophical content of Marx's thought is acquired and defined, is lost when the crucial distinction between praxis and theory, reduced to an ideological distinction, is robbed of all importance and when one reserves the right to distort this thought completely by claiming to reduce it, and Marxism along with it, to epistemology or, better yet, to "a theory of epistemological history."

It is quite useless to attempt to do away with the philosophical work as a whole by subsuming it in its entirety under the concept, if it may be so termed, of "humanism," by declaring that "the philosophy of man . . . had served as his theoretical basis during the years of his youth (1840–45),"[20] by assimilating this foundation to the "old couple individuals/human essence,"[21] as if the rejection of the latter meant equally the exclusion of the former and the definition of all individual reality as ideological—whereas the collapse of the ontology of the universal, of *Gattungswesen,* and of human essence was conveyed in 1845 by the sudden appearance at the heart of the problematic of "living individuals," in terms of which the real presuppositions of history are defined, whereas humanism, as we shall see, is itself equivocal in the extreme, to the point of being contradictory. This contradiction persists throughout the entire philosophical work and can be considered inseparable from its intelligibility. Everywhere one and the same intention is displayed, giving rise to and comprehending the entire problematic: the quest for what is to be understood as reality and, at the same time, as a ground. It is because Feuerbach and, at the beginning, Hegel himself—in opposition to Fichte[22]—appeared in the eyes of the young Marx as thinkers who reflected upon this reality that they momentarily served as his guides before being rejected for the same reason, because far from revealing or defining this reality, on the contrary, they overlooked it and let it escape them, for, as Marx understood, *reality is not identifiable within an ontology of objectivity*.

The singularity of Marx's philosophical project is what confers upon all his works, and not just the philosophical ones, their extraordinary unity. The successive set of concepts and, even more so, the set of themes which are displayed there, can only be explained on the basis of this fundamental project and as the mode of its gradual realization. This is why if it is correct to recognize in Marx's work a history of these concepts, it can be interpreted only in light of the teleology that secretly animates it. It is solely in terms of their adequacy with respect to this history that these concepts are criticized, corrected, ratified, or eliminated. The only concepts that disappear are those whose entire content is borrowed from Hegelianism—or its Feuerbachian subproduct. This is the case, for example, of the concept of man, of the first concept of history, of the primacy of the political essence, of society, and so on. On the contrary, the concepts that remain or that appear in the course of the theoretical elaboration are those that have a fundamental reference to praxis, as, for example, the concepts of the individual, of subjectivity, of life, of reality, and so on. One must therefore be extremely careful not to confuse the elimination of the Hegelian meaning with the definitive exclusion of a given concept if it is capable of receiving or acquiring a fundamental reference to reality in the new problematic resulting from the Feuerbachian reversal. Far from ending in its definitive abandonment by Marx, the critique of the concept of alienation, for example— which is announced in the third manuscript and is realized in the polemic directed against Stirner and which determines the economic investigation— marks the transition from the ideological alienation found in the neo-Hegelians and in Hegel himself, which characterizes consciousness and is defined by it, to real alienation which concerns existence and which makes existence the issue. It is not alienation but the ontological horizon from which it was taken that falls outside the field of the problematic. The same thing is true for all of Marx's fundamental concepts: the concepts of the individual, of history and of praxis itself, which serves as the ground for future developments only when, having escaped the presuppositions of both objectivity and sensibility, it is thought in itself as such and as the innermost determination of being.

A transcendental history is not a linear history but a genesis. Not an historical genesis but, precisely, a transcendental genesis. It is therefore no longer a matter of simply recognizing the appearance and the disappearance of concepts and of their various functions at different points in the problematic, nor is it a matter of indicating mere modifications in terminology which leave the real object intact. Marx, moreover, was aware of this himself as, speaking of the march toward reality, toward the "real material presuppositions" which constitute the teleology and the content of his philosophical reflection, he wrote in *The German Ideology:* "This path was already indicated in the *Deutsch-Französische Jahrbücher*—in the *Einleitung zur Kritik der Hegelschen Rechtsphilosophie* and *Zur Judenfrage*. But since at that time this was done in philosophical phraseology, the traditionally occurring philosophical expressions such as 'human essence', 'species', etc., gave the German theoreticians the desired reason for misunderstanding the real trend of thought and believing that here again it was a question merely of giving a new turn to their worn-out theoretical garment. . . ."[23] A transcendental history of concepts reflects this march toward reality and presents the results in a systematic manner. Far from being restricted to ascertaining the order of the succession of the concepts, it establishes the order of their foundation and performs the radical discrimination between ultimate concepts, that is founding concepts, and those that have their foundation in the former. Concepts that accompany one another in Marx's work, those found, for example, in the same texts, are by no means situated on the same plane; their power of theoretical explanation is different since it rests in every instance on their ontological meaning and refers to this. It is by analysis that the decisive discrimination between founding concepts and those that derive from them is performed, and, inasmuch as this ultimately consists in exposing the levels of being and in recognizing the ultimate essence of being, it is philosophical. It is the interpretation of being as production and as praxis which in the end determines the order of foundation among the concepts along with the order of their respective functions within the body of the problematic. In *Capital,* for example, the disassociation between, on the one hand, the opposition, characteristic of the English school, between fixed capital and circulating capital and, on the other hand, the opposition Marx substitutes for it between constant capital and variable capital in order to explain the movement of capital, that is capital itself, refers beyond the ideal realm of economics to reality itself and to its ultimate constituents.

The reason it is absurd to claim that Marx's thought marks the end of philosophy and consists in substituting for the inoperable concepts of German philosophy concepts that are scientific, economic, sociological, and so forth is because the concepts upon which the analysis in *Capital* is based are exclusively philosophical concepts, and in a radical sense as *ontological concepts*. This is why one cannot draw "breaks" in Marx's work along strictly chronological lines, according to the mere presence—or absence—of certain concepts in the succession of texts. And even then, this chronology must first of all be respected. When it is claimed that Marx's work can be divided into two periods, the first of which is defined by the reign of the concepts of man, of the individual, of alienation, of alienated labor, and so on, while the second is held to witness the disappearance of the ideological concepts and the appearance in their stead of new theoretical concepts proper to Marxism, such as productive forces, relations of production, classes, and so on,[24] the fact is overlooked that the concepts of class and of production are present in the early writings, while, except for the concept of man, the philosophical concepts are found throughout the entire corpus. The only question of interest to a transcendental history—and not a simple history—of the concepts of Marx's thought is the question of determining the fundamental concepts and the relation that is established between the different concepts inasmuch as it is philosophically founded. Now, what appears with respect to a question such as this is that *the concepts of productive forces, of social classes, and so forth—the fundamental concepts of Marxism— are by no means the fundamental concepts of Marx's thought*. This means that just as the realities they designate are not original ones on the level of being, so too are they, as concepts, incapable of providing the premises for theoretical analysis. We then see in the economic work the reversal of the relation established between the scientific, economic, social, historical, etc. concepts on the one hand and, on the other, the philosophical concepts: far from disappearing from the problematic, the latter are presented there as foundational concepts. And this is not just by accident, if indeed the general concepts are robbed of their substance when the ontological horizon of Hegelianism falls outside the field of Marx's thought. *Productive forces and social classes are neither primary realities nor principles of explanation but instead they are, precisely, what has to be explained, mere terms to be analyzed*. The entire aim of Marx is to show that the problematic of productive forces, for example, ends in their decomposition in the subjective element of individual praxis, which alone founds value and accounts for the capitalist system, while the objective element plays only an illusory and purely negative role in the history of the essence *(historial)** of capitalism. *The history of the subjectivity of these forces is their own history, the history of capitalism, the history of the world*. In the same way, the classes imply a productive principle, a *naturans*, and, consequently, a genealogy which, as we shall see, also has its origin in praxis. Situating these forces or these classes at the origin of the analysis, hypostatizing them and even the capitalist regime itself as a *naturans* generating all that is produced within it, is to reverse the order of explanation, to substitute for Marx's thought its résumé by Engels and by Lenin, the old catechism which is only too familiar under the already faded colors of "structuralism."

The preceding indications are intended to serve only as a rough outline of our approach: no theory of texts could ever precede a reading of the texts in question as their condition but instead can only result from this reading. The *épochè*† of Marxism is but the negative condition of this reading. On the positive side, an

---

*By the term *historial*, with its Heideggerian overtones, the author refers to an internal history, to an unfolding of essential determinations (in this case, those essential to capitalism), which also involves the notion of destiny.—TRANS.

†The phenomenological term *épochè* means putting in parentheses, bracketing.—TRANS.

understanding of Marx's thought consists, as we have suggested, in repeating the intuitions and the fundamental evidences* found there. Repeating in this way is reactualizing the meanings which together form Marx's work. In the course of this reactivation, the evidences and their actual† phenomenological content are not simply presented anew to the gaze of philosophical reflection; instead they lead into one another along the paths that are marked out within them and that constitute their systematic explanation. Thus, they serve mutually to situate one another in accordance with the relations of analytical implication and, ultimately, of their essential foundation. Then, due to the apodictic nature of the evidence displayed in these relations, the fundamental texts and concepts can be recognized, not those which are declared fundamental by virtue of an arbitrary or whimsical interpretation but by reason of the essential, that is to say founding, character of their content. Those texts and concepts are fundamental which explain the others and cannot in turn be explained by them.

A method such as this, certainly, is not without its presuppositions. In brief, it implies that Marx's thought not be treated as an ideology, that is to say, that it is to be grasped in and through itself, through its own intuitions and evidences, precisely in the act of repeating these and not in the form of a causal explanation, that is, a set of theoretical propositions external to the intrinsic content of this thought and different from it. What makes Marx's thought a philosophy is the fact that it accounts for itself and constitutes for itself its own theoretical foundation. This means, once again, that none of its fundamental propositions is established on the basis of another order of knowledge and that the thesis of the dissolution of philosophy in Marx into the various positive sciences is decidedly absurd. The status ascribed to Marx's philosophy here naturally does not conflict with his ideology critique, any more than it secretly leads back to Hegelianism. To say that the content of the fundamental evidences is given only in the act of the intuitive grasp and in its concrete realizations is not to make the content depend on such an act; and, consequently, in line with the essential thesis of the critique of German idealism, thought is powerless. Thought, in Marx, is the vision of being, whose internal structure is irreducible to the internal structure of this vision, irreducible to theory; it is praxis.

So we shall be taking Marx seriously here. For us Marx is not some patient stretched out on the analyst's couch, someone whose babblings would serve simply as hints or as symptoms in discovering the truth. It is not through the lacunae, the silences or the blank spots in his discourse that we shall claim to learn more than what Marx himself said or to reach another level of knowledge, another discourse which would have been concealed under the apparent discourse and which would come to us only through his lapses or his shortcomings. This would-be "symptomatic" reading of Marx not only faces, in this case, the

---

*Evidence(s) is to be taken in the phenomenological sense of that which is brought into the clear light of consciousness, given in itself.—TRANS.

†The author's terms *effectif/effectivité* have been rendered throughout by actual/actuality. —TRANS.

ridicule of appearing presumptuous, it itself relies on an only too obvious mode of psychoanalysis if it merely attempts to re-create, under its "manifest" content, the latent content of Marxism.

The philosophical repetition of Marx's thought does not simply project once more the content of its decisive evidences, organized according to the tie of their fundamental interconnection, into the sphere of phenomenological actualization. With a tie such as this, the hidden principle of their unity is, ultimately, wrested out of the inexpressed domain in which all thought finally reposes and brought closer to the light. It is in this way that, as Kant and Heidegger have dared to say, the philosophical interpretation of the thought of philosophers is finally always directed toward "what they intended to say."[25] That this aim and this final intention of a given thought inevitably serve as its unifying principle is attested to by the fact that, grasped within the field of intelligibility opened up by this principle, all of the written statements of a given thinker have, despite their apparent contradiction or their diversity—despite even the heterogeneity of the conceptual systems they develop or to which they address themselves— one and the same meaning. This becomes strikingly apparent to any understanding of Marx's thought which is achieved through the mode of repetition. Through this internal understanding we are able to perceive how, through the various "periods" and their philosophical presuppositions, through Hegel, Feuerbach, and their reversal, through the essential discovery of praxis and the new problematic set up on the basis of praxis, *what Marx meant* takes shape, emerges and is finally rigorously determined.

A word, finally, about the usefulness or the timeliness of "Marxology." Of what good are all these scholarly expositions when men are dying of hunger? But the drama of the twentieth century is not only the result of the fact that poverty persists in the modern world. It also strikes those regimes that were built in the name of Marx and, so it is said, in light of his thought. And what if the principles of this thought—*living individuals*—were to explain the failure of these regimes, the abstraction upon which they have claimed to be established, the inflexible law of their deprivation and their horrors?

Let us, then, allow Marx his turn to speak.

Chapter 1

THE CRITIQUE OF POLITICAL ESSENCE: THE 1843 MANUSCRIPT

The repetition of the essential evidences through which Marx's thought is gradually constituted, and which will define the ground upon which the economic analysis in its turn will be built, necessarily has its starting point in the systematic elucidation of *The Critique of Hegel's Doctrine of the State*, which is presented to us as Marx's first great theoretical work. What is at issue here is not, in fact, simply an initial phase in the thinking of the "young Marx," but rather, from 1842–43 on, the emergence of the decisive intuitions which will direct the entire work to come and which, by placing it from the outset in contact with the real, will thus determine it from the beginning as a philosophy of reality. *The Critique of Hegel's Doctrine of the State* is a paragraph-by-paragraph, sentence-by-sentence, and at times word-by-word commentary on Hegel's *Philosophy of Right*. The part of Marx's manuscript that has been preserved is an analysis of paragraphs 261 to 313 of Hegel's work. In this extraordinary text of unlimited philosophical import, we begin by following step-by-step what was actually Marx's own personal dialogue with Hegel, the initial working out of a thought which simultaneously succumbs to Hegelianism and makes a radical break with it and with the principles which, since ancient Greece, have dominated Western philosophy.

Paragraph 261 of the *Philosophy of Right* states: "In contrast with the spheres of private rights and private welfare (the family and civil society), the State is from one point of view an external necessity and their higher authority; its nature is such that their laws and interests are subordinated to it and dependent on it. On the other hand, however, it is the end immanent within them, and its strength lies in the unity of its own universal end and aim with the particular interest of individuals, in the fact that individuals have duties to the State in proportion as they have rights against it." Marx's immediate position with respect to this text provides us with the initial and final presupposition of his entire analysis: this presupposition is Hegelian; it asserts that the State is not superimposed on civil society or on the family like some synthetic addition to their being, some external principle intended to organize, to rule them from outside; quite the contrary, the State is the *very reality* of the spheres that are placed under it. It is the State which animates them, which defines their life and, as a result, their end as an "immanent end." This idea that the ontological reality of the State constitutes the reality of civil society and of the family is expressed in Hegelian terms as the *homogeneity of the particular and of the universal,* a homogeneity which alone makes possible and defines concrete freedom, that is, the identity of the system of private interest, which is displayed in civil society, with the system of general interest, which is none other than the State—a homogeneity which is, however, to be understood in the sense we have just stated, that is, as a *radical determination of the particular by the universal.* It is with this thesis taken from Hegel, one which is still Marx's own, that he overturns the Hegelian edifice. Marx himself *wants* the identity of the particular and the universal, and what he reproaches Hegel with is having affirmed this identity without being able to establish it, as becomes apparent in his discourse itself. For how could the State present itself as a necessity *external* to the family and to civil society if it truly constituted their *internal* reality and their "immanent" end? But how does Hegel account for the affinity of the particular and the universal on the level of being; how does the State *determine* the concrete spheres of society and the family?

Paragraph 262 of the *Principles of the Philosophy of Right* answers this question: "The actual Idea is mind, which, sundering itself into the two ideal spheres of its concept, family and civil society, enters upon its finite phase, but it does so only in order to rise above its ideality and become explicit as infinite actual mind. It is therefore to these ideal spheres that the actual Idea assigns the material of this its finite actuality, viz. human beings as a mass, in such a way that the function assigned to any given individual is visibly mediated by circumstances, his caprice and his personal choice of his station in life." This means that, *in order to realize itself, to be mind and to manifest itself, the mind divides itself, sets itself in opposition to itself, not just in the form of an empty horizon but poses something vis-à-vis itself, being, the opaque determination it requires in order to reflect its own light, so that in this reflection it returns to itself, emerges into actuality, into the infinity of being-for-itself*—what Hegel terms, precisely, the real idea, infinity. Hegel's fundamental thesis—namely that the Idea is not a mere concept but includes reality, empirical reality, within itself, that the *Idea realizes itself*—becomes transparent when it displays its ultimate phenomenological motivation. Once the reality of the Idea is admitted, the family and civil society are posited within the State. With the help of his recent reading of Chapter VIII of the first part of *The Essence of Christianity* in which Feuerbach presents—in a cursory manner, certainly—the thought of Schelling and, especially, of Boehme, Marx recognizes what is at the root of German philosophy, what constitutes the ultimate explanation of its "pantheism," of *the necessity of including nature within mind in order to make it possible.* His commentary is explosive: "The family and civil society appear as the dark ground of nature [*der dunkle Naturgrund*] from which the light of the State is born."[1]

Posited as included within the development of the Idea and willed by it, necessary for this development and within it, the family and civil society are to be understood as "ideal spheres" and also as "finite" ones. They are finite inasmuch as they do not find their reason for existing within themselves but only outside of themselves, precisely in the Idea, that is; in the final analysis, in exteriority as such and in the conditions for its actual phenomenological becoming.

Let us place ourselves, however, along with Marx in the perspective of these spheres which designate nothing other than the concrete activity of individuals; their life within the family; their work to provide for it; the relationships they enter into with other individuals in the exchange of labor and of products; meetings; conflicts that arise within the workings of these relationships; in short, what we call civil society. It then appears that, in his philosophy of the State, Hegel does not describe these spheres for themselves; he does not grasp their reality as it is, in itself; the laws he recognizes are not their laws but the law of the Idea; the determinations he confers upon them are not their own determinations but the predicates of something else; the life he grasps within them is not their life with its demands, its immanent, individual, and genuinely life-oriented motivations, but the life of a different essence; their mind is not their own but an alien mind and, to be blunt, it is simply not their existence that is in question. Still under the influence of Feuerbach, but with a tone more reminiscent of Kierkegaard, Marx writes: "Reality is not deemed to be itself but another reality instead. . . . (it) is not governed by its own mind but by a mind alien to it."[2] ". . . it is not the course of their [the family and civil society] own life that joins them together to comprise the State, but the life of the Idea which has distinguished them from itself. They are moreover the finite phase of this Idea; they are indebted for their existence to a mind other than their own; they are not self-determining but are instead determined by another; for this reason they are defined as 'finitude', the 'real Idea's' own finite phase. The goal of this existence is not that existence itself."[3]

Because the interplay of individual activity which is displayed in the family and in society does not have its principle in the individual himself, in his needs, but in the real idea, in the State, it is nothing more than an "appearance" of the universal essence in the sense of a simple "phenomenon" of this essence, whose self-realization then unfolds "behind the scenes"—so that the entire development becomes *at once ideal and unconscious*. The mediation between individuals that constitutes this real interplay is nothing more than "the appearance of a mediation which the real Idea performs on itself"; the acts that make up this interplay "are not regarded as true, necessary and intrinsically self-justified; they are not as such deemed to be rational. If they are held to be rational it is only in the sense that, while they are regarded as furnishing an illusory mediation and while they are left just as they were, they nevertheless acquire the meaning of a determination of the Idea. . . ."[4] And Marx continues: "Thus . . . reality . . . is even declared to be rational. However, it is not rational by virtue of its own reason, but because the . . . fact in its . . . existence has a meaning other than itself."[5]

Here, the Hegelian claim to identify the real and the rational is reversed, along with the affirmation of the homogeneity of the particular and the universal. Or rather, *the very place accorded to reason and, in just the same way, to reality is shifted*. For, in taking a closer look at this, Marx in no way contests that the real is rational, but, quite the opposite, he affirms this; more precisely, he affirms that the rationality belonging to the real resides in it. "In it" and not outside of it in some other reality. What is the reality which is external to the real, foreign to it, the reality which is not its rationality, which is not rationality and which, by the same stroke, is not genuine, is not reality? This is "the light of the State"; it is light itself, that which is produced in the internal process of self-opposition by which the Idea realizes itself by objectifying itself—it is objectivity as such, otherness, ideality. And objectivity is ideal not only because it is produced in the internal development of the idea and so belongs to it, but precisely because it is not reality. However, according to Hegel, the Idea does not only produce objectivity, the light of the State; it also produces through its own development and, consequently, posits by itself the "materials of the State," namely, the family and civil society.

Marx contests this. The unveiling of the concrete activity of individuals and of the interplay of this activity within the family and within civil society may well take place in the light of ideality and through it; however, the origin of this activity, its nature, its power, its development and its product are not *the origin, the power, the development, the product of the internal process of the concept, of the movement by which the Idea realizes itself through objectifying itself*. This is why the law of the Idea has nothing to do with the law of this concrete activity, why the power of the Idea is powerless with respect to real power, namely the power of individuals to produce and maintain their life through organizing into the family and into society. *Real activity is not objectification*. Objectification allows what is to exist but changes nothing about it, and as Marx said regarding individuals and the intersecting of their activities, "they are left just as they were."[6] And, moreover, this is why the mediation of objective appearance is the "appearance of a mediation,"[7] because it has had no part in what has really been produced. If what is really produced in the family and in civil society through the activity of individuals, which is concrete, circumstantial, and seemingly arbitrary, does not stem from the movement of the idea, then it cannot be understood as the Idea in the being that it has become through its objectification as ob-ject;* and Hegel's sophism is thereby denounced. "The real subjects," says Marx, "—civil society, the family, 'circumstances, caprice, etc.,'—are all transformed into unreal, *objective moments of the Idea* referring to different things."[8] They are not real and cannot be as long as they are the *objects of*

---

*Ob-ject: the hyphen is used here by the author to remind us of the sense of the prefix ob- as that which is placed before, over, and against.—TRANS.

objectification; they have a different sense, one different from their true sense or rather from their reality as long as this sense refers to the way in which they proceed from the idea. In short, objectivity contains reality as that which it does not contain, does not explain, does not produce, as that for which it does not represent the reason. In the movement of the Idea's objectification, reality, which is allowed to exist as ob-ject, is mere "caprice"; it is arbitrary.

The *Critique of Hegel's Doctrine of the State* is first and foremost the radical critique of all subsumption, namely the subsumption of the particular under the universal, the belief that reality is really explained, exposed in its being when it is exposed in the light of the Idea. This exposition, however, is never itself the reason for what is exposed in this way, for its own internal, specific, particular reality. Hegel conceives of the Idea's development as organic, but why is this organism called the political organism, the organism of the State rather than the animal organism or the solar system?[9] The Idea is not the yardstick of the real; every ideal subsumption is arbitrary. And yet every subsumption is ideal: *subsumption is not only arbitrary, it is the source and the foundation of the arbitrary as such, the source and the foundation of contingency.* Hegel's ekstatic* rationality forms the horizon of contingency and is identical with it. Within the horizon of this subsumption all *"differentia"* "are and remain uncomprehended because their specific nature has not been grasped"[10]—this includes all *differentia*, political *differentia* as well, executive power, for instance. "The only philosophical category introduced by Hegel to define the *executive power* is that of the '*subsumption*' of the individual and particular under the universal, etc. Hegel rests content with this. The category of the 'subsumption' of the particular, etc., must be realized, and so he takes an empirical instance of the Prussian or modern State (just as it is—lock, stock, and barrel) which can be said to realize this category among others, even though this category may fail to express its specific nature."[11] Anything at all can be "subsumed," and any ideal unit of measurement is an illusion. Marx contests the claim that a mathematical investigation of the real can be undertaken and criticizes in advance the "scientific" development of the "human sciences." "After all, applied mathematics is also a subsumption."[12]

If the real is arbitrary in the *ekstasis* of subsumption, as ob-ject, it is, however, rational in itself, in the immanence of its own being; and the place accorded to reason is found in and through its identity with the real. Marx discovers the concept of a reason which is unrelated to the development of the Idea, to universality, to thought. What, then, is this reason, what is the real with which it is identified? As we have seen, this is individual activity, the need in which it is rooted, life. The life of individuals is reason because it is this life which explains and produces the formation of the family and of civil society.

---

*We have rendered by *ekstasis* Henry's term *ekstase*, which, with its Heideggerian overtones, is intended in its etymological sense as opening an original dimension of exteriority in which something can then be posited.—TRANS.

The life of individuals is true reason because its explanation is not fully explicit, allowing what is to be spread out before us, a mere theory involving what Marx called "deference,"[13] an interpretation which leaves what it interprets unchanged precisely because it produces what it explains and because in this way it constitutes the reason in the ontological sense of foundation, of grounding.

The political State too has its origin in the specific activity of individuals and can be understood only on this basis. Hegel interprets the State as the objectification of the Idea but the State offers a particular content, an internal distinction; it is divided into diverse powers; its organization is expressed and summed up in the constitution. Do all of these political *determinations* stem from the movement of the Idea and are they to be explained on the basis of it? Is it enough to describe the legislative power as the thought and the definition of the universal, the executive power as classifying individual cases under this universal and, finally, the crown as the power of decision to which the supreme authority of the State is always submitted? In other words: does the self-development of the universal essence in objectification through which it is realized actually contain within it—in addition to positing law as the universal legality to which everyone is submitted and which is held to express the general interest—the emergence of the particular, namely the cases which the executive and the administration subsume under the law, the emergence of the individual at last, namely the individual who actually performs the subsumption and, in general, makes the final decision in all the matters of State? Does the prince who governs, in whom the political essence in its active actuality is concentrated and whom, for this reason, Hegel called the "crown," does he too proceed from the Idea?

It is remarkable that Marx's critique focuses on this last point, on the problem of the individual grasped in his irreducibility to the ideal essence of universality. *The ontological heterogeneity of reality and of ideality is reaffirmed here at the very moment when this reality is grasped and defined unequivocally as the individual*. Just when Marx's problematic seems to move toward a more precise analysis of the specificity of political power, its ontological meaning suddenly appears. In the guise of a critique of monarchy, masked by the polemic against the King of Prussia, the status of reality is at issue; its insertion in ideal objectivity is once more in question.

The impossibility of deducing an individual, this individual, from the internal process of the concept may seem self-evident. If Marx's manuscript begins with the commentary on paragraph 261 of the *Philosophy of Right*, we must not, however, lose sight of the earlier development in this same work, in which Hegel intends to justify his political philosophy and, indeed, to provide the conceptual genesis of all the real determinations of the State. The fundamental concept on the basis of which philosophy, and no longer history, reveals the political determinations in their rational necessity is that of free will. Will is the universal essence of which the Idea, or the realized concept, is, precisely, the State in the fullness of its completion and of its organization. So it is the development of the universal essence of will, without any outside assistance, which thoroughly accounts for the particularity and the individuality which lend the State its actual content and which accounts first of all for particularity and individuality as such. The universal essence founds particularity in the sense that the will is able to emerge from the nothingness of its original indetermination only inasmuch as it wills, that is to say inasmuch as it determines itself as this or that act of will and, consequently, as a given, particular act. However, the actual will in its particularity includes within it, if it realizes itself and to the extent that it realizes itself, a monadic structure; it is a will in the sense of someone's will, and individuality is the third moment of universal essence. Particularity and individuality are originally neither limitations on nor external, incomprehensible alterations of the universal essence of the will but instead moments in its positive becoming and, precisely, its realization. In particularity and in individuality the will becomes Idea, that is, goes beyond the simple level of conceptual existence in order to be reality.

However, the ideal conception of free will is overdetermined in Hegel by a still further ontological presupposition, namely that the internal actualization of the will by which it becomes a particular and real will is its objectification. This is the reason why the self-development of the notion is identical with the emergence of objectivity; why, too, individuality is defined in paragraph 7, γ of the Introduction to the *Philosophy of Right* as the relation between particularity and universality.[14] Individuality is neither simply nor essentially what comes to be in an actual act of will, that is, its internal monadic form, but instead the immersion of particular determinations in the medium of objectivity which is real universality: the self-reflection of the particular. The individual becomes once again what he has always been within the tradition of Western philosophy: a thing to which thought is added, a being in the ekstasis of the horizon that frees him. It is then that the individual determination becomes a determination, properly speaking, in the sense of a negation and that particularity and individuality take on the basic character of finiteness.

The theory of the monarchical State reiterates these presuppositions. The State is the true, completed realization of the universal essence of the will. This means that the will develops its being to its utmost in the State, that it develops each of its determinations, that it pushes each to its limit, draws out of it the entire reality contained in its possibility, "condenses" it, as Hegel says, and thus brings it to a radical realization at the furthest point of its reality, to the point of existence. "The State," Hegel declares in paragraph 279, "is precisely this totality in which the moments of the concept have attained the actuality correspondent to their degree of truth"; in it, "each of the three moments of the concepts has its explicitly actual and separate formation." The third element of the concept is thus also carried back to its ground; it is not just individuality but, more precisely, that which ultimately realizes it, its existence, the individual, or rather—since the individual does not yet exist and is still only individuality—*an* individual, a person, if you like, but "the person enshrines the actuality of the concept" and constitutes someone in particular. The State, the will's ultimate reason, is therefore presented as necessarily monarchical. "Hence this absolutely decisive moment of the whole is not individuality in general, but a single individual, the monarch."[15]

The bulk of Hegel's demonstration is found in the following text: "personality, like subjectivity in general, . . . has its truth . . . only in a person, in a subject existing 'for' himself. . . ."[16] With this last statement Hegel demolishes his own philosophy; he not only affirms the eidetically monadic character of subjectivity; he also posits that subjectivity can in every instance be nothing other than an individual. But if subjectivity in the sense of an ideal determination, in the sense of personality, can exist only as a real individual, it is because its original existence is found here and only here. Instead of the action of the will as it produces its own determinations being able to produce the existence of an individual, it presupposes this existence. Moreover, how could the internal process of the Idea, the action of universal will, produce an individual since, as Marx bluntly states, the will does not act?[17] One cannot pass, then, from ideal universality and its determinations, from personality, to the real individual, but only from the latter to its own concept. Or, to use the terminology that Feuerbach (who himself borrowed it from Thomas Aquinas) has just taught Marx: personality is not the subject of which the individual would be the predicate but instead the subject is the individual, who in every instance is a particular individual, a real individual; individuality *and universality* are only predicates.

It can be clearly demonstrated that Hegel, in affirming that "what exists 'for' itself is just simply a unit," leaves his own philosophy behind, if we consider the context of this passage; there we see that real existence is removed from the initial spheres of the objective mind, from the family, the community, civil society, and entrusted to the State only insofar as the State itself ceases to be understood, in reality, as a sphere of the objective mind, as a moral personality. Moral personality, the objectification of universal essence, is swept aside in favor of a single individual. For the person exists no longer in the concrete being of a transcendental totality in which he participates and of which he is a member, but now he really exists as an individual, as a determined and isolated individual. Hegel states: "A so-called *artificial* person, be it a society, a community, or a family, however inherently concrete it may be, contains personality only abstractly, as one moment of itself. In an 'artificial person', personality has not achieved its true mode of existence," and yet the philosopher, whose well-known, explicit thesis—which he so often returns to and reiterates—is that the individual is real only in the State, writes quite to the contrary: "It is only as a person, the monarch, that the personality of the State is actual."[18] The rigorous philosophical content hidden under the questionable political theory is, in fact, blindingly obvious: it is the monadic structure of being.

It is in the name of this philosophical content that Marx rejects the political theory, monarchy. For it is to be noted that Marx supports Hegel's views as long as he strives to reduce the ideal essence of personality to a reality which it neither contains nor founds. The reality to which the "personality," the "individual," refers is monadic; this means that *it is, in every instance, an individual,* not an ideal unity but a real plurality. So that it is not only absurd to claim to deduce a real individual from personality, but it is just as absurd to deduce from it just a single individual. Hegel plays on the sense of the word "unit" and grossly deceives us. Because "what exists 'for' itself is just simply a unit," it in no way follows that there is but a single for-itself. Quite the opposite, the internal gathering together of being in the phenomenological actuality of its monadic structure is identical with its dispersal in the radical diversity of numerous monads. In order to attribute a sense to personality, that is, in order to find its reality outside of it, one can only move from personality to all individuals. Here is Marx's text: "It is self-evident that since personality and subjectivity are only predicates of the person and the subject they can exist only as person and subject, and the person is certainly but *one*. However, Hegel should have gone on to say that this *one* truly exists only as *many ones*. The predicate, the essence, can never exhaust the spheres of its existence in a *single one* but only in *many ones*."[19] Here, then, Marx presents the metaphysical foundation of the theory of democracy.

To begin with, this theory has a twofold signification. On the one hand, it involves the rejection of the unreasonable claim that a single individual be considered the real element of the State—and why this particular individual?—rather than all individuals, and, on the other hand, it involves the understanding that the political substance, namely universality, is indeed not the real moment of the State, its founding reality, since the latter resides precisely in the "individual" in the sense of all individuals. We see that the reality of the State resides in individuals and that ideal universality—no more than its determinations, for example, abstract personality—cannot be considered a principle of this reality, due to the fact that the individual intervenes everywhere in the State and not just in the concrete decision of a single man mysteriously deduced from the Idea. "Hegel," Marx writes, "should not be astonished to discover that the *real person* reappears everywhere as the essence of the State—for people make the State. He should rather have been astonished at the reverse, and even more at the fact that the person who appears in the context of his analysis of the State is the same threadbare abstraction as the person found in civil law."[20]

If people make the State, if the political substance is founded in them rather than itself founding them, Hegel's political philosophy is turned upside down along with his ontology. In place of the parts being determined by the whole, on the basis of their substantive homogeneity, is found instead the genealogical thesis, that is, the thesis of their difference, the thesis of the formation and the production of ideal universality out of a heterogeneous reality. By no means can the State, any more than the family or civil society, the great transcendent masses which structure the objective mind, be considered to be primary; none is explained by this mind as its internal distinctions; they all contain, instead, a fundamental reference to a reality of another order. The genealogical thesis then places us before an open question: what is the being of the real considered as the ground of all possible ideality? In the 1843 manuscript we find only the scattered, partial elements of an answer, and these concern only the political aspect which still refers, as in Hegel, to the consciousness of individuals as political individuals, as citizens. That this consciousness belonging to individuals is to be explained by their life is as yet merely intimated.[21] The sense, at least, of the relation established between the individual and the political essence is reversed. The latter no longer designates, as in Hegel, the substantiality to which individual consciousness is submitted as it aims at the general, in its "political disposition," in order itself to become substantial, but rather, through the mediation of their consciousness, individuals themselves produce this substance; it is their work.

This is why democracy is the truth of the political organization, of the constitution, because democracy explicitly ties it to individuals, to "the people," and presents it as produced by them and as having to be produced by them. "Democracy is the solution to the riddle of every constitution. In it we find the constitution founded on its true ground: real human beings and the real people . . . [and] posited as the people's own creation. The constitution is in appearance what it is in reality: the free creation of man."[22] The refusal, in appearance on ethical grounds, to let individual life be determined by the political essence and, in general, by an ideal legality, has its basis in ontology, if it expresses the genealogy of the universal and results from it. This refusal is expressed in the critique of monarchy: "In monarchy we have the people of the constitution, in democracy the constitution of the people." But the ultimate philosophical signification of this critique is constantly recalled, just as it will be throughout all of Marx's later works. "Democracy relates to all other forms of State as its Old Testament. In democracy, man does not exist for the sake of the law, but the law exists for the sake of man, it is human existence, whereas in other political systems man is a legal existence."[23] And yet this legal existence, the political constitution, and politics itself as such are themselves only an appearance if in every instance they presuppose, if the monarchy itself presupposes, reference to the individual. This is why "democracy is the generic constitution. Monarchy is only a variant and a bad variant at that."[24]

The inevitable reference of ideal universality to its real foundation is not only found in the theory of the monarch; it is expressed involuntarily throughout all of Hegel's thought. When political substantiality has been posited as principle, as absolute essence, and, precisely, as substance, as a self-sufficient reality in which everything that is must participate in order to find its being there, we then see this alleged autonomy dissolve in the movement of this alleged substance. Substance *is also* subject. The State, which is supposed to express and to contain the concreteness of being, in reality never attains this except insofar as it empties itself, making itself into subjectivity. Political substantiality is not only "objective substantiality," that is, the organism of the State and its constitution; it is also "subjective substantiality," that is, "political sentiment"

(§ 267). In paragraph 270 this substantiality is further defined by Hegel—and here we are quoting Marx's commentary—"(1) as the universal end of the State and then (2) as its various powers . . . (3) as the real mind that knows and wills itself."[25] In his ideal order Hegel may well invert the real genealogical order, positing first the general interest, then the powers responsible for realizing it, and, finally, the real mind which is directed at this interest and *in reality produces it* before preserving it, precisely, by instituting the powers of the State; he nevertheless cannot fail to include this third term, real mind, the concrete life of individuals in which political determinations are elaborated as so many ideal, transcendental meanings constituted in and by this concrete life. Once the universal has been hypostatized, it must be returned to its primary origin. The synthetic addition of subjectivity to political "substance" demolishes its claim to *Selbständigkeit*. Marx's text is resplendent in its serene simplicity. "Thus sovereignty, the essence of the State, is first objectified and conceived as something independent. Then, of course, this object must again become a subject."[26] "If Hegel had begun by positing real subjects as the basis of the State he would not have found it necessary to *subjectivize* the State in a mystical way."[27] "Hegel proceeds from the State and conceives of man as the subjectivized State; democracy proceeds from man and conceives of the State as objectified man."[28] Ideal objectivity is everywhere carried back to founding subjectivity. Hegel's God has need of men.

Marx's analysis, however, should be understood here in its radical meaning. For what is in question is not only the sense of the relation established between political substance and subjectivity. In reality, it is not a matter of knowing which is first, the subjective motivation of individuals who want to and who have to provide for themselves the conditions for their existence in common, or those conditions which Hegel conceives as the objectification of the universal. The genealogical thesis moves toward a more fundamental problematic, which no longer concerns simply the relation between the foundation and that which it founds but which, in a truly original way, concerns the internal structure of this foundation itself, the structure of subjectivity. This decisive meaning is presented to us in the discussion of the problem of the form or the being of the general interest, the "matters of general concern,"* which refer to nothing other than the political essence. As it repeats the elucidation of this essence, the 1843 manuscript provides us with its most essential philosophical contribution.

The elucidation of the "form" of the matters of general concern reproduces first of all that of political ideality in general. Political ideality necessarily refers back to a concrete subjectivity which produces it. "The universal thought of this ideality. . . ," Marx stated in his commentary on paragraph 279, "must be the self-conscious creation of the subjects and must exist as such for them and in

---

*To conform to the author's analysis, we have translated *"allgemeine Angelegenheit"* as matters of *general* concern rather than matters of *universal* concern and have correspondingly modified the quotes from the English-language edition of *The Critique of Hegel's Doctrine of the State*.—Trans.

them."[29] Indeed, it is only to the extent that political ideality is carried back to all subjects as their conscious work that it can in reality be a *general* concern, that is, the concern of each and every one. *The generality of the general concern does not exist in itself*; it is not a substantial essence, concrete in and of itself, but rather its being is constructed and takes shape only in and through its relation to individuals whose concern it is. This generality, then, exists only for them and through them. The generality of the general concern is not generality as such; it is not enclosed within the ideality of an autonomous and self-sufficient genus; it exists only in the for-itself of individuals, of "many individuals." Having hypostatized general concern in the transcendence of an objective essence, Hegel, on the contrary, cannot but add subjectivity to this concern in order to grant it being in the for-itself; subjectivity arrived at in this way presents a twofold nature. On the one hand, it no longer designates the concrete subjectivity of individuals who assemble themselves together into the State; instead it is none other than the *subjectivization of universal essence*, the simple demand by this being-in-itself for a becoming-for-itself. Here again Marx's text is crystal clear:

> The development of "matters of general concern" into the subject, and thus into independent existence, is represented here as a moment in the life-process of these "matters of general concern." Rather than make the subjects objectify themselves in "matters of general concern," Hegel causes the "matters of general concern" to extend into the "subject." The "subjects" do not require "matters of general concern" for their own true concern, but matters of general concern stand in need of the subjects for their formal existence. It is a matter of concern to the "matters of general concern" that they should also exist as subjects.[30]

Because the "subject" is but the formal existence of the general concern, the mere positing of the becoming-for-itself of the being-in-itself of the general, it itself remains general and completely undetermined, and anything at all can be subsumed under the exigency of this becoming. Who, then, will be conscious of the general interest and will be entitled to determine it? Should we mention in this regard the people itself? But for Hegel the people is as yet an inorganic mass that does not know what it wants and shows itself to be incapable of perceiving the path that it must take to realize its own interests. Or should we seek this consciousness of the general interest in the "estates," that is, in the assemblies of the different orders? But the latter are prisoners of their own particular interests and are unable to elevate themselves to the clear disinterested vision of what is truly the interest of the State. Dignitaries, offices, those in government, and, above all, the king alone know what must be done to maintain the universal interest above and beyond particular interests and, if need be, against them. And it is in this way that the general interest has in reality become something quite different from a general interest—everyone's interest—namely, a private concern, the monopoly of a few, of the monopolies for instance. In order to provide a content for the general demand for a becoming-for-itself issuing from the being-in-itself of the universal, Hegel turns to the empirical organization of the Prussian State and what exists here or there, here and now, as the mere result of history and of circumstances, is passed off as the very form of rational ideality and the rationality of the State vanishes in the bluntness of the fact.

In this way, the form of the general concern, its being-for-itself, or what is subsumed under this form—those in government, senior officials, monopolies—"the formal existence or the empirical existence of the general concern" is separated from its content, from the genuine general concern which would be everyone's concern; the general concern hypostatized by Hegel is not really general. The form is alien to the content, the content is alien to the form. Marx sums up his critique in these terms:

> "Matters of general concern" already exist "implicitly," in themselves, as the business of the executive, etc.; they exist without really being matters of general concern; they are in fact anything but that for they are of no concern to "civil society." They have already achieved their essential, implicit existence. If they now really enter "public consciousness" and achieve "empirical generality," this is purely formal and amounts to no more than a symbolic achievement of reality. The "formal" or "empirical" existence of matters of general concern is separate from their substantive existence. The truth of the matter is that the implicit "matters of general concern" are not really general, and the real, empirical matters of general concern are purely formal.[31]

However, it is not just because matters of general concern are in fact the privileged domain of a few that they are not matters of general concern, or that the form (the intention of a few) is in opposition to the content (the universal); *it is the form of the universal which in itself and in principle is inadequate to it*. In the text quoted above Marx says: "The 'formal' or 'empirical' existence of matters of general concern is separate from their substantive existence." These are not the same things; "or" here means neither exclusion nor equivalence. The "empirical" existence of matters of general concern means those in government, officials, those who take it upon themselves to work for the public welfare. The "formal" existence of matters of general concern originally designates nothing of the sort. The formal existence of matters of general concern is the becoming-for-itself of universal existence, the general presupposition of a subjectivity which is in general implied in substance inasmuch as the latter attains the concreteness of being only in the actuality of being-for-itself. It is not without importance that an empirical existence, and moreover a variable one, is subsumed under the formal existence of matters of general concern. This means that the form of the matters of general concern is of itself empty, that by itself as form it has no content. The form of the matters of general concern is purely formal. But what, then, is this purely formal form belonging to matters of general concern? As we have seen, it is the becoming-for-itself of the being-in-itself of the universal. *The universal essence is objectivity, the luminous milieu in which what is there is there for everyone, the condition and the reign of the "general." The universal essence's becoming-for-itself is its objectification. The subject's subjectivity which substance "is also," its becoming-for-itself, is the movement of self-positing by which the Idea renders itself phenomenal by setting itself in opposition to itself in the form of an object. Subjectivity is opposition. The opposition of the form and the content of the "matters of general concern" is not due to the empirical organization of the Prussian State, it is rooted in the structure of subjectivity and is identical with it*—in the structure of subjectivity as Hegel understood it. Marx writes: "Hegel thus separates content and form, being-in-itself and being-for-itself, and admits the latter only formally and externally."[32] Being-for-itself is added on externally to the in-itself as a formal element because it is the form of exteriority, exteriority itself as exteriorization and as ekstasis. The critique of formalism is the critique of ekstatic subjectivity. Against the backdrop of an ekstatic conception of subjectivity, no criticism of formalism is possible. Hegel vainly attempted to overcome formalism. He affirmed the immanence of the subject and of being. Substance itself, in itself is subject. But what matters is the nature of subjectivity. As long as subjectivity is ekstasis, it allows what is to exist in exteriority and as external. The immanence of subjectivity in being signifies the exteriority of being in relation to itself. Posited in this way in the self-positing of its exteriority in relation to itself, being is forever external, and its form—the form of this self-positing which cast it into exteriority as external to itself, as other than itself—is forever empty. An external content, an empty subjectivity—such is the metaphysical situation which Hegelianism assumes once more as its own and which Marx unceasingly attacks. "Subjective freedom is purely formal for Hegel. . .";[33] and even more explicitly: "it is inevitable that the real subject of freedom should be assigned a purely formal significance. The separation of the in-itself from the for-itself, of substance from subject, is a piece of abstract mysticism."[34]

Abstraction, which Marx calls mysticism, is not the product of an operation performed by the subject, it is the subject itself. Abstraction is the subject because it is the act of withdrawing itself, of abstracting itself from the content. And it is in this act of abstracting itself from the content that the form is constituted as an empty form, as subjectivity and as purely formal freedom. In this act, however, the form relates to the content and is inextricably bound to it. The form is but the abstraction of the content; it exists only as an abstraction of that from which it has removed itself, an abstraction of that which it is not, whereas the content exists only in this form which repudiates it. The indissoluble tie between form and content resides in abstraction. In abstraction, the form and the content are posited as opposing terms, as extremes, but in such a way that each leads back directly to the other, finds its being in the being of the other, and is the other. In abstraction lies the power and the essence of the dialectic, and through this power "every extreme is its opposite." As the poles of abstraction, as opposing terms each of which leads back directly to the other, form and content are, however, clearly defined. Form is an abstraction, objective ideality, the not-being-content in which the content exists as what the form is not and yet as that whose being it is—as finite being in its object-condition. Form is mind, content is matter. Mind and matter are not in opposition as two terms opposing one another in themselves; they are in opposition only in the unity of one and the same essence, in the unity of abstraction. The opposition of materialism and spiritualism is prephilosophical; it does not carry back to the ultimate ontological presupposition, for which matter and mind conjointly produce one another in the unity of a single event and a single structure, in the event of objectivity and in its ekstatic structure. Marx has not yet uttered the cry of his most extreme theoretical demand, his call for a philosophy which "differs both from idealism and materialism,"[35] but the conditions for this demand have already been posited. Right after writing that "every extreme is its opposite," he adds: "Abstract spiritualism is abstract materialism; abstract materialism is the abstract spiritualism of matter."[36] The conceptual genesis of the dialectical unity of materialism and of spiritualism as having its basis in abstraction and as constituted by it is stated explicitly by Marx: ". . . the issue turns on the fact that a concept . . . is viewed abstractly, that it is not treated as something autonomous but as an abstraction from something else and that only this abstraction has meaning; thus, for example, mind is only an abstraction from matter."[37] This dialectical unity explains "the inevitable transformation of the empirical into the speculative and the speculative into the empirical. . . ."[38]

The dialectical unity of spiritualism and of materialism, of idealism and of naturalism, points up the difficulties Hegel encounters in his attempt to determine the form of the matters of general concern. "The 'formal' *or* 'empirical' existence of the matters of general concern . . . ," Marx wrote in his commentary. We must now say instead: "The formal *and* empirical existence. . . ." For the opposition between form and content is established not only between the form and the content of the matters of general concern, between the for-itself and the in-itself of the political essence. Inasmuch as there is an attempt in a political philosophy to give a content to the very form of the general interest, for example, to the constituting power, this form then falls under the sway of the pitiless dialectic of abstraction, under its own dialectic. The form itself is split in two; it is at once formal existence and empirical existence, namely that of the estates, the bureaucracy, the government, the prince—every concrete existence which one might wish to subsume under this form in order to give it a content. Everywhere true existence is shattered; it breaks apart in ekstasis and is, in the light of ideality, no more than a dead, opaque, indifferent content. For reality itself becomes this content when it leaves its own ground, its own reality outside itself, in exteriority. Existence slips away when that which confers upon it its phenomenological actuality, and which makes it what it is, no longer stems from its own mind but now resides in an "alien mind." All existence is alienated in objectivity; its law is no longer within itself and the real is no longer rational. Marx leads us to understand that the abandonment of that which is unfolded in the light of objectivity refers to the latter and to the way in which it is unveiled in every instance, to the structure of ekstatic subjectivity itself. Marx states this in a proposition which encompasses the destiny of Western philosophy: "The profundity of Germanic subjectivity becomes manifest everywhere as the barbarism of mindless objectivity."[39] The critique of the matters of general concern leads us back to the ontological presuppositions with which Marx's manuscript began, and it gives them their decisive meaning. By refusing to oppose form and content, his critique outlines the concept of original existence which is not separated from itself, which remains within itself and finds therein its motivation, its legitimation, its actuality, its mind and its life. Marx's thought encounters here the ontological ground upon which all the subsequent developments will be constructed and, in particular, the rejection of all transcendence, the ever-continuing critique of alienation; this thought can already be understood and defined as a philosophy of radical immanence, a philosophy of life.

The paradox of the Critique of Hegel's Doctrine of the State lies in its claim to apply the concept of original existence—in which the separation of form and content does not occur, in which life is grasped in itself prior to any subsumption under an ideal horizon—to ideal existence, precisely to the political essence. Whereas the general was understood as a meaning produced by the consciousness of individuals on the basis of their real existence and in order to establish the possibility of this existence understood, consequently, as an objective meaning different from this real existence, Marx, on the contrary, rejects a difference of this sort. Whereas the universal essence was posited in its ideality, in its fundamental heterogeneity in relation to reality, Marx now wants to make them identical, to restore the homogeneity of the universal and the particular. Whereas exteriority was recognized as the form of the general concern, as constituting its being, Marx claims to conquer this exteriority, to conquer the transcendence of the political, and demands that the substance of the State become the individuals' very life. In this last presupposition, the 1843 manuscript attests to the fact that Marx's thought continues to be influenced by Hegelianism, and that reality continues to be the political totality in which the individual must participate. But in Hegel, the place of this reality is that of ideal objectivity, for it is in and through objectivity that universality becomes possible and is realized. What is present for each and every one is what is before them all; it is in the light of ekstasis that the individual relates to the essence and makes it consubstantial to himself. By claiming, on the contrary, to apply the structure belonging to life and its radical immanence, which he has just discovered, to political universality, Marx slips into an insurmountable contradiction. This same contradiction determines all of his analyses in the Critique of Hegel's Doctrine of the State and runs throughout this work.

The thesis on democracy, for example, is contradictory. On the one hand, it affirms that the State is produced by individuals, and this is done through opposition—"The State is objectified man"—hence as something different, as something derived. The people is the determining element, the State that which is determined; the people is the subject, the constitution is the predicate, and this is why the constitution evolves, inasmuch as the individuals themselves evolve. This, too, is why there is no need to subjectivize the State, to form a subjectivity that would be proper to it—the universal in its becoming-for-itself—because subjectivity existed before it in the concrete life of individuals and as this very life. But even though Hegelian presuppositions *still* dominate, so that what is held in common appears to be what is most essential, Marx—beyond whatever paltry preoccupations and particular interests he may display in line with the presuppositions that are *already* his own—cannot accept that what is essential is to be found precisely in some beyond, beyond real life, in ideality. The critique of the doctrine of the State then carries the meaning it truly has in the 1843 manuscript. What is at issue there is no longer the conception of the State as what is essential, the conception of political substantiality, but its status. The political element is the essence, but precisely because it is the essence it cannot be separated from us. What now dictates the preoccupations of the analysis is a philosophy of immanence; it is the rejection of separation, of all privation and of all alienation, the rejection of opposition as the opposition of form and content, of the opposition which allows the form to exist outside the content and the content outside the form. The State, precisely, cannot be a formal, ideal principle alien to the concrete life of individuals, to the real "material" content of society. "In democracy," says Marx, "the formal principle is identical with the substantive principle."[40] And it is in this that democracy differs from the other political forms. It differs from them in that it is itself no longer a form. "Every other political formation is a . . . form of the State,"[41] says Marx. The republic, for example, is distinguished from the monarchy as the government of all in opposition to that of just one, but this sort of distinction remains purely formal because it concerns only the political constitution and not the real content of the State. "Property, etc., in short the whole content of law and the State, is broadly the same in North America as in Prussia. Hence the republic in America is just as much a mere form of the State as the monarchy here. The content of the State lies beyond these constitutions."[42] This means that the real State is not political, or, again, that in the State there is a political sphere alongside other spheres which are not political and which, as a result, cannot be determined except in an external, formal, and apparent fashion by the political sphere itself, by the constitution. "In all forms of the State other than democracy the State, the law, the constitution is dominant, but without really dominating, i.e., without materially penetrating the content of all the non-political spheres."[43]

In this way the critique of the political element is redirected: it is no longer the critique of the political element but instead the critique of that which is not political, not yet political, and which has to become political. The opposition directed at Hegel—the philosophy of immanence—leads to a hyper-Hegelianism, to political totalitarianism. The State is no longer what is determined and, in accordance with the genealogical thesis, the product; instead it is what determines, it must determine, determine radically, "penetrating" all the spheres of the State. To tell the truth, no nonpolitical sphere can be allowed to remain in this sort of State. Individual activity, private life, affectivity, sensibility, sexuality must themselves be political. *The rejection of all transcendence establishes the undivided reign of transcendence itself*, and all that exists must be displayed, present to the gaze of all.

It is not without interest to note that this properly demential requirement, the unlimited reign of the political essence, is presented by Marx and legitimated by him in light of a dialectic borrowed from Hegel. If indeed the political element remains a mere form, leaving outside of itself a content which is unchanged in its own being, it is no longer the universal but a particular reality. This is the reason why political formations other than democracy, "political forms," are called "determinate, particular."[44] This is also why in democracy the political constitution does not exhaust the entire political reality; it is only one particular political reality, a part of the entire political reality of the State. In this way we may explain these apparently enigmatic lines: "In democracy the State as particular is only particular, and as universal it is really universal; i.e., it is not something determinate set off against other contents."[45] The claim that the political essence reduces the totality of the real to itself is identical with the refusal to allow the political essence to be circumscribed within the sphere of the constitution alone, inside the "political sphere," its rejection of the predemocratic state in which "the sphere of politics has been the only [real] state-sphere in the State, the only sphere in which both form and content was that of the species [*Gattungsinhalt*], i.e. truly universal. At the same time however, because politics was opposed to all other spheres, its content too became formal and particular."[46]

The claim that the political essence is no longer just a simple form, a particular sphere, but that it reduces the totality of the real to itself because it is now ratified and assumed by Marx as his own explains the nostalgic gaze he casts in the direction of the States in which this claim might seem to have been realized, in the direction of what he calls "original" *(immédiats)* political regimes. "In the original models of monarchy, democracy and aristocracy there was at first no political constitution as distinct from the real, material State and the other aspects of the life of the people. The political State did not yet appear as the form of the material State." This is the case in Greece—which offers us a new example of the ideal common to Hegel and to Marx—where "the *res publica* was the real private concern of the citizens, their real content," where "the political State as such was the only true content of their lives and their aspirations," where "a substantive unity [existed] between people and state."[47] This is also the case of the Middle Ages, where the organization of concrete life— serfdom, feudal property, guilds—is originally a political organization, the very organization of the State, so that here too "property, trade, society and man were political; the material content of the State was defined by its form; every sphere of private activity had a political character, or was a political sphere, in other words politics was characteristic of the different spheres of private life."[48]

Certainly the Middle Ages is presented as an era of "unfreedom"; it is considered nonetheless, in the sense of the 1843 manuscript, a "democracy."

We have been speaking of "Marx's hyper-Hegelianism." For Hegel himself was more realistic. Hegel's realism,[19] in the case we are considering, consists in this—that although the concrete spheres of civil society are posited by the movement of the Idea which is objectified in the State and are thus given as "Ideal," they nonetheless preserve a specific character which lies in the opacity of natural instincts and in the arbitrary character of individual will. Despite the fact that it is permeated with the universal, which secretly animates it, Hegel's civil society conforms to the description of the English moralists and economists. This is why there is, at the very least, a problem with respect to the homogeneity of civil society and the State, with respect to the reduction of the particular to the universal. The Hegelian conception of the State concerns, precisely, the means by which this homogeneity is to be established, the whole set of mediations through which the particular is carried back to the universal as to its true, albeit hidden, essence. And Marx's critique of the Hegelian conception of the State is precisely the *critique of mediations*. Now, in all its detours, in its complexity, which indeed reflects that of the political organism, the critique of mediations places us face-to-face with its constant presupposition, its rejection of all separation, the refusal to allow a true opposition to be established between particular individuals and the political essence, between civil society and the State. For it is indeed this prior difference between the terms which the mediation is then to relate which is implied in the idea of mediation and which motivates Marx's rejection.

The first and the most important of the mediations established by Hegel between civil society and the State is constituted by the "Estates" in the medieval sense, that is by the representative assemblies of the various groups into which society is divided by virtue of the concrete activity of their members. The Estates constitute the mediation that Hegel was seeking between the particular interest and the general interest because, as is stated in paragraph 289,

> at the same time the corporation mind, engendered when the particular spheres gain their title to rights, is now inwardly converted into the mind of the State, since it finds in the State the means of maintaining its particular ends. This is the secret of the patriotism of the citizens in the sense that they know the State as their substance, because it is the State that maintains their particular spheres of interest together with the title, authority and welfare of these. In the corporation mind *the rooting of the particular in the universal is directly entailed*, and for this reason it is in that mind that the depth and the strength which the State possesses in sentiment is seated.

But how can the corporation mind, which always represents a determined condition, the state of the shoemaker or the tanner, expressing particular preoccupations and interests, "the sense and temper of 'individuals and particular groups,'" ever be changed into the intention of the general and the universal as such, uniting with "the political and administrative sense and temper"? "The Estates," says Marx, "are the synthesis of the State and civil society. There is no indication as to how the Estates should go about reconciling the two opposed tempers."[50] The conception of the Estates as mediating between private interests and the general interest, far from being able to resolve their contradiction, on the contrary, presupposes and establishes it. "The Estates are the incarnation or contradiction between the State and civil society within the State. At the same time they symbolize the demand that this contradiction be resolved."[51]

It is true that in Hegel's view private interest does not directly run up against the general interest. Because it is divided from the start into corporations, orders, etc. and because the latter are themselves organized into "Estates," civil society's own interests are displayed only through the mediation of its political assemblies; it is on the level of these assemblies that the particular interest confronts the general interest and is then in a position to join together with it. As Marx recognizes in his commentary, "Only in the Estates as an element in the legislative power does it [civil society] acquire 'political significance and efficacy.'"[52] But, precisely, this "political" efficacy, which has as its aim the general and the universal and which is nothing other than the efficacy of the universal itself, represents something entirely new in relation to the efficacy of the state, which is of its very nature a private state.* The private state is the state of civil society and has nothing to do with the "general state"; far from being able to join together with the general determinations, with the general as the end of its essential activity, it is directly opposed to this. The private state (der Privatstand), says Marx, "is the [state] [der Stand] of civil society against the State [den Staat]. The [state] [der Stand] of civil society is not a political [state] [Stand]."[53] In order to become political, to have the universal as its aim and to be integrated into the State, the private state "must rather abandon what it is, viz. its private status."[54] This self-renunciation remains absolutely inexplicable on the basis of what this state is; the political act of civil society is a "thorough-going transubstantiation" and, for this reason, completely unfounded. "Civil society," says Marx, "must completely renounce itself as civil society, as a private [state], and must instead assert the validity of a part of its being which not only has nothing in common with, but is directly opposed to, its real civil existence."[55]

It is remarkable that in order to make the Hegelian antinomy apparent, Marx transposes it to the level of the individual, who thus appears at once as the criterion and as the place where the opposition between civil society and the State is to be found. "What we see here in the individual case is in fact the

---

*The term "private state" (état privé) refers to the private life of the individual; state (état) in lowercase is to be taken in the sense of a condition or situation, while the uppercase form, State, refers to the political entity, in particular to the Hegelian State. Since the author employs "état privé" as the translation of Privatstand and develops in his own text the notion of state as condition in contrast to State as political body, we have kept this distinction in our translation and have modified the passages quoted to correspond to this terminology.—TRANS.

general rule. Civil society is separated from the State. It follows, therefore, that the citizen of the State is separated from the citizen as a member of civil society."[56] Because the citizen of the State and the simple citizen are one and the same individual, it is therefore in him that the opposition now resides, an opposition which is no longer that between two different terms but an opposition within life, sundering it. Henceforth, the individual leads a double life; "he finds himself in a double organization," citizen on the one hand, a private person on the other. Only, as a private person the individual is actually outside the State. To enter political life, he must renounce his real life; he cannot draw from the latter the property that makes him a member of the State. "If he is to become effective as a real citizen of the State, if he is to acquire true political significance and efficacy, he must abandon his civil reality, abstract from it. . . ."[57]

The argument by which Hegel thought he could found the transposition from the civil to the political upon his ontology is inverted here. In fact, in accordance with this ontology, the transposition to the political realm is by no means made on the basis of a state which would be of its essence different from the general state: *the universal reigns in civil society before it is realized in political society*. The reign of the universal in civil society is manifested by the ever-widening series of concentric "circles" or "spheres" within which the concrete life of men is spontaneously organized: family, corporation, etc. It is on the basis of these spheres, which themselves are already general realities, modes in which the universal is realized, that the properly political edifice of the State takes shape; and it is for this reason that these spheres truly are and are capable of being the "bases" of the State. Hegel's political thought has always rejected the notion of an immediate sphere composed of an atomistic multitude of individuals, and this is what motivates, for example, the polemic against Rousseau. With this prior condition of an immediate sphere, which already involves mediation, organization, totality, and idealism, Marx's critique in the 1843 manuscript finds its proper ground and the intervention of the individual finds its true sense. The private state which must be reunited with the political state is precisely not that of isolated individuals; it is a state common to a great number, a state which is a genus, the Estate of the peasant, the tradesman, etc. The private state is the state of individuals organized into society. "The [private state] is the [state] of civil society, or, civil society is the [private state]."[58] Civil society may then well be presented organically in the "available forms of community"; it nevertheless remains in itself private, nonpolitical. Its internal distinctions, the different spheres, the "available forms of community" are nonpolitical as well. "Now if Hegel counterposes the whole of civil society as a private [state] to the political State, it inevitably follows that all distinctions within the private [state], i.e. the various classes of citizens, have only a private significance in respect to the State and no political status at all."[59] To the extent that the communities in which the individual exists immediately are private, nonpolitical, the emergence into politics, the transubstantiation through which what is not political becomes so, thus bears a well-determined form: it is only in and through the annihilation of these private communities that politics can be born; it is only by breaking out of the concrete spheres of civil society that the individual can become a citizen, can exist and live in line with the State. Hegel did not think nor did he intend that the aim of the general should originate in solitary individuals, but this is what he is forced to do to the extent that the immediate organization of civil society is that of the private state. "The atomism into which civil society is plunged by its political actions is a necessary consequence of the fact that the community . . . in which the individual exists, civil society, is separated from the State, or in other words: the political State is an abstraction from civil society."[60]

Such is now the sense of the individual as he enters in here: he is no longer the foundation, the sign, and the place of the real, on the basis of which politics is constituted. The universal is primary, the individual arises only in and through his decomposition in the dissolution of the primitive organic masses of society. This dissolution, which is at the same time the abandonment of the individual to his atomistic condition, is an event; it is prepared for by the absolute monarchy with its bureaucratic centralization, which, bit by bit, takes all political power away from the Estates, leaving them to fend for themselves, cut off from the meaning of the universal; it is realized under the French Revolution, which pulverizes these Estates themselves, in the sense that the tie existing between the private state, the social state, and the individual becomes an external, contingent tie. At work, the individual is no longer rooted in a true community; he is not sustained "as a member of a community, . . . an objective community, organized according to established laws and standing in a fixed relationship to him."[61] He no longer works just because he is spurred on by need; the relationship he maintains with his Estate involves both chance and vital necessity: "the principle of the civil (state) or civil society is enjoyment and the capacity to enjoy."[62]

In this way the historical situation described by the Hegelian theory of the State is actually realized. "Hegel should not be blamed for describing the essence of the modern State as it is, but for identifying what is with the essence of the State."[63] What exists is a shattered, disjointed reality which has allowed the universal to attain the condition of being-for-itself, to attain effective political consciousness, but in an external fashion, as a mere form. "In the modern State, as in Hegel's Philosophy of Right, the conscious, true reality of the universal interest is merely formal. . . ."[64] How then can reality, which has slipped back into natural contingence and which has been left to scatter into atomistic elements, be reunited with a rationality which itself has withdrawn into ideality, into the irreality of the political heavens? The second mediation established by Hegel between civil society and the State has the merit of no longer referring to an archaic situation, to Estates which in modern times have lost all political and even social significance, but of being based instead on the real world. For this very reason, however, the second mediation established by

Hegel is doomed to failure because, relying on the real separation of civil society and the State, it too can do no more than express it.

The second mediation is constituted by the body of functionaries whose activity is characterized not by an interest stemming from some personal individuality but by service to the State. The second mediation is based on the real world because it starts with the isolated individual, because it offers to each individual considered separately the possibility of acceding to the universal. "This opportunity to join the class of civil servants, available to every citizen, is the second bond established between civil society and the State; it is the second identity."[65] We know the irony with which Marx discussed this "identity." By positing that the service of the State requires that men forego "selfish . . . satisfaction" and "subjective ends," Hegel recognized the right to find this satisfaction in the discharge of one's duty, along with the civil servant's right to earn his living from this work. "There lies the link," said Hegel, "between universal and particular interests which constitutes both the concept of the State and its inner stability." "In § 294," says Marx, "Hegel derives the payment of salaries to officials from the Idea. Here, in the payment of salaries to officials . . . the real identity of civil society and the State is postulated."[66] Polemics aside, the paradox of the second mediation consists in the fact that access to the universal is reserved to those who have entered public service. Access to the universal is the privilege of a closed group. But on what does this privilege rest? On the one hand, on caprice—it is the prince who appoints the civil servants; on the other hand, on examinations, whereby those who want to serve the State have to prove their capabilities. Leaving irony aside once again here ("it is plain that in every examination the examiner is omniscient"), the critique of the examination brings us back to what is essential, to the division into two sorts of knowledge, "the knowledge of civil society and the knowledge of the State,"[67] the examination being the initiation into the latter, "the official recognition of the transubstantiation of profane knowledge into sacred knowledge."[68] However, the possibility for a few to reach the knowledge of the universal essence in another sphere through their initiation, the break which allows a transubstantiation, presupposes an earlier state in which the others still remain, each suffering his obscure fate. The mediation of the examination, of public service, has the same sense as all the mediations constructed by Hegel, that of referring back to a primary and insurmountable division. Division, "mediation" permeate the entire edifice. The bureaucracy, which should establish the bond between civil society and the government, expresses only their conflict and is itself an element of this conflict. The bureaucracy prevents the Estates from having their particularity recognized for what it is in opposition to the State, whereas the Estates prevent the bureaucracy from foundering in its own caprice. What is more, the bureaucracy must not only be protected from itself by the Estates, which it protects from themselves, it must also be protected from itself by itself, by its hierarchical organization, by "the sovereign working . . . at the top." Finally, each civil servant must be protected against himself, for his existence is twofold, and in him the service of the State must win out over private interest. But the service of the State itself leads to the "'mechanical' nature of bureaucratic knowledge and work"; it must therefore be corrected by the personal development of the civil servant, by the "direct education in thought and ethical conduct" (§ 296), so that, as Marx says, "The human being in the official is supposed to save the official from himself. But what a unity! . . . What a dualistic category. . . !"[69]

And, constantly referring to the opposition between civil society and the State which it presupposes, the mediation, far from being capable of surmounting it, attests to the fact that the political essence was unable to reduce the real to itself, that it is not the essence of the real. *That the political essence is the essence and the ultimate reality of the real, that it must as a result restore reality to itself and make it homogeneous with itself in the adequation and the transparence of a perfect consubstantiality, this is, on the contrary, the presupposition of the 1843 manuscript, a presupposition borrowed from Hegel but which Marx wants to render actual.* But what if, instead of coinciding in an original ontological unity, the real and the political are prey to an opposition which makes them spring apart as if they were separate poles, "[if] it cannot have escaped Hegel's notice that he has established the executive as an antithesis of civil society, and indeed as a dominant polar opposite. How then does he prove the existence of an identity?"[70]

The critique of primogeniture—which is just one more mediation that Hegel has borrowed purely and simply from the Prussian State—is interesting because it makes more obvious and more imperative the requirement that the actual reign of the universal, the actual political penetration of civil society, be established, but above all because *it allows us to perceive for the first time an economic definition of this society.* The relation between the political and the economic is therefore also posited explicitly for the first time in Marx's work, and there is no mistaking the solution proposed. *The economic element is not the essence, it is not reality and can neither define reality nor determine it, the economic element cannot be a principle of determination.* Far from constituting reality, the economic element is, on the contrary, the loss and privation of reality, alienation from reality. Now this initial characterization is found not only in the 1843 manuscript and is due not only to the very peculiar way in which the economic element intervenes at this point in the problematic. All of the subsequent work will attest to the fact that the economic element is never, for Marx, the determining element, the principle in the sense of an ontological productive principle, a *naturans*, or a founding power, that it is never true and original reality but instead, for the thought that moves back to reality, simply an effect, a determination that has been produced and engendered, a *naturata*. Certainly, any critical elaboration of the concept of economy is as yet lacking in the 1843 manuscript, or rather the concept is elaborated here in such a naïve fashion that it will later be explicitly rejected. At least the status of the economic element receives a determination that will prove to be decisive, although it still remains purely negative, that of not being reality.

In the 1843 manuscript, reality is political reality. The relation of the political to the economic is precisely the relation of what is real to what is not real. And Marx's critique of the Hegelian interpretation of primogeniture is precisely the critique of a conception which, by making the economic the determining element, thereby grants it a role, a status, an unreasonable and out-and-out scandalous claim. It is true that Hegel wanted to show the same thing as Marx—their presuppositions, once again, are identical—namely that the State determines the organization of civil society, including, for example, the institution of primogeniture, which he posits as a mediation in the process of its own realization. Only, Hegel showed the contrary: not that the State determines primogeniture, but that primogeniture, or the landed property it represents, determines the State. Against his wishes, Hegel's analysis produces the inadmissible theory, which is ontologically false, that the economic determines the political. Let us turn to the texts in question.

Primogeniture is the institution whereby the family reserves its landed property for the firstborn, who then receives it as his inheritance. This allows the firstborn to be independent of "the uncertainty of business," of the fluctuations in possessions that are generally observed in civil society, independent too of governmental power and its favors and, finally, of the very will of the firstborn himself, since he cannot dispose as he likes of the possessions he has received. Through his independence, which rests on that of his fortune, the firstborn is free to assume the tasks and the problems of the State, and in this way the order of primogeniture is, as § 306 states, "more particularly fitted for political position and significance. . . ." Ever faithful to his realism, Hegel thinks that he can find in the family and in nature itself the conditions for realizing the universal. The order of primogeniture forms a "class . . . whose ethical life is natural, whose basis is family life. . . ." (§ 305).

However, the principle of family life is love, "equally loved children," which grants to each member of the family an equal share in its possessions. Far from being able to rest on the principle of family life, from expressing its "spirit," primogeniture is its radical negation. The sacrifices entailed for political ends which Hegel asks of the family means sacrificing the family itself, its liquidation. "The state which is called family life," says Marx, "is thus deprived of the basis of family life."[71] Moreover, according to the *Philosophy of Right*, property is held to be the expression of free will, its realization, objective becoming in the world. It is in this way that property has a moral, rational, even spiritual significance. In primogeniture, however, landed property falls outside the freedom of the will, outside the will of the father, of the other members of the family, and of the firstborn himself. Property cannot be shared, divided up; it is inalienable, so that "the 'inalienability' of private property implies the 'alienability' of the universal freedom of the will and of ethical life."[72] Primogeniture should mean independence, but, in fact, it means absolute dependency, the dependency of everyone and of the whole social organization with respect to property, which is set up as an absolute, and to its own proper law. "Property is no longer mine in so far as 'I put my will into it'; it is truer to say that my will only exists 'in so far as it exists in the property.' My will does not possess, it is possessed."[73] Or we might say that the arbitrariness of the owner has become the specific arbitrariness of private property and, to borrow once again from the language of Feuerbach, that "private property has become the subject of will, the will survives only as the predicate of private property."[74] As a matter of fact, it is not only the will which is now no more than the predicate of private property; the entire social organization, the political organization itself, and the State along with it are only the expression of this reversal. It is private property which designates those who possess the right of primogeniture, those who participate directly in the affairs of the State, and, consequently, it is private property which defines the esential element of constituent authority, for it is the stability of landed property that confers upon the State the stability which models and determines its constitution. "The political constitution at its highest point is thus the constitution of private property."[75] And again: "What makes the glories of primogeniture appear in such a romantic light is that private property . . . is made to appear as the highest synthesis of the political State."[76]

In the analysis of primogeniture found in the 1843 manuscript, the concept of alienation is divided into three different levels. Alienation designates: (1) the condition in which love is thwarted, prevented from acting in accordance with its own law and made, on the contrary, to accept this transgression of its law— love itself refers here to the "family spirit," to a manifestation of the objective mind rather than to the life of the individual; (2) the condition in which the will is kept from accomplishing what it wills, that is to say, is unable to objectify or to realize itself—the will here being individual will in the sense of a particular determination, in the sense of "arbitrary"; (3) the condition in which the authentic moral life, the becoming-for-itself, of the universal essence in political consciousness, in consciousness of the State, is itself thwarted in the sense that the real elements of the State are precisely not of the same nature as this consciousness, are not the objectification of the universal—for the real elements of the State no longer designate here the monarch, civil servants, or the various Estates but, in fact, the right of primogeniture. The three terms which serve as the reference for the definition of alienation and which function in each case as its criterion—the spirit of love, arbitrary will, and the effective self-consciousness of universal and rational will—are borrowed from Hegel and are comprehended and defined in light of his ontology. These are Hegel's own presuppositions which Marx then turns against Hegel, not in order to question them once more but in order to demand their radical realization.

Of the three modes of realizing the concept of alienation as these are implied in primogeniture and which, in turn, determine it, the third is the most important because it concerns reality itself, universal will and its realization in the

State, the political essence. To say that by virtue of primogeniture landed property prevents the realization of a rational State and, quite the opposite, makes it merely the formal expression of private property, all this means that the economic element is what in the State prevents the realization of the universal and keeps it at the level of an empty structure. And this in turn means that *the economic element is the alienation of the political element.* At the time he wrote his *Critique of Hegel's Doctrine of the State,* Marx had not yet begun his studies on political economy, and this is why we have asserted that, in the 1843 manuscript, the determination of the concept of the economy remains as yet naïve and, for the most part, negative. This determination is naïve because it purely and simply assimilates the economy with material things, with landed property, with the land. It is especially negative because, in this material, opaque, and determinate element, it grasps only what is opposed to the realization of the universal, to the consciousness of the State.

On the other hand, is it not obvious that the determination of the economic element is actually neither naïve nor negative, since this concept does not arise in Marx's problematic in complete isolation but, precisely, in connection with the political essence? And it is this relation, the one existing between the economic and the political, which is straightaway in question. And this relation receives, no less immediately, an interpretation in terms of a schema which is far from naïve, that very schema by which Jacob Boehme attempted to understand the relations between God and the world and to which Hegel will return. We have presented this schema because it in fact directs the *Critique of Hegel's Doctrine of the State.* This is the schema of opposition. The political and the economic elements are placed within this framework with, on one side, the phenomenal essence of spirituality and, on the other, the opaque determination of matter, raw being. The political element is the "light of the State," universality in the actuality of its being-for-itself, pure consciousness; the economic element is the earth, its determination restricted to landed property, the "soil." And the paradox of primogeniture lies in positing as the principle of the State not the State itself, the luminous will of the universal, the being-for-itself of the general, the mind, but rather the absurd claim attaching to a piece of land, the deaf stubbornness of an obscure element, the bluntness of the fact of the matter and the hardness, so to speak, of the ground itself. Here again Marx's text is enlightening: "The 'substantial will manifest and revealed to itself' becomes transformed into a mysterious will broken on the soil, a will intoxicated by the very opacity of the element to which it is attached. The 'assured conviction with truth as its basis' which is . . . 'political sentiment' is a conviction based [literally] 'on its own ground.' "[77]

In the 1843 manuscript Marx gives the name of religion to the naked, brute fact, to its claim to be something in and of itself, matter's claim to take the place of mind. Religion designates materialism. This is why Marx writes in the same passage: "Because primogeniture is the religious form of private property we find that in our modern age religion has generally become an integral part of

landed property. . . . Religion is the highest conceptual form of this brutality."
And again: "Primogeniture is private property enchanted by its own independence and splendor, and wholly immersed in itself; it is private property
elevated to the status of a religion."[78] Religion represents the primacy of the
economy.

By subsuming the relation between the political and the economic under the
schema of opposition, Marx has not entirely forgotten the dialectical relation
which never fails to refer the form back to the content. "At every point Hegel's
political spiritualism can be seen to degenerate into the crassest materialism."[79]
This relation, however, is no longer comprehended in its necessity, as the very
structure of opposition; *this structure is no longer questioned*. Quite the contrary,
Marx himself takes over the Hegelian presupposition of objective universality
without admitting as a result just what this objectivity implies, *what it is*, that is,
the liberation of finite being, the *manifestation* of an *obscure* element. German
philosophy continues to reign although its sense has been lost. For what Jacob
Boehme wanted to account for was precisely the manifestation *of finite being*. In
his pathetic effort to justify the world on the basis of the concept of mind,
Boehme indeed interprets finite being as the condition of manifestation itself
and so thereafter he is able to understand manifestation as the manifestation of
finite being. In this way opposition, objectification, and the alienation of mind
in the world receive as their decisive meaning the mind's own proper realization, its capacity to become itself in the emergence of phenomenality. Becoming
other is the self's becoming itself. Consciousness of the object is self-
consciousness. The concept of alienation which also—and above all—means
realization is nevertheless none other than the Hegelian concept of alienation.
This concept secretly determines the entire philosophy of mediation and, on the
level of political philosophy, dictates the possibility and the necessity for the
objective mind of the State to include within itself natural, material determinations, to posit them as its own condition, as "ideal" determinations.

The moment has now come to state explicitly for the first time: between Hegel
and Marx stands Feuerbach. Indeed, it is in Feuerbach that the concept of
alienation undergoes a decisive modification. Alienation no longer means realization but, in the ordinary sense of the word: loss, privation. Starting with
Feuerbach, then, the concept of alienation in the sense of simple privation
dominates neo-Hegelian thought and, through it, the subsequent development
of modern philosophy. The second sense of the Hegelian concept of alienation—alienation in the sense of loss or privation—comes thus to cover and to
hide the essential determination, that is, alienation in the sense of realization.
This is the case notably in Marx. Marx's entire work—not just the early writings
but the later texts as well—is commanded by the privative, negative meaning of
the concept of alienation. The opposition is from then on nothing more than a
mere opposition. Far from being the condition of light, the earth signifies its
suppression. Far from being integrated into the actual becoming of the self-
consciousness of the universal, in the State, landed property is its very anti-

thesis, but an antithesis lacking movement, its extreme opposite but a nondialectical opposite, the term frozen in itself, petrified, forever irreducible, the irrational. "In reality primogeniture is a consequence of private property in the strict sense, private property petrified, private property [*quand même*] at the point of its greatest autonomy and sharpest definition."[80] And Marx even speaks of "the barbarism of private property as opposed to family life."[81]

With the decisive modification of the concept of alienation, nature—of which private property is at one and the same time a part and the symbol—thus loses all possible political significance, all spiritual significance, since it has ceased to be the condition for the realization of the concept of mind, one of its elements and, as Jacob Boehme (even before Hegel) would have it, its "basis." The critique of naturalism that continues throughout the 1843 manuscript derives from this conceptual mutation. Paradoxically, it is under the influence of Feuerbach's "materialism" that Marx's radical political spiritualism, his hyper-Hegelianism, is developed. The denunciation of primogeniture then links up with the great critiques developed in the *Critique of Hegel's Doctrine of the State*, thereby enabling us to recognize one of its major themes, the impassioned rejection of any material element which could claim to participate jointly in the constitution of the State organism or even to serve as its ground. The denunciation of primogeniture connects up with the critique of monarchy. In primogeniture, nature claims to define legislative power since those who possess this right are designated by natural birth. "Participation in the legislature is then an innate right of man. Here we have born legislators. . . ."[82] As if the position of ideal universality and, above all, the designation of the legislator himself had to refer back to a natural determination rather than to the very form of universality, to thought, to conscious and free will, as this is expressed, for example, in elections, for "elections, the conscious product of the trust of the citizenry, stand in quite a different necessary connection to the political end than does the physical accident of birth."[83] In monarchy nature is held to define sovereign power and, through it, the executive since the king is determined by birth, and it is sexual activity that produces kings just as it determines who will benefit from the right of primogeniture. In the project of the universal, nature is everywhere substituted for mind. "In this system nature creates kings and peers directly just as it creates eyes and noses. What is striking is to discover the product of a self-conscious species represented as the product of a physical species."[84] And again: "At the apex of the political State birth is the decisive factor that makes particular individuals into the incarnations of the highest political office. At the highest level political office coincides with a man's birth in just the same way that the situation of an animal, its character and mode of life, etc., are the direct consequence of its birth. The highest offices of the State thus acquire an animal reality."[85] This is why it must be said of the very principle of the Hegelian State what Marx said of the nobility and its "secret": it is mere "zoology."[86]

The critique of naturalism therefore now includes an attack on the concept of the individual understood as a natural, "empirical" individual. The naturalistic definition of the individual is borrowed from Feuerbach's materialism. Not only is the individual tied to the natural functions that take place in him—drinking, eating, procreating—but his essence is constituted by them, *the essence of individuality is corporeity*. If "the understanding is the power which has relation to species,"[87] if it is the consciousness of the species and in this opens us to the universal, no actual existence can ever arise in the milieu opened in this way; *the species is ideal and finds its existence only outside itself*, in an existence which in its very principle is determined, individual, corporeal. The body is just this very principle of individuation, that is to say, the principle of reality as well. "Individuality and corporeality," says Feuerbach, "are inseparable."[88] And again: "The body is the basis, the subject of personality."[89]

However, if the individual is defined in terms of his body—as this is naïvely understood by Feuerbach, that is, as an empirical object—and if the body's most representative activity is its sexual activity, then the question of its relation to the supreme essence, to the essence of political universality, arises once more with even greater urgency. Now, Marx never ceased to affirm the primacy of this essence. Not only do universality and its objectification in the State, and these alone, define that which is to be considered—and which truly is—rational and substantive, but it is repeatedly stated that this essence is not and must not be something ideal, that it cannot continue to develop outside the real, outside of actual existence, precisely, outside of the individual. Eating, drinking, sex, and the activity through which these functions continually seek their satisfaction together constitute civil society, but civil society must not be something different from the State, from the species, from the universal. If the individual and the State are cast time and again as opposite poles, as the individual, precisely, and the universal, as the real and the ideal, as the empirical and the spiritual, how then can this structural ontological heterogeneity, on the contrary, be overcome; how can a homogeneity be reestablished between them? The 1843 manuscript itself creates a divide of the highest philosophical tension; to Marx must be put the question he himself posed to Hegel: "How is unity to be established?"

The question of how the individual enters into the sphere of the universal is the theme and the content of Hegelianism in general, and this question finds its formulation on the level of political thought in § 308 of the *Philosophy of Right:*

> To hold that every single person should share in deliberating and deciding on political matters of general concern on the ground that all individuals are members of the State, that its concerns are their concerns, and that it is their right that what is done should be done with their knowledge and volition, is tantamount to a proposal to put the democratic element without any rational form into the organism of the State, although it is only in virtue of the possession of such a form that the State is an organism at all. The idea comes readily to mind because it does not go beyond the abstraction of "being a member of the State," and it is superficial thinking which clings to abstractions.

The quality of being a member of a State is abstract in a democracy because it is presented as immediate, as self-evident. Hegel wants to say that an individual attains universal life only at the end of a process, the process of internal self-negation through which the individual denies his natural determination in order, in this negation and through it—that is, in the negation of the particular which is the work of the universal and which institutes it—to make himself homogeneous with the universal and to participate in its life, *to become* a member of the State. This sort of process is one of mediation, the final example of which we find here: elections. For everyone cannot participate directly in the affairs of the State but can do so only through the intermediary of elected delegates who, as part of a *political* assembly, will be able to overcome their natural determinations and their immediate interests. Consciousness of the State passes by way of political representation. We are thus led back to the problematic of the "Estates." But the critique of elections cannot be a mere repetition of the critique of mediations, which always presuppose the separation they wish to overcome. To the question of the relation between the political essence and the individual, the 1843 manuscript must now provide a response.

This response consists in the metaphysical *coup d'état* by which the universal is presented straightaway as the essence of the individual. The identity of the civil and of the political no longer remains to be established; it is already given in their very source. The individual *is* a member of the State. This is why from the outset Marx's text contests the claim that the determination which consists in being a member of the State must itself be abstract. Is this not the most concrete determination in Hegelianism itself? "In the first place Hegel describes 'being a member of a State' as an abstraction, although even according to the Idea, and thus the tendency of his own theory, it is the highest, most concrete social determination of the legal person, of the member of a State."[90] It is therefore not a "superficial" thought, lost in "abstraction," which considers the individual as a member of the State. It is only in Hegel's analysis *and, it is true, in the modern State* that the individual is only abstractly a member of the State, and this is so precisely because the modern State is itself an abstraction, because the political essence is located beyond the reach of real society. It is therefore necessary that this society in itself, that is in its very reality, become "political" and that the individual in himself be "political." But how is this to occur? "In a really rational State one could reply: 'Not all, as individuals should share in deliberating and deciding on political matters of general concern,' for 'individuals' do share in deliberating and deciding on matters of general concern as 'all,' i.e. within society and as members of society. *Not all as individuals, but the individuals as all.*"[91]

With "the individuals as all," Marx avoids the Hegelian dilemma: either all participate in the affairs of the State—but this is impossible—or else—and this is, consequently, inevitable—only a few: the delegates. But whether all or only a few participate in the affairs of the State, the condition of Hegelian individuals is in every instance identical: the political essence is located beyond them, and this is why they must strive, through a magical transformation, through the internal self-negation of what they are, to arrive at this essence—no matter whether all or only a few ever reach it. It is this metaphysical condition, in which the individual finds himself from the outset separated from the universal essence in the Hegelian world, that Marx attacks; this is why he can say that, in this world, participating in the affairs of the State "either all the individuals act, or a few. . . . *In either case* 'all' refers only to an external multiplicity or totality of the individuals. [Universality] . . . is not an essential, mental, real attribute of the individual."[92]

What is meant by "all the individuals" becomes clear. What is important is not the plural form, not the multitude of individuals. It is not a matter of considering a collection, a sum, the plurality of individuals, their external totality. "External," that is, as this totality is developed in exteriority, as external precisely to each individual. It is a question of each individual, of each individual considered in himself, in his internal essence, in his inner quality. Universality denotes this quality at the same time as it defines reality. And it is to the extent that the individual has this quality in himself that he is real. As long as he does not possess this quality, the individual can only be defined in terms of "abstract individuality." Inasmuch as he contains this universality, and with it reality, the individual has no need to acquire this quality and, in fact, he would be incapable of acquiring it by joining together with others, by making up a totality together with them, one external to his being which would go beyond the individual in some sense. Universality is not a composite, as in the Hegelian State, in which universality is "only the complete sum of individuality. One individual, many individuals, all individuals. One, many, all—none of these determinations affects the essence of the subject, of the individual."[93]

What is in question is therefore the being of the individual, of his essence. The essence of the individual is the political essence. It is on the grounds of this essence in him that the individual is a member of the State, that he not merely shares in the State but that the State is his share,[94] his substance, the reality of his particular reality, his individual reality. In the final analysis, democracy is founded on the essence of the individual understood as the political essence. The theory of democracy says that "each is really only a moment of the *demos* as a whole."[95] It is in the political essence of the individual that the problem of the form of the general concern finds an adequate solution. In § 277 Hegel wrote: "The particular activities and agencies of the State are its essential moments and therefore are proper to it. The individual functionaries and agents are attached to their office not on the strength of their immediate personality, but only on the strength of their universal and objective qualities. Hence it is in an external and contingent way that these offices are linked with particular persons. . . ." Marx calls into question the concept of an individual who would not be defined by his "universal and objective qualities," who would not be a member of the State, along with the idea of an "immediate personality" the essence of which would not as yet be the political essence. There is indeed a natural element in the individual, but this element could not be the basis of his

personality, which is constituted only within the light of the State. "The activities and agencies of the State," says Marx, "are bound to individuals . . . but
not to the individual conceived as a physical being, only as a being of the State;
they are bound to the state-like qualities of the individual. It is therefore
ridiculous for Hegel to assert that these offices are 'linked with particular
persons in an external and contingent way.' On the contrary, they are linked to
the individual by a *vinculum substantiale*, by an essential quality in him. They
are the natural outcome of that essential quality."[96] And again: Hegel "forgets
that the essence of the 'particular person' is not his beard and blood and abstract
Physis, but his social quality, and that the affairs of State are nothing but the
modes of action and existence of the social qualities of men."[97] Is it necessary to
call attention here to the fact that the definition of the individual in terms of his
"essential quality," understood as "social quality," as the whole of his "universal and objective qualities," is really nothing but the hypostasis of the universal
with which Hegel was reproached earlier by Marx himself? The general character of the general concern no longer consists in a meaning placed on the horizon
of real concerns and intended to render them coherent within a possible unity, a
meaning produced by the individuals themselves through the numerous activities of their lives; rather, it defines this very life as its essence, its substance.
The life of the individual is no longer the diversity of needs and of labors; it is
the universal in and for itself, and this is why it is recognized only in the State.
The genealogical thesis, that is to say, the constitution of the political by a
reality that precedes it and that is different from it, collapses under the weight of
Hegelianism. But the determination of reality is not so easily forgotten, the
political concern itself is always a particular concern, and its "general" form,
the meaning it possesses, that of being everyone's concern, enters into contradiction with its concrete content just as, within the individual himself, his
alleged universality confronts the actual determination of life in him. What then
is the real relation of a particular individual to the being of a real political
concern, which is itself something particular?

"On the other hand," says Marx, "when we speak of specific affairs of State,
of a single political act, it is again obvious that it cannot be performed by all
people individually. If this were not so it would mean that the individual was
himself the true society and thus would make society superfluous. The individual would have to do everything all at once, whereas in fact society has him
act for the others, just as it has them act for him."[98] We now see more clearly
just what the political element is at the moment when the political essence of the
individual is confronted with his reality, with real individuals and with their
concrete activity. In the first place, the political element has lost its specific
character; it now refers neither to a State nor to a specific State activity but
instead to the activity of civil society itself. The political significance of an
individual's activity no longer consists in his participation in "specific affairs,"
in a "single political act," but instead it characterizes his individual activity as
such, his daily activity, both personal and professional. This decisive mutation
by which the political element is carried back to the social sphere is, of course,

not something foreign to Marx's discussion; rather, it is implied in it, if indeed the political essence is not to remain outside civil society but is to penetrate all its various levels. But how does this "penetration" occur concretely?

This penetration consists in the fact that each individual acts within civil society and, consequently, in his own particular activity for "the others," just as the others act "for him." The fact that the individual acts for the others consti-tutes, however, a meaning which transcends the effective content of his action. When I walk or when I run, when I carry a burden or eat something, the reality of my act does not yet contain in itself, in its mute subjectivity, the "generality of the State," any more than it represents "private interest" or "egoism." That the aim of the general is not included analytically in the reality of individual actions is apparent in the fact that such actions can take place, and indeed initially and most often do take place, in the absence of this aim: such is, precisely, the civil society of which Hegel and Marx speak.

Or must we say along with Hegel that individuality is not as bad as it may seem and that, without knowing it, each works "for all"? But what can be the meaning of ideal universality, of the phenomenology of the City, when its status is carried back in the most absurd fashion to that of the unconscious, *that is to say, to nature*? Marx reproaches Hegel, precisely, with allowing the universal to be lost in the dark, to fall outside of the actual everyday life of civil society and to be experienced only in the exceptional times of "war or a situation of ex-igency." ". . . the ideality of the State [exists] . . . as blind, unconscious substance."[99]

To say that the "ideality of the State" exists in civil society only as blind substance, this means precisely: *the immanent phenomenality of individual activity which constitutes the fabric of civil society, the effective phenomenality of action in its subjective tonality, in its reality for the individual who performs it or experiences it, is not ideal universality nor does it contain ideal universality*. By looking within the concrete life of the individual, within the structure of the original experience in which the experiences that are his happen to him and through which this life continues, the philosopher does not find what he is looking for, and what to him has never ceased to stand as the essence, rational universality, the being of that which is the same for all. What is the same "for all" is precisely not what is first of all for each one, namely one's need, one's hunger, one's desire, nor is it the effort or the labor by which one tries to carry these through to their fulfillment. It is just because labor or need are first of all the reality of one individual and belong solely to him that they possess an external relationship to the labor and the need of another individual. This radical exteriority finds its representation in ideal objectivity. Now that this exteriority is hypostatized as a *selbständig* substance, and now that it is placed within the individual himself as his very reality, *exteriority is thus no longer the exteriority of two prior realities, it no longer presupposes them as its condition*, it has instead become *their* condition, preceding them and determining them; it is their inner being. Each individual is essentially this relation to the other; each of his particular determinations bears the mark of this relation and is defined by it, by the universal. Of the individual it must now be said: ". . . his mode of life, his activity etc. [make] him a member, a function of society."[100] Need, each and every need in its particularity, has become "social." In this way Marx poses "an essential requirement that every social need, law, etc., should be investigated politically, i.e. as determined by the totality of the State, in its social meaning."[101] It is indeed the State as a whole, the relational totality, which henceforth determines each particular activity, each of the modalities of civil society, each need. Each need is not only social; it does not only contain an essential relation to the other; it actually defines itself in terms of this relation. Because each need defines itself in terms of this relation, it is the relation that defines need, and need thus constitutes the expression of this relation, one expression among others. Because every particular activity expresses the single ideal relation, it also expresses all the other expressions of this relation, just as the others express it; it represents them. Representing in every instance all the other determinations of one and the same essence, it is in every instance this essence that is represented. Every particular activity of civil society is the expression and the "representation" of the human species. ". . . every definite form of social activity, because it is a species activity, represents only the species. That is to say, it represents a determination of my own being just as every man is a representation of other men."[102]

It must be explicitly stated once more: between Hegel and Marx stands Feuerbach. It is to Feuerbach that the 1843 manuscript turns in an attempt to overcome the contradictions in which it has become entangled as a result of having carried through its own presuppositions, in an attempt to overcome the contradiction of reality, recognized in its specificity, and of ideality, which continues to be posited as the essence. It is the Feuerbachian concept of "species" which is to make possible and to show the unity sought with respect to civil society and the State, the individual and the universal, the finite and the infinite. Feuerbach's concept of species is, precisely, the universal; it is the common being, the general, but this universal presents a very peculiar nature. Although it is ideal, it is constituted by *the sum of all the concrete individual determinations of existence, by the totality of all the affective, sensuous, and intellectual modalities capable of being actualized in the real life of men*. Constituted by the totality of the concrete determinations of existence—an existence which is, in principle, empirical and as such not ideal—the species is ideal nevertheless because these determinations do *not*, properly speaking, *exist* in it but are held in it and make up its being only as virtual, potential, unreal determinations. It is always outside the species that these determinations are capable of really existing, in really existing individuals, who, as such, are empirical, material.

What, then, could be simpler, more inevitable, and more obvious than to consider the multiple determinations and activities of individuals as but so many realizations, so many expressions of a single species, a single essence—the human species, the essence of man. "Thus," says Feuerbach, "the human nature presents an infinite abundance of different predicates, and for that reason it presents an infinite abundance of different individuals. Each new man is a new predicate, a new phasis of humanity."[103] The shoemaker's activity thus realizes and expresses the human species in its own way, just as does the activity of the painter, the activity of the philosopher, or, yet again, sexual activity, which is considered particularly important (whence the decisive influence of Feuerbach's work and its widespread echo today as a precursor of Freud). Because all of these activities express one and the same species, they mutually express and represent one another; they are "social" says Marx, "human" says Feuerbach, and the civil society they constitute thus finds in the species from which they all proceed at once its essence, its universal and properly political meaning, and its unity.

The species, however, is only the external grouping together and the mere gathering up of the real activities of different individuals, and their projection into the ideal sphere of representation. How could this representation of diverse activities actually forge them into a real unity, a unity other than that of representation, which consists simply in being represented together? For activities which are not only diverse but even incompatible among themselves can well be represented together. It is on the plane of reality that the unity, or at least the complementarity, the coherence, of these activities must be shown. *Far from being able to found the unity of civil society, its immediate political meaning, the species, on the contrary, presupposes it and can at the very most only represent it.*

Indeed, it is not only the unity of civil society, the unity of the multiple activities that make it up, which the species is powerless to found, but these very activities themselves. For the species is ideal, according to Feuerbach himself.[104] How then could it posit an existence that is located outside of it and that is, in principle, structurally and ontologically heterogeneous with respect to it? And yet Feuerbach makes this absurd deduction, this deduction of the real from the ideal, when he conceives of the species as the primitive unity, as an originary power of multiple determinations, as a productive principle *(naturans)* which is expressed and realized in them, when, speaking of the "idea of the species" in relation to personality, he says that it "forever unfolds itself in new individuals,"[105] and when he writes: "Doubtless the essence of man is *one,* but this essence is infinite; its real existence is therefore an infinite, reciprocally compensating variety, which reveals the riches of this essence. Unity in essence is multiplicity in existence."[106]

These texts would hardly be worth citing if they had not exerted a direct influence on the 1843 manuscript. It is not only the solution that Marx claims to provide for the problem of the immanence of the political essence in civil society which rests on these texts; the critique of monarchy, despite its deliberately anti-Hegelian stance, was already dangerously inspired by them. Although the final philosophical sense of this critique was, as we have shown, the opposition of monadic reality to ideal universality, Marx, in order to deny Hegel the right to include sovereignty within a single individual to the detriment of all the others, thought he had to pass by way of the mediation of the concept of species in presenting his argument. *This was the starting point* in order to show, after the manner of Feuerbach, that from the species one must then move to all individuals. Marx said that "the essence can never exhaust the spheres of its existence in a single one but only in many ones."[107] This was to reverse the sense of the founding relation which is established between the real and the ideal, to posit at the origin not the real itself, individuals, but precisely the essence, personality; the universal or their Feuerbachian substitutes: the species, "man."

The 1843 manuscript ends with this reversal. But the substitution of the concept of species for that of rational universality is not a simple return to Hegel, for what we find in Feuerbach is rather a caricature of Hegel. *For Hegelian universality is based on an ontology in which ideality defines existence itself,* if it is true that the latter emerges at the same time as phenomenality in the process by which the Idea sets itself in opposition to itself. But when ideality, instead of founding existence, happens on the contrary to be explicitly opposed to it, when ideality signifies nothing but the non-real, the imaginary, in order, finally, to designate the realm of illusion and of dreams, then the primacy of the species becomes quite simply absurd. For how could the species be the foundation of civil society if civil society is the real and if the species is itself, as ideal, outside of existence: the non-real as such?

In 1843 Marx believed he could counter Hegel by borrowing from Feuerbach because the absurdity of the Feuerbachian concept of "species" had not yet become evident to him, because he had not yet understood that Feuerbach's philosophy, just as neo-Hegelian philosophy in general, is but a laughable sub-Hegelianism, an Hegelianism emptied of its substance, robbed of its ontological substratum. In fact it is to Hegel that the 1843 manuscript is addressed, and it is out of this dialogue with Hegel and with him alone that this text receives both its sense and the numerous contradictions in which it flounders, inasmuch as, under the mask of Feuerbachian anthropology, it is through a return to Hegel that this text finds its completion, as is shown in the persistence of the teleology of the universal.

From Hegel to Marx, the *Critique of Hegel's Doctrine of the State* is a dead end that finally only leads back to Hegel. However, by obstinately showing, like a student set against his teacher, that Hegel was able neither to make the real homogeneous with the development of objectivity nor to reduce the real to objectivity, what Marx questions is indeed the ontological claim of ideal universality, the grounding of objective communities and of transparent totalities; it is the ground of all political thought, that of past Hegelianism as well as that of the Marxism to come, which is shaken and which slips out of sight, while, at the same time, the stage is set for the overthrow of Western philosophy.

Chapter 2

THE HUMANISM OF THE YOUNG MARX

To the Feuerbachian concept of species is related what could be called the humanism of the young Marx. To the extent that the Feuerbachian concept of species is equivalent, with a mere change in terminology, to the Hegelian concept of mind, the humanism of the young Marx is just a camouflaged repeat of Hegelianism. To the extent, however, that the Feuerbachian concept of species allows, on the other hand, the very substance and content of the Hegelian ontology to escape it, it is empty and so appears absurd. To this extent, it is noteworthy to see that Marx is instinctively preoccupied with the attempt to give a sense to this concept once again and, in order to do this, to restore to it precisely the Hegelian philosophical content which was lost in Feuerbach, who retained only remnants of it.[1] This is where Marx is closest to Hegel, and materialism but another name for idealism. But just as in the *Critique of Hegel's Doctrine of the State*, the other texts of 1843 and especially those of 1844, in which the humanism of the young Marx is expressed, contain a deep-seated contradiction. This is due to the fact that in them a thought moves in search of itself, one which, despite the Hegelianism with which it it burdened still and in a certain way more than ever, has as its sole aim the rejection of this burden.

The main themes which together constitute the humanism of the young Marx are: the critique of religion, the concept of humanism as such and the affirmation of the identity of humanism and naturalism, the theory of revolution and of the proletariat, and the mythological concept of history.

Humanism properly speaking: the identity of humanism and naturalism

In Feuerbach the critique of religion leads to anthropology. What is substituted for the God of theology and what claims to take its place is the species. However, the actual content of the concept of species in the 1844 *Economic and Philosophical Manuscripts* can be easily recognized; it is the relation between man and nature. It is from Feuerbach that Marx borrows the interpretation of the species as the relation between man and nature and, to an even larger extent, the manner in which this relation is understood. What characterizes the relation between man and nature according to Feuerbach is that this is first of all and at one and the same time a relation of man to man. The first relation, in fact, that

54

can be grasped in man himself is his relation to the woman. This relation is a natural relation; it rests on a natural determination, virility, and addresses itself to a natural determination, femininity, in such a way that, obeying nature and aiming at nature, it opens, precisely, onto a human being. The first nature which, conforming to its nature, offers itself to man is thus a human nature. And it is in this way that, from the very start and in its very origin, the humanism of the young Marx appears as a naturalism and, reciprocally, this naturalism as a humanism.[2] How is this natural relation, properly speaking, a species relation? How does this sensuous fact contain already in itself the ideality of the universal? This is a question that must not be overlooked. For the human species is defined by its relation to the species as such. Inasmuch as the natural relation of man to woman is a species relation, it is not originally a relation to the individual, to this woman considered in herself and for herself, in her empirical individuality, in her irreplaceable singularity, but, precisely and simply, in relation to the species, to the "human." The Thou is, as Feuerbach says, only the "representative of the species." Man needs some "Other," whoever this may be; in his relation to a Thou it is to this Other in general, in reality, that he addresses himself. The so-called sensuous and concrete relation of a man to a woman signifies opening up to a universal. This opening resides in the individual as such and defines him insofar as he is this need of the Other. In this way the secret ontological homogeneity of I and Thou appears in the relation that defines them. Insofar as he is the need of the Other, the individual attests to the fact that he is more than an individual, more than a self-sufficient determination—the error of Christianity lies precisely in conceiving of the individual in this way—but that he is instead inhabited by the species, in such a way that what is experienced in him is nothing other than the will of the species to realize itself. Just as Thou, I, finally, is but the representative of the species and the place of its advent. This immanence of the species in the individual can indeed be seen in the *isolated* individual. Not only in his need but also in his language, in thought, in that metaphysical situation in which man constantly perceives himself in light of the universal as relating to himself, as being other than himself, as being able to take the place of the Other as the Other can take his place, as being *a* man. The *immanence* of the species in the individual is what defines man's *inner* life and makes it possible. "The inner life of man is the life which has relation to his species, to his general, as distinguished from his individual, nature. Man thinks—that is, he converses with himself. . . . Man is himself at once I and Thou; he can put himself in the place of another, for this reason, that to him his species, his essential nature, and not merely his individuality, is an object of thought."[3]

Under its apparent naturalism, the Feuerbachian thesis, taken up again by Marx in the 1844 *Economic and Philosophical Manuscripts*, according to which the relation to nature is identical with the relation to man, thus refers to a dialectic of the universal. The relation of man to nature and to man is not maintained only in the polemic against Christianity; it is not intended only to recall the force of nature in the face of the presumptuous attempts to raise man above nature and to ignore it.[4] The effective character of the species is not limited to sexuality,[5] to the natural relation between men and women[6] which, precisely, forces the individual to consider himself as but a part of the species.[7] In Feuerbach himself, the theme of nature originally grasped as the other man is rooted in German metaphysics, and we are reminded of this by the commentary on Boehme's thought proposed in *The Essence of Christianity*, to which we have already referred in our study of the 1843 manuscript. For Boehme, it is known, the generation within God of the Son is the process in which the absolute sets itself in opposition to itself in order to present itself to itself as object. "The second Person (the Son) is God distinguishing himself from himself, setting himself opposite to himself, hence being an object to himself. The self-distinguishing of God from himself is the ground of that which is different from himself. . . . God first thinks the world in thinking himself: to think oneself is to beget oneself, to think the world is to create the world."[8] In Boehme, this self-differentiation of God is, according to Feuerbach, only the "mystic paraphrase" of the "unity of consciousness and self-consciousness. . . ."[9] Self-consciousness objectifies itself; it thus sets before itself another self-consciousness so that the latter constitutes, precisely, the first object. The first countenance offered to me by the world is that of a self. More specifically: the self as object is the world as such. Consciousness, that is to say, consciousness of an object, is, therefore, first of all self-consciousness. This original unity of consciousness and self-consciousness is expressed in turn by Feuerbach's anthropology: "The first object of man is man."[10] Feuerbach develops this thesis in psychological language: "The *ego* first steels its glance in the eye of a *thou* before it endures the contemplation of a being which does not reflect its own image. My fellow-man is the bond between me and the world."[11]

The thesis of the identity of naturalism and humanism thus finds its explicit ontological ground in the affirmation—borrowed from Hegel by Feuerbach but which here attests to an earlier origin—that objectivity rests on intersubjectivity. However, the fact that objectivity is founded upon intersubjectivity reveals no less explicitly the nature of intersubjectivity itself and allows it to appear as constituted, precisely, by objectivity and as having its own ground in the latter. Objectivity, then, is constituted first of all by a self, but how? It is because self-consciousness *objectifies itself*, because the original structure of consciousness is indeed objectification, opposition, and differentiation itself, that that of which it is conscious is at one and the same time an *object* and a *self*. In this way, what is expressed in the human figuration of nature is nothing other than the metaphysical nature of an original power which is objectification itself, which is the *power of objectivity*. It is because objectivity reigns in the first place as objectification and internal self-differentiation that what is produced under this reign is the relating of a self to itself, of one Self to a Self in the form of an object, "intersubjectivity." Right after stating that "the first object of man is man," Feuerbach adds, "The sense of nature, which opens to us the consciousness of the world as a world, is a later product; for *it first arises through the distinction of man from himself.*"[12] And again, even more explicitly, if this be possible: "The last distinction that I can think is the distinction of a being *from* and *in* itself. . . . The cosmogonic principle in God, reduced to its last elements, is nothing else than *the act of thought* in its simplest forms *made objective.*"[13]

The act of objective thought, the internal self-differentiation of being understood as self-consciousness, this is the metaphysical content at which Hegel aims. In returning to Boehme, whom he finally reproaches for no more than a "mystic" transposition of the metaphysics of self-consciousness, Feuerbach, far from breaking with German philosophy, continues it, liberates the horizon of his own problematic and, with apparent modifications in the vocabulary, transmits it intact to Marx, who in 1844 takes it up again in its most profound and most fully developed form, in its Hegelian form. Hegel conceives of objectivity in a radical manner, as the self-objectification of consciousness. Inasmuch as objectivity—the world, "nature" in Feuerbach's terms—must be understood as the objectification of consciousness, it is not an in-itself, it is nothing that can stand by itself, but only the result of a process, its product. The means of access to objectivity, consequently, is not itself anything stable, a set essence, but precisely this process itself and its completion. *Hegel understands Being-in-the-world immediately as production.* To say that this production is that of consciousness and that it stems from it signifies: (1) it is consciousness itself which realizes this production, and this production is the work of consciousness; (2) because it is the work of consciousness, this production is realized in accordance with the nature of consciousness, it is an "objectification," a making into an object; (3) what results from this production, finally, is consciousness itself in the form of the ob-ject, since the objectification of consciousness is a *self*-objectification. That the result of the objectification of consciousness is consciousness itself—that, in the language of anthropology, "nature" is "human"—this is, in its turn, to be understood in two ways: consciousness as result designates, on the one hand, being-conscious, the fact of being conscious, and this, precisely, as an object, as the objective condition as such, and, on the other hand, "nature," what offers itself as ob-ject, in this condition of objectivity, namely, consciousness again, the first natural being, what anthropology recognizes immediately as its object, "man."

Hegel also interprets the objectification process as "negativity" because it is purely and simply the negation of being, of beings, or, yet again, the self-negation of being which allows it to exist as object. Understood as negativity, the objectification process is again described as "labor," a term by which Hegel underscores the specifically active character of objectification itself as such. It is in this way that he speaks of the "labor of the negative."[14] Labor understood in this way does not yet refer to the specific human activity by which men produce the objects required for their subsistence: this is instead the internal structure of being as it has been perceived in German metaphysics since Boehme, this is the objectification process understood as internal self-differentiation which Hegel thinks of first of all under the concept of labor, this is the nature of consciousness itself. But when Hegel, as a reader of Adam Smith, encounters labor in the specific role it is prepared to play, and which it is already playing, in nineteenth-century society, the role it has in fact played since the origin of humanity, since men have "labored" in order to live, he immediately interprets labor as negativity. *With the interpretation of concrete labor as negativity and as objectification, German metaphysics enters the realm of economics.* The latter, conversely, or rather the vital elementary phenomena which serve as its basis— need, activity, production in its relation to manufactured products, etc.— provides this metaphysics with a new field, one that is no longer constituted by the simple sphere of thinking and of representation but precisely by that of existence, of life coming to grips with nature in need and in labor. The year 1844 is precisely the time when the young Marx throws himself passionately into his studies of political economy, pursuing them in the light of Feuerbach's anthropology, that is, in the light of Hegelianism as well. Because the human species has finally no content and no meaning other than self-consciousness, the latter, its internal structure, its self-completion as self-objectification, the understanding of this completion as production, negativity, and labor, the definition of the object as the Self's own product and as constituted by the Self itself inasmuch as it is the production of the Self by itself, all of this defines the condition of man and of what happens to him in such an obvious manner that Marx himself becomes aware of this. "The importance of Hegel's *Phenomenology* and its final result—the dialectic of negativity as the moving and producing principle—lies in the fact that Hegel conceives of the self-creation of man as a process, objectification as loss of object *(Entgegenständlichung)*, as alienation and as supersession of this alienation; that he therefore grasps the nature of labor and conceives objective man—true, because real man—as the result of his own labor." And yet again: "He [Hegel] sees labor as the essence, the self-confirming essence, of man."[15] Thus man is the product of his own labor in the same way as and on the basis of one and the same process of self-objectification; the object of consciousness is consciousness itself in the identity of consciousness and self-consciousness. The "self-creation of man" is a "process"; it is both "objectification and "loss of object" *(Entgegenständlichung)*, that is to say that it produces man as object but in such a way that the object produced is precisely man himself. Marx indicates even more specifically that the object, that nature, is man by presenting this object as the externalization and, consequently, as the exhibition of "species-powers," that is, of the very essence of man. It is against the background of objectification, of externalization, that man's manifestation and realization are possible, his being-for-himself, giving himself to himself as object. In this self-givenness, against the backdrop of an externalization which identifies this self-givenness with a creation, the species of man finds its source and its completion. "The real, active relation of man to himself as a species-being, or the realization of himself as a real species-being, i.e. as a human being, is only possible if he really employs all his species-powers."[16]

In this way the opposition of man and animal is explained. Whereas the latter is identified with its activity, which it performs in a sort of immediateness, human activity is, on the contrary, a conscious activity, which means that man distinguishes himself from his activity, sets himself in opposition to it and takes it, precisely, as an object. The internal structure of species labor is that of consciousness as an oppositional structure. "Man makes his life activity itself an *object* of his will and consciousness. . . . Only because of that is he a species-being. Or rather, he is a conscious being, i.e. his own life is an object for him, only because he is a species-being."[17]

The opposition between consciousness and life against the background of consciousness understood as this very opposition determines the first formulation of the concept of alienation that appears in the *Economic and Philosophical Manuscripts*, making its Hegelian character most evident. Because species-activity is the conscious activity to which life activity, animal activity must be subordinated—since the axiological relation of the subordination of life to consciousness is the expression of the ontological definition of consciousness as the negation of life—alienation consists precisely in the reversal of this relation, in the submission of species-activity to life activity. The situation of the worker who works to eat and not to liberate within himself the being of labor as such, namely becoming oneself in the world in the form of self-consciousness, is the concrete expression of this alienation, in which one can read the very meaning, although now inverted, of the struggle between consciousnesses, namely the definition of oneself as a conscious being and not as a mere "living thing": "In the same way as estranged labor reduces spontaneous and free activity to a means, it makes man's species-life a means of his physical existence. Consciousness, which man has from his species, is transformed through estrangement so that species-life becomes a means for him."[18]

In what, more specifically, does species-labor consist? We have seen that the human species is defined by the relation to the species as such and so implies an opening to the universal. It is this very opening which defines species-labor. Whereas animal activity is urged on by need as an activity that is partial, one-sided, and individual, so that its result is of significance only to the animal itself, providing only a sensuous, individual satisfaction which remains part of its body, human labor, on the contrary, is modelled on the pattern of things, taking as its law of construction the universal laws of nature, creating objects in accordance with these laws, objects standing in and of themselves, possessing their own inner finality, that is to say, universal objects. By creating objects in accordance with the laws of nature, the objects of nature itself, man reproduces nature, and his action has an objective and universal significance.[19] However, acting in this way, creating in accordance with the aesthetic laws of nature, man realizes his own essence, an essence which is precisely the relation to the species as such, the opening to the universal. "The practical creation of an objective world, the fashioning of inorganic nature, is proof that man is a conscious species-being, i.e. a being which treats the species as its own essential being or itself as a species-being."[20] By creating in accordance with the laws of the species and by making these laws apparent in the object he creates, by making them objective, man thus renders objective his own capacity for creation following the laws of the species, making objective his relation to the species. It is this relation to the species that is displayed in the reproduction of nature; it is the essence of man, who objectifies himself in the object of human labor. "The object of labor is therefore the *objectification of the species-life of man*."[21] *It is in this way that human labor is truly realized as self-consciousness by virtue of the fact that its object, the object that it creates in the objectification which constitutes it, is nothing other than the objectification of the relation to the universal as such and, consequently, the objectification of consciousness itself*. In the object of his labor, in nature reproduced, man, says Marx, "can contemplate himself in a world he has created."[22]

Alienation then names what takes place when, taking away from man the object of his labor, at the same time one takes away his own Self, his true species-life, takes it away precisely to the extent that this true life does not exist for itself, does not exist for man except as an object, as objective species-life. "In tearing away the object of his production from man," says Marx, "estranged labor therefore tears away from him his species-life, his *true species-objectivity*."[23] This true species-objectivity, however, is none other than nature, what nature has become for man, a nature which makes the various species apparent and the species of man within these. What is torn away from man in the object of his labor is at one and the same time his nature and nature itself, so that now deprived of all nature, he is more destitute than the animal. Alienated labor, Marx again states, "transforms his advantage over animals into the disadvantage that his inorganic body, nature, is taken from him."[24]

Because in the object of his labor man gives himself his own Self, because he himself becomes this object, objectification has the radical meaning of self-realization, it is positivity. Because alienation is produced only to the extent that man is robbed of the object of his labor, that is to say, of his own self as object, such alienation is tied to a contingent condition, to that situation in which, precisely, the worker works for another, for the industrialist who robs him of the product of his labor and appropriates it for himself. It is in a determined historical situation that objectification signifies alienation. If this situation is eliminated, then alienation will disappear, while objectification, on the contrary, will be able to be carried out fully, to be the radical ontological realization that it signifies. *The dissociation of alienation and objectivity implied by the* Economic and Philosophical Manuscripts *of 1844, which is taken up again by Lukács in particular and which is held to characterize Marx's own position in opposition to that of Hegel, belongs in fact to the horizon of the Hegelian problematic and unfolds within it*. Defining being in terms of self-objectification, the possibility of alienation, if not its actual realization, understood as located within this very objectification (when my being is constituted as an object, then it can be taken away from me and handed over to the fate of the world), these form the prior framework within which—and within which alone— the question of the connection between objectivity and alienation, their possible unity and dissociation, can arise. Just when thought finds itself in the presence of a decisive "economic" problem, that of the relation of the worker to the product of his labor and to his labor itself, it seems obvious once more that this problem is shaped and argued against the background of German metaphysics, which itself is never elucidated. Lukács's alleged reexamination of Hegelianism is simply another example of this.

Marx described more precisely the conditions under which objectification is positive, but he still secretly borrows the conditions and the content of this positivity from Hegel. This is the reason why these conditions prove to be directly and at one and the same time the conditions of a *possible* alienation. By "assuming the positive supersession of private property," that is, by considering objectification in its positive aspects, leaving aside all alienation, the claim that "man produces man"—a claim by which humanism gives a positive sense to the critique of religion—is now made more explicit in the claim that he "produces . . . himself and other men."[25] Man produces himself not only because he creates the object required for his subsistence but precisely because this object is the objectification and the realization of his capacity to create in accordance with the species-law. But this object is offered to another for his contemplation or his consumption. In the second case, man has produced the existence of other men, he has kept them alive. In the first case, *which also includes the second*, man offers an object to others to experience, an object which is the realization of the human essence, the objectification of human labor, of the ability to create in accordance with the species-law. What is given to others to experience is therefore this very ability; it is this essence which is each person's own essence, the essence of man as universal essence. Inasmuch as the other experiences in and through this object the creative essence of the species, the universal essence, his own essence, it is the essence of experiencing which is modified within him and which becomes the experiencing of the universal, self-consciousness. What is meant by the fact that man "produces himself and other men" is therefore to be understood in the strict sense. Summing up a part of the manuscript that has been lost, Marx says of man that "the object, which is the direct activity of his individuality, is at the same time his existence for other men, their existence and their existence for him."[26] Existence here does not mean sheer existence, subsistence, but, precisely, the existence *of man*. This is not life, it is the ability to work according to the laws of the species, it is the possibility of the relation to the universal and of the universal itself which is realized and brought into existence. The object that I create is my existence for the other; this means that in it I make manifest what I am and what I do—a species-being working in light of the universal. It is the other's existence, because the species existence it displays is precisely the other's essence and, in providing him with the opportunity to experience his own essence, it provides him with his own proper existence in addition to the consciousness of what he is. The object is, therefore, the existence of the other man for man, that is for me, as the one who created the object because as the other finds his existence in the object I have created, he thus finds in it his existence for me.

The object, says Marx, is social. By this it may seem first of all, and most often, that the object is created by me for the other, that the object of my work is the object of his need. And in the same way, the object of my need is the object of his work. To say that the object is social means that it carries this origin in itself, that it comes from the other for me and from me for the other. In this origin lies the object's "social and human nature," which is nothing but the objectification and realization of man's social nature. In the production which escapes alienation, in which each person realizes himself in the object of his work while satisfying the needs of the others, "I would have the joy of having produced in the individual manifestation of my life the direct manifestation of your life, and so of having affirmed and realized directly in my individual activity my true nature, my social, human nature."[27] Still speaking of nonalienated production, Marx further states: "The supersession of private property is therefore the complete emancipation of all human senses and attributes; but it is this emancipation precisely because these senses and attributes have become human, subjectively as well as objectively. The eye has become a human eye, just as its object has become a social, human object, made by man for man."[28] Just what is meant by "made by man" and "for man" must nevertheless be kept constantly in mind. "Made by man," precisely, does not mean "coming from an individual" and intended for an individual, coming from a living being and intended for a living being, intended to maintain life within him. Made by man means coming from one who works in the light of the laws of beauty, one who indeed has this relation to the laws of nature. Coming from man means making this relation objective, making the universal itself an object so that in this object the other can recognize his own essence, his species essence, recognize himself as man. This is why "I can only relate myself to a thing in a human way if the thing is related in a human way to man,"[29] if it is the objectification of the universal and its becoming-for-itself.

It is true that the social object carries within it the relation obtaining between individuals and that it expresses this relation. Coming from one *individual* and being given to another appears as the first characteristic of the object of labor. Is not the putting into relation of different individuals, intersubjectivity, the very essence of the "social" and its definition? But why is it that the object of my labor is capable of being given and is in fact given to another and why must this be so? Why, if not because it is first and foremost precisely an ob-ject? It is inasmuch as the object is spread out in the extendedness of exteriority that it is there in front of us, bathing thus in the light of being, that it is there precisely for each and every one and can be there for all. It is because labor is objectification that its object can be social. Objectification does not only objectify the species-essence of man, his ability to relate to the universal; it first of all opens the milieu in which this essence can appear and be given, the milieu of objectivity which is the universal itself. So it is against the background of the universal itself and of its unfolding that the universal becomes apparent and can be experienced. It is in this radical sense that labor is the universal's self-objectification and its becoming-for-itself. In the *Economic and Philosophical Manuscripts*, the concepts of the social, of society, and of the human express nothing other than this absolute ontological event.

The individual himself is only the place of this event—the self-fulfillment of the universal as objectification and self-manifestation—which constitutes his very life, his species-life, "social" life. "The individual is the social being. His vital expression—even when it does not appear in the direct form of a communal expression, conceived in association with other men—is therefore an expression and confirmation of social life. Man's individual and species-life are not two distinct things. . . . Man, however much he may therefore be a particular individual . . . is just as much the totality, the ideal totality, the subjective existence of thought and experienced society for itself,"[30] that is to say, the "subjective" existence of the universal, its becoming-for-itself in objectivity. And just as Feuerbach, who defined the individual in terms of his relation to the species, was able to present the actual existence of another individual as contingent, so Marx affirms in the above-cited text that the social manifestation of "individual" life is neither necessarily nor in the first place a "collective" existence; rather it is precisely the manifestation of the universal upon which, as in Hegel, all possible intersubjectivity is founded. "Social activity and social consumption," Marx again states, "by no means exist *solely* in the form of a *directly* communal activity and a directly *communal* consumption . . . even if I am active in the field of science, etc.—an activity which I am seldom able to perform in direct association with other men—I am still *socially* active because I am active as a *man*. It is not only the material of my activity—including even the language in which the thinker is active—which I receive as a social product. My *own* existence *is* social activity. Therefore what I create from myself I create for society, conscious of myself as a social being."[31] "Society" is finally nothing other than the "objective mind." It is the place in which the universal becomes objective, in which the essence of man is there for each and every one.

Because society is this place where the essence of man is there for man, where man attains self-consciousness, nature is made really homogeneous to man only when it is identified with, precisely, man's self-consciousness, with society. "The *human* essence of nature exists only for *social* man; for only here does nature exist for him as a *bond* with other *men* . . . only here does it exist as the *basis* of his own *human* existence. Only here has his *natural* existence become his *human* existence and nature become man for him. Society is therefore the perfected unity in essence of man with nature, the true resurrection of nature, the realized naturalism of man and the realized humanism of nature."[32] What ultimately exists, being as it is understood and defined by the identity of naturalism and humanism, is "natural existence become human existence," it is nature become society, and it is society itself as the objectification and the realization of the species-essence, as the mind's self-realization. The theme of society has played a decisive role in the modes of thought stemming from Marx, but it is only in the most absurd manner that this theme of the "social" subsists in Marxism inasmuch as the latter presents itself as a materialism, inasmuch as that which is thought under the term "social," or rather that which thinks the social dimension, is a metaphysics of the universal.

The theory of the proletariat and revolution

Feuerbach's critique of religion serves only as a *starting point* for Marx's own problematic, which immediately goes beyond it in the direction of something else, namely of reality. This is why all of Marx's texts concerning religion evince a sudden break, that is, they break with the plane which encompasses both religious thought *and the critique of religion itself*, to the extent that this critique connects religion, understood as a set of representations, to consciousness, understood as the source and basis of these representations. As early as 1844 Marx's thought attempts to break with the notion of consciousness as basically incapable of displaying within itself the origin of religious representation as well as its liquidation, and so to break explicitly with the philosophy of conscious-ness. This is the apparent sense of the Introduction to the *Contribution to the Critique of Hegel's Philosophy of Right*. Man, as Feuerbach showed, projects his own essence onto God. But why? Because this essence is not fulfilled *on the plane of reality*. Religion is an illusory realization of the human essence, illu-sory because it is produced on the plane of representation, of mere thought, of the imagination, and so a representation that is not really one, a "fantastic" realization. As such, as the fantastic realization of the human essence, religion is the expression of its genuine nonrealization and at the same time a compensa-tion for this, the imaginary satiation of that which is not really satisfied. Under these conditions, the problematic can only turn away from the sphere of the imaginary and illusory realization of the human essence in order to turn toward the sphere of its real nonrealization, toward the actual situation "which has need of illusions." Thus the critique of religion in fact takes leave of religion itself and of its relevant problems in order to turn toward something else, toward the life of men here below, precisely toward reality, understood as the reality of society.[33]

On the Jewish Question expresses this same movement of thought in the direction of reality. Whereas Bruno Bauer wanted to solve the paradox of the Christian State by asking both Jews and Christians to give up their religion, that is to say, their particularity, in order to open themselves, precisely, to political universality, to become full-fledged citizens of a State which itself would be a-religious, that is, capable of being this universality fulfilled, the rational State, Marx, on his part, shows that this dialectic is inoperative because it is still foreign to reality. To ask both Christians and Jews to give up their religion is to postulate a mere change in their consciousness. The fact that this consciousness, relinquishing its particularity on either side, opens itself to the universal in free citizenship, this is just what remains foreign to reality to the extent that reality resides not in the State but in civil society. In this way, the elimination of religion on the level of the State, the atheist State, which allows private religion to subsist along with, in general, whatever is affirmed or recognized on the plane of the State, this is flatly contradicted on the real plane of civil society. The political emancipation of religion is an illusion because political emancipation as such is an illusion. All that counts is real emancipation, which Marx continues to call, following Feuerbach and Bauer himself, "human" emancipation.[34]

Therefore, if the critique of religion always leads to reality, the question of knowing what this reality is can be formulated as follows: what is the reality discussed in the 1844 *Economic and Philosophical Manuscripts*, inasmuch as this is social reality?

This has already been answered in the problematic: it is the reality of self-consciousness. We are then presented with the following indisputable self-evidence: the *passage* that the critique of religion wants to make in the direction of reality, in the direction of a sphere foreign to that which encompasses both religion and the theological critique of religion as we find them in Bauer and in Feuerbach, is purely an illusion, if the reality to which it leads does not differ from that which it claims to escape. It is true that Marx explicitly rejects Bauer's atheism, considered a pure modification of consciousness, and that he explicitly calls for a different sort of ground for religion itself. Is not civil society basically different from the *representation* of a God external to man? *But in the 1844* Economic and Philosophical Manuscripts *society is the development and the result of the self-objectification of the human essence, which itself is nothing other than this self-objectification which defines at one and the same time the structure of consciousness and that of labor:* "The object of labor is therefore the objectification of the species-life of man; for man reproduces himself not only intellectually, in his consciousness, but actively and actually, and he can therefore contemplate himself in a world he has created."

In the Introduction to *A Contribution to the Critique of Hegel's Philosophy of Right*, this reference to reality is no less ambiguous. Indeed, it is not reality itself that is taken as the theme of reflection but its expression in law and in politics. To say that "the criticism of heaven turns into the criticism of earth" means that "the criticism of religion" turns into "the criticism of law and the criticism of theology into the criticism of politics."[35] Marx gives as the reason for this thematic shift, in which philosophy is substituted for reality, the backwardness of Germany in relation to other peoples, a backwardness which leads the Germans to experience, for example, the Restoration without having had a Revolution. It is only on the theoretical level, in its philosophy, that Germany is able to maintain a relation with the real and to manifest its contemporaneity with history. German philosophy, however, is the critique of religion. The passage from the critique of religion to reality, to the extent that reality now designates in a precise manner German reality, is thus nothing other than this passage to the critique of religion. The problematic is contained inside a circle which Marx, it is true, immediately breaks. If theory, namely the critique of religion, is in German reality the only real element corresponding to history and to the internal requirement of its fulfillment, should not the whole of German reality be made homogeneous with what it already includes that is present and living? Does not German theory then contain the "principles" upon which the rest of German reality is to be organized and constructed? "We must then ask ourselves: can Germany attain a practice *à la hauteur des principes*, that is to say, a revolution that raises it not only to the official level of modern nations but to the human level that will be their immediate future?"[36]

Attaining a practice that measures up to its principles means for German reality: becoming homogeneous with philosophy, and for philosophy this means: becoming German reality itself, realizing itself therein. By following the path that leads from the critique of religion to reality understood as German reality, understood in the first place as the critique of religion itself and in the second place as the reality of German society which must come to conform to this critique, to philosophy, the problematic is not, properly speaking, contained inside a circle for it has achieved the following self-evidence: the reality to which the critique of religion leads is not a reality of an order other than that of the reality of this very critique, other than the reality of consciousness, other than the reality of philosophy; quite the contrary, its structure is the same. Only on this condition will German reality be able to realize German philosophy, the philosophy of self-objectification, of alienation—on the condition, that is, that this structure indeed be its own. Such is, once again here, the inevitable presupposition of the surprising meeting of thought and reality: the secret homogeneity of their common essence. A homogeneity such as this renders illusory the opposition—even the mere difference—between German theory and practice; it signifies their profound affinity and, precisely, their homogeneity. The question Marx poses to Germany thus becomes fully transparent: "Will the theoretical needs be directly practical needs? It is not enough that thought should strive to realize itself; reality must strive towards thought."[37]

However, German reality does not strive toward thought and is not homogeneous with its theoretical requirements. Marx's entire analysis will show, precisely, in the break that opens up between, on the one hand, the German philosophical requirements that are adequate to contemporary history and so to its immediate future and, on the other hand, the archaism of German society, "the enormous gap that exists between the demands of German thought and the responses of German reality."[38] The demands of German thought are contained in the radicalism of its theory, in the critique of religion to the extent that this ends in "the doctrine that for man the supreme being is man." Such a doctrine, overdetermined as it is by both the idealist conceptions of the autonomy of consciousness and the Hegelian descriptions of mastery and servitude means that man's total liberation is called for, that is to say, it involves the no less radical rejection of his alienation and, precisely, of all servitude. This meaning is made all the more obvious if we refer, with Marx, to "Germany's revolutionary past," which, just as its present, "is also theoretical": the Reformation. We are familiar with the famous text on Luther, who "certainly conquered servitude based on devotion, but only by replacing it with servitude based on conviction. He destroyed faith in authority, but only by restoring the authority of faith. He transformed the priests into laymen, but only by transforming the laymen into priests. He freed mankind from external religiosity, but only by making religiosity the inner man. He freed the body from its chains, but only by putting the heart in chains."[39] Germany's "revolutionary" past signifies the inner servitude of man, that is, his most radical alienation, and this is why it is the condition for Germany's theoretical revolutionary present which signifies the most radical liberation, because, by eliminating the external God, it eliminates precisely the inner faith in this God. Germany's revolutionary theoretical demand is, therefore, the demand for a radical alienation as the condition for a radical liberation.

The response of German reality to its theoretical demand is nonexistent. Where in German society do we see the growth and development of a "radical" alienation, a situation which gets bogged down in an ever greater, ever graver contradiction, letting a wall build up before it, a wall growing ever higher until it becomes insurmountable, until the only solution lies in the brutal destruction of this wall, the total suppression of this alienation? Where is the passion for the universal, the will to carry things through to the end, which alone could call for, demand an absolute dénouement? What class in Germany bears within itself the violence of this passion or actually possesses this will? Let us take a look: "What a spectacle! A society infinitely divided into the most diverse races which confront one another with their petty antipathies, their bad consciences and their brutal mediocrity."[40] Marx strives in vain to present this mediocrity as the sum of the failings of all other regimes and of all other peoples, as if an accumulation of particular wrongs could take the place of the absent cause of a radical revolution.[41] The fact that German reality does not constitute a response to the demands of German thought is acknowledged as the analysis progresses, when, unable to find in this reality the conditions for "universal human emancipation," the condition for at least "the partial, merely political revolution"[42] is sought. A partial revolution means that a class emancipates itself but only by establishing its domination over the other classes. In so doing it makes the others believe that it struggles not for itself but for society as a whole, that its goals are universal goals. Only on this condition is it able to arouse general enthusiasm, to captivate the rest of society. And yet this illusory realization of the universal is brought about only against the background of opposition. One class can sum up and embody in itself the positive goals of society only if another class gathers together in itself the wrongs and vices of this society. The latter erects the barrier, defines the obstacle, constitutes the opposition which has to be overcome so that what is positive in the positive class of society can be liberated and brought to completion.[13] Thus in 1789 the French bourgeoisie not only needs to make itself believe and to have others believe that in its goals and in its ideals it represents and realizes the emancipation of the whole of society; at the same time it must also show what must be destroyed if these goals and these ideals are to be realized, that is to say, there must exist some "negative representation of society"—namely the clergy and the nobility along with their "privileges"; the suppression of these privileges will thus permit the advent of the universal and the establishment of "general rights." The suppression of the negative, the negation of the negation as the possibility of the advent of the universal and of the liberation that will accompany it, this is already the condition for political revolution, of all revolution, even "partial" revolution.

The conditions for a simple political revolution do not exist in Germany any more than do the conditions for a general revolution. Due to the practical mediocrity of the German classes, there is not one that possesses the idealism which would allow it to claim to stand for the whole and to reshape the entire society in its own image, nor is there any German class capable of standing as an obstacle to this project of general emancipation, which itself does not exist. Whereas in France "each class of the people is a political idealist" and so claims to be directed toward the general interest and to realize it, so that "the role of emancipation therefore passes in a dramatic movement from one class of the French people to the next," in Germany, "no class of civil society has the need and capacity for universal emancipation."[44] There is really no response in Germany to the demands of German thought or to the necessity for a revolution.

This is why Marx will construct it. To construct a response to the demands of German thought means to address oneself to reality, to turn to it not in order to display it or to recognize it—it does not exist—but precisely to turn to what does not exist in order to sketch the framework, the form, the structure of what should be and will be, that is, what will fit into this framework, take on this form, comply with this structure. The German question is the rough draft and the mold of a "reality" which will be shaped by this very question. The German question is not a simple question. As the rough draft and the mold of what will be and what will occur, of the being to come, the German question indeed defines the condition of its occurrence, of its possible-being, of its ontological structure. The German question is the *being* of the response. The German question is German theory, theory as such. The response is practice, as the practice of theory, a practice which is made possible and defined by it. To the extent that practice is constructed in accordance with theory, finding in theory its rough draft and its mold, practice—reality—is the object of a construction *a priori*. How then is German reality constructed insofar as it is constructed *a priori* by German theory? German theory, in its completed form, is the critique of religion, the theory of a radical liberation considered as the suppression of a radical alienation. Since it finds its law of construction in the *a priori* of German theory,

German reality has to or will have to offer itself as this radical alienation whose negation will be radical liberation, that is, it will be German emancipation but as "universal human" emancipation.

Marx states explicitly that German theory determines what its practice must be: "The only liberation of Germany which is *practically* possible is liberation from the point of view of that *theory* which declares man to be the supreme being for man."[45] The fact that practice is determined by theory and that this, in turn, leads to a concept of emancipation which is defined and realized as the suppression of alienation, all this is no less clearly affirmed: "The criticism of religion ends with the doctrine that for man the supreme being is man, and thus with the categorical imperative to overthrow all conditions in which man is a debased, enslaved, neglected and contemptible being."[46] However, these social conditions do not exist, German reality does not respond to the German question. This is why we say that Marx constructed this reality *a priori*. And the reality constructed *a priori* in accordance with the demands of German theory, which, in accordance with the theses of German philosophy, is nothing other than the law of this construction, is the proletariat. The construction *a priori* of the proletariat is contained in the following text: "So where is the positive possibility of German emancipation? This is our answer. In the formation of a class with radical chains, a class [*Stand*] which is the dissolution of all classes, a sphere which has a universal character because of its universal suffering and which lays claim to no particular right because the wrong it suffers is not a particular wrong but a wrong in general; a sphere of society which can no longer lay claim to an historical title, but merely to a human one, which does not stand in one-sided opposition to the consequences but in all-sided opposition to the premises of the German political system; and finally a sphere which cannot emancipate itself without emancipating itself from—and thereby emancipating—all the other spheres of society, which is, in a word, the total loss of humanity and which can therefore redeem itself only through the total redemption of humanity. This dissolution of society as a particular class is the proletariat."[47]

Because its reality is constructed *a priori* in accordance with the prescriptions of German philosophy, the proletariat manifests in its being its compliance with the structure of theory, a compliance which founds their affinity and which appears in this affinity as the way in which they mutually serve one another: the proletariat enables philosophy to be realized by giving itself an actual, "material" content; the proletariat provides philosophy with its weapons while, reciprocally, finding in philosophy its law of construction, along with its law of development and thus its law of action. "Just as philosophy finds its material weapons in the proletariat, so the proletariat finds its intellectual weapons in philosophy; and once the lightning of thought has struck deeply into this virgin soil of the people, emancipation will transform the Germans into men."[48]

The reality of the proletariat, insofar as it is constructed *a priori* in compliance with the prescriptions of German philosophy, is presented as a particular reality which becomes universal—a particular class which ceases to be a particular class—in such a way, however, that this is the universalization of the negative, that it is itself the development of alienation—not a "particular wrong" but a "wrong in itself"—and that it is precisely in and through the development of this radical and universal alienation that liberation and regeneration take place, as a liberation which is itself universal, as the liberation not of one class of society but of all classes, not of one nation, Germany, but of "man." As we see, Marx still conceives of liberation in the same way as did Bauer in *The Jewish Question*, as a passage from the particular to the universal; the particular determination that has to be abolished is, however, no longer that of the Jew or of the Christian but of the particular class on the one hand and of the nation on the other. With respect to the term in which the particular is resolved in its suppression, this is once again here, as in Bauer, the universal, and its advent is also thought of by Marx as the advent of "man." However, the presuppositions which guide Marx in his analysis go back much farther than this. As the movement from the particular to the universal, a movement taking place through the mediation of negation and the suppression of this negation, the reality of the proletariat is dialectical. What then is the dialectic?

The dialectic is usually presented as a concept whose meaning is held to have been first of all ideal, spiritual, the model of which was said to have been proposed to Marx by Hegel, who himself took up the grand theme of the dialectic as it had found its most celebrated and most remarkable expression in Platonism. The dialectic is first and foremost the dialectic of ideas, their necessary interconnection following the schema of opposition and synthesis. Marx is supposed to have maintained this schema, while at the same time radically changing its sense by applying it to another domain, no longer that of ideal determinations but that of reality, that is to say, of nature or, yet again, of "matter." Actually, it is Engels who explicitly realized this mutation in the concept of the dialectic, or rather its simple transfer from one region of being to another by constructing and proposing a "Dialectic of nature." Did not Marx himself, however, claim to have set the dialectic back on its feet, that is, precisely, to have sought and to have located its movement in reality before finding it in what is but its reflection, in the movement of ideas and of the mind?

One may venture the gravest doubts concerning the legitimacy of such an interpretation of nature and of the role of the concept of the dialectic in German philosophy at the beginning of the nineteenth century. First of all, it is false to suppose that in Hegel the dialectic had solely an "ideal" meaning, involving only the world of consciousness or of thought, the "human" world, in contrast to the domain proper to nature,[49] as if the latter remained in itself foreign to the dialectical movement and outside it dominion. Quite the opposite, it is only within the dialectical process that nature reaches being; and this is so, on the one hand, because the alienation of mind is realized only if this alienation becomes truly radical, if nature exists not only *for consciousness* which is alienated in nature, that is for the mind and as its own proper alienation, but *in itself*, in the actuality of absolute opposition, as the term that is really other, foreign to the mind; on the other hand, this is so because beings attain being only in this condition of opposition, only to the extent, then, that they are penetrated by the negativity of the dialectic. Because it grounds the being of nature and so belongs to it and constitutes it, the Hegelian dialectic in no way allows itself to be bound up inside the sphere of "consciousness," a sphere which for Hegel does not exist as such, in its alleged separation from the sphere of being. Instead, consciousness is being itself in its actuality, nature itself in its condition of object, the unfolding and the reign of nature in accordance with its own proper structure.

Because it refers to nature, the Hegelian dialectic allows the trace of its real origin to appear in itself. This origin is definitely not to be found in Platonism. It is always after the fact, and only in order to confirm what it considers to be self-evident that German thought refers to ancient philosophy and, for example, to Plato. The original character of the German dialectic can be seen, precisely, in its specific origin, which lies in medieval alchemy, where intuitions or illuminations, research, and work reach their culmination in the circle of thinkers and philosophers grouped around Paracelsus. By claiming to make gold out of lead, alchemy implies directly as the prior theoretical presupposition supporting its practical undertaking that the ground of reality is not made up of fixed things, of immutable elements, but that it is instead *change*. Or again: change cannot be understood as the mere substitution of one element for another, as replacing one body with another, as will be the case in Cartesian mechanism, with its conception of movement as a chain of bodies which move together.[50] Quite the opposite, change as it is considered by alchemical practice and as it is presupposed by this practice, is a change in the body itself; it is the internal and real transformation of one being into another, in such a way that this "other" is nothing but the transformed-being of the first, the *becoming-other of the being itself*. A becoming such as this, the becoming-other of a being, is inscribed in it as its very reality, as a constitutive potentiality of its being and which determines this being. To the extent, then, that the being of beings is understood as becoming, as the potentiality of becoming other, reality can thus appear and be understood as "dialectical."

Given this becoming which is immanent in reality, this universal movement of things as they pass into one another, it is then only too easy for man to base his action upon this fact in order to effect transformations in bodies which are already inscribed in them virtually. These transformations are in no way indifferent; they are ordered on the basis of a teleology which is immanent in each thing and which places within it as constituting the very nature of the thing the uneasiness and suffering of waiting. The alchemist is attentive to this uneasiness and this suffering; his knowledge of nature is truly metaphysical, it goes beyond stable appearances and moves back to the obscure will which inhabits each thing and which is directed at fulfilling its being by transforming itself into what for it will be, precisely, its fulfillment. This hunger, this painful desire, this incompleteness, and this unfulfillment characterize, for example, the being of lead and determine it as "dark," "bereft," "unconsoled," as long as it has not become gold and has not taken on its glorious brillance.

The concept of the dialectic originally understood in this way as a dialectic of beings, as an ontic dialectic, received a radically new meaning when Jacob Boehme had the unprecedented intuition—an intuition which was decisively to determine the German metaphysics of the great post-Kantians and, through this, the entire history of Western thought—the intuition that passing into the other does not lead to the production of a new and privileged being in which the dark element finds its consolation, but instead to the advent of that which is more than any particular being, to the advent and to the actual becoming of being itself in its phenomenality. For the passage of one being into another is its passing into the condition of ob-ject, its coming into the light of the world. The dialectic of nature no longer has a limited meaning; it no longer concerns the play of its elements and their mutual transformation; rather it is nature as a whole, it is the whole of what is that attains being to the extent that the reign of the other is established, the reign of objectivity which is that of nature itself. Inasmuch as it no longer designates the transformation of one particular thing but rather the liberation of its being, the dialectic of beings has become the dialectic of the object, and ontic dialectic an ontological dialectic. This is precisely the sense of the dialectic in Hegel.

To the extent to which the dialectic has an ontological meaning and to which becoming other defines the becoming of objectivity in which the being of nature unfolds, the structure of the dialectic appears at one and the same time to be the structure of consciousness itself, such as Hegel understands this, that is to say, not as a sphere closed in upon itself in the silent tautology of identity but precisely as the development of objectivity in the movement of alienation. This is why alienation, in Hegel, has a positive meaning, because it defines the very structure of being; this is also why alienation must be radical and mind be brought down to the level of nature, because the extreme point of alienation is at one and the same time the being of mind, as it is the being of nature itself. This is not all: in the movement by which a being is alienated as it becomes an object, it enters into the realm of universality and bathes in its light; the dialectical process is the passage from the particular to the universal. Finally, because alienation is the original formation of objectivity and because it liberates this objectivity along with the being which is in the latter, alienation is at one and the same time this liberation and the actual becoming of mind. The thesis of a radical emancipation which would have its condition in a radical alienation is rooted in the very structure of the dialectic, understood as the structure of consciousness, of experience and of being. Feuerbach was to confer upon the concept of alienation a purely negative meaning, but its original ontological meaning secretly subsists in German metaphysics. To this original meaning, in any event, is connected the dialectical interpretation of the proletariat in the 1843–44 Introduction to the *Critique of Hegel's Philosophy of Right*, an interpretation in the light of which *the structure of the proletariat appears as the structure of consciousness itself such as this is understood in German metaphysics.*

The concept of dialectic in German metaphysics is, however, overdetermined by conceptions of another order. Actually, the dialectic, to the extent that it signifies change, cannot have its exclusive and truly primary origin in nature, inasmuch as the latter offers instead the image of a certain permanence and of stable being. The very movements and diverse changes which affect the being of nature display a certain regularity, when they do not present a cyclical form in which the idea of change moves beyond itself in the direction, precisely, of permanence. The alchemist's intuition of a transformation that takes place within things and that constitutes their true nature had to be fought for and had, in a certain sense, to be postulated in the face of appearances to the contrary. If it does not lie in the content of external experience, where can one find not the idea but above all the actual experience of change and of transformation considered real, immanent and lived change, internal transformation, if not in life itself? It is individual subjective life as it occurs in the immediate experience of its radical phenomenological immanence which reveals this change within itself, inasmuch as it changes and as it is itself "change," in the flow of its impressions and of its hidden affective tonalities; and in this flow the latter never stop passing into one another in an incessant movement that is life itself. We are unable to show here how, in this passing which is not in time but which is time, the affective modalities of life do not originate and occur therein by chance, how they stem not from the world and its future but from life itself and its essence, as modalities which are willed and ordained by it, as the very modes of its realization and as the history of its essence *(historial)*.[51] Let us simply state: it is because these modalities originate in the ontological passivity which determines the essence of life and which constitutes it from the outset as affective that these modalities are themselves presented and are posited as affective, more precisely, as suffering and as joy and as their incessant "passing back and forth." For the essence of suffering lies in the radical passivity of life and in its sufferance and as such includes, to the extent that life's sufferance is its original self-givenness in the adequation of an undivided immanence and the experience of its own plenitude, the possibility and the essence of the opposite determination, the possibility and the essence of its unceasing transformation into joy. The original essence of the dialectic lies in life to the extent that it contains within itself the *a priori* and pure possibility of its fundamental tonalities and along with this the possibility of their reciprocal transformation.

It is in the original essence of the dialectic, inasmuch as it lies in life and expresses the eidetic regularities of its fundamental tonalities, that one should seek the determinations it will later possess in an explicit manner on the level of thought such as, for example, the law of opposites. The more life is caught up in the suffering of its being as it is limited and tied to itself, and the more it experiences as a burden the absence and the impossibility of any transcendence, of any overcoming, the more this overcoming is realized, the more one can feel in and through this very suffering the emergence of one's own being, its silent advent and the experience of its ultimate ground. In this way, Kierkegaard was able to conceive of the extreme point of suffering, despair, as leading the self to the most radical test both of itself and of the life within it, to delve through its own transparence into the power that has posited it. Thus, generally speaking, we can explain the religious or mystical conceptions which express the metaphysical essence of being understood as life and which relate the history of its essence *(historial)* in the simultaneous or successive blossoming of opposites in the dramatic passing from negative to positive, from destitution to plenitude, from suffering to joy. From the nearest to the farthest, *per angusta ad augusta*. The higher the star is in the heavens, the deeper is its reflection in the sea. It is this dramatic passing between opposites that provides the religious idea of sacrifice with its force and perhaps with its ontological content as well. If we now call suffering "alienation" and use "liberty" to refer, on the contrary, to the positive expansion of affectivity, then alienation is the condition for all liberation and the primary mode of its fulfillment. If we call it death, then death is the condition for life. In Christ's passion and in his sacrifice the metaphysical law of life is revealed and is expressed, insofar as its essence lies in affectivity, insofar as the blow struck against life lays bare its intangible essence, insofar as the wound made in the soft, white flesh gushes with blood, insofar as suffering reveals what it is that suffers at the very heart of this suffering, the absolutely living being of life.

As has been rightly said: the proletariat is Christ. The proletariat is the one—for, just like Christ, the proletariat is a person—who must go to the very limit of suffering and of evil, to the sacrifice of his being, giving his sweat and blood and ultimately his very life, in order to reach—through this complete self-annihilation, through this self-negation which is a negation of life—the true life which leaves all finiteness and all particularity behind, which is a complete life and salvation itself. "He who wants to save his life shall lose it, and he who wants to lose it will be truly alive." In its own way, the proletariat is involved in the dramatic history of opposites and fulfills this history, fulfills the sacrifice, strips itself down, loses itself completely and so has access to redemption, which constitutes the recovery and the reconquering of true being, revival and regeneration. "A sphere," states the text we are discussing, ". . . which is, in a word, the total loss of humanity and which can therefore redeem itself only through the total redemption of humanity." The critique of religion claimed to take us out of the religious sphere and to release us from its fantastic constructions, claimed to lead us into the domain of reality and, more precisely in the 1843–44 Introduction, into the domain of German reality, of German history, and of the proletariat which is being formed there. But the proletariat is just a substitute for the Christian God, the history that it animates and will fulfill is merely the profane transcription of a sacred history.

However, it is far from the case that the religious and mystical conceptions to which we have been compelled to refer have themselves had any direct influence on the texts we are analyzing. Instead, this influence is exerted through the mediation of German metaphysics. It is by way of the remarkable works of G. Cottier, on the one hand, and of de Negri, on the other, that we are able to specify just how German metaphysics became imbued with these religious themes to begin with, so that in their turn Marx's 1844 texts and finally Marxism itself were determined by these same themes. At the source of what he terms the kenotic schema—in accordance with which reality, in order to reach its fulfillment, must first of all annihilate itself by passing into its opposite so that, out of the annihilation of this opposite and in this way alone, the schema of realization understood as self-negation and as the negation of this negation can at last emerge in its plenitude—Cottier rightly cites the passage from Saint Paul's Epistle to the Philippians (2: 6–9) in which he recounts in the following terms what could be called the history of Christ's essence, that is to say, at once his personal history and his being: "For the divine nature was his from the first; yet he did not think to snatch at equality with God, but made himself nothing, assuming the nature of a slave. Bearing the human likeness, revealed in human shape, he humbled himself, and in obedience accepted even death—death on a cross. Therefore God raised him to the heights and bestowed on him the name above all names. . . ." ἐκένωτεν in Greek denotes the act by which Christ strips himself, empties himself of his divinity, that is to say, of his very being, and thereby annihilates himself in order to take on the human condition, in such a way, however, that this privation is pushed to the extreme, that it constitutes the act of taking on humanity in what in it is most extreme, its limiting situation, death, and even more, death in its most ignominious form, the death reserved for those sentenced to death and for slaves. For it is only in this way, when it is pushed to its own limit and to the end point of its being, that the opposite is itself annihilated to permit the return of the full positivity of the absolute in regeneration. Cottier's presentiment concerning the role Luther played in transmitting this "kenotic schema," that is to say, in the formation of German metaphysics as dialectical thought, has its source in the fact that Luther translated ἐκένωτεν by *hat sich selbst geeussert*, thus taking Christ's privation as his alienation.[52]

Actually, it is the entire Lutheran problematic which can appear in many respects as a prefiguration and at times an explicit preformation of dialectical thought. Indeed, the founder of the Reformation rises to this level of thought in his effort to resolve the difficulties of the Christian *paradox*, difficulties which all converge on the question of the *possibility of uniting opposites*, of presence *sub contrario* or yet again of *communicatio idiomatum*. The problems that lead to this question and that occupy all of Luther's attention are notably those concerning Christ on the cross and the Eucharist. They are posed in this way: how can it be that in a slave who has been crucified and has died a God can exist and can live, or rather, God himself; how, then, under this contrary appearance *(sub contrario)* can the divine essence be present? And likewise in the Eucharist, which Luther termed the *impanatio*, how is the real presence of Christ in the bread to be understood? That one and the same person, namely Christ on the cross, could be at one and the same time spiritual and carnal, sinner and just, bad and good, thus both dead and living, suffering and blessed, active and at rest, just as the bread is itself also the body of Christ, is explained by the *communicatio idiomatum*, that is, by the union of opposing properties. In this union each of the properties remains itself and, consequently, the properties continue to oppose one another, but in their meeting they form a new essence which contains these opposites and reunites them in a higher union. Luther, in one of his last treatises, called *De praedicatione identica de diversis naturis*, which is analyzed by de Negri, strives to justify rationally the *communicatio idiomatum* by showing that understanding it implies giving up syllogistic logic and replacing the copula "is" with a thought of becoming, of *werden*, in which the passage from one property into another and even into its own opposite is realized. To the objection that this passage from the same to its opposite is irrational, Luther replies, and in this strikingly foreshadows Hegel, that such a passage defines, precisely, true reason, that which conceives becoming and not identity as the essence of things, in short, a dialectical reason.[53]

The properly spiritual meaning of Luther's thought must not, however, be forgotten. It is not only the ontic properties of things that are involved in the *communicatio* and are thus submitted to the power of the dialectic. The law of opposites, its paradox, and its supersession concern and define first and foremost the life of each believer, his experience along the road to salvation. What characterizes this road is that it can by no means be considered to be a progress, a continuous improvement of moral life as a result of personal effort and will. Quite the contrary, it is only with heartfelt contrition, by slipping into absolute despair and by giving oneself up to the revolt against God, in and through this spiritual death, that faith and salvation can be born. In this, one element of the subsequent idea of the dialectic becomes apparent—the radical nature of opposition as the condition for its radical suppression and for the advent of universality, since it is by losing everything and only by absolute fault that everything can be recovered. This is the sense of the criticism of indulgences, which is not directed at the mere fact of this trade but at the Catholic conception of graduated penitence, proportional to the wrong. It is the very idea of proportioning and of measuring that appears inadequate and completely unrelated to salvation if the latter implies, as the sphere in which it emerges, total evil, the abyssal consciousness of sin in the soul of the sinner. It is obviously under the influence of Luther and of Lutheran theologians that Kierkegaard conceived his dialectic of the *Treatise on Despair* to which we have alluded.

Recognizing the spiritual significance of Lutherian thought leads us to the origin of the dialectic, to lived experience. This sheds new light on the evidence that has already been encountered in our own problematic, according to which the primary reality of passage and the very place where its concept arises is in life, in the passage which is itself understood as a lived experience, as the experience of the transformation of life in its own proper and fundamental tonalities. For it is precisely when life, in the very course of its experience, is lived as modification and, what is more, as radical self-modification in the passage from despair to certainty, that it is elevated to the intuition of spirituality. But then it must be said that already in Luther, and consequently from its inception, the concept of dialectic allows its basic ambiguity to appear. This consists in a μετάβασις εἰς ἄλλο γένος in the incontestable μετάβασις by virtue of which what is considered to be a law of the spiritual world and which is discovered in it is found to have been transferred to another region of being, to the domain of material things and their properties. For the identical predication of opposites no longer concerns only the phenomenological becoming of the *Erlebnisse*, their silent growth out of life and its essence; identity no longer designates this original and concrete essence as the condition of the possibility of what happens to it and thus happens *in it*; it is to the whole of what is, and first and foremost to material beings, that the *communicatio idiomatum*, the new "reason," is alleged to apply. The dialectical schema is isolated from the conditions that give it its original validity; it becomes a formal structure under which anything and everything is alleged to be subsumed. The possibility of subsumption lies neither in the nature of what is submitted to the schema nor in its prior examination, in making evident at least a possible adequation of the latter, of this particular nature, to the former, to that schema. It is the schema itself, the formal structure of the dialectic, which justifies the subsumption by reason of its own and somewhat magical power. Form has become content. Being itself, whatever it may be, whatever concrete form it may possess in each instance, comes to be in self-negation and comes to be to the extent that this negation is carried to term, that is to say is, in its turn, negated. Everywhere and always the negative signifies the genesis of being and its advent. Everywhere and always: not only when the negative designates the suffering of sacrifice, or despair, and the upsurge in it and through it of the limitless experience which thought cannot name, but also when what is involved is an objective event inscribed in the course of nature or of history—when what is involved is the advent of objectivity itself, of "nature" and of "history" as such and as the whole of being.

However, the founding power of the negative is coupled with an axiological meaning which, like this power, is ascribed to its secret origin, to the capacity of suffering to liberate in itself the being of life, to the capacity of evil *grasped in its phenomenological actuality*, just where it is indeed an "evil," to be a "good." Just like the power of the negative, its positive axiological meaning is transferred along with it and so comes into play along with it, plays where it plays. On the one hand, the simple course of events, whether natural events or human events, is not indifferent but is always oriented toward the coming of that which, as the negation of its condition, is more than it, and history has a "sense." As we have seen, even the alchemical transformation of things obeys an immanent teleology which leads to what is considered an "end" and a completion in terms of all the earlier modifications. On the other hand, to the extent that the concept of dialectic adds to the initial ontic meaning it has in alchemy or in Luther the decisive ontological meaning it contains in Boehme or in Hegel, it is now the production of objectivity, the phenomenology of mind, which is presented as the finality of the entire process, as the result which secretly drives it.

German metaphysics acquires and conveys three meanings of the concept of dialectic: (1) its original affective meaning, in accordance with which it designates life and the dichotomy of the tonalities within it, their sudden mutation, the paradoxical bond of suffering and joy, of love and hate; (2) an ontic meaning, in accordance with which the transformation is extended to "things" and alleged to define the being of every being; (3) an ontological meaning, by virtue of which the dialectic defines and determines this being as it is thought and grasped in itself, the opposition of objectivity and the world. The ontic and ontological meanings are the μετάβασις of its original meaning, the tardy and precritical extension to all that "is" of the original essential history of being in the life of radical subjectivity. In the μετάβασις the properties that belong to the single region of being in which they have been perceived, that is, to the original being of life, are also extended to the whole of being and are held to constitute its structure. We must not simply repeat the brilliant critique which Kierkegaard was to address to Hegel and say that the negative cannot be used to designate anything and everything, cannot function at one and the same time as an ethical, metaphysical, ontological, and, we might add, ontic concept, for the problem lies in the way in which the negative operates in each case, and this cannot be resolved by the equivocation of homonymy. Producing a nature, objectification, cannot be the same thing as what despair destines us for—and which signifies, precisely, the impossible objectification of life—nor is the history of the world that of the individual.

The threefold meaning of the concept of dialectic conveyed by German metaphysics is present in the construction *a priori* of the proletariat and secretly determines it, determines the German question to which German reality has to respond, the reality of Prussian society during the first half of the nineteenth century. To determine the reality of a particular society, even of society in general, on the basis of the concept of dialectic as this happened to be constituted in the movement of Western metaphysics as the result of various and sundry conceptions, of religious, theological, theosophical, alchemical, ontic, and ontological conceptions, and even more as the unrecognized expression of the essence of life, is to accomplish a new μετάβασις, the μετάβασις of the dialectic itself in a domain totally foreign to its place of birth, and is to give to the elements that constitute it a sense they do not possess. The first philosophy of labor presented in the 1844 *Economic and Philosophical Manuscripts* marked the invasion of economics by German metaphysics; the construction *a priori* of the proletariat and the theory of revolution that it defines mark the invasion of politics and history by German metaphysics. This is what is stated involuntarily and yet with sharp clarity by a famous proposition: the proletariat is the inheritor of classical German philosophy.[54]

Following the shift to the domain of material things, what can be the meaning of the structure of the objectification process of consciousness or of the affective dialectic of life, the "power of the negative"? If it is not the simple German designation of their objective condition, can the negation of a bridge or a house then mean only their destruction, sheer annihilation? In what way does this process of destruction, in itself and of itself, the quality and the force, so to speak, to make something new surge forth, something that is greater in the order of reality or of perfection, a wider bridge, a bigger house? And yet this is the really magical quality belonging to the negative in the concept of revolution. Revolution is nothing other than the negative in its claim to perform itself the work of being, the negation which is to define and to produce all positivity. The concept of revolution reflects the metaphysical identity of being and nothingness but by transposing it, absurdly, onto a level where it loses any possible sense, onto the ontic level.

Given this, is there any reason to say, in the absence of any reference to actual material reality, that the concept of revolution is empty, robbed of all possible effectiveness? However, the concept of revolution gathers within itself the constituent elements of the dialectical schema. The revolution performs the redeeming catastrophe, the life-giving radical negation, and in this resembles the proletariat whose history it concentrates in a dramatic summary. And yet, as has been sufficiently demonstrated, it is from life that the dialectical schema as it is presented in the concept of the proletariat, which is summed up in that of the revolution, is secretly borrowed; it is the dichotomy of affectivity which founds its oppositional structure and its pathos. From this moment on, the political heaven loses its transparency and its lightness, the empty concept of revolution is filled all at once and becomes a sphere of total investment. In it, all the powers of life are represented and find an imaginary prolongation: in destruction the death instinct, in regeneration the life instinct, in the loss of alienation suffering, in the victory over alienation and reconquest joy, in the passage from destruction to regeneration the very movement of life, of life which is always ahead of itself, in the ambiguity of attraction and repulsion, in the secret connivance of anguish and happiness. Revolution is the imaginary representation of what is produced and can only be produced in us. Revolution is a fantasy of life.

The mythology of history

The concept of revolution, just as that of the proletariat which is its agent, if not to say its officiating priest—the proletariat, Marx writes in *The Class Struggles in France*, comprises "the high dignitaries of the revolutionary interests"[55]—names no particular reality which would be limited to a moment in time and in history. Not only does the proletariat bring about the advent of the universal, since it is that particular class which denies itself as such and in so doing abolishes all the other classes, thus taking man out of the finiteness or restrictive and oppositional determination and giving him back to himself—inasmuch as the being of man is, precisely, the universal—but for this very reason, because the proletariat realizes the essential history of the universal, it is the essence of history that is accomplished in it, if indeed history has a sense, if it is that metaphysical adventure in which the poverty and the limitations of origins are gradually overcome and finally superseded in the major event of total realization. To the extent that history finds the condition for its possibility, along with its sense and its essence, in revolution, history also borrows from the latter its structure, the structure of temporality proper to it. History's time is thus in no sense the homogeneous milieu within which a succession of events unfolds; it is not an evolution but a revolution; it does not occur as a progress but as its opposite, as the development of the contrary, the opposite, the obstacle, as the slow construction of the wall whose sudden collapse will free being in all its fullness, will inaugurate the new Kingdom. This is why the coming of the universal, the establishment of a human order, is not the result of a linear progress at the end of which man would gain possession of himself; it is not winning man over *(le gain de l'homme)* but his "revival" *(son "regain")*, a new conquest which occurs by way of the "total loss of man." The time of history, history itself, is the development of alienation as the condition for reappropriation. Moreover, this is why the present of history is not a simple present, that which is here and now, purely and simply, a state of things, but the moment of a fall, a time of distress, for it is only out of the excessiveness of this distress and only when suffering becomes universal that salvation will come. The present announces this salvation and recognizes its coming in the very coming of catastrophe. All of history is held in this present which gathers history together within itself and which dominates history; history is the instant in which the contradiction is condensed, in which amid collapse and general upheaval the past all at once swings into the future.

The extent to which this apocalyptic and messianic conception of history is an offshoot of German metaphysics could be easily demonstrated if we had the time here to recall the grand themes of German Romanticism as these appear, notably, in Schilling, Novalis, Hölderlin, Hegel, or Schelling.[56] In the latter, for example, becoming commences by positing an initial bastard principle destined to be suppressed; thus it is presented as a strange process which begins by pursuing the slow construction of what it will then tear down and which undoes what it has already done. This way of getting at the definitive and the true by first of all asserting the contrary appearance, this disguising of one's deep intentions, is what Schelling calls the irony of God,[57] an irony which Marx, in his turn, thinks he recognizes at the heart of history. Significant in this regard are the historical-political writings—in particular those composed at the time of the 1848 revolution and during the rise to power of the future Napoleon III.

Examining the revolutionary process in France during the years 1846–51, Marx divides this period into two parts, the first of which has just ended before his own eyes and thus belongs to the past, leading to the December 2 *coup d'état;* the second is just in the process of occurring, and its description is at the same time a prophecy, and this Marx interprets, precisely, as the construction of a secret finality in the guise of an apparent counterfinality. "It [the revolution] goes about its business methodically. By 2 December 1851 it had completed one half of its preparatory work; it is now completing the other half. First of all it perfected the parliamentary power, *in order to be able to overthrow it.* Now, having attained this, it is perfecting the executive power, reducing it to its purest expression, isolating it, and pitting itself against it as the sole object of attack, *in order to concentrate all its forces of destruction against it.* And when it has completed this, the second half of its preliminary work, Europe will leap from its seat and exultantly exclaim: 'Well worked, old mole.' "[58]

The construction of the contrary which, in turn, is handed over to destruction, this "method" which is the method of revolution and of history, is presented by Marx in the opening lines of *The Class Struggles in France,* where he explicitly offers it as the object of his demonstration. Only "by creating a powerful and united counter-revolution; only in combat with this opponent did the insurrectionary party mature into a real party of revolution. To demonstrate this is the task of the following pages."[59] It is as this contrary necessary for the development of the process that the bourgeoisie intervenes and develops, assembling together within itself all the contraries, all the property-owning classes in order to constitute the absolute obstacle. "The first task of the February republic was rather *to complete the rule of the bourgeoisie* by all the property-owning classes to enter the political arena along with the financial aristocracy."[60] Because this opposition is necessary for the development of the revolutionary process, that is for its own development, the proletariat must participate in its formation, assist in the ascension of the bourgeoisie, pursue along with it the common struggle against the archaic element which continues to oppose the triumph of the bourgeoisie. "At this stage, therefore, the proletarians do not fight their enemies, but the enemies of their enemies, the remnants of absolute monarchy, the landowners, the non-industrial bourgeois, the petty bourgeoisie."[61]

However, if the proletariat, whose actions are like those of Schelling's God, can secretly savor the setting up of this complex system of which it is to be the ultimate beneficiary, the bourgeoisie, on the other hand, caught up in the ineluctable process of this strange history of which it understands only the short-term positions and consequences, finds itself in an uncomfortable and, in a word, dialectical situation. The bourgeoisie constitutes the contrary which is posited only to be destroyed, and its destruction begins with its inception.[62] In 1850 the bourgeoisie's self-destruction passes by way of the rise to power and the triumph of Bonaparte, and Marx shows with subtlety how, in order to defend itself, the bourgeoisie throws itself into the arms of its enemy and is forced, in order to ensure its survival as it confronts the people and the "Montagne" which represents the latter, to sacrifice its own parliamentary regime.[63] The irony of history does not simply hand the bourgeoisie over to Bonaparte; it establishes Bonaparte's reign only to isolate it in turn and to set up in opposition to it the whole of the people, so that "the overthrow of the parliamentary republic contains within itself the germ of the triumph of the proletarian revolution."[64]

In addition to the divine irony which continually poses the contrary of what it wants to do and so does what it wants only in and through the annihilation of what it does not want, in Schelling we also find the reason for this irony, which is therefore not sheer madness. This kind of "reason" resides in the divine will or, if one prefers, in the law of being according to which "all possibilities must occur."[65] It is not a matter of choosing from among all possibilities the best one and abandoning the others to the nothingness of that which will never be, but instead of bringing it about that all possibilities are realized and come into being so that the great law of being is indeed accomplished, the law of the total exhibition and the total realization of being. *History is precisely the milieu in which this law is accomplished.* This history will thus be a total history, the history in which all that can be does occur, the history of all virtualities, so that everything shows itself and can show itself, so that nothing remains hidden. This is why history is the history of contraries, why it provokes their occurrence and requires that each blossom forth fully, that each unfold completely all of the potentialities that it implies, because it is important that all of these potentialities[66] come to fulfillment and be displayed in full light. This is why the work of history is radical; it cannot tolerate anything within itself that is unfulfilled or obscure; it seizes the secret in each thing, uncovers it and in this assigns to it its end; it realizes all possibilities and destroys them in one and the same movement, and as a great purifying fire, it consumes everything along its path and leaves nothing standing. "History," says Marx in the 1843–44 Introduction to his *Critique of Hegel's Philosophy of Right*, "is thorough and passes through many stages while bearing an ancient form to its grave."[67] Inasmuch as it is the archaic German regime that is identified suddenly, on the contrary, with the historical present and with history itself, Marx, accordingly, writes in the same text: "Germany, which is renowned for its thoroughness. . . ."[68] Being thorough, in this context, is to make revolution not merely by overthrowing what is in the summary and brutal negation of a state of things but, rather, by the much more subtle interplay which allows a situation to develop, leads the contrary to its term and the contradiction to its greatest degree of tension, thereby exhausting the possible. "But," Marx will again state in *The Eighteenth Brumaire*, "the revolution is thorough."[69] Indeed, in the revolution the process of exhausting possibilities, which strews them one after the other like empty carcasses along the road it follows, is accelerated.

> In the first French revolution the rule of the Constitutionalists was followed by the rule of the Girondins, and the rule of the Girondins by the rule of the Jacobins.

Each of these parties leaned on the more progressive party. As soon as it had brought the revolution to the point where it was unable to follow it any further, let alone advance ahead of it, it was pushed aside by the bolder ally standing behind it and sent to the guillotine. In this way the revolution moved in an ascending path. In the revolution of 1848 this relationship was reversed. The proletarian party appeared as the appendage of petty-bourgeois democracy. It was betrayed and abandoned by the latter on 16 April, on 15 May, and in the June days. The democratic party, for its part, leaned on the shoulders of the bourgeois-republican party. As soon as the bourgeois republicans thought they had found their feet, they shook off this burdensome comrade and relied in turn on the shoulders of the party of Order. The party of Order hunched its shoulders, allowed the bourgeois republicans to tumble off, and threw itself onto the shoulders of the armed forces. It believed it was still sitting on those shoulders when it noticed one fine morning that they had changed into bayonets. Every party kicked out behind at the party pressing it forward and leaned on the party in front, which was pressing backward. No wonder each party lost its balance in this ridiculous posture, and collapsed in the midst of curious capers, after having made the inevitable grimaces. In this way the revolution moved in a descending path.[70]

It is, in truth, the process of history itself which becomes more evident when it gathers itself together and accelerates in the revolutionary process. History in general is this radical movement which actualizes possibilities only in order better to exhaust them and to lead them, by way of their power, to their impotence and to their death.

Because it does nothing halfway and because it is thorough, because it forces each possibility to produce all the virtualities it holds within itself and to display them in the light of developed-being, history, which is the place of this exhibition and its essence, is also the place and the essence of truth. What is characteristic of truth is that it appears when its time has come, as Hegel states in the preface to *The Philosophy of Right*. History, however, is this time of truth in which every particular being has to prove what it truly is. By unmasking each thing down to its innermost being, history evaluates it in terms of what it contains of actual positivity; history judges it. *Weltgeschichte ist Weltgericht*. In a talk he gave as part of the celebration of the London Chartist organization on April 14, 1856, Marx, alluding to the secret court of Saint-Vehme, which in the Middle Ages avenged the evil deeds committed by the powerful, marking a red cross on the houses of those to be punished, stated in conclusion: "Today the mysterious red cross marks all the houses in Europe. History itself renders justice and the proletariat will carry out the sentence."[71]

How does history render justice? The truth of history is the objectification of being in which being arrives at itself in the actuality of its object-condition. The truth of history is the unfolding of the world. History is, precisely, the history of the world. History is a foreground bathed in light, the stage upon which that which cannot remain enveloped in the night of virtuality steps forward in order to account for itself and to be developed. History is a theater, the theater of the world. On the stage of this theater, possibilities, one by one, come to play their role; these are the figures in which the absolute appears, the successive forms in which it is realized. The characters of history, Hegel's peoples or empires, Marx's classes, even individuals insofar as they speak in the name of these peoples or these classes or of some great cause and thus incarnate them, have only a short time, the time to say what they have to say and to play their role. History reclaims them and collects them in the mausoleums it erects to their glory, unless it relegates them to its dungeons or its wastebins. Certain characters, it is true, do not want to leave the stage; others try to make a comeback; they then recite empty lines and go through the motions of a second death. History is also a history of ghosts; death the second time around is comedy.[72] Marx was obsessed with the aesthetic categories of Hegelian romanticism, and it is from them that he takes the opening lines of the *Eighteenth Brumaire*: "Hegel remarks somewhere that all the great events and characters of world history occur, so to speak, twice. He forgot to add: the first time as tragedy, the second as farce."[73]

In truth, all the Hegelian categories, as if they too wanted to play their role a second time, little by little invade this "materialist" history, giving it an air of *déjà vu*. And it is not only words but concepts as well which, here and there, confer upon history a common structure, an identical way of being realized. This realization takes on, everywhere and in all cases, the form of dialectical opposition, of the titanic confrontation of contraries and of their fight to the death. Against the backdrop of this tragedy, in the perpetual play of birth and death, at the heart of this "bacchanalian revel, where not a member is sober," the ridiculous heroes and their empty gesticulating appear for but a moment, as a crest of foam on a vast wave before it breaks and is no more. However, the obstacle and evil are the secret motor at the heart of this process. The opposition of antagonistic forces is a spiritual combat. The schema of redemptive negation can be recognized under the materialist gangue of the dialectic; it continues to shine forth in these lines added onto *Capital*: "In history, just as in nature, putrefaction is the laboratory of life."[74]

What indeed could be the relation between history which obeys the kenotic schema, which is nothing other than this very schema—history pursuing the slow construction of the contrary and suddenly collapsing in the liberating catastrophe—and real history, the history of individuals, of their needs, of their works, of the instruments with which they produce? In particular, how is it that the perfecting of these instruments, the innumerable inventions that in every instance appear under particular conditions with respect to particular problems, precise technical problems, how is it that the series of these specific modifications, where each calls for the other, where each is situated as a prolongation of another, how is it that this slow transformation of activities which are diverse and yet which always complement one another and coordinate with one another to some extent, in short, how is it that this whole positive development could signify sheer negativity and the growth of the negative, of evil as such, the formation of the "contrary," in a word, an increasing alienation and, in this alienation and through it, in the sudden destruction of this contrary, the liberation, the blossoming forth of all the essential potentialities of life—how could this actualize in succession or rather at one and the same time, in the same instant, "the complete loss of man and the complete revival of man"? Let us ask once again, more precisely, by what miracle the historical present comes to offer itself as the first term in a process which German metaphysics elaborated at an earlier time in the philosophical act by which it thematically posed other problems? How can one hide the arbitrariness of the decision which ascribes to this particular present rather than to another the task of realizing the negative and first of all of identifying with it? Does not this identification of the present with a moment of the dialectical process presuppose the secret ontological homogeneity linking all of real history, to which the present belongs, to a process such as that which defines the structure of ideal objectivity, the ontological homogeneity of reality and of pure ideality as such? It is said that Marxist materialism wants precisely to transfer the dialectic from the spiritual sphere to that of reality. But is it not this transfer which is an aberration and which carries the absurdity of the μετάβασις to its extreme? And then just what could be meant by the opposition of "materialism" and idealism?

The dialectical conception of history implies, however, other presuppositions which, in the final analysis, concern the metaphysical problem of being, presuppositions which Marx's thought, all at once discovering the anti-Hegelian intuition that has secretly animated it from the start, will now recognize and denounce.

Chapter 3

THE REDUCTION OF TOTALITIES

The transcendental theory of history: "historical materialism"

The ultimate—although most often unobserved—presupposition of the dialectical conception of history is metaphysical; it is the presupposition that, in and of itself, history constitutes a reality in the literal sense of the word, namely, on the one hand, an actual, substantially existing reality defining a dimension of being and perhaps being itself and, on the other hand, precisely *one* reality, a unitary and ultimately unique reality, one single substance, one single essence, one single existence which unfolds itself and whose unfolding is thus nothing other than its self-unfolding, the unfolding of itself by itself, exhibiting by its own act its own reality. The origin of the metaphysical interpretation of history which can be found in the 1844 texts resides in the concept which serves, precisely, as a ground for these texts and which, in general, determines the humanism of the young Marx, that is, in the concept of *Gattungswesen*. The human species is this unitary reality which constitutes both the subject and the object of history, its principle and its content. History is the History of Man, the history of his ruin and his recovery, so that it is one and the same essence, the human essence, which is alienated and which overcomes its alienation. To the extent that history is the objectification of the human genus, its being is more or less the same as that of society. The 1844 *Economic and Philosophical Manuscripts* only made more precise the ways in which this objectification occurs in labor. The affinity between the concepts of "society" and "history" is obvious; both are part and parcel of a metaphysics of ideal universality or of its Feuerbachian counterpart; they are based upon the Hegelian ontology and simply reveal the essence that supports it.

In 1845 Marx's anti-Hegelianism, which had secretly inspired the 1843 manuscript and, as we shall see, remained implicit in the 1844 texts, attains the level of thought, becomes explicit, and is formulated conceptually. This abrupt awakening may well have occurred through the contact with Stirner's thought—it directly follows the reading of *The Ego and His Own*—nevertheless it simply brings out the initial and fundamental intuitions; or rather, for the first time, they are thought and this thought involves in the same stroke the deliberate and brutal rejection of the Hegelian concepts and of their substitutes. And first and foremost among these are the concepts of "society" and of "history." *The fact*

that this decisive conceptual mutation is not simply produced, without our know-
ing why this is, within an epistemological field but that it rests, on the contrary,
upon ultimate ontological presuppositions in accordance with which the ideal
universality of objectivity defines the sphere of existence and of reality—this can
be seen precisely in the fact that henceforth, for Marx, neither "society" nor
"history" "exists" as an ontological reality whose unity stems from the universal
process of objectification and which is produced by it as unitary and substantive
objective realities. Unable to display a reality which would be adequate to them,
a reality whose actual existence would attest to itself and allow itself to be
recognized as an actual and not merely a formal unity, the concepts of history
and society allow us a glimpse of their vacuity, destroy themselves as simple
concepts and show themselves to be no more than *words*.

In the *Poverty of Philosophy* (1847), Marx, engaging in polemics against
Proudhon, who reproaches the economists with not having understood that
society is a reality *sui generis, a general and as such unitary reality,* a "collective being" whose structure and whose laws would therefore have nothing in
common with the determinations of the individuals who make up this generic
reality but who are in fact determined by it, replies in these terms: "We have
pleasure in confronting him with the following passage from an American
economist, who accuses the economists of just the opposite: 'The moral entity—
the grammatical being called a nation, has been clothed in attributes that have
no real existence except in the imagination of *those who metamorphose a word*
into a thing. . . . This has given rise to many difficulties and to some deplorable
misunderstandings in political economy.'"[1] This text is all the more remarkable
in that it appears with reference to the problem of the surplus left by labor, at
the very moment when Marx recognizes that the production of the "social
individual," of "associated individuals," goes beyond that of the isolated individual, of nonassociated individuals. From this moment on, the collective productive force that plays a decisive role in *Capital,* as in every real society, has a
clearly defined philosophical status, allowing no possible equivocation. *The*
collective productive force, which is superior to the whole of the individual forces it
comprises, does not as such constitute any particular being possessing stability or
self-sufficiency. The "collective being," the social as such, is not autonomous, or
rather simply is not; the ontological dimension of existence is not constituted by it.

To confer existence in the sense of a substantive, unitary, and actual existence upon the collective being, upon the common being, upon the "social" as
such *independently of the individuals whom it comprises and whose own ontolog-*
ical reality constitutes the only possible reality of society, is to hypostatize the
latter, to treat as a specific being something that does not exist. Marx said: "This
is to treat society as a person." *The rejection of society as a person apart has a*
rigorous ontological meaning; it explicitly challenges the claim of the universal,
the whole, the organism, the set, the structure, all the modes and all the declen-
sions of the general as such to constitute reality in and of themselves. This
rejection is so vehement in Marx that it constantly takes the form of a polemic, a

polemic which in no way conceals but, quite the opposite, underscores the essential, metaphysical nature of the problem encountered. If there is a polemic against metaphysics itself in Marx, it is aimed precisely at the hypostasis of reality in a place other than its place of origin, in a dimension which no longer constitutes the condition for its possibility and in which it, consequently, is able neither to unfold nor to take shape. "Metaphysics" is the name for what is beyond reality, the site where reality can no longer be situated, where nothing that is actual can occur. This is the case for society, inasmuch as in it one sees something other than a word, something other, too, than the individuals who make it up and who indeed define the place of reality, inasmuch as one attributes to society laws that would not be the laws of these individuals themselves, laws that express them and that are grounded in them and in them alone, inasmuch as society is treated, on the contrary, as an original reality with its own determinations, with structures and determinations that belong to it alone, revealing its specific nature, revealing its reality precisely as an autonomous and unitary reality, as the unitary power of structuration and of determination.

It is in fact in a polemical manner, in the bluntness of the essential discourse, that the ultimate presuppositions of Marx's thought burst forth, the metaphysical thesis which destroys all "metaphysics" and denounces the poverty of philosophy, the poverty of the philosophy of the universal, represented at that time by Proudhon as its French subproduct. In the passage that directly precedes the one we have discussed and that deals with the surplus-product, Marx writes, "To prove that all labor must leave a surplus, M. Proudhon personifies society; he turns it into a *person, Society*—a society which is not by any means a society of persons, since it has its laws apart, which have nothing in common with the persons of which society is composed, and its 'own intelligence,' which is not the intelligence of common men, but an intelligence devoid of common sense."[2] The fact that the hypostatization of society, "the fiction of the person, Society,"[3] represents the claim that to society belong its own particular laws, which would not be those pertaining to the individual and, in the same motion, confers upon society a reality different from individual reality, this is unconditionally affirmed in the following text: "Surplus labor, he says [this is Proudhon speaking], is explained by the person, Society. *The life of this person is guided by laws, the opposite of those which govern the activities of man as an individual.* He desires to prove this by 'facts'."[4] But precisely because the laws of the individual cannot be opposed to, or superimposed upon, the laws of society, Proudhon can only prove the opposite of what he wants to prove, namely "that the profits and losses of society are not in inverse ratio to the profits and losses of individuals."[5]

The polemic against Proudhon simply takes up once more the critique levelled against Stirner, in which for the first time Marx presents his thesis that society does not in itself constitute a reality but instead is precisely the hypostasis of something that lies elsewhere, namely in individual existence. It is precisely for this reason that reality, because it is presented in every instance as the reality of an individual, is in its very origin a splintered, multiple, plural reality, a reality which can be formulated solely in a collective plural, and yet only in such a way that the unity of this formulation cannot fool us, in such a way that it does not name any actual, real unity but just the opposite of unity, an absolute diversity of monads. Stirner's paralogism, the source of the metaphysical belief in society, consists in substituting for this indefinite plurality of individuals, through the effect of the illusion proper to language, a real and substantive unity, a determination of the universal. "Who is this person you call everyone?" asked Stirner, and he replied: It is "society." And Marx comments on this assertion in these terms: "With the aid of a few quotation marks Sancho here transforms 'all' into a person, society as a person, as a subject. . . ."[6]

Marx's critique is all the more radical, its interest all the greater, as it is aimed at Stirner, who claimed, precisely, to oppose the individual to society and to deny the latter the right to set itself up as a real or normative absolute confronting the individual, imposing its laws on the individual, and dictating to him its own prescriptions. Stirner indeed wants to reverse this relationship of dependency, to consider society merely as an instrument in the service of the individual and no longer as a superior moral reality which the individual should serve.[7] But if Marx subscribes to the Stirnerian rejection of a hypostatized society, what could be the substance of his own critique of Stirner? It lies in the fact that Stirner, like the anarchists, brings about the hypostasis of society just when he believes he is combatting it. For Stirner initiates an opposition, the naïve opposition *par excellence*, between society and the individual; he considers the relation that he establishes between them a conflictual relation which is to be resolved no longer for the benefit of society but this time for that of the individual, by giving free reign to the egoism as a result of which the Unique will henceforth "make use" of society. But society does not exist. The opposition between the individual and society presupposes the existence of the latter outside of the individual and independent of him, that is to say, precisely, its hypostasis. Stirner does what he reproaches the socialists for doing. "Saint Sancho has quite forgotten that it was himself who transformed 'society' into an 'ego' and that consequently he finds himself only in his own 'society.' "[8]

The hypostatization of society outside of the individuals who constitute its only possible reality is laden with consequences. Because society now exists as a reality in its own right in opposition to the individual, the problem of a relation between these terms previously posited as different inevitably arises. If this relation is no longer understood in Stirner's sense, in a naïve and quixotic fashion, as the opposition of the individual to society and his refusal to allow himself to be determined by this sanctified society, by the "saint," the relation is then simply reversed and becomes the determination of the individual by society. However, this "evident" determination presupposes along with the Stirnerian relation, of which it is the mere inversion, the mutual exteriority of the terms between which it is established. It is this exteriority that Marx challenges, rejecting in the same stroke the very possibility of an external relation between the individual and society, the possibility, to tell the truth, of any relation between them; and this is so for the further reason that society as such does not exist. For it is not only the status of society, its transcendence, for example, that Marx rejects; it is instead, as we have seen, the very reality of society as a unitary and actual reality. *A relation between society and the individual is impossible in principle; the relation of individuals to themselves alone exists and alone can be rendered problematic.* Such is the first decisive consequence of the radical critique of the concept of society.[9] Long afterwards, in the general Introduction to the 1857 *Critique of Political Economy*, Marx will write: "To regard society as one single subject is, in addition, to look at it wrongly; speculatively."[10]

No more than society is history a "single subject," a universal reality possessing being and as such capable of acting, the source and principle of determinations. In 1844 Marx said: "History does nothing halfway." A few months later he writes: "History does nothing."[11] The rejection of the conception of history understood as an ontological reality unfolding itself, integrating actual determinations as mere mediations in the process of its self-development, consequently, realizing itself, realizing its own aims through the apparent aims of the complex activity of individuals—this is expressed by the vocabulary already employed in the critique of society and which now translates the refusal to hypostatize "history," the refusal to treat it as a person, as a particular character. Immediately after having said that history does nothing, the text we are discussing adds: "it 'possesses no immense wealth,' it 'wages no battles.' It is man, real, living man who does all that, who possesses and fights; 'history' is not, as it were, a person apart, using man as a means to achieve its own aims; history is nothing but the activity of man pursuing his aims."

That the aims of man, and by this one must now understand the multitude of individuals—"the activity of real mankind is nothing but the activity of a mass of human individuals"[12]—have nothing to do with the aims of history can be seen in the fact that, whereas these individuals pursue the achievement of their own plans, consequently obeying motivations included within their individual phenomenological life and inscribed therein as actual lived determinations, needs, desires, etc., the history at issue here, Bauer's history just as that of Hegel, of which it is but the pale reflection, aims at the advent of truth which, precisely, defines the finality proper to it. History is nothing other than, as it were, the process through which truth is realized, the movement of its becoming, a movement inseparable from its essence and constituting this very essence. It is against this conception of history as essence and as the history of the essence of truth that Marx now consciously commits himself. To Bauer's question: "What would be the purpose of history if its task were not precisely to prove these simplest of all truths. . . ?" Marx supplies the following commentary: ". . . history exists in order to serve as the act of consumption of theoretical eating—proving. Man exists so that history may exist, and history exists so that the proof of truth may exist. In this critically trivialized form is repeated the speculative wisdom that man exists, and history exists, so that truth may arrive at self-consciousness."[13] That, for Marx, it is not simply a question of denying the teleology of history that is situated traditionally in theology but of going back to the ground which makes this teleology possible, to the metaphysical conception of a universal reality whose self-unfolding in the form of objectification is its becoming for itself as truth, to the hypostasis of this historical essence of truth which takes the place of the real "subject," that is to say, of living individuals who themselves are cast in the role of a mere mediation—posited mysteriously—of this absolutized essence, this is what Marx explicitly states: "That is why history, like truth, becomes a person apart, a metaphysical subject of which real human individuals are merely the bearers."[14]

The critique of history understood as a substantive and autonomous reality paves the way for Marx's thesis according to which *the reality of history is to be sought outside of it, outside of the unitary process which is represented in its concept,* according to which *history admits of presuppositions.* What these presuppositions are is stated outright: living individuals. Here and now a crucial evidence becomes apparent with respect to the essential philosophical problem of the evolution of Marx's thought: *Marx's abandonment of the Feuerbachian concept of genus, of the human species, of the universal as the subject of history and as progressively realizing itself through its objectification in history, the abandonment of the* Gattungswesen *in no way means the correlative abandonment of the concept of the individual but, quite the contrary, its emergence, its conscious, deliberate, and explicit situation at the center of the problematic as the guiding concept of the search for and, above all, of the understanding and the elaboration of the concept of history.*

Marx refers to the founding premise of history in an insistent, repetitious, and apparently monotonous fashion: "The first premise of all human history is, of course, the existence of living human individuals."[15] And further on: "This manner of approach is not devoid of premises. It starts out from the real premises and does not abandon them for a moment. Its premises are men. . . ."[16] And again: "The premises from which we begin are not arbitrary ones, not dogmas, but real premises from which abstraction can only be made in the imagination. They are the real individuals. . . ."[17] Pursuing his systematic examination of the presuppositions of history, Marx distinguishes three; the last two, however, can be carried back to the first and serve merely as its explanation. They are: (1) the activity by which the individual satisfies his needs; (2) the production of new needs; and (3) the reproduction of the individual himself in the family.[18]

Referring history to its founding presuppositions is not as simple as it seems. It means that the succession of events formed by the multitude of diverse human actions, the interplay of the complex connections to which they give rise and in which they are caught, is not only a "succession" which takes place before our eyes and which we would have only to witness, but instead something which has to be explained. And the principle of this explanation, *the ground of history,* resides precisely in "living individuals." Is not this sort of "explanation" a pure tautology? Does it not designate as the condition for the development of individuals these individuals themselves? Or does it not rather pose the tautology to which all alleged positivity is confined, the simple hypostasis of the succession of events and of what occurs? By presenting living individuals as the presupposition of history, Marx explicitly situates the principle of all economic, social, political, and cultural phenomena which "occur in the world" and which we call "history" in individual phenomenological life and in the necessity proper to it, consequently, in what this life is and in its essence, in life which wants to live and which in order to live must satisfy its needs and which in order to satisfy them must work. Individual phenomenological life, all these lives or, to speak as Marx does, "living individuals," although they enter into history and are determined by it, themselves, on the contrary, determine history in an ultimate sense: not because each life in its own modest way, in its own infinitely small way as it were, shares in producing the course of the world and in fashioning its physiognomy as a whole, but because these lives constitute *its necessary condition, that without which history would not exist*. Inasmuch as it constitutes the necessary condition for history, life, although it belongs to history, does not belong to it and must be understood as metahistorical and as that heterogeneous ground with respect to the positive nature of the development it founds, that is, as metaphysics. There is no such thing as history; there are only historical individuals. Moreover, individuals are historical in two ways: first, insofar as they belong to history and as their actions constitute its course; and second, insofar as they do not belong to it, insofar as, subordinated to the power of life in them, they found history. "Historical" has, therefore, two senses designating in turn the infinitely varied content of history but also, and above all, its ground. The second meaning, where it is no longer a question of factitious history but of its *a priori* necessary condition, is the essential meaning; it aims at a "reality" which is not what occurs but which brings it about that "what occurs" can occur, must occur, and actually does occur. It is to this essential meaning that the "presupposition" of history which Marx has in mind refers, that which denotes the radical concept of the "historical fact" as an originary founding fact *(fait proto-fondateur)* of history, as opening the field of history in its prior possibility. After having stated that life as the presupposition of history implies drinking, eating, and the production of material life, and after having designated this production as the "first historical act," Marx adds, "and indeed this is an historical act, *a fundamental condition of all history*."[19]

That life constitutes the fundamental condition of all history, its *a priori* necessary condition or, as we may again say, its transcendental condition, that it is, consequently, to be understood as a metahistorical condition, in no way signifies that it is situated outside of history. Transcendental condition signifies a condition immanent in everything it makes possible, an internal condition, an essence, and, finally, a substance. Life, the transcendental condition for history, enters in at every point of this history and in every instance makes it

possible. Right after having asserted that the production of life is "indeed . . .
an historical act, a fundamental condition of all history," Marx's text adds,
"which today, as thousands of years ago, must daily and hourly be fulfilled
merely in order to sustain human life." The originary founding nature of life,
however, characterizes all of its determinations, need, production—precisely—
and labor. "The labor-process . . . is human action with a view to the production
of use-values, appropriation of natural substances to human requirements; it is
the necessary condition for effecting exchange of matter between man and
Nature; it is the everlasting Nature-imposed condition of human existence, and
therefore is independent of every social phase of that existence, or rather, is
common to every such phase."[20] The determinations of life, however, as transcendental determinations of history, do not determine it indiscriminately; they
prescribe for it their own proper order of determination as an order which is
itself transcendental. It is because in life need precedes activity that, on the
level of factitious history, this precedence itself takes on an historical form, the
form of an actual succession. Still in *Capital*, Marx says: ". . . ever since the
first moment of his appearance on the world's stage, man always has been, and
must still be a consumer, both before and while he is producing."[21]

What, precisely, is the meaning of the immanence in history of its metahistorical necessary condition? How can life at one and the same time belong to
history and not belong to it? For life, belonging to history means being in every
instance in it, at every moment *or rather in every individual* the condition for an
effective production, a production made necessary by this life and for it. Not
belonging to history means: this condition for all history is not something that
could be submitted to history, carried along and finally abolished by it; it is not
an historical state, that is to say, precisely, a state of things in the process of
transformation, slated, finally, to disappear. *The repetition alike unto itself,
against the background of its own proper essense, of individual phenomenological
life and of its fundamental determinations, the indefinite repetition of desire, of
need and of labor—this is what, as the always new and always present condition,
allows there to be a history.* That the necessary condition for history is individual
phenomenological life, this means further that this condition is not a formal
condition, which would be incapable of displaying reality in itself, compelled to
find reality outside of itself and to receive it, tracing out no more than the empty
form of this possible reception. Quite the opposite: the necessary condition for
history is already a real condition, it is reality itself in its most elementary and
most essential determination, namely, to be specific, life in the positivity of its
phenomenological actuality. More real than history is that which makes it
possible. It is against the background of the absolute ontological reality of its
necessary condition that history is itself real.

It is therefore reality itself, absolute ontological reality which, as the necessary condition for history, is and must be understood as metahistory. Metahistory, consequently, is the theory of this reality, the theory of the necessary
condition for history. The theory of the necessary condition for history is not

history, the factitious science of the events that constitute the course of the world, historical science *(Historie)* which has historical reality *(Geschichte)* as its object. The theory of the necessary condition for history is the theory of history itself, it is Philosophy. As the *a priori* theory of the *a priori* necessary condition for history, philosophy considered here as the philosophy of history, is itself metahistorical; it has, precisely, nothing to do with history, whether history is understood as historical reality or as the science of this reality. The implicit confusion of philosophy and history or, again, the explicit attempt to identify them is meaningless *a priori*. Consequently, it is meaningless to reduce philosophy to an ideology, that is, to a moment of history, to a theoretical ensemble which itself is part of a factitious historical formation and which can be explained in terms of it. It is equally meaningless to identify philosophy with historical science; for example, consider this statement by Gramsci: "The identity of history and philosophy is immanent in historical materialism."[22]

Because the production of life is the condition for all possible history, it is not an historical condition in the ordinary sense of the word, that is, a condition for a particular historical event, a condition which itself would belong to history and be situated within it preceding this event and determining it as its cause, a cause of the same nature as the effect and like it destined to occur and then to disappear. Thus when Marx says that "the capitalist mode of production—its basis being wage-labor . . . can assume greater dimensions and achieve greater perfection only where there is available in the country a quantity of money sufficient for circulation,"[23] it is obvious that such a "condition" for capitalism is itself a product of history, that this cause is also an effect. The capitalist system presupposes a good many other conditions, all of which, however, are found to be with respect to history in the same situation as the growth of a sufficient money supply, that is, in the situation of belonging to history, *of being historical conditions and not conditions for history*. For example, the capitalist system still presupposes the separation of the worker from the means of production. The worker's appearance on the market as an exchangeable commodity, the fact that he offers himself indeed implies that he has nothing else to offer, that he lacks any instrument of production. This situation, which constitutes the most important historical premise for capitalism, is, however, no more than an historical situation which itself is the result of earlier conditions. It results from the seizure of land by the large landowners who, by taking it away from the peasants, forced them out—proletarians with neither home nor hearth—onto the labor market. This rural exodus itself resulted from replacing cultivated fields with grazing land, which brought a greater profit and which necessitated the consolidation of large domains and required fewer laborers. All of these "conditions" for capitalism, which Marx describes at length, are obviously merely historical conditions which, once again, determine the course of history but in no way constitute the necessary condition for history itself. This is why, just as these conditions belong to history, make up historical reality, the study of these conditions, their analysis, and the evaluation of their role and their importance is part of historical science, of the science that studies this reality *but not of the philosophy of history which studies the necessary condition for this reality*. It is not historical materialism, it is history as science which thematizes the "historical premise" of capitalism, for example, and Marx, to the extent that he pursues this thematics, is doing the work of an historian.

Other, more general, conditions which, moreover, seem to escape history insofar as they comply with the fundamental law of reiteration which defines the *a priori* are still, in reality, simply historical conditions. This is the case, for example, of the condition that is thought under the title of "class struggles." "The history of all hitherto existing society is the history of class struggles."[24] "All hitherto existing society": it happens that if we take a backward glance at the actual history of past societies, we are led to think that this history is dominated by conflicts between the groups which make up these societies. To this factitious history belongs class struggle as a character which is itself factitious. In "all hitherto existing society" it has been so. There is nothing to prove that this must be so. There exists no *a priori* condition which would make it have to be so. Marx intends, precisely, to show that factitious history commits itself to a different path. The statement "The history of all hitherto existing society is the history of class struggles" is an assertoric proposition which states a property of completed history and which, as such, belongs to the empirical science of this factitious science. It is external in relation to the apodictic content, which defines the necessary condition for all history in general. *The theory of class struggles is foreign to "historical materialism."* Likewise, all the more specialized theories that relate to the more general theory—the theory of the proletariat, of revolution, etc.—even if these were correctly understood and were no longer considered in the light of the mythological conception of history which we have denounced, would nevertheless continue to lie outside the domain of the philosophy of history and of the thematic proper to it. It is, precisely, the hypostasis of history as a universal reality, the comprehension of opposition and, finally, of struggle as belonging to the process of self-development of this universal and as required by this process, which have made people believe that opposition—precisely—struggle, class struggles were inscribed in the very possibility and in the essence of becoming and of "history" as such.

The opposition between history as science and the philosophy of history, between the history of historians on one side and, on the other, historical materialism, whose fundamental premises are indicated by Marx at the start of *The German Ideology*, becomes obvious if we compare the propositions, or rather the types of propositions which belong to these different "sciences" and which determine them. To the assertoric character of the propositions of history is opposed the apodicticity of the theoretical content of "historical materialism." To the observation concerning class struggles in the history of past societies is opposed the thesis that *history, all possible history inasmuch as it is grounded in individual phenomenological life, in a life which exists as need and as activity directed toward satisfying this need, is found necessarily to be a history of production and of consumption.* And so, consequently, is any possible society. Of course, the radical opposition of the philosophy of history to history itself as science does not mean that such a philosophy has no relation to this history. This relation resides precisely in the fact that the philosophy of history elucidates the necessary conditions for history, opens the ontological dimension in which this history will unfold, marking out at the same time the thematic object of historical science. The determination of history *a priori* as the history of production, for example, belongs to the constitution of the field defining historical reality and, therefore, the theme of history as science. As a result, historical materialism does not simply impose upon the science of history a particular style of research, a type of problem, etc.; by defining its object *a priori*, at the same time it defines it in its specificity and constitutes it as the particular science that it is. Even before historical science becomes involved in its varied and, moreover, infinite investigations, it receives a share of the *a priori* belonging to historical materialism, the transcendental element which underlies each of its endeavors and which, removing it from the basic indetermination of an inquiry lacking any ground and any particular object, makes it efficacious and, above all, possible. The transcendental grounding of history both as reality and as historical science, this is finally what is meant by Marx's thesis that history allows presuppositions.

Marx's conception of history loses its apparently naïve character when it appears as the prior refutation of the Heideggerian interpretation of historicality. It is true that an "historical" object—for example, a piece of furniture in a museum—can be understood only in relation to an historical "world" in which it once belonged.[25] It is, however, the nature of this "world" that causes a problem. Does it allow itself to be reduced to the whole ensemble of projects, to the projects common to those who were the "inhabitants" of this world? But the specificity of these projects, which defines the specificity of a given historical world, can in no way be explained on the basis of the formal structure of the "project" in general, on the basis of the formal structure of historicality which is, in fact, reduced by Heidegger to the structure of time itself. What is involved is the movement by which existence, understood as transcendence, ecstatically moves beyond itself toward the finite horizon of the future in order to return, having run up against this horizon, from it back upon itself in such a way that this act of "returning back upon" opens up the dimension of the past in which existence discovers itself, an existence handed over to the world in order to die there. However, if in every instance the untiring activity of this movement ahead-of-itself toward the horizon of its death and of this return back-upon-itself uncovers a world, it is nevertheless incapable of founding the content of this world. The reason why the form of time is powerless to account for the content of history or, rather, for history itself must, however, be shown. It is precisely the initial presupposition of the project, the definition of existence as *ekstasis*, which renders incomprehensible the actual determinations which this existence always presents in reality and by virtue of which it engenders a determinant history, irreducible indeed to the colorless schema of self-projection and self-understanding. Only a philosophy which from the start makes a place for the positivity of life can account for both the possibility and the positivity of history, a philosophy which recognizes that what is at the origin is not a project but hunger, need, life as it is experienced in the actuality of the living present, in affectivity. Only that which is affective can have and, above all, can actually found a history. There is no history of the object, there is no history of the mind. Thus, before the project of feeding oneself, before the project of clothing oneself, there is cold, the subjective experience of discomfort; after the project, the concrete subjective activity through which life attempts to abolish its negative determinations, its "suffering." Afterwards? To tell the truth, affectivity immediately determines action and is continued in it; the "project" as such is never more than a mediation which intervenes in accordance with the conditions of experience. In any case, it is in the determination of life that preoccupation finds its own determination; the possibility of defining an historical world by repeating the projects of those whose world it was necessarily refers back to the immediate prescriptions of life in them.

The irreducibility of existence—which founds history—to a project, the irreducibility of life to the transcendence of an *ekstasis*, puts into question the secret homogeneity which is established in Heidegger between historical reality and history as science and makes it impossible. According to the teaching of *Sein und Zeit*, in fact, it is because the *Dasein* of the historian is historical, permeated by the work of temporality, it is because, returning back upon itself starting from its finite future, *Dasein* in this "returning back upon" opens up the ontological dimension of the past that it is able, precisely, to enter into a relation with this past, to discover itself and to discover the other *Dasein* as having-been-there. The structure of having-been-there, "having been present," is itself, however, nothing other than this projection toward a future and this return upon the self. This is why in understanding men of the past the historian understands their projects and the way in which they understand themselves in light of these projects. The ontological structure of the *Dasein* of the historian is homogeneous with the structure of the *Dasein* that he discovers. *Ekstatic* self-understanding defines both history as science and historical reality. *But, for Marx, one cannot understand a society in light of the understanding which that society had of itself, and this is so not primarily because this understanding would be falsified or mystifying but for the more ultimate reason that the original life of the men who formed this society was not an understanding and does not permit itself to be defined in terms of one*. It is because the life of the men who form a society, the life that produces history, insofar as it produces itself in the immanent movement of affectivity and of action, is not reducible to self-understanding in the development of temporal *ekstasis* that real history, which is this production of life, is not reducible to history as science, to the *ekstatic* understanding of oneself in the transcendence of the temporalization of temporality.

The radical heterogeneity of historical reality and of history as science includes the heterogeneity of the ultimate structure of being and expresses it. By relating history to its real presuppositions, to immanent life, Marx makes inevitable a radical mutation of all the concepts that are tied to it. Because history is no longer time, the development of original exteriority,[26] it no longer signifies what this sort of development would satisfy, the birth of phenomenality, the unfolding of truth understood precisely as objectivity and as world—it is no longer the history of this truth, the history of mind. To say that history is not time, the *ekstasis* of a horizon, this also means that it no longer stands beyond the real as the empty place of its manifestation, beyond the living individuals who live it and who make it, who *are* this history; this means that history is no longer foreign to them. The reference of history to individual phenomenological life and to its concrete determinations finds its expression in the terminology employed by Marx, and this is all the more significant as it is the same terminology used at the same epoch—and not by chance—by Kierkegaard in *The Concept of Anguish:* history is no longer that of the mind; it has become the history of generations.[27]

The genealogy of the classes

The critique of the hypostatized social totality endowed as such with its own reality and specific effectiveness, the critique of the person, Society, takes the form in Marx of a reduction of that society into the classes that compose it and that constitute its real and determinant elements. In his polemic against Proudhon, who "gives the person, Society, the name of Prometheus, whose deeds he glorifies," Marx said: "What then, ultimately, is this Prometheus resuscitated by M. Proudhon? It is society, social relations based on class antagonism."[28] Such is therefore the reality of society, the reality of the classes which compose it and which form at one and the same time its anatomy and its physiology, so that the "movement of society," just like that of "history," is in reality only a process resulting from the prior existence of these classes and of the struggle that sets them in opposition, a struggle which at times exists in a latent state in the background of "society" and at times manifests itself in an obvious fashion in a conscious and brutal confrontation.

However, to the extent that they enter into conflict, the classes do not explain only the structure of societies and their history. If, as has been stated, this history is always that of living individuals, *the classes can determine history only if they first determine the individuals,* so that it is not, in reality, these individuals who "make history," who are its true "premise," but instead, precisely, the classes, the individuals if one prefers, but *in the situation and the determination conferred upon them by the class to which they belong.*[29] Such, then, is the concept of class, that of an ensemble, of a totality which alone is concrete and real, capable of being a principle of determination with respect to the vaster ensemble in which it is inscribed, namely a given society, but above all with respect to the individuals of which it is the class. This determination of the individual by the class to which he belongs is rigorous and, in a certain manner, radical; it signifies that an individual is what he is only in and through his belonging to a class, which class confers upon him the whole of its features, its social features at any rate. The latter, however, are essential; they concern and define his concrete and everyday existence as well as his way of thinking.

It was in an abrupt, biting, and, one might have thought, decisive manner that Marx had rejected the well-known concepts which we have just recalled and which together constitute one of the major themes of both traditional Marxism and its alleged renewal under the banner of "structuralism." In the margin of the manuscript of *The German Ideology* Marx wrote: "With the philosophers *pre-existence* of the class."[30] Who are the "philosophers" who so absurdly affirm the primacy of the class in relation to the individuals who compose it? The context clearly indicates who they are. There is Stirner, there are all those whose thought constitutes the "German ideology" properly speaking, and the neo-Hegelians in general. And indeed the concept of class is an Hegelian concept, not because it is in fact found in Hegel,[31] in particular in the *Philosophy of Right* on which Marx meditated at length, but because it presupposes in general an Hegelian-type ontology in which actual existence is defined by the objective totality and the participation in this totality. The objective totality which defines existence, the concrete totality out of which the individual draws his being is, doubtless, no longer the State, the unitary and homogeneous essence in which universal life circulates and is gathered together, nor is the individual any longer the citizen. But the determination of the "concrete" individual by the class which confers upon him its own proper characteristics and now constitutes his being, so that one must understand the individual on the basis of the class, is analogous to the determination of the citizen by the Hegelian State. In all cases an objective totality in which the ontological weight of reality is concentrated ordains with respect to the elements "which comprise it" but which are, in reality, simply its exemplars, not only the structure which governs their properties but, first and foremost, these properties themselves. This is what is explicitly denied by Marx's text which lies opposite the marginal notation that we have just quoted: "The statement which frequently occurs with Saint Sancho that each man is all that he is through the state is fundamentally the same as the statement that the bourgeois is only a specimen of the bourgeois species; a statement which presupposes that the bourgeois *class* existed before the individuals constituting it."[32] *This decisive affirmation by which the concept of class is dismissed along with that of the State and for the same ontological reason, namely the refusal to define reality as general, that is to say, as transcending individual reality,* does not turn up here by chance in Marx's writing. It can also be found in the polemic against Stirner, where it is a question of showing, this time with respect to private property, that it is impossible to explain an individual determination on the basis of anything other than individual life itself, on the basis that is of an alleged generic reality, whether it be that of the State or of the class. Against Stirner, Marx writes: "The transformation of private property into state property reduces itself, in the final analysis, to the idea that the bourgeois has possessions only as a member of the bourgeois species, a species which as a whole is called the state and which invests individuals with the fief of property. Here again the matter is put upside-down."[33]

To set things back on their feet—to use an image of which Marx was fond—to reestablish reality and the true order of foundation of the determinations which are produced starting from reality is to provide a genealogy of the class as well as of the properties that define it. In the passage following the text we have just quoted, this genealogy is presented with the simplicity of a discourse that eliminates any possible equivocation: *"In the bourgeois class, as in every other, it is only personal conditions that are developed into common and universal conditions. . . ."*[34] And, still in *The German Ideology:* ". . . personal relations necessarily and inevitably develop into class relations and become fixed as such. . . ."[35] The genealogy of the class does not simply reverse the traditional Marxist formulation according to which the class determines the individuals. By affirming on the contrary that the properties of the class are nothing other than those of the individuals that constitute it, than "personal conditions," under its apparent simplicity, a metaphysics is concealed. In accordance with this metaphysics the reality of a social class is not proper to it, is not, strictly speaking, its reality, a generic reality. The reality of a social class is constituted by a set of determinations; *the reality of these determinations lies in individual phenomenological life and here alone finds its possibility and its effectiveness*. Social determinations are not simply "borrowed" from monadic subjective life, they are the determinations of this life, their substance is its substance, their particularity is its particularity, they are precisely its determinations, the modalities of its fulfillment or its nonfulfillment. Social determinations are determinations such as "getting up early or late," "performing this or that action," "doing this or that work"—a pleasant or disagreeable work—"being able to read, to learn" or "not being able to do so," "feeling one way or another," etc. Determinations such as these are not individual simply in the sense that they are comprehensible solely on the basis of the subjective life of an individual but for the further reason that they can "exist" only within this life, within an essentially monadic life, that they are in every instance the determinations of a given particular individual. Social determination is not possible unless there exists an individual, not so much to "incarnate" it, to be its "bearer," its "exemplar," or even to provide it with the place of its "possible realization"— this would be, precisely, to reestablish the ideological "preexistence" of the class—but rather in order to constitute the original ontological reality of this determination, in order to be, as this "determinate" individual, the living, singular and concrete, existing and actual determination, for which the "social" determination is just another name.

The fact that a social determination is always in reality that of a given individual, a singular determination situated within a monadic flow and belonging to it as "its own" does not, of course, signify that it therefore is or can be the determination of a single individual. Quite the opposite, a determination is social, belongs to a class, defines it and constitutes it only if it is lived by several, by "many individuals." "Personal conditions," said Marx, "have simply become common and general conditions." What does "general," "becoming general," signify here? For a personal condition, becoming general in no way signifies changing oneself, modifying one's being; the status of this condition is not transformed because of the fact that it henceforth appears as the lot of "several." *A personal condition does not cease to be personal at the moment it becomes general; this becoming is completely external to it and in no way affects it, in no way changes the monadic structure of experience with which it is fused, nor does it change the specific content of this experience.* Nor could one say, at least if one wishes to speak with any rigor, that such a content is found in several individuals because, precisely, this is not "the same"; the contents of experience which belong to a "living individual" are as unique as his very life. To say that personal conditions become general therefore means that similar contents of experience are produced in individuals placed in similar circumstances.

Is the class nothing but the sum of determinations whose reality lies in each instance in a given individual? Is its unity limited to the formal and empty unity of a mere collection, in the external assembling together of a multiplicity of elements which, in the insurmountable dispersion, concentrate in themselves all possible ontological actuality? Is what is real, therefore, simply a scattering of individuals of whom one knows only that they do and think more or less the same thing, but in such a way that this knowledge exists only for us, for an outside observer, while each "member," so to speak, of this class lives as if buried in his activity, lost in thoughts that are but his own? The very interesting theory that Marx develops concerning the French peasant class during the first half of the nineteenth century replies explicitly to these questions. Within the framework of a general analysis of the political situation in France at this time, it is a question of understanding the causes that make the December 2 *coup d'état* possible, and it appears that the peasant class constitutes, precisely, the principal force supporting Napoleon III. In what, then, does this force consist? Precisely in a scattering of individuals without any tie among themselves: peasants owning small portions of land. Without any tie, that is, other than *similar individual* living conditions, namely the fact that each family farms a portion of land by its own means, without any division of labor except that which arises spontaneously among the family members—that, consequently, "each individual peasant family is almost self-sufficient . . . and therefore obtains its means of life more through exchange with nature than through intercourse with society."[36] Between these families as a result there exists no relation which is not strictly local and limited, no relation on the national or political level. ". . . the identity of their interests fails to produce a feeling of community, national links, or a political organization."[37] *The original reality of the class is thus neither a community, nor an organization, nor a unity; it cannot be understood as a totality, as a general reality that is concrete and real by itself, autonomous, internal with respect to the members of the class; on the contrary, it is reduced to the individuals that already compose it despite their absolute dispersion.* The historical description of small peasant proprietors in France in the nineteenth century resembles an eidetic analysis;* it strikingly confirms the ontological theory of the genealogy of the class as finding its reality in the isolated and determinate individuals who, properly speaking, constitute it.[38]

One finds in Marx, it is true, a second concept of class, in which the latter is defined, on the contrary, by its unity, its true unity, which is no longer the simple adding together of dispersed and independent elements. This sort of unity is produced when the various individuals living under similar conditions become conscious of the similarity of their conditions and represent this to themselves. The representation of similar subjective conditions is at one and the same time that of common objective characteristics, of objective characteristics which together form the concept of a class.[39] The second concept of class that arises in Marx's thought expresses the moment when a real class attains its own concept. The unity of the class which then appears and which can serve to define it is actually itself defined with the utmost clarity; this is the ideal unity of a concept. Rather than being substituted for the original reality of the class, this sort of unity presupposes, on the contrary, the radical multiplicity of living individuals and their concrete determinations. The objective unity of the class rests upon its subjective reality for the reason that it can neither found nor determine the latter but instead is itself determined by it. The theory that the foundation of the objective unity of the classes is to be sought in their original subjective reality is part of a general theory of ideology, which will be presented later. Let us simply say here that the theory of ideology will show that the possibility for a class to become conscious of itself as such resides in a potentiality included within and belonging to subjective life, the potentiality for producing a self-representation. The concepts of the various classes are not *a priori* elements given to reflection; they do not fall out of the heavens, nor can one understand them as ideal variations of an ideal reality—society, structure, any organized complex, etc. It is rather the individuals themselves who form the concepts of their own existence; "class consciousness," consciousness of a given "class" is their own consciousness, the consciousness that they have of themselves. Naturally, this process of becoming-conscious takes place gradually and is subject to a wide range of circumstances. Because it remains,

---

*Eidetic analysis is to be understood in its customary phenomenological sense as an essential analysis.—TRANS.

nevertheless, a continuing possibility of subjective life, the *complete concept of class* necessarily includes, in addition to the concrete determinations of this life, a process of becoming-conscious at the end of which the class then exists as an ideal reality.

The theory of the genealogy of the classes must therefore make a very clear distinction between: (1) the original ontological reality of the class as an ensemble of subjective determinations, and (2) based upon the latter, the representation of these determinations, "class consciousness." This consciousness alone confers upon the members of the class a true unity, an ideal unity, one which, nevertheless, is intended and desired by them. Marx explicitly distinguished between the *original concept* and the *complete concept* of class when he wrote in *The Eighteenth Brumaire of Louis Bonaparte*: "In so far as millions of families live under economic conditions of existence that separate their mode of life, their interests and their cultural formation from those of the other classes, they form a class. In so far as these small peasant proprietors are merely connected on a local basis, and the identity of their interests fails to produce a feeling of community, national links, or a political organization, they do not form a class."[40] The question of knowing whether the class is a political or simply a social concept can be elucidated only in light of the distinction that has just been made. The complete concept of class, which implies the class's becoming-conscious of itself, develops into a political concept when this becoming-conscious reaches its term, when the class thinks of itself and intends itself as a unity, when it thinks and acts as such.

The distinction between the original concept and the complete concept of class explains the rhythm of history; more precisely, it explains the difference that arises between the history of real classes and that of political classes. Although its possibility lies in principle in subjective life, there is no properly political form, no form which gives rise to the thematic intention of a general interest, except under certain conditions, for example, when life becomes "unbearable," but this intervention can be quite sudden and brutal. The process of becoming-conscious offers a striking contrast with the slow formation of real classes; there then occurs an acceleration of history which is simply that of these classes which have become political. In *The Class Struggles in France*, Marx writes: ". . . the different classes in French society had to count the epochs of their development in weeks as they had previously counted them in half-centuries."[41]

The distinction between the original concept and the complete concept of class, however important it may be, must not give rise to a misunderstanding. *By becoming political a class does not change its nature;* its reality is not transformed into an ideal reality but continues to be constituted by individual subjective determinations. To say that a class acquires a political signification means: among all those determinations which by their essence are individual, one must now recognize the existence of a new determination, namely the intention of the general as such, the consciousness of a class interest, but in such a way that intending the general in this way is in each case the subjective intention of a specific individual. The coherence of the class, its concrete unity, is in no way constituted by the ideal unity that is intended but by the fact that all the individuals who constitute this class—at least a certain number among them—realize this intention and act as a result in compliance with what it prescribes, acting with the aim of this ideal unity which they represent to themselves, with the aim of the "general interest."

As the 1843 manuscript has decisively shown, not only does the notion of the general imply a reference, that is to say, not only can the general interest be defined solely on the basis of all of the individuals *of whom it is the interest, the individual interest,* but the consciousness of this interest and the action aimed at realizing it are in every instance those of these individuals themselves. The coherence of a class—whether with respect to its original coherence, that is, the similarity of its living subjective determinations, needs, work, etc., or with respect to its political coherence, that is, once again, the concordance of the actions which aim thematically at the common interest and are ordered on the basis of the representation of its ideal unity—is in all these cases the coherence of the individuals who constitute it, and this is why the class unceasingly makes and unmakes itself. Finally, the determinations which form the ontological reality of a "class," including the intentionalities that are directed toward the universal, whose transcendence is never other than that of a correlate, the correlate of an intention which is of its very essence subjective, are precisely all subjective determinations that are immanent to the flow of individual life and belong to it.

Is not the ontological interpretation of the reality of the social determinations of a class—considered originally and of their essence subjective—rendered problematic when it appears that the class, on the contrary, is what is set over against the individual, what is made autonomous before him, what stands before him only to place constraints upon him and to determine him? There are numerous texts to this effect. After having declared, decisively it is true, that *"individuals have always proceeded from themselves,"* Marx corrects this by adding: "But in the course of historical development . . . social relations inevitably take on an independent existence."[42] And again: "The illusory community in which individuals have up till now combined always took on an independent existence in relation to them. . . ."[43] That this "independence" is another name for objectivity is still evident when, in the same passage, Marx speaks of "the transformation . . . of personal powers (relations) into material powers. . . ." This objectivity of the class presupposes, in its turn, the dependence of the individual in its regard: "On the other hand, the class in its turn assumes an independent existence as against the individuals, so that the latter find their conditions of life predetermined, and have their position in life and hence their personal development assigned to them by their class, thus becoming subsumed under it."[44] In the Preface to *Capital* Marx goes so far as to treat individuals as "the personifications of economic categories": "My standpoint, from which the evolution of the economic formation of society is viewed as a process of natural history, can less than any other make the individual responsible for relations whose creature he socially remains, however much he may subjectively raise himself above them."[45]

As we find once again here the themes which were to become classic in Marxism, it is important to recall Marx's central intuition, namely that economic and social structures find their actuality and their law in individual subjectivity. This is why, in order to dispel any misunderstanding, it is advisable at this time to cite, in contrast to the passage from the Preface to *Capital* that we have just quoted and which is too often quoted out of its context, a context that is none other than *Capital* itself, along with other similar texts—for example, the following: "Every individual capital forms . . . but an individualized fraction, a fraction endowed with individual life, as it were, of the aggregate social capital, just as every individual capitalist is but an individual element of the capitalist class"[46]—this other passage, also taken from Book Two of *Capital*. This text, however, is located on a more essential level, no longer on that where economic structures are already constituted and hence presupposed so that one is able to represent to oneself the "relation" these structures maintain with the individuals which they subsume, but on the deeper level of reality for analysis, where it is a question of the genealogy and of the essence of these structures themselves: "That which is true of a commodity produced in some individual industrial establishment by any individual laborer is true of the annual product of all branches of business as a whole. *That which is true of the day's work of some individual productive laborer is true of the year's work set in motion by the entire class of productive laborers.*"[47] However, these decisive indications, in which the socioeconomic configurations of the whole are unequivocally carried back to the particular activity of an individual considered in isolation as if this were the source of their structure and their history, are premature.

With respect to the problem with which we are more directly concerned here, that of knowing how the determinations which are held to be those of the individual himself can indeed be imposed upon him by an "objective power," let us first of all note that the formulation of this problem cannot be ascribed to the inadequate set of postulates presented by a philosophy of subjectivity; *this problem is Marx's very problem, it is formulated by him*, and the problematic that recognizes this problem as its own confirms its fidelity to the thought proper to Marx and to its implicit or avowed presuppositions: "How is it that personal interests always develop, against the will of individuals into class interests, into common interests which acquire independent existence in relation to the individual persons. . . ? How is it that in this process of private interests acquiring independent existence as class interests the personal behavior of the individual is bound to be objectified [*sich versachlichen*], estranged [*sich entfremden*], and at the same time exists as a power independent of him and without him, created by intercourse, and is transformed into social relations. . . ?"[48]

Let us now make a second remark which has a decisive ontological bearing on our problem: the fact that determinations must finally appear as independent of the individual, as "opposed" to him, as powers that determine him and place constraints upon him, in no way signifies that such determinations cease to be his own, cease to be the modalities of his own life, that they cease to belong to the sphere of subjective existence. *Despite the fact that it is his own, is not this very existence, the existence of the individual, independent of him in general and in principle?* It is true that Marx is not concerned with the metaphysical thesis which recognizes the groundlessness of life, the fact, which constitutes its essence and which may serve to define it, that life never acts as its own ground but experiences itself, on the contrary, in its radical passivity with respect to itself, experiences its own coming into itself and its growth as something that does not depend upon it. Marx is concerned with social determinations such as "going to work in the factory," "performing certain specific gestures," etc. Although they are imposed upon the individual, these sorts of determinations are nonetheless modalities of the individual's own life and, like it, are subjective. The idea that the independence of social determinations with respect to the individual can signify their objectivity in the philosophical sense of the word, in its proper and strict sense, in the sense of a reality transcending the immanent flow of phenomenological life and, as a result, belonging to the outside world and finding in it its power and its constraining force—this is an absurdity. If they were situated in the objective universe, social determinations would constitute no more than a spectacle spread out before the individual; far from being able to affect him, they would leave him totally indifferent. It is precisely because social determinations are subjective that they strike the individual at the center of his life.

It remains the case that these social determinations, insofar as they are, for example, the determinations of a line of work, are imposed upon the individual.[49] Marx attempted to think of the determination of the social activity of individuals on the level of reality and not on that of ideological verbiage. That this determination is grounded in the individuals themselves, in what they do in order to produce their life and in the way in which they do it, that social activity is nothing other than this immediate living activity,—this is what is explicitly stated by the thesis according to which *the production of social relations can be carried back to the production by individuals of their own life and is identical to this.* "Monsieur Proudhon has very well grasped the fact that men produce cloth, linen, silks, and it is a great merit on his part to have grasped this small amount! What he has not grasped is that *these men, according to their abilities, also produce the social relations* amid which they prepare the cloth and linen."[50]

The hypostasis of social relations and the alleged explanation of individual activity in terms of the latter are no longer possible when the genealogy of these relations is explicitly supplied by and carried back, precisely, as to its place of birth, to individual activity itself. To the extent that individuals produce their social relations, which at every moment of their history constitute the essential part of "historical circumstances," the individuals are the cause of these relations. After having stated that the conditions under which individuals relate to one another are conditions belonging to their individuality, Marx added: ". . . conditions under which alone these definite individuals, living under definite relations, can produce their material life and what is connected with it, are thus *the conditions of their self-activity and are produced by this self-activity.*"[51]

The fact that social conditions are produced by the activity of individuals does not, however, prevent them from being presented at the same time as the conditions for this activity, as the forms in which this sort of activity is realized. Does not the latter, after having been presented as the cause of these forms and social conditions, ever appear as their effect? Can the difficulty be dispelled by declaring that individuals are at one and the same time the cause and the effect of the conditions in which they live, or yet again, as Marx does, that "circumstances make men just as much as men make circumstances"?[52] In the same way, in reference to the historical genesis of the bourgeois class, Marx said: "The citizens created these conditions insofar as they had torn themselves free from feudal ties, and were in their turn created by them insofar as they were determined by their antagonism to the feudal system which they found in existence."[53]

Does one escape from the circle of the reciprocal causality of individuals and conditions by declaring that individuals *first of all* instituted these conditions— for example, the bourgeois in their struggle against feudalism—and that they were *then* determined by them? But how is one to conceive of this subsequent determination of individuals by social conditions if the myth of their objectivity has been rejected, if they are nothing "external" to individuals, if all causal relation is abolished along with the exteriority of its terms? Does the schema of reciprocal causality indeed suffice to exorcise an exteriority of this sort? Is it not instead the final expression of this exteriority? The sense of the texts that conform, whether explicitly or not, to this schema of reciprocal causality is clear at any rate. The aim of the problematic is always the same, whether in the case of the polemic against Stirner which we have discussed, or of that levelled at the true socialists, who cannot help but establish an external relation between society and individuals, or whether, more generally and more conclusively, in the case of the critique of eighteenth-century materialism, of the naïve belief that one must first change the whole of social conditions, that is to say, change the education given to individuals so that they are themselves changed—a critique which musters its full strength in the third thesis on Feuerbach: "The materialist doctrine concerning the changing of circumstances and upbringing forgets that circumstances are changed by men and that it is essential to educate the educator himself. This doctrine must, therefore, divide society into two parts, one of which is superior to society." By rejecting the transcendence of social conditions, that is, precisely, their exteriority—and doing so in order to think their immanence, "the coincidence of the changing of circumstances and of human activity or self-changing," as the third thesis continues—does one not in the same stroke reject the concept of causality, of which reciprocal causality is only the most recent variant?

This rejection is effective when the determination of the social life of individuals is no longer presented as the effect of an external cause—even if this cause were itself an effect—of an objective power *which does not exist*, but as a synthesis which takes place within individual life, a passive synthesis, analogous to that which can be found, for example, in all perception. The individual finds the conditions for his activity, he finds his activity itself as an activity already performed by others and which offers itself to him so that he can engage in it in his turn; *he finds it precisely inasmuch as he performs it himself, inasmuch as it is his own life*, and so inasmuch as it would be nothing outside himself, nothing that would determine him from outside. Marx attempted to conceive of a situation such as this when, as we have seen, he represented history as a succession of generations within which each generation, and consequently each individual, receives the conditions of its social existence, *conditions which result from the activity of the preceding generation and yet which are nothing but the activity of the present generation, an activity to which it is submitted but which is, nevertheless, its own activity*.[54] The fact that in this transmission from one generation to the next of the social conditions of existence which constitute the "circumstances" what is in question is always the concrete activity of individuals, an activity which is repeated by those belonging to the succeeding generation, so that in this way the reality of these conditions never ceases to be that of the individuals themselves, is confirmed again in the text of the letter to Annenkov, dated December 28, 1846: "Because of this simple fact that every succeeding generation finds itself in possession of the productive forces acquired by the preceding generation, which serve it as the raw material for new production, a coherence arises in human history, a history of humanity takes shape. . . . Hence it necessarily follows that *the social history of men is never anything but the history of their individual development. . . .*"[55]

Conceived of in the light of the succession of generations and as "transmitted" from one to the next, social conditions have lost all possible objectivity, since at whatever level they are grasped in history, in every instance they disappear completely within the immanence of individual activities. One must not believe, therefore, that the first generation *creates* the social conditions to which the following generation is then subjected. In the first place, this cannot be so because no generation creates social conditions, as if it were not itself in the position of finding existing social conditions, as if "creating" these conditions were to mean positing them outside oneself in the exteriority of a thing existing in itself, as an objective structure which would determine the following generation. There is not a before of causality and an after of passivity, but instead every generation finds itself in the same situation as all the others, and so does every individual: *each is the creator of social relations to the very extent to which he suffers them, to the extent to which he performs the activity that is his own*. The social condition is a heritage; there is no break in the process, no transcendence by which to reintroduce causality but only, as has been said, a repetition in which each life re-creates the social relation to the extent to which it realizes once again the activity that was once that of another life. Here again Marx's text shines with the light of philosophical evidence: ". . . it was, therefore, precisely the personal, individual behavior of individuals, their behavior to one another as individuals, that created the existing relations and *daily reproduces them anew*."[56]

Beyond the conception of history as the succession of generations and as repetition, an essential problematic in Marx will now establish that the social determination of individuals must be conceived of on the basis of the individuals themselves, on the basis of subjectivity and of the structure proper to it, that is, the structure of the division of labor.

The division of labor

If classes are produced, if, far from being an ultimate principle of explanation, they must first themselves be explained, and if this explanation can be nothing other than the theory of their production and, consequently, of their disappearance as well, the theory of their genealogy, then the division of labor presents itself precisely as the ultimate sphere upon which this genealogy can be based, as the ground of all social classes, past, present, and, possibly, to come. This is why the critique of the division of labor has nothing to do with a simple ethical or existential "critique," because it is the unveiling of the origin of the fundamental determinations in their very being, determinations which, in their turn, constitute social determinations, the "classes."

First of all, Marx explicitly situated the origin of social classes in the division of labor, an origin which is not, of course, historical but which is to be taken in the sense of an essence and a ground. The first division of labor, properly speaking, is that which occurs between material labor and intellectual labor.[57] Now, it is precisely this division which founds the first great social distinction, that between town and country.[58] Stressing the importance of this opposition that dominates history, placing on one side the concentration of the population, of needs, of production, and of capital, and on the other side, dispersion and isolation, Marx declares: "The antagonism between town and country . . . is the most crass expression of the subjection of the individual under the division of labor, under a definite activity forced upon him." But this is not all: the division of labor spreads little by little, and along with it begin to appear a wide number of social distinctions and oppositions, the separation of production from commerce with the formation of a particular class of merchants, a separation which, in turn, brings about a specialization in production among the various towns, followed by a greater division of labor within each production branch, the organization of activities within the shop, within the factory, and, finally, within heavy industry. The great types of society—patriarchal society, caste society, feudal society, corporative society, etc.—are defined on the basis of the forms that the division of labor takes in each one.[59] It is due to the division of labor that the personal conditions of activity take on the aspect of objective conditions forced upon the individual.[60] And, finally, it is this division of labor that determines the various forms of ownership, so that the latter can be abolished only by suppressing the division of labor.[61]

If the division of labor constitutes the origin of all social formations, of their distinctions and of their determinations, if it founds ownership and along with it, as Marx again states, the contradiction between private interest and the general interest and, on an even more essential level, the possibility of exchange, that is to say, of the market economy, and, finally, of capitalism, and if socialism has as its principal goal the suppression of the division of labor, then the question arises: what then is the division of labor; in what does this decisive and ultimate phenomenon consist?

It should be noted that when he approaches thematically the problem of the *nature* of the division of labor—and this is the case in his polemic against Proudhon—Marx rejects straightaway the idea that this division of labor might be likened to a law, a category, that is to say in the final analysis, to a structure capable of determining reality, of accounting, precisely, for its determinations. *The* division of labor does not exist. The reduction of what is called the "division of labor" to the unity of a category or a law is identified by Marx with its reduction to a concept, to an idea, and, finally, to a word. To the ideal and ultimately verbal unity of *the* division of labor is opposed its reality. The reality of the division of labor, which Marx conceives of in opposition to its concept, is presented in the form of an actual plurality—the forms of the division of labor are multiple and diverse—and, in the same stroke, in an historical form. It is this plurality of the concrete forms taken by the division of labor throughout the course of history which Marx opposes to Proudhon's conceptual interpretation.[62]

In *The Poverty of Philosophy*, as in all of Marx's subsequent works, the reference to history signifies, generally speaking, the reference to reality. For, in accordance with the way in which its concept is divided, history is no longer the self-development of an autonomous totality but that of individuals. *The reality of the concrete historical forms of the division of labor is that of the individuals themselves.* It is starting from the reality of the individual that the specificity of the division of labor is defined. Doubtless, Marx's analysis may seem here to follow that of Proudhon, who envisaged the "advantages" and the "drawbacks" of the division of labor. Advantages and drawbacks for whom? For the individual, no doubt. But this is precisely a consequence of the division of labor, the effect of a law, of a system, and the individuals—*what they are*—represent, precisely, this effect. The reversal of the Proudhonian concept is radical in Marx because it is no longer the division of labor which, as a preexisting law or even as a structure, would determine the reality of the individuals subjected to it; it is, on the contrary, the reality of these individuals which defines, which *is* the division of labor, so that the analysis of the latter amounts to the phenomenological elucidation of individual subjective activity and is henceforth indistinguishable from it. It is no longer a question of the ethical or practical consequences for the individuals of a given society of a phenomenon which, of its essence, is different from them. It is the essence of a phenomenon which, in reality, is exhausted in monadic subjectivity and in the determinations proper to it. The analysis of the different forms taken by the division of labor is in every instance that of a given subjectivity.

Let us consider the division of labor in manufacture. It replaces that observed in the workshop, which consisted essentially in assembling together in the same spot a wide number of workers with different skills. This is why the division of labor in the workshop only reproduced that which preceded it in the organization of the guilds; this means that the activity of each individual remained what it had been in the exercise of his specific craft. Thus it is the nature of this individual subjective activity that defines the nature of the division of labor in the workshop. And it is precisely because this individual activity is changed when the workshop becomes a factory, manufacture properly speaking, that the industrial division differs from the division of labor in the workshop as such. In what does this difference consist? It consists in the fact that the individual worker, who up until then performed in the exercise of his craft a whole series of diverse and coherent activities leading to an intended result, now sees his personal task limited to just one of these activities. The task of performing the other activities is now the job of other individuals, each of whom is, however, placed in the same situation, each specialized in performing one small operation and, finally, in making one single and self-same monotonous and indefinitely repeated action. When one speaks of the "division of labor," one is, in fact, thinking today of the division of the manufacture, to the situation in which labor that was originally synthesized as a result of the aim pursued and which is nothing other than the unity of the object produced is, on the contrary, divided, broken up, parceled out so that in place of this synthetic labor one henceforth finds "piecemeal labor." In what, exactly, does this division consist?

It has no objective meaning. Objectively, the labor required to manufacture a product still consists in a plurality of different activities which contribute to the intended result; it naturally divides itself among these various activities. Objectively, labor has always been divided. Thus it is not this objective division of labor, its decomposition into different processes, which is intended by the concept of the division of labor, of its industrial division, for example. The division of labor concerns the fact that the diverse activities that constitute synthetic labor are no longer performed by the same individual but by different individuals, in such a way that, as has been said earlier, one individual no longer performs any more than one of these partial activities. It is only at this moment that labor is divided. The division of labor is its division among different individuals. In what does this new division consist?

It has in itself no objective meaning. Of course, if one places oneself in the superficial perspective which consists in looking at things from outside, one can easily imagine that the division of labor in the sense in which it is now understood as the fact of entrusting to different individuals the different activities of a global work is itself something objective, a fact to be precise, and one which is, moreover, observable by all. But this illusion is dissipated if one actually considers the reality of the labor "objectively" divided in this way. This reality is exhausted in the reality of the partial activities that constitute it, in the reality of the individual subjectivities of which these activities are the concrete determinations. It is within each of these subjectivities that one must place oneself if one is to grasp the reality of divided labor, the reality of its division. It then appears that the reality of the division of labor is nothing other than the division of this subjectivity, than the division of the individual himself.

Marx explicitly posited: (1) that the division of labor has nothing to do with the simple decomposition of an objective process into partial processes of the same nature and with respect to which it would be the recomposition, the synthesis; (2) that this decomposition of global labor into the sum of the partial activities of which it is composed is a division of labor only inasmuch as these partial activities are performed by different individuals; and (3) that, as a result, the intended phenomenon designates nothing other than the state of a given subjectivity, which henceforth is forced repeatedly to perform a "fractional operation," and that in this fundamental reference to a determinate subjectivity, the division of labor, stripped of any objective meaning, unrelated to the milieu of exteriority, definitely irreducible to any "objective law," in fact signifies and presupposes the division of this subjectivity itself, the division of the individual. This is what is stated in this exceedingly dense text: "Not only is the detail work *distributed to the different individuals, but the individual himself is made the automatic motor of a fractional operation.*"[63]

How exactly could the individual, who is undivided and indivisible, be broken up, divided? And certainly Marx understands the division of labor as harming the very being of the individual: "it converts the laborer into a crippled monstrosity";[64] it "cuts down the laborer";[65] "it attacks the individual at the very roots of his life."[66] The division of labor is an illness befalling life, and this illness is so serious that it necessarily, or so it seems, leads to death. And Marx takes as his own these words of Urquhart: "To subdivide a man is to execute him, if he deserves the sentence, to assassinate if he does not. . . . The subdivision of labor is the assassination of a people."[67]

Generally speaking, to divide is to break the unity of a prior totality; division can be comprehended only on the basis of this totality, which it presupposes before the "elements," thereafter "separated out," are given. But, as we have seen, in Marx the division of labor has no objective meaning, and neither does the totality to which it is applied. The totality that constitutes the ontological presupposition of the "division" of the division of labor is monadic subjectivity itself. Let us therefore consider subjectivity, not the subjectivity of idealism, which includes no more than thought or "consciousness," but the concrete subjectivity of the individual. *It presents itself to us phenomenologically as a totality to the extent that it carries within itself, in the form of potentialities, a multiplicity of possible activities and intentionalities.* Marx calls these subjective potentialities "personal powers."[68] Subjectivity as individual subjectivity is the subjective unity of these powers, which are themselves subjective, which define its original being and which are willed by it, which are its needs. To live is necessarily to develop these possibilities. In *Capital* Marx speaks of the "free-play of . . . bodily and mental activity."[69]

Restored to the milieu in which it develops and from which it draws its ontological possibility and its actuality, elaborated within the framework of a phenomenology of subjective life and inscribed within it, the central phenomenon sighted by Marx's analysis becomes crystal clear: in the division of labor the actualization of the subjective potentialities of individual life comes about in such a way that only one of these potentialities is found to be realized. The realization of one potentiality signifies at one and the same time the nonrealization of the others. This, it is true, is the situation of the life of subjectivity in general, but in life potentialities imply one another; the actualization of one brings about, leads to, the actualization of all the others, so that, as it follows its spontaneous course, life takes the form of the gradual unfolding of all its powers, even if this unfolding is necessarily in the form of a succession. In the division of labor, on the contrary, the actualization of one potentiality does exclude, not just in the instant but decisively and definitively, the realization of other powers of life instead of awakening them or giving rise to them. In life the positive character of an actualization resides not solely in the positive nature of the phenomenologically lived experience that it brings into being but also in that of the actualizations to come, whose realization is nevertheless directly tied to the living present, so that if we consider corporeal life, performing an action, for example, has its continuation in the unfolding of the powers that are connected to it by a series of correlations, which together constitute the very nature of the subjective body in such a way that it is the entire corporeal nature that comes into play, the entire body that is alive. In the division of labor these natural correlations play no role; the actualization of a potentiality is limited to reiteration, and this repetition prevents rather than brings about the realization of these potentialities, in the rigidity of an activity that is henceforth isolated from its living context, which is nothing but absolute subjectivity along with the totality of its potentialities. It is through this reduction of subjective life to the actualization of a single one of its potentialities that the division of labor in manufacture mutilates the worker to the point of reducing him to a portion of himself.[70]

What this division of labor signifies now becomes clear in the phenomenology of monadic life, and in it alone. However, does not the category of objectivity inevitably arise in connection with the essence of the division of labor when the question of the actualization of potentialities arises, the question of those potentialities that are not realized in a given individual but only outside him and, consequently, in exteriority? Marx strikingly described how in the manufacturing workshop all the forces of life and, in particular, its superior powers are lost by the worker and are now massed together as if to confront him, assuming a monstrous solidity in the form of a vast machine which contains within itself and seems to constitute the realization of the synthesis of which the workers are but mere elements determined by it. "The knowledge, the judgment, and the will, which, though in ever so small a degree, are practiced by the independent peasant or handicraftsman . . . these faculties are now required only for the workshop as a whole."[71] This paradoxical hypothesis concerning intelligence outside of the subjective life to which it originally belongs appears in a text by Thompson, quoted by Marx, in which knowledge becomes an instrument capable of being separated from labor and set in opposition to it.[72] The fact that this hypostasis of the synthetic power of the intelligence outside of the individual locates the synthesis, precisely, in objectivity and in the mechanical form of the workshop is affirmed in this text of Fergusson, which is assumed by Marx for his own purposes: "Ignorance is the mother of industry. . . . Manufactures, accordingly, prosper most where the mind is least consulted, and where the workshop may . . . be considered as an engine, the parts of which are men."[73] And this is why, as Marx himself notes, one seeks to employ "half-idiotic persons." How this transfer of the power of synthesis into the mechanical process of the workshop, becoming one and the same with it, signifies an objectification would seem to be stated in the following text: "What is lost by the detail laborers, is concentrated in the capital that employs them. It is a result of the division of labor in manufactures, that the laborer is brought face to face with the intellectual potencies of the material process of production, as the property of another, and as a ruling power."[74] Objectivity, now understood in its ontological sense as exteriority, does in fact signify domination. Hegelian mastery finds its concrete expression when it designates, precisely, the exteriority of a power which is situated outside of individual subjectivity and which the individual has lost when this external power takes on the form of a gigantic machine: "The separation of the intellectual powers of production from the manual labor, and the conversion of those powers into the might of capital over labor, is, as we have already shown, finally completed by modern industry erected on the foundation of machinery. The special skill of each individual insignificant factory operative vanishes as an infinitesimal quantity before the science, the gigantic physical forces, and the mass of labor that are embodied in the factory mechanism and, together with that mechanism, constitute the power of the 'master'."[75]

It is not surprising that the problematic here encounters the question of the status of social determinations, of their "objectivity," if it is true that the division of labor constitutes the ground of these determinations. The hypostasis outside of the individual of the subjective powers which, consequent upon the division of labor, are no longer realized in him, is precisely the formation of the social forces that are apparent in the workshop. "In manufacture, in order to make the collective laborer, and through him capital, rich in social productive power, each laborer must be made poor in individual productive powers."[76] A little farther on Marx says, still speaking of the division of labor, that "it increases the social productive power of labor . . . for the benefit of the capitalist instead of for that of the laborer."[77] Does not the objectivity of the social forces which are unequivocally situated outside of the individual subjectivity of the laborer, and this as a result of the division of labor, call into question in the most thoroughgoing way the radically subjective interpretation of the "division" that has been proposed?

But as the problematic of the classes has sufficiently shown, social determinations, the social forces of labor for example, do not for one instant cease to be individual. This decisive fact is seen to be evident in the *ontological condition of the social as such*, in the analysis of the division of labor. The subjective potentialities that are not actualized in the individual are realized outside of him. Of course. But just where is this realization to be located? Is objectivity as such the sphere in question; does it constitute the region of being in which this actualization is produced and in which it attains, precisely, being? This is just not so. The potentialities that are not actualized in a given individual are realized in another individual; *a subjectivity is in every case the place of this realization*. The division of labor does not signify the projection of certain activities into the inert milieu of objectivity *in which no activity can take place*, but instead their insertion into different monadic spheres. This essential passage from *The German Ideology* deserves our reflection: "The division of labor implies the possibility, nay the fact, that intellectual and material activity, that enjoyment and labor, production and consumption, devolve on different individuals."[78] The division between labor and rest, between labor and nonlabor, is only one consequence and, finally, only a particular case of the division of labor itself: in all cases, that which is external with respect to one subjectivity is internal with respect to another from which it draws its reality. The exteriority of the potentialities that are realized outside of an individual has no ontological signification. *It is only for the individual, in his representation, that what is not realized within him is realized "outside of him." The exteriority of the realization is simply that of its representation*.

Can the objectivity of social forces be reduced to the appearance of a representation which is not of the same nature as the reality of these forces? Is the industrial mechanism of the workshop, with its multiple cogwheels and its complex assemblies, really simply a subjective representation? Does it not stand there facing the laborer inside the shed which is filled by its irrefutable mass? From this it would then follow that the various activities which are separated, but also unified, by the division of labor are, precisely, unified and coordinated in the objective process which is the result of the interplay of the machines, a process in which each participates in his modest way, performing that share of the work allotted to him by the mechanism as a whole. *This is Proudhon's thesis which is explicitly refuted by Marx*. Indeed, according to Proudhon, the machine would be the recomposition of divided labor, its synthesis as opposed to its analysis. To which Marx replies: "Nothing is more absurd than to see in machinery the antithesis of the division of labor, the synthesis restoring unity to divided labor."[79] What makes this absurd? The fact that the machine is objective, as are its parts. The machine is the combination of a certain number of instruments of labor which, when joined together, permit the execution of complex processes—these processes, these instruments and the machine, which is indeed their synthesis, all belong in and of themselves to the dimension of spatial objectivity and find their being there. *If we hold that global synthetic labor cannot be identified with the machine, any more than the fragmented elements of labor can be identified with the instruments that constitute the various parts of the machine, this is because labor in general, regardless of the way in which it is performed—whether it be the realization of one subjective potentiality or whether it imply a synthesis of these potentialities—is in itself and of its essence subjective.* It is for this reason that the nature of divided labor, of the detail operations which set in motion the various elements or instruments that compose the machine, has nothing at all to do with these instruments or with the machine itself; nor does the relation which is established between these partial operations performed by different individuals or by the same individual have anything to do with the objective relations between the instruments themselves and their connection within the machine, which itself is this very connection. "The machine," Marx says, "is a unification of the instruments of labor, and by no means a combination of different operations for the worker himself."[80] *The machine does not work.*[81] The problematic of labor and of its different modalities, the problematic of the division of labor takes its place within subjectivity. Confusing the subjective determinations of fragmentary labor with the instrumental division of the industrial apparatus understood as an organization of the ensemble and as an objective totality results from the total disregard of the decisive ontological categories that compose Marx's thought and make a philosophy out of it.

It is indeed the idea of an objective totality that is challenged—radically challenged—by the problematic of the division of labor. If, in fact, one affirms the primacy of the Whole or of the universal, *totality and universality transcending the individual and in this sense radically "objective,"* then the critique of the division of labor no longer has any sense. From the viewpoint of the Whole and regardless of the way in which it is conceived—whether it be thought of as the totality of the organism, of the structure, or even of an historical world—each part or element is in its proper place, performs its function, plays its role within the economy of the whole. The division of the potentialities and of their effectuation among the various members of the organic totality signifies harmony, constitutes, precisely, the organic character of this totality, and defines both its essence and its internal finality. It is with good reason that Agrippa obligingly explains to the plebeians that a body is made up of the head and the members, which must live and work together, while their separation, the secession of the plebeians, means death. We know Marx's furor concerning this fable,[82] which, in a word, advised everyone who had a hand and a foot to reduce himself to that alone and to do without a head, realizing in this way the situation of the detail laborer in the mechanical workshop. But in Marx this indignation is not first and foremost of an ethical nature; it reveals a metaphysics. In fact, it is only if the part, the element, is posited as absolute and *the individual himself as the whole*, that all that is realized outside of him directly signifies an infringement of his own being and so represents something of which he has been deprived. In this way, the fulfillment of all the potentialities of life, the realization of the universal, can no longer take place through the mediation of diverse individuals, the one actualizing one of these potentialities, the other another, each being integrated in this way in a totality as one of its members, as an organ in an organism. Different existences no longer complete one another and no longer find beyond themselves, in a whole greater than themselves in which they would be integrated, in a world in which and of which they are held to live, their realization as a moment of the realization of this great Whole, as a moment of a reality that supersedes them. The beautiful ideal of the ancient city has seen its day.

This is why the situation that is created by the division of labor must at last be understood. In this situation, let us say, the actualization of the potentialities of life takes place in such a way that only one of these potentialities is realized in a given individual, the effectuation of other potentialities occurring in different monadic spheres. But the life which bears all these potentialities within it and which constitutes their synthesis is not, as in Hegel, a universal essence transcending the individual, the current of life which would be indifferent to the nature of the wheels it causes to turn; this life is the individual as such, and the totality, as has been said, is identified with the monad itself. What keeps all the realizations from being dispersed indifferently among the individuals in which they are realized in accordance with the division of labor, composing in this way a satisfying objective totality, is the fact that these realizations all belong to one and the same subjectivity, at least inasmuch as they are virtualities willed and ordained by it. This is why whatever is not realized within the individual is not simply realized outside of him (that is, in fact, to say, as we have seen, in another). It is in him that what is realized "outside of him" is not realized; the "not realized in himself" of that which is realized outside of him *is a mode of realization of his life, his lived experience, his need, his lack, and his suffering.* The objectivist interpretation of the division of labor according to which what is not realized here is realized elsewhere, in another, is totally incapable of accounting for the single thing that has any importance for Marx—"lack," need. There is no objective lack but only lack for a subjectivity and within it. This is why Marx demands, assuming an attitude that would appear to be sheer lunacy, that everyone be hunter, fisherman, shepherd, painter, sculptor, critic, because his analysis is a phenomenological analysis of absolute subjectivity.[83] The reduction of totalities, which has just been presented, is only the effect of this problematic of subjectivity, which appears in Marx's work beginning with the 1843 manuscript and leads to the decisive turning point in the "Theses on Feuerbach" and *The German Ideology*. This problematic is at one and the same time that of reality. It is to the movement of taking hold of reality that we must now return in order once again to live its unfolding in the essential philosophical act of repetition.

Chapter 4

THE DETERMINATION OF REALITY

Practice and theory

The determination of reality is the central theme of Marx's thought, his primary and exclusive preoccupation. It is in light of this impassioned search for what truly exists that Hegelianism is rejected in favor of Feuerbach's anthropology. With Feuerbach, reality is at first designated as "practice," to which is opposed "theory." Practice understood in this way, Feuerbachian practice, has as yet no evident relation to action properly speaking; it designates nothing more than what is real in general, whereas theory signifies, no less generally, irreality, inasmuch as the latter is constituted by "representations." It is this opposition between reality and representation understood as the opposition between a thing and its image, the original and its copy, being and appearance that is expressed in Feuerbach by the opposition between practice and theory.[1] On the side of representation we find religion, politics, the realm of the imaginary, illusion, the dream in all its forms, the dream which, according to Feuerbach, has no content other than the real universe, which is the real itself but transposed in the light of representation and of irreality.[2]

What then is the reality which is opposed to representation? What is "practice"? It is sensuous reality. "The real in its reality, that is to say, as real, is the real as the object of the senses. The real is what is sensuous. Truth, reality, sensuousness are identical. The senuous being alone is a true being. Sensuousness alone is truth and reality."[3] It is this definition of the real in terms of sensuousness which motivates both the *critique of religion*, that is, of the reduction of being to a being-in-thought, and the conception of "true philosophy": "This philosophy . . . (includes) the eye and the ear, the hand and foot; it does not identify the idea of the fact with the fact itself . . . but it separates the two. . . ; it recognizes as the true thing, not the thing as it is an object of abstract reason, but as it is an object of the real complete man,"[4] that is, as an object of the senses.

The paralogism upon which Feuerbach's sensualist ontology rests must now be recognized and denounced. Sensuous being, in terms of which Feuerbach defines what is real, has two clearly distinguished meanings. In fact, it designates two different things: on the one hand, sensuous being as that which is sensed—rocks, the moon, machines—consequently, every being that is part of nature, this nature itself, what Feuerbach calls material being, "matter"; on the other hand, sensuous being means capable of sensing, bearing within oneself the capacity of opening up to external being and, furthermore, actually being this very capacity of opening up, identifying with it, being defined by it. To open oneself up to external being is to receive it, to live in the relation to being, a relation which exists as such, as this possibility of relating to something and as its actualizing, as the pure possibility of experiencing and as *experiencing itself*, precisely as sensuousness in the sense, that is, of transcendental aesthetics, in the sense of an ontological power which is originally directed to being and to which being gives itself, to which it gives itself "to be sensed." To the extent that sensuous being designates the rock, the moon, etc., that is, designates beings, it has an ontic meaning; to the extent that it designates the power of opening up to beings, the power of sensing, its meaning is ontological. The ontic meaning and the ontological meaning of sensuousness are not merely different; they are incompatible. Sensuous being in the sense of natural beings does not sense, it is insensible. Sensing can belong only to that being which bears sensuousness within itself in the sense of a transcendental power of opening up and of unveiling, sensuous being in an ontological sense.

Feuerbach continually shifts from the ontic meaning to the ontological meaning of the concept of sensuousness and mixes them up to the point of no longer being able to keep them separate. When he opposes to the object reflected upon by philosophy the real object, sensuous, "material" being, what he has in mind is beings, and it is the ontic concept of sensuousness that underlies his discourse. When he writes: "I feel and I feel feeling . . . as belonging to my essential being . . . as a . . . power," it is the ontological power of sensuousness that he has in mind and that he considers as one of the "perfections" of man, as that which makes him what he is, a being that maintains a relation to Being. "What would man be without feeling?"[5]

It is the transcendental concept of sensuousness which supplies the elements for the "materialist" critique of religion. Religion, as we know, "immediately represents the inner nature of man as an objective, external being."[6] What is this innermost essence of man that religion improperly projects onto God? It is the ontological power of opening up to being, the power of sensing, of feeling. It is because this power is lived by him at one and the same time as his own proper being and as what constitutes the essential character of life in him, as sacred and holy—"that alone is holy to man which lies deepest within him, which is most peculiarly his own, the basis, the essence of his individuality"[7]—that man, who, precisely, experiences this power as a divine possession, projects it onto God, provides himself with a God who is a feeling God. That the essence of sensuousness, the essence of man that man professes in God, has, as transcendental sensuousness, nothing to do with "sensuous" being, which Feuerbach opposes to being as it is thought by philosophers, is unwittingly betrayed in what he says: "Have I any sympathy for a being without feeling? No! I feel only for that which has feeling."[8]

To what extent a sensuous being, a being which has feeling in the sense of being able to feel, has nothing to do with sensuous being which, as material being, is nothing but an opaque and mute entity, locked up within itself and as such incapable of feeling, "insensible," this is clearly shown by the context, in which, rather than merely presupposing sensuousness in its transcendental meaning, sensuousness is posited within this determination only as a mediation permitting the development of that which is more than it, permitting the development of feeling itself in its most elevated forms, in its religious forms. For sensuousness enters in, finally, only as a condition for suffering, and the latter, in its turn, only as the condition for loving others. After understanding God's sensuousness as the possibility of his suffering—"God suffers," "A suffering God is a feeling, sensitive God"—Feuerbach entrusts to Saint Bernhard the task of unveiling the ultimate teleology of this sensible structuring of being: *"Pati voluit, ut compati disceret; miser fieri, ut misieri disceret."*[9]

It is sensuousness understood in this way as the power of feeling and, consequently, of submission, suffering, and compassion which continues to be the source of the critique of morality that is found in Feuerbach, the source of the philosophy of forgiveness. For, as we have seen, morality is incapable of forgiving.[10] Only compassion, which finds its foundation in sensuousness, can perform an act of clemency and, in the same stroke, reject abstract justice. In presenting a series of religious themes, in which everything in this strange critique of religion is in fact borrowed from Christianity, "material" being is thus finally to be understood as the capacity to feel, the capacity to suffer, the capacity to love. Feuerbach's materialism does not designate as real being only opaque beings which are opposed to the subjective representation of thought; *his avowed theme is subjectivity itself in its original form, as sensuous and affective subjectivity*. The concept of materialism thus repeats the basic ambiguity of the concept of sensuousness which identifies "material" beings with the power that allows them to be given as such.[11] In this confusion resides the absurdity of Feuerbach's materialism and of Marxist materialism in general to the extent that the latter is determined by that of Feuerbach. This determination can be observed in the 1844 *Economic and Philosophical Manuscripts*, where, in his effort to grasp reality, Marx purely and simply repeats, to the point of appearing to recopy them, the Feuerbachian themes that have just been recalled.

"Man is directly a natural being,"[12] says the third manuscript. But, as the entire context shows, "natural being" is thoroughly equivocal. On the one hand, since reality is defined as sensuous reality, precisely as nature, man is real to the extent that he belongs to nature, to the extent that he himself is reality or, better, to the extent that he is a sensuous object. It is being a part of nature in this way that makes him a "natural being," no different in this, however, from a stone, a plant, or the sun. But "natural being" does not only mean being a part of nature, bearing within oneself the opaque materialness of what is, possessing the same essence as other beings. Natural being also means opening up to nature, to the totality of beings, maintaining with them a relationship such that in this relationship beings are given to feeling, *become sensuous, become phenomena, objects;* as Marx himself says in this regard, "Externality here should not be understood as *self-externalizing sensuousness accessible to light and to sensuous man.*"[13] Natural being now designates the transcendental sensuousness within which the world becomes a world. It is this sensuousness as the phenomenological opening up to the world which is at work and which makes its essence prevail when man relates to the objects that surround him *in such a way as to feel them,* as to have them as *his* objects. "When real, corporeal man, his feet firmly planted on the solid earth and breathing all the powers of nature. . . ,"[14] the sensuousness of these sensuous forces secretly determines the reality of this real, corporeal man as a subjectivity, as the transcendental subjectivity that opens up the field of experience and makes it possible, phenomenologically actual, that which makes it "sensuous" experience.

The ambiguity of the "natural being" discussed in the third manuscript is apparent in the fact that it is not just any natural being that is sighted by the problematic and taken as its proper theme. The naturalism in question is inseparable from a humanism. "Consistent naturalism or humanism."[15] Naturalism thus becomes consistent when, among all natural beings, it surreptitiously comes to consider that particular being for which to be a natural being means to have a nature, to have a world, to live in the intuition of being. It is true that this privilege, which belongs to man, *against the background of a transcendental sensuousness in him,* is carefully masked by a comparison with plants and the sun, on the one hand, and, on the other—and in a more decisive manner—by a definition of natural being that claims to have a universal bearing and, consequently, to concern every natural being. According to this definition, natural being means having its nature outside of itself, having an object outside itself and, in the same stroke, being itself an object for this external object, for this nature in which the natural being then participates. "A being which does not have its nature outside itself is not a natural being and plays no part in the system of nature. A being which has no object outside itself is not an objective being. A being which is not itself an object for a third being has no being for its object, i.e. it has no objective relationships and its existence is not objective."[16] Inasmuch as the natural being is objective, has an object outside itself for which it is itself an object, it is "suffering, conditioned and limited,"[17] even if the forces of nature are also present in it making it—inasmuch as they penetrate it through and through and to the very extent to which they do so—"active" as well. It is here that the plant and the sun enter in; each has outside itself an object for which it itself is an object in turn—the sun is the object of the plant inasmuch as it gives it life; the plant is the object of the sun inasmuch as it displays the force of the latter.

What is meant by the expression "to have an object outside itself" must now be clarified. In the strict sense, to have an object means to have a being before the self, to represent this being to oneself and to do this in the mode of sensuous representation, precisely, *to feel* it. It is in this sense that man is a natural being and that he has an object outside of himself. This transcendental meaning of exteriority which sights the phenomenological givenness in the form of the object is absent, however, when it is said that "the sun is an object for the plant . . . just as the plant is an object for the sun. . . ."[18] What permits this shift from the transcendental sense, in which the object is an ob-ject, a being given as something sensuous, to the meaning, which is but sheer nonsense, according to which the sun and the plant are objects for one another, sensuous objects—and this in the absence of any sensuousness—is a third thesis, also recopied from Feuerbach and according to which the "object" of a thing manifests the essence of this thing, represents what this thing is in reality. It is in this way that the sun, for example, which seems to be an object common to all the planets is not the same object for each of them; it does not light and warm Uranus in the same way as it does the earth. This is why the *earth's sun* is in fact the object proper to the earth, expressing its distance, its position, etc., in short, its own essence. "The relation of the Sun to the Earth is therefore at the same time a relation of the Earth to itself, or to its own nature, for the measure of the size and of the intensity of light which the Sun possesses as the object of the Earth is the measure of the distance which determines the peculiar nature of the Earth. Hence each planet has in its sun the mirror of its own nature."[19]

How does one move from this physical and, as it were, material theory, which, in the vestiges of a medieval vocabulary, expresses nothing but the reciprocal causality of natural bodies, to a philosophy which, while claiming to limit itself to "material" presuppositions, surreptitiously includes transcendental sensuousness among these? This is what is shown by its generalization in Feuerbach. "The essence of a being is recognized . . . only through its object; the object to which a being is necessarily related is nothing but its own revealed being."[20] In a more explicit fashion, *The Essence of Christianity* had already stated: "But the object to which a subject essentially, necessarily relates, is nothing else than this subject's own, but objective, nature." The "object" does not only reveal the inner and secret nature of a being—as the plant does with respect to the sun's life-giving power and to the field of its action—but, precisely, it reveals this nature and makes it actual in phenomenological appearance. This is why that which finds in the "object" the "mirror" of its own essence is no longer just any sort of being, is no longer the sun, but a "subject," as Feuerbach's text states; it is man. In truth, the theory of the object as revealing the essence of the subject shows its real sense when it is placed in its context in *The Essence of Christianity*, at the beginning of the book as a direct introduction to the thesis that is to be demonstrated, namely that God is the object of man. By this what is asserted in the first place is that God's being exposes the true being of man and itself contains nothing more than this. It is as a comparison, and nothing more, that the earth and the plant were said to be the object of the sun. This is, moreover, an unsuitable comparison. For God does not simply repeat the essence of man, but, precisely, he manifests it and makes it visible, and this is the only reason for the reduplication of man in God, since it adds nothing to man on the level of real predicates. Instead, it adds phenomenality to him. The reduplication occurs as man's self-consciousness, and the object now signifies this consciousness, signifies the dawning of actual experience. The ambiguity of Feuerbach's materialism becomes evident: the sensuous object designates manifestation as such. Right after speaking of the sun, the earth, Uranus, Feuerbach writes: "In the object which he contemplates, therefore, man becomes acquainted with himself; consciousness of the objective is the self-consciousness of man."[21]

The phenomenological meaning of this thesis, according to which it is the object of a being that reveals its nature, remains hidden to the extent that this thesis also means: the object of a being is what is indispensable to it, what it needs; and a being that is part of nature has its object outside of itself inasmuch as it has outside of it what is necessary for its existence. "A being that breathes," said Feuerbach, "is unthinkable without air, a being that sees, unthinkable without light." It should be noted, nevertheless, that the natural being in question, one which must seek outside itself the object that it requires, is, precisely, man and that, consequently, *need is, as it will be throughout all of Marx's work—and to begin with the following year in* The German Ideology—*a subjective need*, that the exteriority of the "object" with respect to the being that has need of it becomes once again, in the same stroke, phenomenological exteriority, the exteriority of an object in the strict sense. That is why the theory of "natural, objective, sensuous being" leads in Marx, just as in Feuerbach, to subjectivity, which as sensuous subjectivity constitutes the secret essence upon which consistent naturalism or humanism reposes. As sensuous *and affective* subjectivity. For to have outside the self the object necessary for existence, *but as a sensuous object, that is to say, by experiencing one's own life as the lack of the object and as the need for it*, is to be determined subjectively as suffering; it is to find the essence of one's being in a subjectivity that is determined affectively and that is constituted by affectivity itself. In the conclusion to his analysis of man as a "natural" and "objective" being, Marx writes: "To be sensuous is to suffer. *Man as an objective sensuous being is therefore a suffering being*, and because he feels his suffering, he is a passionate being. Passion is man's essential power vigorously striving to attain its object."[22]

The fact that subjectivity, as transcendental sensuousness, is the ground of the "naturalism" of both Feuerbach and Marx is also shown in the theory of the senses, to which what follows in the text refers when it is affirmed that the sensuous object is not the immediate natural object—and by this must be understood an object properly speaking, "natural objects *as they immediately present themselves*"[23]—but an object coming out of the history of man's sense, that is, out of the actuality of his subjective development. The thesis of the subjective development of the senses and, consequently, that which serves as its premise, the thesis of the subjective essence of sense in general, are presented at length in two other passages in the third manuscript. Another essential text asserts first of all that under the title of anthropology and of naturalism what is actually thought is nothing other than the structure of being, a structure by virtue of which being is given as a sensuous object to a power which is, as this givenness and this receiving of being, an ontological power, not a mere anthropological determination, the property of a being called "man." "If man's feelings, passions, etc., are not merely anthropological characteristics in the narrower sense, but are truly ontological affirmations of his essence (nature), and if they only really affirm themselves in so far as their *object* exists *sensuously* for them. . . ."[24] Because it is sensitive to feeling and to passion, the sensuous object, the *natural being*, is not a stable being; the modalities of its existence are those of sensuousness and of passion themselves, the modalities according to which they take place in every instance in their concrete subjective effectuation. This is why the being of the sensuous object is in every instance nothing other than an affective determination, a specific mode of gratification. "The mode in which the object exists for them is the characteristic mode of their gratification."[25] As essential ontological affirmations, sensations and passions allow the object to bathe in the freedom of its variable sensuous determinations only inasmuch as they themselves constitute this determination, only inasmuch as this freedom is precisely their own, the freedom of sensuousness and of affectivity as living powers that continually modify themselves and assume one modality or another. Of these powers Marx says, furthermore, that "their mode of affirmation is by no means one and the same, but rather that the different modes of affirmation constitute the particular character of their existence, of their life."[26]

Because sensuousness and passion are living powers that continually modify themselves and assume different modalities, they are capable of evolving; they have a history that is none other than the history of the senses, their gradual subjective development. "The cultivation of the five senses is the work of all previous history."[27] The history of the senses, however, is no different from that of the object itself, from the history of nature, to the extent that the object *is sensuous*, to the extent that nature exists in and through sensuousness. Marx describes this correlation between the senses and nature which is the result of the ontological power of sensuousness and which directly expresses it. To a sense that is not well developed corresponds an impoverished object, that of "crude practical need."[28] It is in this way that someone who "is starving" is incapable of perceiving the sensuous richness of food, its form, its taste, the nuances of its savor, etc., is incapable of sensing but simply grasps something that can stave off hunger, food in "its abstract form." Likewise, a man burdened with cares cannot see the beauty of a performance, "the dealer in minerals sees only the commercial value, and not the beauty and peculiar nature of the minerals."[29] The critique of private property rests on this phenomenology of sensuousness to the extent that the fact of considering something as mine amounts to considering it not as it is in itself, in the unfolding of its own richness, to substituting for the development of all the senses the single "sense of having."[30]

Marx attempted to pursue this correlation between sense and nature, which prefigures the noetico-noematic correlations that Husserl was to recognize at the heart of the relation to being as the specifications and the fundamental determinations of this relation. Speaking of sensuous objects as they relate to individuality, Marx writes: "The manner in which they become his depends on the nature of the object and the nature of the essential power that corresponds to it; for it is just the determinateness of this relation that constitutes the particular, real mode of affirmation. An object is different for the eye from what it is for the ear, and the eye's object is different from the ear's. The peculiarity of each essential power is precisely its peculiar essence. . . ."[31] The peculiarity of each essential power is none other than the structure of a sense which, in every instance, determines that of its object. Feuerbach's thesis, according to which the nature of a being is revealed by its object, finds its evident and precise phenomenological significance when it points to this structural determination of the object by the corresponding sense. Against the background of this determination, however, a history is produced, the history, as we have seen, of each sense, the history in terms of which "the eye has become a human eye, just as its object has become a social, human object," and "the human eye takes in things in a different way from the crude non-human eye."[32] Marx attributes the source of this history at times to the development of the senses, at times to that of the object. With respect to the development of the object: "only music can awaken the musical sense in man . . . only through the objectively unfolded wealth of human nature can the wealth of subjective human sensitivity . . . be either cultivated or created." This is why the development of the senses depends upon the degree of development of a society, on the types of object that a culture proposes at a given moment of its history. But by virtue of the ontological meaning of sensuousness, the determination of the sensuous object can, in the final analysis, only be that of sensuousness itself, that of the sensuous faculty of which it is the object. "Because my object can only be the confirmation of one of my essential powers, i.e. *can only be for me in so far as my essential power exists for me as a subjective attribute* (this is because the sense of an object for me extends only as far as my sense extends, only has sense for a sense that corresponds to that object)."[33] In any case, the reference of materialism to subjectivity is evident here in the radically subjective definition of sense by which nature exists only as a sensuous object.

It is this ontology of sensuous reality that constitutes, in 1844, the source of the critique directed against Hegel. It is because Hegelianism understands reality as the concrete being of the Idea, precisely as its reality and, consequently, as an ideal reality, that it allows what constitutes, on the contrary, the essence of true reality to escape it, namely the singularity and the individuality that belong to sensuous being as such. Because being, however, is given as sensuous, that is, in the phenomenological actuality of its singularity and of its individuality, Hegel could not fail to recognize the undeniable character of its givenness, but he interprets it as a moment of the Idea and in this way falsifies its nature, just when he pretends to acknowledge it in its own right. It is on the basis of the universality of thought that singularity and individuality are themselves explained;[34] this is so inasmuch as negation constitutes the inner structure of being and as universality, as a result, attains being only against the background of this structure in it, that is, in the concrete and singular being that it posits in order to rise out of its negation. In this, thought recovers and presents as belonging to it, as moments of its own development, what belongs in reality to being, and it is in this way that it claims to reduce being to itself. "Thought overleaps its opposite; this means that thought claims for itself what belongs not to itself but to being. Particularity and individuality, however, belong to being, whereas generality belongs to thought. Thought . . . makes the negation of generality . . . into a moment in thought."[35]

The mystification through which being is recognized in its singularity and in its individuality only to be reduced thereby to a moment of the movement of the Idea is apparent in Hegel's *Logic,* which claims to restore ideal necessity to this movement. In order to reach truth, that is, to reach phenomenological actuality, the Idea, insofar as it is this actuality, as it is intuition, must, in accordance with the presuppositions that have been sufficiently elaborated on, give itself to itself in the form of otherness, and this other-being, which itself is the reflection of the Idea, is the phenomenon; the immediate in its peculiarity, objective determination, is nature. Marx cites the text in the *Encyclopedia* where Hegel states how in "its unity with itself," that is, as "intuition" *(Anschauung),* that is, moreover, "in its own absolute truth," the Idea "resolves to let the moment of its particularity or of initial determination and other-being, the immediate idea, as its reflection, issue freely from itself as nature."[36]

The truth of this movement of the Idea is not, however, as Hegel believed it to be, its truth in the sense that has just been stated, namely the manifestation and the full realization of a being that would be its own; this truth, on the contrary, lies in what is not a temporary but instead a fundamental insufficiency, the radical failure of the Idea to define being and the necessity in which it finds itself of seeking being outside itself in that which differs substantially from it, in sensuous being. It is in this way that Feuerbach interprets critically the "logical" movement of the Idea, as the necessity of abandoning the Hegelian philosophy of the Idea, idealism, and of substituting for it his own philosophy, a philosophy of nature, "materialism." Here again Marx follows Feuerbach: the boredom of an empty thought which in itself lacks any ontological signification forces it to seek being outside itself; it is the "longing for a content" that leads it to make itself into intuition—that is, to receive a content which it is, precisely, incapable of supplying by itself—into something other than itself. This inability to constitute being by itself is what designates thought as abstraction, and the way in which thought grasps hold of itself is nothing other than its self-awareness as abstraction. "But the abstraction which comprehends itself as abstraction knows itself to be nothing; it must relinquish itself, the abstraction, and so arrives at something which is its exact opposite, nature. Hence the whole of the Logic is proof of the fact that abstract thought is nothing for itself, that the absolute idea is nothing for itself and that only nature is something." And further on: "This entire transition from the *Logic* to the *Philosophy of Nature* is nothing more than the transition—so difficult for the abstract thinker to effect, and hence described by him in such a bizarre manner—from abstracting to intuiting. The mystical feeling which drives the philosopher from abstract thinking to intuition is boredom, the longing for a content."[37]

The thesis that now sums up Hegelianism in the eyes of Feuerbach and of Marx and appears to them as the most obvious and purest illustration of "idealism" is formulated as follows: *thought creates the object*. A thesis such as this presupposes another, one which is not explicit but which Marx hastens to recognize, namely the prior substitution of thought itself, as process and as the subject of the process, for the only real being that is entitled to fill this double role: man. Or yet again, what amounts to the same thing, the definition of man as self-consciousness. Everything stems from this: "The positing of man = self-consciousness."[38] "For Hegel human nature, man, is equivalent to self-consciousness."[39] "Because man is equivalent to self-consciousness,"[40] etc. Once consciousness has been substituted for man, every real process is then a process of thought. Yet, still in line with the Hegelian presuppositions, this process is a process of objectification; what it produces is an object and, inasmuch as it is a real process, this is a real object. And thus it is that nature, which designates this object in its reality, is reduced to the objectification of thought. Thought is alienated in nature; it posits itself as other, but this alienation, as a result, is no different from the act peculiar to thought, from its objectification. Alienation and objectification are identical in two ways: thought posits its own self in the form of otherness, thus it itself takes on the appearance of exteriority and of nature, but on the other hand, it itself also performs this positing, this positing of itself in the other. The upshot of this is that what is posited by the objectification of thought is not, in reality, anything other than this thought; it is its product and, what is more, it is itself in another form. So that this other form is a pure appearance, the appearance of an otherness which is, in fact, only thought itself, not a real thing but what Marx calls thingness, that is, on the one hand, a thing for thought and only for thought and, on the other hand, a thing that is still simply thought itself, under the appearance of exteriority and of otherness. And since this exteriority and this otherness, this thingness, do not constitute a true being, a true thing, something truly other than thought, truly external to it, do not constitute an actual content different from pure thought, they are therefore as such, as lacking true actuality, "abstract"—to stick to Marx's own words—that is, they constitute an abstract exteriority, an abstract otherness, an abstract thingness. "A self-consciousness, through its alienation, can only establish thingness, i.e. an abstract thing, a thing of abstraction and not a real thing. It is also clear that thingness is therefore in no way something independent or substantial vis-à-vis self-consciousness; it is a mere creature, a postulate of self-consciousness. And what is postulated, instead of confirming itself, is only a confirmation of the act of postulating; an act which, for a single moment, concentrates its energy as a product and apparently confers upon that product—but only for a moment—the role of an independent, real being."[41]

Precisely because the process that has just been described and to which we must give its true name, which is the *action of thought*, is only an abstract process and because what it postulates is merely a pseudo-exteriority, a pseudo-otherness, a pseudo-reality, and in no way a reality really different from thought, because the objectification it produces is only an apparent objectification to the extent that the object is still only thought itself, because alienation is itself only an apparent alienation—for all these reasons, then, thought retains the possibility of taking back what it has postulated, of overcoming its alienation, of reducing to itself this object which is but the appearance of an object, which is nothing but thought itself under this objective appearance. In this way, then, what is before consciousness, before knowledge as its object, is no more than this knowledge itself, is not separate from it, is only in appearance something other than itself. What appears to it as an object is merely itself. When knowledge knows this, it knows precisely that this object is nothing different from it, is but itself and, through this knowledge, knowledge reduces the object to itself, reduces otherness, overcomes the latter and all possible alienation. *The supersession of alienation is not only possible, it is identical to alienation itself, or rather it is only the consciousness of alienation.* To supersede alienation is indeed no more than this: it is to know that the object which thought posited in its objectification as other than itself, as nature, is in reality nothing but itself. "[Consciousness] knows the nullity of the object, i.e. that the object is not distinct from it, the non-existence of the object for it, in that it knows the object as its own *self-alienation;* that is, it knows itself—i.e. it knows knowing, considered as an object—in that the object is only the *appearance* of an object, an illusion, which in essence is nothing more than knowing itself which has confronted itself with itself and hence with a *nullity*, a something which has *no* objectivity outside knowing. Knowing knows that when it relates itself to an object it is only *outside* itself, alienates itself; that it only *appears to itself* as an object, or rather, that what appears to it as an object is only itself." Or again, consciousness "in this alienation *knows* itself as object or . . . the object as itself."[42]

Because the supersession of alienation is identical to alienation itself, or rather to its conscious grasp of itself by virtue of which consciousness knows that what it opposes to itself in the act of self-objectification which constitutes it is nothing really different from itself, but that in this form of opposition and of exteriority it is in reality itself which it gives to itself—therefore, superseding alienation in this way is identical to maintaining it and allows what is opposed to subsist as it is, in its opposition, since *there is no question of really superseding it but only of knowing that what is opposed to thought in this way is still only thought itself*, its own objectification. Because the opposite of thought is simply objectified thought, by remaining close to this opposite, thought remains at home with itself. "Consciousness—self-consciousness—is at home in its other-being as such . . . it is therefore, if we abstract from Hegel's abstraction and talk instead of self-consciousness, of the self-consciousness of man, at home in its other-being as such."[43] Remaining at home with itself in its other-being, indeed having no need to supersede the latter since this is nothing different from itself, thought must instead maintain and allow to subsist this other-being, which is but the manifestation and the confirmation of thought itself, and this is why, by confirming itself in the other-being, thought in reality confirms the latter; it "reaffirms" it, says Marx, and "restores" it. Thus is recovered the signification of the Hegelian *Aufhebung*, in which, as the third manuscript says, "negation and preservation [affirmation] are brought together."[44] The negation of the nega-tion, the negation of the other-being, is in fact only *the negation of the signification it had of being other*, but, once its true signification is recognized, the signification it has now for consciousness, that of being itself, it is hence-forth posited in this new signification; it is legitimatized and, consequently, preserved. Whether this other-being be nature or the cultural world, it must be said that "self-conscious man, in so far as he has acknowledged and superseded the spiritual world . . . as self-alienation, goes on to reaffirm it in this alienated form and presents it as its true existence, restores it and claims to be at home in its other-being as such."[45]

Hegel's "apparent criticism" lies in this restoration of that which has not truly been negated but only in its apparent signification of being other and which, once this signification has been modified and turned into the signification of being the same, is then "preserved." And it is in this way that everything that was thought as an alienation of consciousness—law, politics, religion—is finally reestablished, insofar as its true signification is unveiled and conse-quently appears as the confirmation of the being of life, as a confirmation of life reduced to that of consciousness. "Man, who has realized that in law, politics, etc., he leads an alienated life, leads his true human life in this alienated life as such."[46] This is also why the Hegelian negation is not a true negation which effectively supersedes its object by showing its illusory character, by positing it as an apparent essence, but quite the opposite—it is the affirmation that this apparent essence has, in reality, the sense of being the realization of true essence, that is of consciousness. And it is in this manner that the apparent essence, that the objective appearance, is no longer the negation of conscious-ness but its incarnation and thus finds itself reduced to this consciousness; it is in this manner that it has itself become the subject. "In Hegel, therefore, the negation of the negation is not the confirmation of true being through the negation of apparent being. It is the confirmation of apparent being . . . or the negation of this apparent being as an objective being residing outside man and independent of him and its transformation into the subject."[47]

A radical clarification of the critique that Marx levels against Hegel here cannot, however, sidestep the ambiguity of this critique to the extent that it necessarily reflects the ambiguity of the "materialism" which determines it and to which it leads. For as we have seen, when Feuerbach speaks of true being, he fails to distinguish between material reality and its phenomenological actuality as sensuous reality, between beings and their condition as object. The problematic developed in the third manuscript takes on its philosophical significance only when it is considered in the light of the distinction we have just recalled, consequently, only insofar as it does not in fact have one meaning but actually two, which, moreover, are fundamentally different: an ontic meaning and an ontological meaning, which henceforth must be rigorously distinguished.

When Marx declares that the objectification of thought is not a real objectification, that the object it posits is not the real object, something really different from thought, really opposed to it, is not "nature," the "sensuous world," "reality," he means that this object is not a being. The illusion of thought is believing that in the becoming-other of its own alienation, in its *self-*alienation, it is capable of founding a being that is truly other than itself, natural determination or, yet again, that of the human world, material abundance, etc. This is the "illusion of speculation" in accordance with which "consciousness— knowing as knowing, thinking as thinking—claims to be the direct opposite of itself, claims to be the sensuous world, reality, life."[48] In this critique Marx explicitly follows Feuerbach—"Thought overreaching itself in thought (Feuerbach)"[49]—echoing his very words: "In his *Grundsätze der Philosophie der Zukunft* (§ 30) Feuerbach writes: 'Hegel is a thinker who over-reaches himself in thought.'" How does thought overreach itself? By presenting its own movement as being capable of producing what is not itself, by proposing itself as the power of growth in which, in the ideal development of the Idea, beings are abruptly included and contained. In short, thought presents and conceives of its own action as an ontic, "real" action capable of producing beings and, for this same reason, of superseding them and abolishing them. And since the beings it claims to create thus belong to its own development, they belong precisely to it, they are its "moments" and its self-confirmation. "And because thought imagines itself to be the direct opposite of itself, i.e. sensuous reality, and therefore regards its own activity as sensuous, real activity, this supersession in thought, which leaves its object in existence in reality, thinks it has actually overcome it. On the other hand, since the object has now become a moment of thought for the thought which is doing the superseding, it is regarded in its real existence as a confirmation of thought, of self-consciousness, of abstraction."[50] The ontic meaning of the critique Marx levels against Hegel is therefore strikingly clear: what is rejected is this *ontic creativity of the action of thought* and hence the power of thought to reduce beings to itself. And it is for this reason that *intuition* is substituted for thought, *that is, precisely, a faculty which is not creative but receptive with respect to finite being*.

But what is intuition? It does not create beings, it receives them, it gives them. It is the power that tears finite being out of the darkness in which it lies in its very principle in order to offer it to the light and to make it phenomenon. Intuition has this ultimate phenomenological meaning; it is this and no more than this. It unveils beings, it is this unveiling as such. *It is due to intuition that being is not simply what is, but that the latter is a sensuous being and this sensuousness characterizing being bestows upon it the positivity, the actuality, the materiality that Feuerbach and Marx recognize in it and by virtue of which it is precisely, for them, being, reality*. The phenomenon of intuition upon which Feuerbach's materialism is founded makes the ambiguity of this materialism clear, since it shows us that the immediate being of a being is precisely its givenness in intuition, its condition of sensuous being. To the ontic meaning of intuition, which has this power to give us beings, is inevitably added its ontological meaning, which refers to this givenness as such. The givenness of beings is intuition itself, transcendental sensuousness as sensuousness which is at one and the same time presupposed and forgotten by "materialism."

The consideration of *intuition as such* leads us to the question we shall now raise: *what is the ontological meaning of the critique Marx directs to Hegel in the third manuscript?* This question must be formulated as follows: in what does the givenness which properly constitutes intuition as such consist? What is the structure of sensuousness? The reply has been provided by all the texts quoted from the *Economic and Philosophical Manuscripts*, and it is unequivocal: beings are sensuous to the extent to which they are objects. "Real," "material" being is the "sensuous object." The power which brings about the sensuous is the power to form the object. Sensuous being, Marx said—and this is how he defined "natural being"—means "having an object outside itself." The essence of sensuousness, intuition as such, resides in the power which gives itself an object outside itself, in the objectification process in which objectivity is objectified. Certainly, the ontic meaning of the critique levelled against Hegel must not be overlooked: the objectification process does not create the object, or rather, the being; it discovers it and it is in this that it is intuition. But this discovery is nothing but the opening up of a dimension of objectivity by which beings are given to us, become sensuous precisely inasmuch as they attain this condition, inasmuch as they are objects. To speak of a "sensuous object" is a tautology: it is as object that being is sensuous.

Thought that defines being as sensuous being—naturalism insofar as it is a humanism—is an ontological thought; it thematizes the structure of being and understands it as sensuousness, as intuition. *Insofar as the structure of intuition resides in the process of objectification in which objectivity as such is posited, it is no different from the structure of thought as Hegel understands it*. By thought, Hegel in no way means a mere representation of things, giving us only their imitation, their copy instead and in place of their real being. Thought and being are identical for Hegel. This signifies that being exists only as phenomenon and exists as such quite precisely to the extent that it presents itself as an object. This is why the structure of being is objectification. To the extent that he identifies thought and being, Hegel understands being as subjectivity. But Hegelian subjectivity is precisely nothing other than objectivity itself as such. To say that being is subjective is also to say that it is objective and that its concrete fullness is at the same time the unfolding of an objective universe, of an objective history capable of containing everything and of expressing every-thing because nothing exists outside of this universe and this history. The object of thought is thus not a being-in-thought, a being that is "represented," imag-ined or dreamed, a "subjective" being; it is real being and the only possible being. It is not thought which creates being but, quite the opposite, being which makes itself "thought," "Logos," which becomes object and does so in order to be, in order to attain the concreteness of its actuality. Thought does not create being, it creates the object. To say that thought creates the object is an assertion that can only be contested as long as one fails to understand it, for this is a sheer tautology. Thought creates the object because it is objectivity as such. It thus creates, if not beings themselves, at least their objective condition, what per-mits them to give themselves to the senses by manifesting themselves. Insofar as it founds the objectivity by which beings are given to the senses as objects, thought is originally intuition. Insofar as the structure of intuition is at one and the same time that of thought, as Hegel understands it, the critique formulated against him by Feuerbach and Marx has no ontological signification.

This is also why the reproach Marx addresses to Hegel, and this is still in the wake of Feuerbach, of wanting to *abolish objectivity*, could be formulated only at the price of a complete misunderstanding of both the profound intentions and the explicit presuppositions of Hegelianism. A reproach such as this becomes apparent in the context of a discussion that thematizes the relation between the objectivity in question here and alienation. Hegel is held to have identified objectivity and alienation in such a way that the teleology which directs his entire system, whereby consciousness aims at overcoming every form of aliena-tion, could lead only to the supersession of every form of objectivity and, consequently, to the supersession of objectivity itself as such. "To recapitu-late," Marx writes. "The appropriation of estranged objective being or the supersession of objectivity in the form of estrangement—which must proceed from indifferent otherness to real, hostile estrangement—principally means for Hegel the supersession of objectivity, since it is not the particular character of the object but its objective character which constitutes the offense and the estrangement as far as self-consciousness is concerned."[51] And again, just as explicitly: "The reappropriation of the objective essence of man, produced in the form of estrangement as something alien, therefore means transcending not only estrangement but also objectivity. That is to say, man is regarded as a non-objective, spiritual being."[52] This claim of radically superseding objectivity is also visible, according to Marx, in the Hegelian conception of nature, which, as has been demonstrated, is merely an appearance of objectivity and, for this reason, is but a temporary appearance. This means that nature's appearance of objectivity is for the real being of the Idea nothing but a flaw, and the realization of this being can therefore consist only in the complete reabsorption in the self of what for a moment was allowed to go outside it, so that once again here the end of alienation signifies the abolition of objectivity. "Externality here should not be understood as self-exteriorizing sensuousness accessible to light and to sensuous man. It is to be taken in the sense of alienation, a flaw, a weakness, something which ought not to be. For that which is true is still the idea . . . this externality of nature, its antithesis to thought, is its defect . . . it is a defective being. A being which is defective not only for me, not only in my eyes, but in itself, has something outside itself which it lacks. That is to say, its essence is something other than itself. For the abstract thinker nature must therefore supersede itself, since it is already posited by him as a potentially superseded being."[53]

To what extent Marx is mistaken when he formulates this interpretation, which will be repeated blindly by all of his followers and all of his commentators, is sufficiently demonstrated by everything that has been said on this subject, by the Hegelian analyses in general and, in an obvious and irrefutable manner, by the very foundations of the ontology upon which they rest.[54] All of the fundamental concepts of Hegelian thought bear objectively within them, not as a temporary and incomprehensible moment of a uselessly complicated history but as the essence which is that of realization, which is therefore their own essence, precisely inasmuch as they make a claim to objectivity and actually attain it. It is in this way that nature is not, as Marx believed it to be, a flaw in the Idea; instead the Idea, if it were not nature, not actual and autonomous nature, if it were not "at the same time a presupposing of the world as independently existing nature,"[55] would be only an abstract concept. Because nature is the reality of the Idea, because, generally speaking, the reality of the Idea is its objectivity and its actuality as objective being, because the Idea of freedom, for example, is nothing "subjective" but the State itself, the world of history, the empires that constitute it, etc., this objectivity in which reality is fulfilled cannot be superseded unless reality itself, as Hegel understands it, is also superseded. This is why the assertion that in Hegel objectivity would be superseded at the same time as alienation is inaccurate. It is true that in Hegel objectivity and alienation, understood in their radical ontological meaning as constituting the internal structure of being, are identical. They are identical inasmuch as they designate in an identical fashion the process by which being is made Logos, objectifies itself in the light of phenomenality. But because this process designates being itself and its realization in phenomenological concreteness, it continually takes place and never ceases to take place, so long at least as being is. *Understood in its meaning as identical with objectivity, Hegelian alienation can no more be superseded than can this objectivity itself.*

Did Hegel not claim, nevertheless, to put an end to alienation? Is not this alienation overcome when, in absolute knowledge, the consciousness of the object finally coincides with self-consciousness? And yet neither the structure of otherness, which defines ontological alienation, nor that of objectivity, which is identical with that of the former, is absent from absolute knowledge. Quite the opposite, *it is in the difference of otherness that the object, which is maintained and preserved by it, offers itself to consciousness with the meaning of no longer being something opposed to it but of being consciousness itself*. The supersession of alienation designates not the supersession of the object but the modification by virtue of which it is no longer given as "indifferent" or "hostile" being, as foreign being, but as "the same." This is why the supersession by which the foreign character of the object but not the object itself is superseded, by which the meaning of being other but not the otherness of its objective presentation is superseded, allows the latter to subsist and presupposes alienation understood in its ontological structure as identical with objectivity as such. Marx's mistake then becomes evident, as when he writes in the above-cited text: "It is not the particular character of the object but its objective character which constitutes the offense and the estrangement as far as self-consciousness is concerned."[56] Because in Hegel the structure of self-consciousness is never other than that of the consciousness of the object, because consciousness signifies in general the objectification of objectivity, its unfolding, this objectivity, *the objective character of the object, can in no way be for consciousness offense and estrangement but, quite the opposite, is the confirmation of itself, or rather, its very being*. It is for this reason that the object is in reality the Self, that the other being reveals itself to be the same, the being of consciousness, because it is nothing other than its objectification, because the objectification of objectivity, the creator of phenomenality, is consciousness itself.

This is what the text of the third manuscript says in reality under the appearance of its explicit opposition to Hegelianism. For what Marx reproaches Hegel with here is not, in the final analysis, that he does away with the object but that he in fact allows it to subsist. Marx's deep understanding of *Aufhebung* has indeed shown us how Hegelian negation was only an apparent negation and how, once the object is recognized in its meaning as being no longer the opposite of but the confirmation of the objectification of consciousness, it then subsists in this role, so that consciousness is henceforth at home with itself in its other-being. Here again one sees that ontological otherness as such is not superseded; only the meaning that it is a foreign being is abolished. *It is precisely insofar as ontological otherness subsists, the becoming-other in which consciousness is realized in the form of objectivity, that the latter possesses the meaning, precisely, of no longer being the other but of being consciousness itself, that the consciousness of the object becomes self-consciousness*.

A rigorous reflection upon the third manuscript thus places us before this twofold certainty: (1) objectivity is neither absent nor abolished in Hegelianism, where it constitutes, on the contrary, the sphere of all realization and of all actuality, as Marx finally understands when, rediscovering the ontological

meaning of the Hegelian dialectic, he grasps negation as *Aufhebung*, as the very
positing of the object; (2) this objectivity interpreted by Hegel as the essence of
phenomenality, as "thought," constitutes at one and the same time the essence
of Feuerbachian sensibility upon which the *Economic and Philosophical Manuscripts* are in large measure based, the essence of intuition, with the sole
reservation that the latter is receptive and no longer creative with respect to the
specific content that it displays. Hegel simply confused the ontological meaning
with the ontic meaning of intuition and, because beings offer themselves to the
senses only as objects, he believed that this creation of the object, the
objectification of objectivity, was in the same stroke the creation of the beings
that it unveils. This was, as we have seen, the ontic meaning of the critique that
Feuerbach and Marx directed at Hegel, the absence of any ontological meaning
of this same critique being expressed in the fact that the givenness of intuition
is, precisely, nothing but Hegelian objectification.

The fact that the essence of sensuousness is identical with that of thought
constitutes the *truth* of the 1844 *Economic and Philosophical Manuscripts*. We
have seen that Marx, following Feuerbach, understands sensuousness as composed of a certain number of "essential forces" which define the modes of its
actualization and which are nothing other than the different senses. In what
does the actualization of these forces—that is, properly speaking, the exercise
of each sense—consist? "The peculiarity of each essential power is precisely its
peculiar essence, *and thus also the peculiar mode of its objectification*, of its
objectively real, living being."[57] It is because as objectification it is identical
with thought that sensuousness too offers us a world of objects and finds therein
its own self-confirmation, the confirmation and the affirmation of "human essence." "Man is therefore affirmed in the objective world not only in thought but
with all the senses."[58] The sensuous world, too, is thus henceforth not a "pure"
world, an original nature, but a "human" nature, the product of the
objectification of each of the essential forces which define man's sensuousness.
The essential homogeneity of nature and of culture which, in Hegel, permits the
movement from one to the other, remains secretly present in the 1844 *Economic
and Philosophical Manuscripts*. It is not even necessary to state that thought is
at work in the first sensuous constitution of nature, which it is held to govern in
the sense of an *a priori* law, since the essence of sensuousness is already that of
thought.

Because the essence of sensuousness is at the same time that of thought, we
see that the meaning of the concept of sense in Marx's text is extended in the
most peculiar fashion. "Sense" no longer designates simply the traditional five
senses, but all the potentialities of subjectivity. Materialism was defined in
terms of its opposition to thought; it now includes within itself all the forms of
the latter, including its "higher" forms. In his critique of private property, Marx
showed that in place of the abstract and impoverished definition of the object as
mine had to be substituted a total opening up to being. But this opening up is
not simply sensuous; it implies an intellectual opening as well, which is *itself*

understood and defined as a sense. "Therefore *all* the physical and intellectual senses have been replaced by the simple estrangement of *all* these senses—the sense of having."[59] The designation of having, that is of a theoretical, even juridical, intentionality as a "sense" presupposes as well the extension of this concept to the totality of the modalities of relating to the object, to consciousness understood as this relation. "The inexhaustible, vital, sensuous, concrete activity of self-objectification"[60] is structurally the same as thought, is only one of the forms of human "sense," of the realization of self-objectification that constitutes this sense, man's humanity. *"For not only the five senses, but also the so-called spiritual senses, the practical senses (will, love, etc.), in a word, the human sense, the humanity of the senses—all these come into being only through the existence of their objects, through humanized nature."*[61] And indeed one sees that nature in Feuerbach and in Marx can no longer be opposed to that in Hegel, that the object of sense in no way exists prior to "consciousness," that it too is the product of its objectification. ". . . immediate sensuous nature for man is, immediately, human sense perception. . . ."[62] This is why nature is part of history, because it exists neither before nor outside of this objectification, neither before nor outside of what Hegel calls "thought." "Nature as it comes into being in human history . . . is the true nature of man."[63] It is nature as a whole which is "human," which is "culture." "It is only when objective reality universally becomes for man in society the reality of man's essential powers . . . that all objects become for him the objectification of himself . . . his objects."[64]

Alienation in no way challenges the universal status of the object, nor does it imply any "absolute" object which would be independent of man, which would not be his objectification, but only describes the negative modality through which this objectification takes place. "Nature as it comes into being through industry, although it is in an estranged form, is true anthropological nature."[65] Here again, far from separating Marx's thought from that of Hegel, the problem of alienation unites them within a common ontological horizon. Here again, it is in following Feuerbach and his theory of the object that Marx is carried back to the presuppositions of Hegelianism. According to Feuerbach, the object in general, and consequently the sensuous object as well, reveals the essence of human nature because it is the objectification of this essence. "And this is true not merely of spiritual, *but also of sensuous objects.*"[66] Because the structure of the object of sense is the same as that of the "spiritual" object, because, against the background of this common structure, the extension of the concept of sense grows to the point of including the totality of the intentionalities of consciousness, which purely and simply coincides with the realm of sense, because the essence of sensuousness appears to be identical with that of thought, the separation of these faculties does not merely pose a problem, it entirely misses the mark. *The hostility between sense and intellect, the third manuscript states, is abstract.*[67]

Along with the separation of sensuousness and thought, however, it is the entire problematic of the 1844 *Economic and Philosophical Manuscripts* that is challenged. What indeed was the aim of this problematic, if not to show the reality that Hegelianism had missed? Practice names the place of this reality, the actual relation to being as it is realized within sense. To practice is opposed theory, which formulates the abstract determinations of the object, abstract because in it they are only the objectification of the forms of thought. This is why nature is not the other-being of thought, because its determinations are those of thought, abstract, logical determinations, because nature is merely the objectification of the forms and the potentialities of the human mind. And it is in this way that for the abstract thinker "the whole of nature only repeats to him in a sensuous, external form the abstractions of logic," and this is also why, when he analyzes nature, he analyzes "these abstractions again."[68] *But is not sensuous praxis, too, simply the objectification of the potentialities of the human essence? Sensuous nature is not the other-being of these potentialities but their form, the form in which these essential powers attain their self-manifestation in and through objectivity, the form in which they attain self-knowledge.* "The particular sensuous human powers, since they can find objective realization only in natural objects, can find self-knowledge only in the science of nature in general."[69] And what are involved in praxis are not even potentialities different from those of thought, not merely because the "practical senses" include the "spiritual senses"—will, love, etc.—but because *the essence of this praxis, of this concrete and actual relation to being, is precisely objectification,* that is, intuition, thought. The reason for this is that the effectuation of sensorial praxis is nothing other than the opening up of the field of visibility constituted by objectivity; *this praxis is at one and the same time vision, a gaze, intuition, contemplation, and theory.* "The senses," the third manuscript states, *"have therefore become theoreticians in their immediate praxis."*[70] This reduction of praxis to theory, after their apparent opposition, corresponds to the thought of Feuerbach, for whom the realization of reality, the realization of man, is the object that gives man back to himself, reflects his image back to him in the illumination of objectivity, in the theoretic festival of contemplation. "The eye of man alone keeps theoretic festivals. The eye which looks into the starry heavens, which gazes at that light, alike useless and harmless, having nothing in common with the earth and its necessities—this eye sees in that light its own nature, its own origin. The eye is heavenly in its nature. Hence man elevates himself above the earth only with the eye; hence theory begins with the contemplation of the heavens. The first philosophers were astronomers. It is the heavens that admonish man of his destination, and remind him that he is destined not merely to action, but also to contemplation."[71] The reduction of praxis to theory is identical with the reduction of materialism to idealism; it places in evidence their common essence as *theoria,* as the opening up of being in the transcendence of objectivity. Here is why: because they are founded upon the essence of objectivity which they claim to oppose to Hegelianism and which the 1844 *Economic and Philosophical Manuscripts* unconsciously reduplicate.

Starting with the 1843 manuscript, however, Marx knew that Hegel had allowed reality to elude him. To say that reality eludes the presuppositions of Hegelianism means, therefore, clearly and undeniably that *reality does not lie in objectivity and is not constituted by it, nor, consequently, is it constituted by Feuerbach's intuition*. In its pathetic striving toward reality, Marx's thought must make a sharp break with itself insofar as it had believed itself to be capable of measuring up to its ontological project following in the steps of Feuerbach; it must abruptly and radically reject, at the same time and in the same motion, both Feuerbach and Hegel, materialism and idealism, the reduction of praxis to theory and theory in general as being fundamentally incapable of displaying in itself the being of reality. It is not because Marx has just read Stirner that he judges it necessary to abandon ship and to leave Feuerbach behind; it is rather because he finds himself faced with essential and insurmountable evidence, which has now become ours inasmuch as we have been able to repeat the internal movement of his thought, its contradictions and its ultimate exigency: to grasp reality in its unsurpassable opposition to theory, to grasp the original essence of praxis. The "Theses on Feuerbach" are not merely possible, they are necessary.

The original essence of praxis

The decisive importance of the "Theses on Feuerbach" stems from the fact that they furnish a reply to the question that inspires Marx's philosophical reflection from its very beginning, and this is, in truth, the question of philosophy itself: what is reality? Reality is lost, as we saw, when thought is everywhere substituted for it, when the ideal determinations of being incorporate within themselves being itself. What is given to us by Feuerbach's intuition is beings, and materialism designates these beings as irreducible to the thought process that produces them, *as heterogeneous to the categorical determinations of theoretical consciousness which constitutes them precisely as the set of these determinations, as scientific objects*. No doubt Feuerbach contradicted himself on this point, since after having defined being in terms of the immediacy of sensuous presence, he then wanted—due to the many contradictions of this sensuous world, notably its contradiction of our aspirations, our consciousness, and our feelings—to grasp it on another level, on the more profound level of its essence, and this is to be accomplished thanks to a more penetrating manner of seeing, which is nothing other than that of philosophical thought. "He [Feuerbach] must," says Marx in *The German Ideology*, "take refuge in a double perception, a profane one which perceives 'only the flatly obvious' and a higher, philosophical, one which perceives the 'true essence' of things."[72] But Feuerbach's error does not lie here. "Feuerbach's error," Engels writes in the margin of Marx's text referring to the passage we have just cited, "is not that he subordinates the flatly obvious, the sensuous appearance, to the sensuous reality established by detailed investigation of the sensuous facts. . . ." Nor does it consist, as Engels himself believes, in the fact "that he cannot in the last resort cope with the sensuous world except by looking at it with the 'eyes', i.e., through the 'spectacles', of the philosopher." Indeed, what does it matter whether reality is displayed in its immediate sensuous presentation or through conceptual determinations formulated by theoretical consciousness in its attempt to grasp what truly exists in beings presented in this way and what it is to be understood as the "true" being, as its "essence"? Whatever the case may be, whether beings are taken as what consciousness does not produce or whether their determinations are, on the contrary, posited by consciousness; *whether what is involved is thought or intuition, it is through the mediation of objectification which constitutes their common essence, which, before being that of thought, constitutes the essence of intuition, that its givenness is realized, the givenness of a being which makes it an object.* The determination of the being of beings as objectivity, the determination of being as a "sensuous" object and then as the object of "thought," this is the ontological presupposition of Feuerbach's materialism. And it is due to this presupposition, common to both Feuerbach and Hegel, that the critique of Hegelianism in Feuerbach, as in the 1844 *Economic and Philosophical Manuscripts*, had, precisely, no ontological significance but only an ontic significance. Once again, Marx will never reconsider this last point; the powerlessness of thought to posit a being in its materiality will remain a constant theme of his problematic, one which will be taken up again and continued throughout his entire subsequent work, starting with *The German Ideology*.

With the "Theses on Feuerbach," however, something quite different is at issue. *What is put into question and, indeed, challenged with respect to its claim to constitute the original structure of being is the intuition itself as the power to receive as its object a being which it has not created.* To the ontic meaning of the critique of Hegelianism is added, as the new and really decisive contribution of the "Theses on Feuerbach," its radical ontological meaning, which no longer refers simply to the alleged creative power of thought with respect to beings but to the capacity to receive them passively in sensuousness, that is, to intuition. What is rejected is "intuitive materialism" *(die Anschaung der Materialismus)*, to borrow Marx's formulation in the ninth thesis. This critique is radical, decisive, and novel because it dismisses not simply the explicit Hegelianism of conceptual genesis but *the very thing that was opposed to it by Feuerbach and, following him, by Marx himself in the 1844* Economic and Philosophical Manuscripts, *namely the necessity for consciousness to sense being, to make itself receptive in intuition.* This is not to say that Marx disputes, either in the "Theses on Feuerbach" or thereafter, the passive character of sensuousness, the radical exteriority of sensuous being. *But this exteriority and, consequently, sensuous being, can no longer define being itself in its original nature, can no longer define reality. Reality is not objective reality.* This is displayed to us in the ever-deepening meaning of Marx's thought inasmuch as it is no longer the critique of thought but of the sensuous world, inasmuch as it now rejects "intuitive materialism."

What is the being that is opposed to intuition, that is no longer dependent on it, that is no longer perceived by it, that is no longer the "sensuous object"? One after the other, the "Theses on Feuerbach" spell it out, untiringly repeating: it is "practice." But it is then clear that if the concept of practice is to enable us to conceive of what is sighted in the "Theses on Feuerbach," that is, the radically new and essential ontological horizon that they trace out, it is on the condition of undergoing a decisive mutation. Not just a change in sense, as if the "practical" reality considered by Feuerbach were still abstract: sensuous man in general in his relationship with a sensuous world in general, affective man in his too general affective relationship—love, friendship in general—with another in general. It is as if it were a matter of substituting for these indeterminate determinations something more concrete, no longer "Man" as he relates to the world, *In-der-Welt-Sein*, but a real man apprehended in the situation that is his own, caught in a network of relations, in the effective web of a preexisting totality, man as part of history and of a given society. Man becomes abstract when he is isolated from the whole within which he is included, and this is when one indeed obtains, as the sixth thesis states, "an abstract—isolated—human individual" which is "Man," the human "genus," man defined by a universal essence which itself claims to define each particular man as one of its exemplars, as if this man could be understood on the basis of this essence, this genus, independently of what he is in each case in a determined historical and social structure. And it is in this way that "to abstract from the historical process" permits one, still in the words of the sixth thesis, to comprehend human essence "only as 'species', an inner, mute general character which unites the many individuals in a natural way."[73]

None of this is false, none of this permits us to understand anything at all about the "Theses on Feuerbach." It is not by simply reading a few sentences taken out of context, which itself remains unintelligible, that we can gain any insight into what is at stake here. The fact of limiting ourselves to these few sentences is instead proof that the rest has not been understood. What is more, it is the indefinite repetition of the same passage and the interpretation that is immediately proposed which definitively place out of our reach the essential sense contained in the "Theses on Feuerbach," a sense they hold locked up within themselves like a hidden and, finally, a lost sense. What in fact is the meaning of Marx's surpassing of Feuerbach according to this partial and distorted interpretation, which has since become the traditional interpretation? It holds that for the abstract man of whom philosophy has always spoken—and in this respect Feuerbach is still only the last philosopher—is to be substituted the real essence of man, *that is, the ensemble of social relations*.[74] However, isolated from the global problematic of *The German Ideology*, which alone can give us the meaning it has for Marx, the expression "the ensemble of social relations" cannot, as we have seen, help but hypostatize a new abstraction which takes the place of reality, namely the *living individuals who among themselves have relations such as these*. Why the hypostasis of "social relations" entails the complete falsification of reality, of the reality of "living individuals" who alone are "concrete" is fully clarified by the "Theses on Feuerbach." In the hypostasis of their abstraction, "social relations" name nothing more than objective relations, and it is in this way that they are thematized by a thought that is *scientific because it is objective*. When the human essence ceases to name, as in Feuerbach, an essence properly speaking, the genus, the universal and general reality that is found in every individual and that makes him what he is, in order to signify, on the contrary, a totality of objective relations that can be discerned and determined according to the place they occupy and the role they play in the system they form, in a "social structure," then indeed the ideological concept of "Man" collapses while, at the same time, the thematic field henceforth offered to the free investigation of "theory" opens up. It does not much matter then that someone like Luporini[75] wishes to correct the formal aspect contained in a structuralist interpretation by reminding us that one can no more consider this system of relations as an in-itself, abstracting from the individuals in which they are embodied, than one can consider these individuals themselves independently of the relations in which they are involved. In this interplay between empiricism and epistemology, the decisive contribution of the "Theses on Feuerbach" is lost as well. Individuals as they are understood *in the same way* by both Luporini and Althusser, *empirical individuals belonging to Feuerbachian reality, to sensuous reality, are recognized and defined in the light of his ontology*. The new epistemological field opened and structured by the "scientific" concepts of social relations, etc., is only "the higher way of seeing" which allows one to go beyond "sensuous appearance" in order to reach "a deeper analysis of the concrete state of things" and, finally, to reach its "structure." Must one then return from the sensuous object back to the object of thought, contrary to the untiring demands of the 1844 *Economic and Philosophical Manuscripts* and confront the ghost of Hegelianism once more in the rags of its contemporary disguises? Or should one recognize that it is only on the ground of sensuous reality and as its determinations that categorial determinations in general, "scientific objects," are constructed and developed, so that concrete singularities, individuals, can indeed be grasped and *known* only within these relations, which themselves, however, have no sense except with reference to individuals?

It does not much matter, we said. In sensuous reality just as in the scientific thematization outside of which it is claimed that one is unable to reach this reality—as if sensuousness were not a particular power alongside that of thought—*in intuition as in theoretical consciousness reigns sight, the primordial theoria which presents being as what is seen, as an object*.[76] This structure of being is what is ultimately rejected by the "Theses on Feuerbach." Such is the radical ontological meaning of the reversal of theory in practice. This reversal has nothing to do with the Feuerbachian reversal which aims at substituting, and in this anticipates Nietzsche, sensuous being for intelligible being, and which recognizes the rights of the givenness of intuition as more fundamental than those of conceptual vision. It is the Feuerbachian framework itself, and consequently the pre- and post-Feuerbachian framework as well, the intuitive relation to being, the intuitive relation or the conceptual relation and *this very alternative*, the intuitive *and* conceptual relation as relations that are properly and essentially ontological, which are overturned in the reversal now performed by Marx.

Since what is overturned in this reversal is contained within the problematic, how does it accomplish this reversal and what is the result of the act of overturning? The reversal of the "Theses on Feuerbach" overturns in its own way, overturns and allows what it overturns to remain intact. Neither the sensible object nor the scientific object is set upside down nor is it annihilated. Both subsist just where they are, *before us*. Only, this "before us" is no longer the theme of the problematic. *The problematic which is directed toward the reality of being no longer takes into consideration the seeing of* theoria, *the seeing of intuition or that of thought, and, allowing this seeing to subsist just where it is, allowing what is seen to unfold just where it is seen, it indicates that the original reality of being lies elsewhere, in some other place, and, henceforth, it consciously directs itself toward this other place*. What is this other place? What is it that is no longer "theory" and, as such, is truly, is being? The "Theses on Feuerbach" affirm no less explicitly: it is action. The thesis of the "Theses on Feuerbach" then surges forth with the brutality of its incoercible self-evidence. *Feuerbach was mistaken because he believed he could grasp the essence of reality in intuition and, as a result, grasp being as an object, whereas the reality of this being, the reality of reality, lies on the contrary in an original and exclusive manner in practice, which itself designates nothing but activity, pure activity as such*. The first thesis declares straightaway: "The chief defect of all hitherto existing materialism (that of Feuerbach included) is that the thing, reality, sensuousness, is conceived only in the form of the object or of contemplation, but not as . . . activity, practice. . . ."

Why then is intuition incapable of displaying in itself the being of action; why can it not give this being to us? Why must it be rejected and why must Feuerbach be reversed in order for action to be? For action, being means acting. The structural ontological heterogeneity separating intuition and action which Marx brings to light and which is thought by him in terms of this reversal is then made explicit in the following way: acting is not intuiting, it is not seeing, it is not looking. Inasmuch as intuition takes place, inasmuch as we live in it, inasmuch as we "intuit," we are not acting. The intuition has an object, it is the theory of this object, it contemplates it. But if the intuition intuits the object, if it "sees" and "contemplates," action does nothing of the sort. No doubt we can well act and *at the same time* intuit, contemplate the world, the sensuous world; we can also have the intuition of the action we are performing. In this case *we look at what we are doing*. It may even seem that this looking is a condition for our action; let us understand by this a way of assuring ourselves that our action is indeed going the way we want it to, in the direction of the goal we are pursuing, and possibly providing a way of correcting it. But action, *considered in itself*, has nothing to do with this gaze of intuition, *with the discovery of a spectacle, with the appearing of an object*. Discovering a spectacle, contemplating it, living in the presence of an object is, precisely, not acting. Inversely, we can well act without having the intuition of our action, *that is to say, without looking at it, without giving it to ourselves as an object*. It is, moreover, in this way that we act most often, that we perform most of the motions of our daily life. This is so with respect to everything we "know how to do," that is, the whole of the professional or private practices which mark out our existence and constitute its fabric, its very substance. This is so of "practice" in general.

This characteristic of practice by virtue of which it is foreign to intuition, whether the latter be sensuous or intellectual, is not, however, to be understood as an habitual characteristic, a property that could be found in most of our actions, that would be present "most of the time." This is why the proposition formulated previously, according to which we could indeed act without having the intuition of what we do, without representing our action to ourselves, must be specified, grasped in its rigorous meaning after the reversal. We must say: *action is possible only inasmuch as it is not intuition, as it is neither intuition of itself nor of any sort of object*. There is a contingency attaching to the relation between action and intuition, and this contingency signifies that action has nothing to do with intuition, that its essence is totally foreign to that of intuition, that it does not contain intuition but instead excludes it and does so in a radical manner in order to be possible, to be what it is, that is, in order to act. The structural ontological heterogeneity of action and of intuition is thus uncovered through the rigorousness of eidetic analysis: in analyzing intuition, that is, the appearing of an object, one cannot find action there, but only its contrary, seeing, contemplation. In the same way, in analyzing action, one cannot find intuition there, since if intuition were present in it, it would not act. This is why when intuition takes place at the same time as action, this "at the same time" defined and determined in a rigorous manner signifies "outside," as this characterizes radical exteriority, signifies that an intuition takes place elsewhere, outside of the action itself. And it is inasmuch as this intuition takes place outside of action and not in it that action can continue, that action, let us say, is possible and real.

The radical exclusion of intuition from action so that action can be possible, so that action can exist, must be carried in thought to its very end. To say that in action there is no intuition, no seeing, means that nothing at all is seen—nor can be seen—in it, means that in it there is no object. What then is action to the extent that in expelling all seeing outside itself, it thereby excludes every object? The first sentence of the first thesis on Feuerbach says what it is: it is subjective. Materialism in all of its forms was, precisely, criticized as grasping reality "only in the form of the object or of intuition but not as . . . activity, practice, *not subjectively*."[77] To Feuerbach's objective intuition—*objective in the sense of the 1844* Economic and Philosophical Manuscripts, *in the sense in which man is an objective being insofar as he has outside himself an object with which he is in relation through intuition, in the sense in which "objective" signifies the relation to the object—is radically opposed subjective action, in which subjectivity designates, on the contrary, the absence of this relation, of any intentional relation in general, precisely, the absence and the exclusion from it of intuition.*

But what then appears before us is an absolutely new sense of the concept of subjectivity; it is its authentic and original meaning; it is subjectivity itself which allows itself to be glimpsed by us in its very being and in its innermost essence. And it is here that Western philosophy, at least in what it possesses that is most constant and most apparent, is turned upside down. For such is the importance of the reversal performed by Marx in the "Theses on Feuerbach," the reversal of Western philosophy itself. In this way, far beyond and far short of Feuerbach, it is the horizon within which philosophy has always posed and solved its problems that is shaken; it is the very concept of being that is made to waver. The concept of being is subjectivity. Subjectivity is what permits beings to be. It has always been the case, in the West at least, that subjectivity permits beings to be inasmuch as it proposes them as objects, inasmuch as it is intuition. It has always been the case, from the time of ancient Greece, that the subjectivity of the subject is but the objectivity of the object. When, with Descartes, subjectivity is understood as "thought," it is still the necessary condition for the object that is sighted; this condition remains the original seeing which shapes and founds objectivity transcendentally, even if the place of this seeing is henceforth located in the intellect and no longer in sensuousness. In the same way, in Kant, the analysis of "transcendental consciousness" is nothing other than a presentation of the *a priori* structures of any possible subject, that is, precisely, of objectivity as such. It is once again as thought and, precisely, in the wake of Descartes and Kant that subjectivity is interpreted by Hegel, when it is identified by him with being, when it is understood as the being of substance. It is this tradition, which he believes he is opposing, that Feuerbach in his turn continues, if it is true that the intuition in which he wants once again to locate the relation to being simply frees, by restoring its original dimension, the "seeing" which constitutes the essence of this relation. This is why, as has been sufficiently demonstrated, the Feuerbachian critique of Hegelianism in fact had no ontological meaning. After all the others, Feuerbach's materialism unawaredly takes up again the presupposition which finds its explicit formulation in classical rationalism and according to which being resides in *theoria* and as such is seen, known, knowable, "rational." It is with this presupposition, which is handed down to him by way of Feuerbach, that Marx abruptly breaks in 1845. The passage from Feuerbach's materialism to Marx's "materialism" is not the passage from one particular conception of matter to another, from a static conception to a dynamic, "dialectical" conception. Nor is it the passage from a philosophy of mind, of the "universal," which is still present in Feuerbach, to a conception capable of producing actual material reality, to true materialism; *it is the passage from a certain conception of subjectivity to another,* from an intuitive subjectivity establishing and receiving the object, an "objective" subjectivity, to a subjectivity that is no longer "objective," to a radical subjectivity from which all objectivity is excluded. According to the first conception, being is an object and, as the objectivity of being is established within the realm of sense, a sensuous object. According to the second, on the contrary, being is nothing that can be presented to us as an object, is nothing objective, nothing sensuous; it is, in a radical— and in a radically new—sense, "subjective."

Taken literally, the first sentence of the first thesis is unintelligible, undermined by an enormous contradiction. It states: the error of past materialism is to have grasped "the thing, reality, sensuousness . . . in the form of the object or of contemplation," that is, precisely, as object, as sensuous world. But *what it means,* beyond this apparent absurdity, is blindingly clear. It says that reality, that which up to the present has been understood as the object of intuition, that is, as object, as sensuous world, and which Marx himself in the wake of Feuerbach names in this way in the first part of the sentence, is originally nothing of the sort, is not constituted in its essence by intuition and so does not present itself as an object, is nothing "objective." It is this reality foreign to objective intuition that constitutes, precisely, reality, which Marx now calls by its true name of subjectivity, and Marx reaches the concept of this reality by considering the phenomenon of action, of practice, because action is possible, acts, only insofar as it carries within itself no intuition, as it has neither an object nor a world.

The question that has motivated the present work and determined our entire investigation has been the following: what is the ultimate sense of Marx's critique of Hegelianism? The clear comprehension of the first sentence of the first thesis on Feuerbach gives us the reply. Why does Marx set himself in opposition to Hegel? Because, it is said, Hegel is a philosopher, because he contented himself with thinking the world, that is, with offering an interpretation of what is and what becomes, a philosophy, precisely, of nature, of history, of right, of art, of religion, etc., whereas the question raised by Marx, an entirely new question generating a new attitude in the spiritual life of humanity, was that of practice. This question substitutes for the traditional teleology of knowledge that of action; it no longer implies a recognition of the laws of being but the radical modifications it is to undergo—science, knowledge cannot help but be subordinated to this end which of its essence is "practical." This is why Hegel was dismissed not as one philosopher among others, as proposing an inaccurate philosophy open to criticism, full of holes and errors, etc., but as the philosopher, as representing philosophy itself. Hegel's philosophy is philosophy not because it contains all the others in the *Aufhebung* of absolute knowledge but because it is this knowledge and obeys it as its inner determination. Hegel: a philosopher, all philosophers. It is the teleology of knowledge that the eleventh thesis explicitly challenges at the same time as it opposes to this teleology, no less explicitly, the new teleology of "practice" and of action. "The philosophers have only interpreted the world, in various ways; the point is to change it."

Only, appearances to the contrary, the eleventh thesis does not provide a reply to our question; it does no more than state it. What is more, it states it in an enigmatic form and renders it insoluble. If it is true that, in Marx's eyes, all philosophies now find their representative in the philosophy of Hegel,[78] and that it is to Hegel that Marx's discourse is addressed, the latter is intelligible only insofar as Hegelianism continues to be understood as a philosophy of thought, as a thought of the world. However, this understanding, which is self-evident, has nothing immediate about it; it is dependent on Marx and on Marxism, dependent on our contemporary cultural universe, which since the beginning of the century has had us repeat that Hegel, philosophers, and philosophy in general have only thought about the world, whereas the point is actually to change it. In the "explanation" that is usually given, the eleventh thesis indefinitely presupposes itself, as an empty tautology. Perhaps it is even a totally unintelligible proposition if it is true that Hegelianism is not a philosophy of thought but, precisely, a philosophy of action, a philosophy which states: *das Wesen des Menschen ist die Arbeit*, the essence of man is labor. It is a philosophy which states that right is not the thought of right but its Idea, that is to say real right, right acting in a given society, determining the ensemble of relations that are produced there, a philosophy which, in the final analysis, is one with these relations, with the social life of which they constitute the very fabric, with the ensemble of social relations. This is a philosophy which revealed its implicit presuppositions precisely with respect to the problem that concerns us, the problem of action; and it did so by the radical critique of traditional morality. By showing that morality, no more than right, is not a thought, the aim of a duty for example, an intention, but that actual morality, which is the Idea of freedom, is "actualized by self-conscious action,"[79] that it is always a matter of going beyond the representation of the goal by realizing it, of "[translating] something from subjectivity (i.e. some purpose held before the mind) into existence"[80] and that this "actualized" and "achieved" aim can be so only "by means of its activity."[81] By showing, too, that this action, consequently, can no longer be understood as a mere "action of thought" but as a real action, an actual modification of the world, imprinting on it its recognizable indelible mark, finding in it at one and the same time the place of its actuality and that of its testimony. ". . . since action," § 132 states, "is an alteration which is to take place in an actual world and so will have recognition in it. . . ." And again, in § 132: ". . . an action, as its aim entering upon external objectivity. . . ." One could invoke a number of other similar quotations.

These quotations, which have been collected at random in our reading of the *Philosophy of Right* concern far more than just this single work, one moment— the last—in Hegel's thought; they contribute to defining far more than just one aspect of this thought. They refer to the fundamental ontology of Hegelianism, and they express its central theme, to the extent that this theme lies in the conception of being itself as action and as production. This is why everything that exists, if it is not to sink into the inanity and the emptiness of the loss of its being, can only be and persevere in being on the condition that it make itself adequate to the condition of being itself, cannot help but act in order to make itself consubstantial to a being that is action and operation. ". . . the act takes place," states a decisive text in *The Phenomenology of Mind*, "because action is *per se* and of itself the essence of actuality."[82] This is why the individual acts, in order to be something rather than nothing, and if substance demands this mediation of the acting individual, what it needs is not, in truth, individuality so much as the ontological force of action itself, of operation as such. It is the fact of acting in itself and for itself to which, negating itself, it gives itself over that makes it, in this self-negation constituting being, the being of actual substance and, as Hegel says, its actualization. "What seems here to be the individual's power and force," states *The Phenomenology of Mind*, "bringing the substance under it, and thereby doing away with that substance is the same thing as the actualization of the substance."[83] We know what becomes of individuality that does not act, of substance that does not make itself homogeneous with the operation of being understood as this very operation, as production. The beautiful soul which turns away from the world, *that is to say, which does not act*, is not the object of an ethical judgment that directs against this soul the negative evaluation it believed it was itself making with respect to things; instead it withdraws from being as such by rejecting its law, and following an ineluctable destiny, through the very will of being which is will and action, it dissolves into the void.

The interpretation of being as production dominates Hegel's entire thought. The manuscript written by Hegel at Iena in 1803 or 1804 and known under the title of "The First Philosophy of Spirit"[84] is noteworthy in this respect. We know that Hegel defined the necessary conditions for consciousness here, that is, for being itself. Language, no doubt, comes to be recognized as the first of these conditions, first in that it tears consciousness out of the abysmal night of sensuousness in which was unendingly swallowed up that which in it strove to give being to itself; language substitutes for this ephemeral sensation the name, in which it finds its ideal and continuous existence. This existence, however, is still only theoretical because if the empirical intuition ideally posited in the name acquires in it the transparence of a universality which tears it out of the obscurity of its intrinsic ineffability, it nevertheless remains unchanged in this very naming. This is why language affords only a theoretical mastery, the aptitude to see and to recognize as the "same" what nature offers us that is continually different. A real mastery of nature, that is, an effective transformation which makes it adequate to human need, can only be the result of action, and by this the young Hegel means the labor performed in the "material" process of producing things. In this way, "the theoretical process passes into the practical process"[85] which alone can give a true reality to consciousness.

Hegel's entire work celebrates the primacy of praxis over theory and affirms the necessity of action. Because action is constitutive of being, it cannot be the object of a prescription nor present itself in the form of an imperative; it cannot *precede itself in an ideal form*. The ideal form in which being is unable to precede itself does not only refer to an ethical imperative, the *Sollen* of having to be; it is philosophy itself as the thought of being or as the thought of the world. To say that action, which constitutes the being of the world, does not precede itself in any way as the thought of being and of the world, this means that it is first realized and that the process of forming reality produces one after the other the successive phases of its own development. This is the reason why Hegelian being presents itself essentially as a process and as becoming. This becoming has been produced and, as Hegel says, the real has matured when the ideal appears before it, when the phases of the process of its formation are reproduced in memory, where they are interiorized, in the empire of the ideas of philosophy. The latter, the ideal form of being, can therefore only state after the fact what has taken place in advance of it. The subordination of theory to practice is inscribed in the structure of being originally understood as production. When one opposes the eleventh thesis—the critique of all of philosophy—to Hegelianism, one forgets that Hegel has already written it, and not just offhandedly but in an effort to convey the substance of his thought, in lines that are quoted too often for them to be really heard: "One word more about giving instructions as to what the world ought to be. Philosophy in any case always comes on the scene too late to give it. As the thought of the world, it appears only when actuality is already there cut and dried after its process of formation has been completed. . . . it is only when actuality is mature that the ideal first appears over against the real. . . . The owl of Minerva spreads its wings only with the falling of the dusk."[86]

If Hegel and Marx both conceive of being, in an original manner, as production and as action, can the opposition of the second to the first signify anything other than an opposition in the way of conceiving of the being of action, than a radical and final opposition in the way of conceiving of being itself? As long as we are not capable of moving back to this ultimate ontological difference, the reversal that the "Theses on Feuerbach" wish to perform remains incomprehensible to us. How then does Hegel understand the being of action? As early as the Iena manuscript, at the moment when action finds a concrete form in labor, the latter is immediately interpreted as that which permits consciousness to change itself into something objective, namely "into this middle term, the instrument." The instrument is thus the very existence of consciousness, its stable and lasting being, universal, objective, real and "material" in opposition to the objective yet still ideal being of the name.[87] It is because the instrument confers upon labor the permanence of real being by situating it in objective universality that Hegel will come to say, paradoxically, of this instrument, which seems to be only a means, that it has a greater value than the end.[88]

This close connection between action and objectivity is recognized in the lena manuscript with regard to the necessity that labor be realized in accordance with a rule that is, doubtless, discovered by the individual, "learned" by him and in this appears as external to him, as "inorganic nature" Hegel says. But the fact that the labor of men conforms to a rule such as this gives it precisely the form of this rule, the form of the universality in which it can alone find its efficiency along with the actuality of recognized-being. This is why this form, this universal method, constitutes the true essence of labor as an objective essence.[89]

The objective universality of labor can also be seen in the fact that the individual does not work directly for the satisfaction of his own need but in view of the needs of all, and that it is only in this way, as "a universal labor for the needs of all," aiming at need considered a universal, that it "may satisfy his [a particular individual's] needs"[90] and, for instance, the needs of the one who performs this labor. This is why labor is not in reality what it is for the individual but what it is for all and so becomes in its being, as in its aim, a "universal."

The objective universality of labor finds its most manifest expression in the Work, which is always a common work, the work of all. In this work, it is true, each becomes external to himself and thus presents himself to himself as other than himself. But this otherness of the Work is only apparent: in it the true other—inorganic nature—is, on the contrary, annihilated, carried back to the nature of the self, produced by it. ". . . but this outward being is their deed, it is only what they have made it, it is themselves as active but superseded; and in this outwardness of themselves, in their being as superseded, as middle, they intuit themselves as one people; and this their work is their own spirit itself because it is theirs."[91]

The connection between action and objective universality must, however, be grasped in its radical origin. The latter resides neither in the instrument itself as such, nor in the universal method followed by all activity that determines itself as labor; nor is this origin to be found in the Work itself, where labor gives itself in objectivity the actuality of universal being. On the contrary, instrument, method, and work possess the meaning that they have and that they will retain in subsequent texts only inasmuch as they bear within themselves what originally links action and objectivity, inasmuch as they actualize this original tie as what makes them possible and at the same time provides their motivation. The original tie between action and objectivity resides in the very being of action understood as objectification. Action has a radical ontological meaning; it is the unfolding of being itself; what is actualized in it is not this or that, the manufacture of a given object, the production of a given content of experience; it is the arrival of the object in its object-condition; it is the production of this content in the light of being. This very light is itself produced in action. And this is why action is produced—in order that light be, in order that being be. This is why action is produced as objectification, because this light is, according to Hegel, the light of objectivity, objectivity itself as such.

It may at times seem that Hegel is speaking abstractly of action and that, failing to recognize the character peculiar to each of the various actions which together make up the course of the world, neglecting to study the specific laws that direct it, the nature of the processes that they determine, he reduces the grand interplay of society and of history to the monotonous schema of alienation and its sublation. To substitute the "essence" of action, "operating in-itself and for-itself" for the various real "practices" and for the positive analysis of their conditions, is this not pure abstraction? The fact is that Hegel has in view the *action of action*, what truly takes place in it, its primary reason and its ultimate motivation; in the flash of metaphysical vision, he realizes that *production is nothing, produces nothing, if it is not the production of being*.

How, for example, does individuality bestow effectivity upon the substance it actualizes? "For the power of the individual consists in conforming itself to that substance, i.e. in emptying itself of its own self, and thus establishing itself as the objectively existing substance."[92] This is why the action of the individual is not really his own, it is the action of action, the self-production of being in objectivity, "the development of individuality *qua* universal objective being; that is to say, it is the development of the actual world."[93] It is in the light of this ultimate ontological proposition that must be read the "self-evident" texts in which the necessity of action is monotonously reaffirmed along with its immediate interpretation as "objective action," that is, as *action which makes what it does enter into the sphere of objectivity and, in this, submits what is done to the laws of objectivity*, to its destiny in the world. Paragraph 118 of *The Philosophy of Right* states that "action is translated into external fact, and external fact has connections in the field of external necessity through which it develops itself in all directions." And §132 speaks of "an action, as its aim entering upon external objectivity. . . ." §9: " . . . its activity of translating its subjective purpose into objectivity." §113: "It is not until we come to the externalization of the moral will that we come to action." And so forth. The critique of subjective will, the radical critique that robs it of the actuality of existence so long as it does not make itself, in action and through it, identical with objectivity and its production, reaffirms, if need be, the ontological meaning of action, its "objective determination." With respect to duty, Paragraph 149 says that through it the individual "finds his liberation . . . from the indeterminate subjectivity which, never reaching reality or the objective determination of action, remains self-enclosed and devoid of actuality."

Grasped in its ontological meaning as productive of objectivity in which each thing becomes visible as object, in which each thing becomes conscious, action then allows itself to be recognized as what it is in its ultimate doing; it is the production of consciousness itself. When action allows itself to be recognized as such, when, as objectification, it is, to be more exact, the production of the object, the formation of the object, and, as a result, the view of the object that it perceives in the very act by which it forms it, then one must say: *what action does is to see*. The opposition between praxis and theory collapses in Hegelianism, where it becomes instead their very identity.

This inner structuring of action which develops as the consciousness of the object and as seeing establishes the latter at the very heart of action, freeing within it a place for thought. For thought emerges and develops within the domain of seeing, and it is properly constituted as thought when what is seen allows itself to be explicitly recognized as the objectification of mind. This situation is realized in culture, where the immediacy of nature is overcome, where the object purified in this way by the negation of its natural immediacy henceforth presents itself in the condition of universality. *In culture, the Hegelian substitution of consciousness for action is presented in a striking manner in the form of a substitution of thought for will*. A substitution such as this, which signifies nothing other than a radical falsification of praxis in its reduction to theory, becomes conscious of itself within the Hegelian problematic itself; moreover, this is what the problematic explicitly calls for in the significant text of paragraph 21, which describes the formation of culture: "The self-consciousness which purifies its object, content, and aim, and raises them to this universality *effects this as thinking getting its own way in the will*. Here is the point at which it becomes clear that *it is only as thinking intelligence that the will is genuinely a will* and free."[94]

Because action carries within itself the essence of self-consciousness, because it opens up the sphere of thought, it is not separate from the latter. In Hegelianism there is no radical distinction between the diverse modalities of existence, between action, thought, language, art, religion, law, no distinction, as is expressly stated in the text we have just cited, between the will and the intelligence. Intelligence, will, memory, etc. designate the different manners in which the process of the self-objectification of being, in which being becomes, takes place. It is for this reason that the dissociation established by the Iena manuscript between language and action has an entirely relative meaning. This dissociation occurs on the basis of a common structure, namely the establishment of stable and permanent being against the background of the abysmal power of the Night. Whether this be the name or the instrument, it is always a question of an objective being. The evolution of the doctrine will only confirm this final ontological homogeneity. In this way, the exchange of roles between language and action is explained. When action fails to produce in objectivity what it intended and when the artist, for example, is disappointed with his work, language exists to state this disappointment. To state, that is, to display in objectivity that which has not yet been able to be accomplished. Conversely, if what is claimed has to be proven by action, this is because action takes place as objectification, thereby allowing its result to be recognized and to be displayed as well in the milieu of being. This is why the dialectics of language and of action are identical and attest to the same destiny.[95]

As to the relation of action to thought, if one wishes to define it at all rigorously, then one must say: this is not, in reality, a question of a relation between two different modalities of existence, but of one and the same thing—of the objectification process in which being produces itself. Action designates this process considered in itself, whereas thought designates the fact that the production of that which is objectified is at one and the same time consciousness of an object. Production is literally the production of thought, action that which makes it possible, produces it, and which finally is thought itself. This action of thought defines the nature and the status of labor in the 1844 *Economic and Philosophical Manuscripts*. It is this action of thought, however, that is criticized in these same manuscripts, more specifically in what, according to Marx, is held to constitute the "final chapter" dedicated, in his own words, to a "critical analysis of Hegel's dialectic and of his philosophy in general." A deeply-lying contradiction permeates the 1844 *Economic and Philosophical Manuscripts;* it determines Marx's theoretical work during these decisive formative years and ends in the brutal dénouement of the "Theses on Feuerbach." What we then understand is the following:

(1) The concept of labor which is developed in the first manuscript and in the first part of the third manuscript of 1844 is the Hegelian concept of action as the action of thought. It is the activity of a consciousness which objectifies itself in a world where it is found and where it finds itself. Where it is found: the production of the object is at one and the same time its consciousness, the advent of beings to the condition of phenomena. Where it finds itself: as the objectification of the generic laws of consciousness, the object reflects back to consciousness its own image; it is the universal elaboration of the inorganic essence of nature. The final obvious result of this text from the first manuscript, in which the distinction between action and intellect is only the means of displaying their common essence, their common origin, is that the praxis which is actualized in labor is identical to consciousness, to self-consciousness, and finally to thought; it is theory. "The object of labor is therefore the objectification of the species-life of man: for man reproduces himself not only intellectually in his consciousness, but actively and actually, and *he can therefore contemplate himself* in a world he himself has created."[96] The comparison between these texts written in 1844 and the manuscript written by Hegel in Iena in 1803–1804 is therefore not foundationless. Why quote at length from *The First Philosophy of Mind* when Marx himself had not read it? Because the situation of these two texts is the same. They both represent what we have termed the incursion of German metaphysics into the economy, namely the interpretation of the essence of labor in the light of the Hegelian ontology of the self-positing of being in objectivity.

(2) The "last chapter" of the third manuscript, in which Marx at last consciously and deliberately strikes out at Hegel, unequivocally, vehemently, and repeatedly sets action apart from thought, described as "formal" and "abstract." " . . . the formal and abstract conception of man's act of self-creation or self-objectification."[97] The action of thought is formal and abstract because thought

is not capable of producing beings, of creating them. What produces beings—not, however, by creating them but by receiving them—is not the action of thought; it is intuition.

(3) Inasmuch as the action of thought is eliminated in favor of intuition, the substitution of theory for practice is not merely latent, as in Hegel, but explicit and avowed; and Marx, along the path he is laboriously following in the direction of reality, suddenly understands that he has gone astray. He understands that intuition, which claims to constitute the inner structure of being and to give it as a sensible object, is still only theory—"Feuerbach . . . only conceives of man as an object of the senses . . . he still remains in the realm of theory."[98] He understands, in the same stroke, that Hegelian action is only pseudo-action, not because it is incapable of positing beings, but because it is itself a seeing, a theory, and it is for this reason that it is, in reality, incapable of positing beings. Marx rejects both Feuerbach's intuition and Hegel's action, and he does this, not by accident, in the mere chronological coincidence of two different movements of thought, but in the unity of a single movement which reverses together sensuous intuition and the action of thought, materialism and idealism, because it reverses the single essence residing in both of them, the essence of objectification, the essence of theory.

But *how* does Marx perform this reversal? We now wish to say: what are the conceptual means at his disposal with which, setting theory aside, to introduce the essence he has in view? The philosophical materialism available to Marx at the start of the year 1845 is supplied to him by the systems of Hegel and of Feuerbach. It is, precisely, the ensemble of categories, notions, schemata, arguments, and types of arguments which he employed in the writings preceding the "Theses on Feuerbach"—in other words, the ensemble of concepts in which sensible intuition and the action of thought have themselves been conceived. This means: in order to think the absolutely new essence that he had in view, the essence of reality, Marx has no concept available to him. In this way is explained the manner in which he proceeds; in this way the text of the second sentence of the first thesis becomes clear. In order to set aside Feuerbach's intuition, which decomposes being by handing it over to the condition of object, which substitutes for living reality a universe petrified by the gaze, Marx opposes to it action, which he takes where he finds it, in Hegel to be precise, in idealism, for up until Marx idealism was the sole philosophy to have thought in terms of action, to have thought action.[99] Moreover, it is in an explicit manner, and with singular lucidity, that Marx refers to idealism in order to reduce the ontological claim of intuition, its claim to produce as objectivity an original manifestation of being. The second sentence begins thusly: "Hence, in contradistinction to materialism, the active side was developed abstractly by idealism. . . ."[100] Only, Hegelian action is not really action; it is only the production of consciousness and exhausts itself there, in *theoria*. Cited in its entirety, the second sentence reads: "Hence in contradistinction to materialism, the active side was developed abstractly by idealism[101]—which, of course, does not know real, sensuous activity as such." After having rejected Feuerbach's intuition by means of the concept of action borrowed from idealism, Marx is now preoccupied with rejecting the idealist concept of action. "But how?" we ask. *By resorting to Feuerbach's ontology.* It is in this way that in the texts we have just quoted, where Marx tries to say what real activity, unknown to idealism, is, he describes it as sensuous. This is to resort to the Feuerbachian definition of being in order to describe the real being of action. Already the first sentence, in which Marx wanted, on the contrary, to reject this Feuerbachian definition of being as sensuous being and to oppose action to it as alone constituting true being, could define the latter only with the help of the definition of being that was to be rejected. Real activity, practice, was said to be a "humano-sensuous" activity. "Human," "sensuous," in other words, the very terminology and the ontology of Feuerbach.

Setting aside Feuerbach's sensuous intuition with the help of the action of thought in idealism, rejecting the action of thought with the help of sensuous intuition, the first thesis seems to move in a circle. This circle is that of the conceptual means available to Marx, means such that each term in its fundamental inadequacy refers to the other, which is, however, itself in the same situation referring us back to the first. What this circle indicates to us in this perpetual back-and-forth reference from materialism to idealism and from idealism to materialism is their common inadequacy with respect to what is to be thought. It would thus be a decisive mistake to take seriously one of the terms between which the first thesis, in the powerless dialectic of its circular movement, ranges. Once again the categories of idealism and materialism have merely a functional significance, each serving only to disqualify the other, each, considered in itself, incapable of claiming any sort of positivity. No more than Marx's thought can be related to idealism under the pretext that its thematic field includes the problem of action,[102] can the materialist definition of this action be admitted as sensuous human action. *The recourse to Feuerbach's ontology in order to think the reality of action in opposition to the simple action of thought from the standpoint of idealism has no motive other than signifying this opposition, which in itself is pure nonsense if it is true that this ontology of intuition is precisely what Marx means to reject.* This is why the concept of *sinnlich menschliche Tätigkeit* must itself be the object of a radical critique; it signifies nothing other than the absurd maintenance of Feuerbach's terminology just when Marx explicitly assigns himself the goal of reversing Feuerbach's ontology.[103]

How could Marx have used repeatedly in the 1845–46 texts the term sensuous activity, if the being of action is heterogeneous to that of sensuousness? Heterogeneity means: analytical non-implication, contingent relation. If action is subjective, if it exhausts itself in the internal experience it has of itself, in the radically immanent feeling of effort with which it is fused, if, considered in itself, it is this lived tension of an existence caught up in the ordeal of its act of pushing, pulling, lifting, or grasping, and if, caught up in itself in this way and wholly self-occupied, performing and undergoing its effort without the slightest respite and without being able to take any distance with respect to itself, then it is blind, opaque, and takes place without the gaze of contemplation being able to lighten the burden it is for itself; and yet it is true that the fundamental possibility remains—and this is what is signified by the contingency of the relation between action and intuition—of looking at this action, of seeing it, feeling it, and, in this gaze that is now directed to it from outside, for this *theoria* contemplating it, action is sensuous action. Action is not sensuous, objective, natural in itself but only inasmuch as it is grasped in intuition, that is, as a content foreign to the power that intuits, as an objective content.

"Sensuous activity" means *praxis as it is presented to the gaze of theory. It is the mode of access to praxis inasmuch as it is no longer constituted by praxis itself, inasmuch as it takes place in the intuition, and first of all in sensuous intuition, which defines not the original and inner being of praxis but its objective appearance as empirical.* It is, as Marx says, "empirical observation"[104] which renders its object sensuous, empirical. Imagine a runner on the stadium track. As the object of intuition, as empirical, objective, sensuous, natural phenomenon, his race is there for each and every one. But the spectators look on and do nothing. It is therefore not the empirical intuition of the race, its objective appearance, that can define it and constitute its reality; it is nothing but its appearance. The reality of the race lies in the subjectivity of the person running, of the lived experience that is given to him alone and that constitutes him as an individual, as this individual who is running, as a "determined" individual, to speak as Marx does. *This is what is signified by the decisive affirmation of the first thesis, according to which practice is subjective.* Because practice is subjective, theory, which is always the theory of an object, cannot reach the reality of this practice, what it is in-itself and for-itself, precisely its subjectivity, but can only represent this to itself in such a way that this representation necessarily leaves outside itself the real being of practice, the actuality of doing. Theory does nothing.

The dissociation of theory and practice does not lead to their sheer opposition; instead it receives its most radical formulation in the founding tie that unites them. By virtue of this decisive tie it appears that the world offered to the gaze of theory does not proceed from it; the object of intuition is not its own but, on the contrary, finds its origin in praxis itself. It is first of all in this sense that praxis founds theory: by providing it with the content it displays in intuition. This foundation is realized in two different ways. In the first place, the object of intuition considered as a natural determination is precisely not a determination of nature but a determination of praxis, from which it takes its predicates. "Even when the sensuous world is reduced to a minimum, to a stick as with Saint Bruno, it presupposes the action of producing this stick."[105] But Bauer is quickly dismissed in *The German Ideology;* it is especially in opposition to Feuerbach that the dependence of the sensuous world as a whole is affirmed with respect to praxis, and this is the case because it is precisely the seeing of intuition that is in question. It is because "Feuerbach's 'conception' of the sensuous world is confined . . . to mere contemplation of it . . ."[106] that Marx takes intuitive materialism as the target of his critique, affirming that the sensuous world that seems to be the correlate of intuition and to be defined as such, as that which is seen, is, despite this appearance, nothing of the sort but simply the product of praxis, of what Marx calls industry, commerce, history. ". . . and so it happens that in Manchester, for instance, Feuerbach sees only factories and machines, where a hundred years ago only spinning-wheels and weaving-looms were to be seen, or in the Campagna di Roma he finds only pasture lands and swamps, where in the time of Augustus he would have found nothing but the vineyards and villas of Roman capitalists."[107] Thus, the aspect of the world, which is related to seeing, is not related to it. Nevertheless, it is not only this immediate view of the world, its immediate and naïve perception, it is science itself and, consequently, theory in all its forms that finds its ground in praxis and reveals itself to be fundamentally determined by it. "Feuerbach speaks in particular of the perception of natural science; he mentions secrets which are disclosed only to the eye of the physicist and chemist; but where would natural science be without industry and commerce? Even this 'pure' natural science is provided with an aim, as with its material, only through trade and industry, through the sensuous activity of men."[108]

The determination of theory does not consist solely in the fact that what is seen is not the result of seeing and does not find in it, in the nature and forms of sight, in the structure of theory itself, the principle of its nature, of its forms and its own peculiar structure, a principle which lies, on the contrary, in praxis. Or rather, it is the very peculiar manner in which the content of intuition now originates in praxis that determines the second mode in accordance with which the foundation of theory is realized. The "natural" object is here no longer the product of human activity, of "commerce" and industry, is no longer a nature henceforth transformed so that "pure" nature no longer exists: there is no nature in any sense at all, no natural object however much it may be mediated by praxis, but instead it is praxis, human activity itself, that constitutes the "object" of intuitive vision. Feuerbach's mistake was precisely to have failed to understand that the object of intuition is finally nothing other than praxis, that what this intuition proposes to us as a world and under the sensuous appearance of this world, are in reality the numerous activities of individuals. "Thus he [Feuerbach] never manages to conceive the sensuous world as the total living, sensuous activity of the individuals composing it. . . ."[109] And again: ". . . he only conceives of him [man] as an 'object of the senses', not as 'sensuous activity'. . . ."[110] Because the substance, the reality, the essence, the inner nature of that which is given in intuition as the "sensuous world" is the substance, the reality, the essence of praxis, then the latter, because it constitutes the true being of the world and of that which gives itself to us as such, actually founds it, founds the sensuous world in a radical manner as the very thing that it unfolds as a world, that it represents and without which it would represent nothing, as that which exists in it and without which nothing would be.[111]

In designating praxis as the ground of being, the "Theses on Feuerbach" discover at the same time the original place of truth. It is trifling to say that a true thought, one which grasps hold of objective truth, recognizes the primacy of practice over theory, the anteriority of being to the gaze that is directed to it. In a thought such as this, theory is situated in its proper place and attains the truth about itself. Truth is then still the province of theory, when it is asked to shine light on what exists before it. Moreover, this is the truth of Feuerbach; it is the truth of intuition understood in its fundamental receptivity. The fact that the being received and illuminated in this reception is no longer that of the brute beings of "pure" nature but praxis changes nothing regarding the nature of this illumination, regarding the essence of truth. Radically opposed to the truth which finds its essence in theory, and which is still only the gaze cast on the enigmatic being of praxis, is a new truth which is no longer the truth of thought, of self-consciousness, or of sensuousness but which lies in praxis itself as such. Henceforth, it is not a theoretical proposition that can enlighten us and, through its transcendental meaning, bear a truthful witness to being, give a statement capable of saying what is. The power of revelation belongs henceforth and exclusively to doing; only he who does something knows, by this doing and in it, what being is about—being, which is this very doing. If a theoretical proposition persists in its claim to express truth, this is in a very peculiar way, insofar as this proposition no longer contains the truth and no longer gives it to be "seen" in itself, but indicates outside of itself and as the absolute other in relation to itself the place in which this truth is realized, refers to this realization which it has nothing to do with except to summon it and to invoke it. *In a radical ontology of praxis, theory ultimately assumes the form of a prescription.*

This is the case with respect to religions, which can be reduced to a theology,[112] that is, to a theory of being, only at the cost of an absolute misunderstanding—such as Feuerbach's, for instance. On the contrary, what characterizes religious saying is the way in which the theoretical content dies out and the commandment abruptly surges forth. "Abruptly" signifies precisely: in the absence of any theoretical context. This, again, is why the religious saying is offered as a naked utterance, an isolated proposition that begins with such and such a word and ends with such and such a different word, and that must be taken as it is. The religious saying resounds from the heavens, erasing the objective universe, arising in doubtful or uncertain circumstances. When the world and its connections are placed out of bounds in this way, who speaks? Is it a man, a prophet, or an angel? Is it Moses or Christ? The word that is heard, the text of the Tablets, the law that is promulgated and bestowed are, in any event, given as absolute, as the divine word. Absolute, divine, the word is bound to nothing, has no extrinsic justification. Does this justification lie in the word itself? But how could an isolated proposition draw a theoretical legitimation from this isolation, which always consists in analytical implication and refers back to the open chain of foundations and final principles? *Or instead might not the legitimation lie outside of theory: in practice?* Practice and it alone, because it constitutes the original dimension of being, can reveal in itself and in the actuality of its doing what being is about. In prescription, theory says its last word, it negates itself and leads outside itself to a being that it summons, invokes, and does not contain. This is why the claim that was made by Husserl to reduce all normative science to a theoretical science manifests the very illusion of theory.[113] Of course, every normative proposition can be converted into a corresponding theoretical proposition, and instead of saying "a warrior must be brave," one can always write "only a brave warrior is a good warrior," or another similar statement. By closing itself up inside of itself, however, theory loses, when it no longer takes the form of normativity, the only tie it can maintain with the original truth of being. Because normativity—when it is not reduced, as Husserl precisely will do, to the apodicticity of the principles of reason—expresses, on the contrary, the decisive limitations of theory; as Idea, it continues to have the value of an ontological index. This is also why the critique of moralism is neither as simple nor as obvious as it seems. This critique forms, as we know, one of the major themes of Hegelianism and we find it again "as is" in Marxism. And in the young Marx too, inasmuch as he is still Hegelian.[114] But if the ethical imperative is vain so long as it leaves reality unchanged and remains itself no more than an empty wish, it at least indicates as a simple proposition at the very heart of theory that the place of reality is not to be found here. Inasmuch as the normative principle is indeed presented as a prescription, inasmuch as it is addressed to a doing, it signifies that the place of reality which transcends all theory is precisely that of praxis. "One must" means "one must *do*" this or that.[115] "One must" is then no longer the empty word floating in the air, mistaking reality and making way for knowledge; it is the essential word which, on the contrary, by challenging knowledge as the way of reaching being, refers us back to being in accordance with the way in which this referring back and this access can be realized, in accordance with the fundamental mode of praxis. The critique of moralism in Marx turns out to be the critique of theory, of thought, allowing the "one must" to subsist and, what is more, it is formulated within this principle. After having been directed at German philosophy of the first half of the nineteenth century, the eleventh thesis gives us its decisive meaning, the essential connection between prescription and praxis. It tells us that philosophers have only interpreted the world in various ways and that *what one must now do* is to change it.

The fact that the original essence of being—and that of truth along with it—lies in praxis, that every true, objective thought—that is to say, thought capable of referring itself to being and of recognizing the place of truth—must recognize at the same time its fundamental incapacity to constitute by itself this place and this original essence of being and of truth, the necessity in which it finds itself to appeal to something other than itself, other than theory, its referential nature, the expression of this essential reference in the "one must" of prescription—all this is contained in the exceedingly dense text of the second thesis, in which the reversal performed by Marx is concentrated, in the ultimate ontological reversal of theory in practice: "The question whether objective truth can be attributed to human thinking is not a question of theory but is a practical question. Man *must* prove the truth, i.e. the reality and power, the this-sidedness of his thinking in practice. The dispute over the reality or non-reality of thinking that is isolated from practice is a purely scholastic question."[116]

The fundamental reference of theory to practice, against the background of their essential difference, opens up the place in which ideology resides and makes the latter possible.

Chapter 5

THE PLACE OF IDEOLOGY

The ontological dimension of irreality

The German Ideology is based entirely on the opposition between reality and representation. At the end of the extraordinary philosophical itinerary that Marx has covered in the three years previous, this opposition takes on a rigorous sense; it is the opposition between praxis and theory. Praxis designates the internal structure of action as it excludes from itself the objectification process, all distancing, all transcendence in general. What is held to be real, consequently, will be whatever excludes from itself this distancing, whatever is subjective in a radically immanent sense, whatever experiences itself immediately without being able to separate itself from itself, to take the slightest distance with regard to itself, in short, whatever cannot be represented or understood in any way at all. What is real, therefore, is need, hunger, suffering, labor too—everything that consists in this inner and insurmountable experience of the self. To the radical immanence of this subjectivity, which now constitutes reality for him, Marx gave the name appropriate to it: life.

The concept of "representation," however, is ambiguous; it includes two different meanings: first of all, to present in the sense of making present, of giving in person. When Kant says that space is a representation, he does not mean that it is the mere appearance of another space that would have its essence elsewhere; it is the being of space itself that is displayed in spatial representation.[1] Representation understood in this way has an ontological value; it offers us being itself in such a way that this being is a "represented" being, that is it is presented in exteriority, as ob-ject.

By "representation" is also meant a "mere representation," that is, a presentation which is no longer that of the thing itself but a mere copy, its tracing, its image, its idea, something that stands for it, indicates it, and reflects it but that is not that thing, something that merely "represents" it. The modalities of "mere representation" are numerous: image, concept, sign, word, index, symptom, trace, etc. The mere representation of a thing can resemble it more or less, but however faithful it may be, an essential discontinuity breaks the tie linking the image to its object: to the reality of the thing is opposed the irreality of its representation.

Ideology is the whole of the representations of human consciousness in the sense

160

of mere representations—the whole of the images, memories, ideas, notions, arguments and types of arguments, categories, and theoretical or practical schemata that this consciousness is capable of forming. *The place of ideology is the ontological dimension of irreality to which every mere representation belongs as such, a dimension which confers upon it its own peculiar status.* What makes ideology what it is, what determines it *a priori* as "mere ideology," as "pure ideology," is thus not the share of inexactness or approximateness that inheres in its representations; it is not their provisional character, their lack of theoretical elaboration (in the case of concepts), their only partial correspondence with the real object (in the case of images or memories); it is the irreality belonging to such representations by their very nature, a characteristic which defines their being. This is why the claim to establish a radical opposition between ideology on the one hand and "science" on the other is meaningless. Science is part of ideology not by reason of its provisional incompleteness but because by its very nature it is located within the milieu of ideality, which is a milieu of irreality. Thus, one would search in vain in *The German Ideology* for this alleged opposition between ideology and science.

As long as Marx remained Feuerbachian and understood reality as sensuous reality, sensuous representation had the meaning of reaching this reality in itself; images, dreams, religion were its "mere representations." But when reality is defined by praxis, *the ontological meaning of original representation, of the representation which presents being as an object and which in this presentation gives it as it is in itself, is lost.* The representation of individual activity as sensuous activity, the representation of life as an objective given, is its mere representation. When, in the definition of reality, life is substituted for sensuous being, the essential distinction upon which Feuerbach's entire problematic and the 1844 *Economic and Philosophical Manuscripts* are based, the distinction between the real thing and the thing in thought is itself abolished. The significance of this reduction of representation to a mere representation must be reflected upon, for it gives us the key concept to the whole Marxian interpretation of ideology. *The representation which reveals itself to be unequal to its ontological claim, which, as it gives us external being, cannot give us being but is only a mere representation of it, this representation is "consciousness."*

The ontological unequalness of consciousness to being is the constant theme of *The German Ideology*; it is asserted in an essential proposition, which attempts to read from the very structure of the German word—*Bewusstsein*—the condition of being, the insurmountable division that occurs between what it is in itself and its conscious representation: "consciousness can never be anything else than conscious being." *"Das Bewusstsein kann nie etwas Andres sein als das bewusste Sein."*[2] What real being is in its opposition to its conscious representation is stated directly thereafter: "and the existence of men is their actual life-process." Here we find abruptly excluded the possibility of granting a radical ontological meaning to the knowledge which is identified by Marx with consciousness, the possibility for this consciousness to constitute the very experience of being and its true givenness as a givenness that offers it as it is in itself. The unequalness of consciousness to being is neither provisional nor capable of being overcome at the end of a progressive development which would be that of consciousness. Because being is life, the immediate internal experience of the self excluding all transcendence, all representation, it in fact cannot give itself in the exteriority of represented being. It is because consciousness is, nevertheless, understood as this representation and is identified with it that it is unable, precisely, to give us being, that it is, as representation, its mere representation.

The fact that consciousness is understood by Marx as representation and, as a result, as mere representation with respect to original reality, the fact that consciousness is, consequently, defined and expressed in the mode of mere representation, in conceptions, ideas, and notions, is what is stated in the following texts: ". . . ideas, views, and conceptions, in one word, man's consciousness. . . ."[3] "The production of ideas, of conceptions, of consciousness. . . ."[4] Consciousness as it is understood by Marx therefore has nothing to do with the original lived experience which constitutes the essence of life and which belongs to it in its very principle, belonging thus to need, to work, to suffering and, generally speaking, to "practice." Far from being able to be identified with the reality of this immanent subjectivity which constitutes the inner being of all that lives, making it in every instance an individual, "consciousness" is instead opposed to it in this opposition which is representation itself; consciousness represents it in such a way that this representation necessarily allows the living interiority of life to escape it. The "consciousness" of an individual is therefore not his life but the way in which he represents it, the idea he has of it, the meaning he gives it. The Preface to *A Contribution to the Critique of Political Economy* states, "Just as one does not judge an individual by what he thinks about himself, so one cannot judge a period . . . by its consciousness."[5] The fact that consciousness designates not the immediate existence of the individual but the way in which the latter understands the world in which he lives and, as a result, understands himself, that far from being identified with this real existence and being able to define it, consciousness is nothing but a manner of representing it and of interpreting it, so that a modification of consciousness does not signify a modification of existence but only of the interpretation by means of which it is recognized—this is what Marx states textually: "This demand to change consciousness amounts to a demand to interpret the existing world in a different way, i.e. to recognize it by means of a different interpretation."[6]

Let us add that this meaning of the concept of consciousness is found throughout Marx's entire work, where it continues unchanged. "Consciousness" always means "to be conscious of," to represent to oneself, to think, to judge, to realize, to become aware of. In every instance the illusory character of this sort of consciousness consists not in its particular content but in the fact that, as a mere representation of reality, it allows reality to escape and to slip away from it without being able to change anything about its real being. To the extent that ideology belongs within the sphere of consciousness, its critique consists in making its powerlessness apparent. This critique is thus initially presented as a mere repetition of the critique of the action of thought developed in the last chapter of the third 1844 manuscript. Except for the fact that, on the one hand, the critique is no longer levelled at Hegel but at Bauer and Stirner and that, on the other hand, the criterion of reality is no longer supplied by the sensuous object but by living praxis. The decisive moment in ideology consists in substituting for the reality of this vital praxis its conscious representation; this is the transposition by which ideology places reality under its dominion by making it of the same nature as itself. Indeed, as soon as reality is composed of representations, any modification of these representations is *ipso facto* a modification of reality. The action of thought is henceforth possible since it now carries the meaning of concerning reality, hence an ontological meaning which it, precisely, does not have. Marx's critique of ideology at this stage is twofold: it is first directed at exposing this substitution, this transposition, considered the mystification by which all ideology begins. Second, it consists in showing that once this substitution is made, the effect one expects from it is purely illusory, because a modification of the conception one has of reality in no way changes the latter. The mystification of ideology is thus to claim to bridge the ontological gap separating reality and irreality, to begin by reducing the first to the second in order then to try to move from the second to the first.

The critique directed at Stirner takes up these themes once again, denouncing first of all the dissolution of reality in the play of representations. It is in this way, according to Stirner, who is awkwardly copying Hegel, that history is the history of the Ancients and the Moderns. The Ancients are those who *represent to themselves*, who interpret the external world as real being, and who understand themselves as participating in this world, drawing from it their reality and their truth. With Socrates and Christianity the representation that man has of himself and of the world changes completely. Man discovers himself and thinks of himself as a spirit; he understands that truth lies in this spirit, consequently in himself, and in the same stroke he considers the world to be nothing. "The person who considers himself a free spirit is neither oppressed nor tormented by the things of this world because he has no esteem for the world."[7] What follows an understanding of the world as essential and of the individual as unessential is therefore a new way of representing the world to oneself, of thinking of it and of judging it—"no longer holding it in esteem"—and this new modality of the existential understanding of the world is only one aspect of the new understanding of oneself that is dawning, an understanding by means of which man is to represent himself and to understand himself as "spirit."

But, and here Stirner's history differs from Hegel's and is turned against the latter and against Feuerbach, the understanding of oneself as "spirit" is inaccurate; it initiates a new form of alienation replacing that from which it claims to free us. The Christian, modern man, has only substituted for the domination of the external world that of the spirit in all its forms—religious, philosophical, moral, juridical, etc.—and this sacralization of the world—henceforth called "the holy"—occurs at the expense of the individual. What motivates Stirner's entire problematic and gives it its radical cast is the rejection of these spiritual powers, the rejection of all reality transcending the individual.

Yet how is the individual to rid himself of all these transcendences in order to be able, finally, to be himself, to be able to be Unique? But, first of all, how are these formed? By an action of consciousness, by the action of thought: in both cases the reply is the same. The individual lives in the presence of a spiritual world that is sacred and holy to him only inasmuch as he considers it to be so, inasmuch as he represents it to himself in terms of these characteristics, characteristics that have their origin in this representation, that are created by it. It is human consciousness which makes the gods, law, and right and which determines that freedom is holy and that everything, including the individual, has to be sacrificed to it. *The "Holy" is the product of a givenness of sense which takes place in consciousness understood as the radical origin of this sense*. The "Holy" in all its forms exists only through the attitude I have with respect to it, by the Respect I show to it, by the submission I attest to in its regard. Before Sartre, who declares that "it is always I who will decide that this voice is the voice of an angel,"[8] in the same way, Stirner affirms: "And yet nothing in itself is sacred but only because I have declared it to be sacred; it is so due to the sentence, the judgment I make, due to my genuflections, finally due to my consciousness."[9] Thus Stirner *attributes to consciousness, to the way in which it represents things to itself, the power of deciding what is sacred, of establishing the "holy" in and through this very representation*. However, what consciousness has made, it can unmake. In order to free oneself from the holy and to abolish it, it is not enough to cease to consider it as such, to cease to venerate God, to cease to respect right or morality, to cease to serve freedom but at the most to make use of it. When this act of consciousness which constitutes the holy by considering to be such ceases, the holy is no more than an empty shell, what Stirner calls a ghost: "The entire spiritual universe is only a ghostly universe once I withdraw my consideration from it."[10]

Property too depends solely upon the way in which I represent the object to myself. By ceasing to consider it as different from myself, as foreign, in order to hold it, on the contrary, to be "mine," it thereby becomes mine by this very gesture. This is what Stirner calls "ideological appropriation," which, it must be noted, *rests on the structure of representation with which it is identical*. It is precisely because the being given in consciousness's representation is an object that it is something foreign and possibly even holy, but as this representation of consciousness is inevitably its own, it is not simply an object but its object, its property, consequently, and something it "uses": ". . . since every object for the 'ego' is not only *my* object, but also my *object*, it is possible, with the same indifference towards the content, to declare that every object is not-my-own, alien, holy. One and the same object and one and the same relation can, therefore, with equal ease and with equal success be declared to be the holy and my property. Everything depends on whether stress is laid on the word '*my*' or on the word '*object.*' The methods of appropriation and canonisation are merely two different 'refractions' of one 'transformation.' "[11]

Just how foreign reality is to this play of representations can be clearly seen if one returns for a moment to the universe of real praxis, where individuals are acting to produce their life. They are caught in a web of relations dictated by their need, relations that are, to begin with, those of the family and of labor. Marx then makes the crucial distinction between, on the one hand, the relation between consciousness and its own representations, representations which depend upon it and which it can modify as it wills, and, on the other hand, the relation between life and its immanent determinations, which are precisely its need and the activity to satisfy this need, relations which are no longer within the power of consciousness and to which the latter can no more than attest. The critique of Stirner is summed up in this text in which Marx denounces "the transformation of real collisions, i.e., collisions between individuals and their actual conditions of life, into ideal collisions, i.e., into collisions between these individuals and the ideas which they form or get into their heads."[12] As a consequence of this substitution of ideal conflicts for real conflicts there results, on the one hand, the illusion that the latter result from the former, and, on the other hand, the belief that by abandoning or by modifying the relation of consciousness to its representation one eliminates at the same time the relation between life and its own determinations. Now this substitution of consciousness for life is not true only for ideologues; every man, to the extent that he represents his own life to himself, makes this substitution in his turn and believes that his behavior depends in the final analysis upon the way in which he represents things to himself—just as jurists imagine, for example, that all of the practical relations of a society obey the ideal determinations of law and its concepts.

One will grasp the full extent of the critique initiated here by Marx if one considers a problem as general as that of the concrete relation of individuals among themselves. *The interpretation of this relation as a relation between consciousnesses, its questioning by the problematic of classical philosophy under the title of the "problem of communication between consciousnesses," is ideological in its very principle*. What is actually involved when the relation between individuals is reduced to the communication of consciousnesses? What is involved is the way in which one individual represents another to himself, the way in which he represents the representation that the other has of him and, consequently, the way in which he represents the relation that is established between them, a relation which exhausts itself in this play of representations. If it happens in this dialectic of "consciousnesses" that the representation which the other forms of him does not suit the first individual, does not seem to him to conform to what he is, *what he is* means what he is for his own consciousness, the way he understands himself. The individual understands himself as a consciousness, but for the other he is only a living thing. It is therefore necessary for him to bring the other to consider him as a consciousness, so that what he is for the other resembles what he is for himself. For the other means in the other's representation. For himself, *"pour soi,"* means in his own representation. The struggle that is engaged between consciousnesses can well be a real struggle, and the individual can well risk his life to show that he is something other than a living thing. *This means that the struggle shifts to another level, that it is situated, precisely, on the level of life, of living and acting individuals who actually combat with their hands and their bodies.* "The spiritual combat is as violent as the battle of men": the first, however, has ceded its place to the second. The dialogue of consciousnesses dons the serious and tragic character in which it is garbed only inasmuch as this essential displacement is accomplished surreptitiously, a displacement which *involves existence* and by virtue of which the struggle is now placed on the plane of reality and no longer on that of representation, on the plane of practice and no longer on that of theory.

The Hegelian dialectic which includes this displacement and which recognizes it as the place of proof, misunderstands it, however, and immediately falsifies its sense. *It is not life which explains the struggle of the living; neither the origin of this struggle nor its end lies within it itself, in its own modalities, in its needs.* It is the play of the representations of consciousness which motivates it as an inevitable though contingent mediation, and the outcome of the struggle is only to establish the adequation of these representations, the adequation of the representation of the other to my own. To say that I am the Master means: that the other considers me as such, that a representation emerges in his consciousness which represents me as a consciousness, as what I am for myself. My Master's being, my Mastery, is due solely to this representation he has of me and will collapse when it collapses. Moreover, this representation that he has of me and that makes me the master has this meaning and this power only *inasmuch as I represent this representation of the other to myself as making me and as capable of making me the master, inasmuch as I bestow this meaning upon it.* For if I cease to bestow this meaning upon it, if I represent to myself as null and void the representation he has of me, if I take all importance away from it in my consciousness and through it, then indeed the system falls apart. I am no longer the master either because the other ceases to consider me as such, or because I cease to consider the representation he has of me to be valid. In all instances, it is the representation of consciousness that creates mastery and servitude, and this is why this dialectic, this struggle, is in fact a struggle of consciousnesses and, more than this, *a struggle whose telos is consciousness itself. For it is precisely the definition of the individual as consciousness, as power of representation, as a totality composed of singularities, that is at stake in the struggle and that the struggle attempts to establish.*

But this is not all. The representation of consciousness not only gives me the representation that the other has of me; *it determines it.* One must not say simply: I represent to myself that the other represents my being to himself not as that of a living thing but as a consciousness, that he understands me as being his master. *It is because I represent the other to myself, because I make him the object of my representation, that he is precisely nothing but an object, my object, the object of which I am the subject; it is for this reason, as a result of my representation, that, being no more than my object, he can actually represent himself as such and understand me, in the same stroke, as a consciousness and as his Master.*

We know that in Sartre this dialectic became that of the "gaze," which possesses the extraordinary property of transforming the inner being of the other and of reducing it to the object-condition. This is a particularly noteworthy example of what Marx denounced as the "ideological appropriation" of Stirner, who, precisely, applied this appropriation to the problem of others. And Marx's critique, untiringly repeating that a modification in consciousness cannot signify a modification in reality, denounces as illusory my alleged action on the other inasmuch as it consists in a way of considering him, in a modification in my "point of view" with regard to him. "Every other person in his sphere of action, too, is his object, and 'as his object—his property', his creature. Each ego says to the other: 'For me you are only what you are for me . . . namely, my object and, because my object, my property'. Hence also my creature, which at any moment as creator I can swallow up and take back into myself. Thus, each ego regards the other not as a property-owner, but as his property; not as 'ego' but as being-for-him [*als Sein-für-Ihn*], as object; not as belonging to himself, but as belonging to him, to another, as alienated from himself."[13] Stirner's entire problematic is thus reduced to the simple variation of "viewpoints" *(Ansehen)*, that is, to the various ways of understanding, of interpreting things. But it is not just Stirner's type of history, it is the entire Hegelian history of consciousness that is struck to the very quick by Marx, if a history such as this indeed consists in the succession of representations in which consciousness refers to the real, if it is the history of *what is for consciousness*, for it *(für es)*, that is, for natural consciousness deceived by its direct knowledge of beings, for us *(für uns)*, as philosophers who know the truth, for it *(für sich)*, finally, when it has reached true knowledge, when what is for it coincides with what is for us.

To what extent this ideological history of consciousness differs from real history and can neither explain it nor *a fortiori* be substituted for it and serve as its ground, can easily be seen as soon as, with Marx, one casts a glance at real life. What is then given to our understanding is that *the determinations of life are always explained on the basis of life*. It is not the struggle to the death of consciousnesses trying to obtain recognition which accounts for the forming of couples, the forming of families, the forming of society or their history; it is instead the transparence of need and the subjectivity of bodies.

The genealogy of ideas and the ideological concept of ideology

The opposition of reality to representation as the radical opposition of reality to irreality is overdetermined in *The German Ideology* by another no less essential thesis, which can be stated as follows: *reality is not only opposed to repre-*

sentation, it grounds it. The grounding of representation in reality can be understood in two ways. On the one hand, it is reality that is represented in representation and that bestows its content upon it. It is in this sense that in the "Theses on Feuerbach" practice grounds theory. *The German Ideology* takes up this assertion once again in a decisive proposition which we already cited when we were attempting to provide an initial framework for the status of consciousness: "Consciousness can never be anything else than conscious existence." Existence, that is to say, the practical living process of individuals—such is the content of this representation which is consciousness itself.

But—and this is what is important to us now—consciousness is not an autonomous representation of reality, an absolute representation, so to speak, its exact reproduction or its certified copy.[14] The way in which consciousness represents living being is something that does not depend upon it. Upon what, then, does the way in which consciousness represents life depend? What determines this consciousness? Marx's reply strikes like a bolt of lightning: it is life itself. "It is not consciousness that determines life, but life that determines consciousness." "Nicht das Bewusstsein bestimmt das Leben, sondern das Leben bestimmt das Bewusstsein."[15] Such is the second modality in which representation is grounded in reality. Grounding representation no longer means simply supplying it with the content it displays, determining this content, but rather determining the way in which it displays the content, the way in which it unveils it or, possibly, veils it. The determination of theory by praxis here comports a rigorous meaning since it is sight itself as such that receives the law of its development from practice. Consequently, not just the content of theory but theory itself, in the positive or negative modalities of its realization, have their ground in praxis and are determined by it.

Thus, the illusion of ideology is twofold. It does not consist simply in substituting for what is real the whole of the ideal productions of consciousness, in believing, for example, that history is the history of these productions, the history of ideas, of right, of morality, of science, etc. So that this ideological history, *the history of ideology*, comes to mask real history, the history of the production of material goods and the history of individuals, which are thoroughly intermingled. The illusion of ideology is to continue to posit this set of representations as an autonomous totality possessing its own authority and stability, drawing from it the laws of its development. Whereas, if representations are grounded, the question which arises is necessarily that of the origin of all the ideas that constitute the field of ideology, as an origin external to this field, foreign to ideology itself. This origin lies in reality. "The production of ideas, of conceptions, of consciousness, is at first directly interwoven with the material activity and the material intercourse of men, the language of real life. Conceiving, thinking, the mental intercourse of men at this stage still appear as the direct efflux of their material behaviour. The same applies to mental production as expressed in the language of the politics, laws, morality, religion, metaphysics, etc., of a people."[16] Numerous other examples could also be cited.

But how can the real produce an idea? When reality is divided into consciousness, on the one hand, and objective being, on the other, into "mind" and "nature," and exhausts itself in these, to what indeed can ideas be connected when they are no longer posited in their alleged independence, when the hypostasis of the intelligible, which in fact renders it unintelligible, ceases? To consciousness? Referred to consciousness, that is, to the form of representation in general, the representations are described, precisely, in their formal structure and not explained in their specificity. The thought that refers representations back to consciousness is locked up inside a tautology: to say that representations are the representations of consciousness is to say that they are representations. Consciousness forms its representations, but why does it form this one rather than that one?

Consequently, the origin of the content of ideology as a content that is in every instance specifically determined is to be sought in the actual state of things. It is the economic and social structure of a society that founds the political, juridical, philosophical, etc. "superstructure" and wholly determines it. Unfortunately, no one has yet explained how a state of things, whether it be that of the forces of production or of social formations, how an objective structure and, in a word, a fact could be capable of producing an idea. The genealogy becomes aberrant or rather it ceases to be possible when the origin it ascribes to the ideal productions of ideology is understood as a third-person determination, as an opaque element lacking any meaning in itself and, *a fortiori*, lacking any power to constitute a meaning. It is to Engels that we owe the basic misinterpretation according to which reality was supposed to have been defined by Marx as matter. It is therefore matter that is responsible for producing ideas, and it does so through the intermediary of the "brain," for in the fantastic constructions of mythologies, when it is a question of reducing one or the other of these irreducible terms, there is always a magical mixture which takes on this function and which is posited as the union of incompatibles. Totally failing to recognize Marx's reversal of Feuerbach's intuitive materialism, Engels relies upon the latter and borrows from him the idea "that the material, sensuously perceptible world to which we ourselves belong is the only reality; and that our consciousness and thinking, however suprasensuous they may seem, are the product of a material, bodily organ, the brain. Matter is not a product of mind, but mind itself is merely the highest product of matter."[17]

Materialism—this simplistic reversal of the external relation of "matter" and of "mind"—is in fact totally absent from *The German Ideology*, as from Marx's work in general. In Marx, "material" does not designate matter, the object of physics, but the real life of individuals, and it is only because reality is understood in this way as life, and not as "matter," that the production of ideas on the basis of reality and through it is something besides nonsense. The ontological interpretation of reality as the subjective essence of praxis alone makes the very idea of ideology possible, that is to say, a genealogy of ideas. This interpretation has to be carried further still if the very concept of subjectivity is to be divided and the problematic to reach the crucial opposition between subjectivity, as it is understood in the very same way by both idealism and materialism—that is, as consciousness itself, as representation, as theory—and original subjectivity, which signifies the radical immanence of life, heterogeneous with respect to all representation and which Marx conceived of in terms of the concept of praxis. Only on this condition is the problematic of the genealogy able to escape both the absurdity of materialism and the tautology of idealism. To escape the tautology of idealism, which claims to deduce representations one from another. To escape the absurdity of materialism, which claims to deduce them from matter.

The crucial opposition between representative subjectivity and immanent life is not only the explicit content of the "Theses on Feuerbach"; it determines the problematic of *The German Ideology*. This is why the reduction which continually occurs there and in which the genealogy properly consists is never the reduction of conscious representation to matter nor to some sort of objective state of things; it is the reduction of this consciousness to life, to real and active individuals. "Men are the producers of their conceptions, ideas, etc.—real, active men."[18] However, is it not consciousness and it alone that can produce representations, if it is the very structure of representation? But the representations *which are consciousness* are not ultimately determined by it; they borrow their structure, not their content, from it. Their content is explained only by the life of the individuals of which they are the consciousness. In this way we see that what Marx criticizes is the *separation of consciousness from the individual life that determines it: "This entire separation of consciousness from the individuals* who are its basis. . . ."[19] We have seen, moreover, with Marx "how a theory and history of pure thought could arise among philosophers *owing to the separation of ideas from the individuals. . . ."*[20] What Stirner was reproached with was having "made the thoughts of individuals into something existing independently,"[21] whereas they can be explained only in terms of the latter. The meaning of the concept of ideology is set before us: a set of representations rooted in life, which is its "expression," its "language." Ideology means genealogy, but genealogy refers to a sphere of personal experience, to the mode of concrete life of an individual, which is the origin and the true determining factor of his representations. If it happens that these form a system, it is not their intrinsic content that motivates their ideal unity; it is the unity of real experience in which they are rooted, the unity of the original phenomenological system which secretly nourishes them and holds them before itself as long as they are adequate to it, that is to say, as long as they answer its need.

This is why it is incorrect to oppose, purely and simply, ideology to reality. Once this opposition is understood in its rigorous ontological meaning as the opposition of the real to the irreal, an essential continuity is established between an individual and what he represents to himself, and this continuity is that of his very life, of what he is, of what he imagines, what he dreams and what he thinks. Speaking of the individual's thinking, Marx says: "From the outset it is always a factor in the total life of the individual, one which disappears and is reproduced as required."[22] The immediate context presents this thinking of the individual as one manifestation of his life among others: ". . . when the individual passes from thought to some other manifestation of life." Taking as a backdrop the inherence of thought within the original phenomenological flow of individual life, every determination of this life is *ipso facto* a determination of this thought. "In the case of an individual, for example, whose life embraces a wide circle of varied activities and practical relations to the world, and who, therefore, lives a many-sided life, thought has the same character of universality as every other manifestation of his life."[23] The same is true for its "narrowness." So that every profound modification of this thought can, in the final analysis, be only a modification of this very life.[24]

The reality that is placed at the origin of ideology is most often designated in *The German Ideology* by the pair "the individual and conditions,"[25] be they social, economic, or world conditions. One should not forget, however, that social and economic conditions are nothing else than the determinations of individual life: "men, developing their material production and their material intercourse, alter, *along with this their actual world* [*mit dieser ihrer Wirklichkeit*], also their thinking, and the products of their thinking."[26] Because individuals constitute, in reality, the substance of these conditions, because what define the economic and social determinations are the determinations of their life, their determinations, because there is, for example, a genealogy of the classes, the foundational relation of ideology does not proceed from classes or from the conditions of production to ideas; it originates in what founds these classes and these conditions. *A single origin, a single creative principle* (naturans) *produces the conditions of production, the classes and ideas*. Naturally, the genealogy of the classes does not coincide with that of ideology. The production of socioeconomic conditions is immediate and takes place on the level of immanent life; the determinations of individuals at work *are* these conditions. The production of ideology by these same individuals implies the mediation of representation; it is this representation, their "consciousness." But *the genealogy of these conditions renders the genealogy of ideology possible*. By moving back from the classes and the conditions of production to their original subjective reality, this genealogy shows that its determination of ideology loses its apparent absurdity. It is because the ultimate creative principle *(naturans)* which produces classes and production itself is life that it can also produce ideas. What is more, the specific modes of life constituting production and defining these social conditions are the very ones that produce ideas; and the relation that exists between a class and an ideology is displayed in its *a priori* possibility in the identity of the creative principle which produces them both. The essential connection between the genealogy of socioeconomic conditions and the genealogy of ideology, the no less essential relation that is established between a type of production, a class, and an ideology, as a relation grounded in their common creative principle, the essential possibility of the genealogy of ideology and of ideology itself as grounded in this creative principle *(naturans)*, which, as living subjectivity, is capable precisely of producing this ideology and of grounding it, all of this is contained in a crucial text of *The Poverty of Philosophy*. After recalling the dependence of social relations upon the mode of production and after defining the latter in terms of the subjectivity of life—"In acquiring new productive forces men change their mode of production, in changing the way of earning their living, they change their social relations"— Marx then adds: *"The same men* who establish their social relations in conformity with their material productivity, *produce also* principles, ideas and categories in conformity with their social relations."[27]

If we cast a backward glance at the series of analyses that pursue the development of the concept of ideology, we can glimpse an ambiguity there. Inasmuch as ideology belongs to the ontological milieu of irreality, its meaning is pejorative; it is indeed no more than pure ideology. But the concept of ideology is overdetermined by the fundamental thesis of the genealogy. *Representations are consciousness; they are not, however, produced by it and, far from being within its power, they escape it*. For ideology is rooted in life; the necessity it displays on the plane of ideality, and which may at times appear to be only an absurd contingency, is actually the necessity of life itself—let us understand by this the necessity inscribed within it, and inseparable from its being, of being life, of living, and, first of all, of surviving. Life's prescriptions are implacable when what is at stake is life itself, when they are its own conditions, and the ideology that conveys them is the most serious thing in the world.

This is why the theory of genealogy reverses the immediate meaning of the concept of ideology, according to which ideology is but mere ideology and, even, a set of prejudices of which we must rid ourselves as quickly as possible. For if consciousness easily undoes the representations it has formed itself, that is to say "freely," *with respect to its own conditions, life has no power except to fulfill them*. And the ideology that represents these conditions has finally as its content not representations but these conditions themselves; representation is the form in which what ideology presents to us is reality. This is why one does not change ideologies as one does overcoats, why consciousness is powerless with respect to its own representations, because what it represents to itself in its representation does not have its source in this representation and is not produced by it, because, despite appearances, ideology is not theory but draws both the motivation for what it states and its substance from the life of individuals and from practice. The conceptual content of ideology immediately negates itself, refers back to its origin and to its true nature and is expressed in the form of a prescription.

It has been shown concerning ideology that it is developed as an action of thought, that it performs a prior reduction of reality to representations in order to be able, by transforming the latter, to modify the former. And the critique of ideology, at this first stage, consisted in showing that reality can neither be reduced to representation nor be transformed by it. The final postulate of ideology, the assertion that consciousness has at least the power to modify its own representations, is now rejected. For this power can no longer be ascribed to it when the content of its representations is prescribed for it, when it can only catch sight of this content instead of producing it, when it is no more than the *theory of practice*. Along with the questioning of this third postulate, that of the autonomy of consciousness, it is the very meaning of the concept of ideology and of its critique that is not simply modified but reversed. For it is no longer a matter of confirming the ineffectiveness of the system within which consciousness is locked up with its representations but, on the contrary, of affirming that this system originates in what is real and is as its text. Ideology is not a dream; it is neither madness nor delirium; it is reason itself, the exposition on the level of reason of the principle that governs all things, of the reason of all reasons, of the reason hidden in the depths of life.

The critique directed at Stirner lays bare this reversal of the meaning of the concept of ideology and its emergence in positivity. For what Stirner is finally reproached with is, precisely, having failed to take ideology seriously, with considering the whole of the representations, prescriptions and interdictions of which it is composed as *"idées fixes"* with which men have "stuffed their heads" and from which they must be freed. These *idées fixes*, this "folly," as Stirner also says with respect to right and to the will to satisfy it,[28] are presented as being "something higher,"[29] as the "rule of thought":[30] this is the "holy." But if ideology is, in fact, presented as a dominant element and most often—and above all—as a set of sacred prescriptions in the history of humanity, *Stirner does not see in this imperious domination the rule of life over thought but, on the contrary, that of thought over life;* he interprets it *stricto sensu* as a "domination of thought," not simply as "dominant ideas," but as ideas that dominate due to the action of thought that is devoted to them *for what reason one knows not*. It is precisely because Stirner does not know why certain ideas are dominant, because their genealogy proceeding from life, that is, their ultimate rationality, escapes him that he holds them to be sheer madness, madness that varies enigmatically from country to country and from epoch to epoch.[31]

One can read in a passage later stricken from the Preface to *The German Ideology:* "There is no specific difference between German idealism and the ideology of all the other nations." German idealism designates, depending on the context, Feuerbach, Bruno Bauer, and Stirner, united by the common assertion that "men have always formed wrong ideas about themselves. . . . The products of their brains have got out of their hands. . . . Let us liberate them from the chimeras, the ideas, dogmas, imaginary beings under the yoke of which they are pining away. Let us revolt against the rule of concepts . . . and existing reality will collapse."[32] German idealism, the German ideology which Marx broadly sums up in its recurrent themes in this introductory text, consists then in holding men's representations, the "phantoms of their brains," to be "false conceptions," "chimeras," "dogmas," and even "imaginary beings." This is why *the German ideology has nothing to do with the ideology of other peoples* and why Marx had to strike out of the manuscript the above-cited assertion of their identity. The ideology of other peoples is the representation of the necessary conditions for their life and their survival. The German ideology is the belief that this representation is misleading. In the German ideology the concept of ideology receives a very particular meaning, which not only does not coincide with the general concept of ideology formulated by Marx but is diametrically opposed to it: ideology, in compliance with this meaning, means illusory representation. To confuse this particular meaning with the general meaning of the concept of ideology is precisely a form of ideology in the particular sense that has just been recognized. *Consequently, any conception of ideology which holds the latter to be mere ideology is ideological. This ideological conception of ideology is the German ideology.*

But the ideological conception of ideology itself belongs to ideology and presupposes it. It is when life, through developing and perfecting the means it has at its disposal, relaxes the pressure it continually exerts upon itself that the ideological apparatus it displays as one of its means loses a little or a lot of its constraining force and presents itself as simply a system of ideas that one can perceive as such and with respect to which one is permitted to take a certain distance. And it is then that ideology, its vital motivation forgotten, is no more than a mere ideology. A society that has attained this degree of development, or of aging, does not simply hold its own ideas to be prejudices; it projects all around itself the gaze it casts upon itself and considers with amused astonishment other peoples, their bizarre beliefs and picturesque rites, their laughable mental structures. But this is an uneasy laughter, since this society knows it too falls under this common law. All is therefore nothing but ideology. But this gaze of relativism is also that of science. It is possible, now that all things are equivalent, to follow, in the naked light of objectivity, the interlacing of these ideal sequences, to describe them rigorously, to grasp their structure, that is, the internal law of their organization. For these ideal systems—whether it is a matter of ideas properly speaking or of the linguistic system that determines them—are, precisely, systems, autonomous ensembles, bearing their principle within themselves, juxtaposed, all on an equal plane. In the eyes of the ethnologist or of the sociologist, ideology once again forms a whole. If one can go beyond the plurality of the equivalent totalities, it is only to recognize the structural unity that dominates them to the extent that it is present in each one of them, namely the fact that each of them forms, precisely, a structure. The Same exhausts itself in the formal idea of an effective formal organization, of a metonymic causality. The Same is no longer the living principle which has produced and organized these ideological and institutional structures as the very conditions, first of all, for its own self-perpetuation, then for its development, as structures and conditions that can be understood in each instance only on the basis of this principle. However, the reason why an ideology is never mere ideology, why it cannot be juxtaposed with another, is the fact that it results from a certain development of the practical and productive activity of given individuals and that this activity, at the evolutionary stage which is peculiar to it, is different from that of a less evolved society, for example. For Marx, there is a progress in the practical life process, namely the very fact of its development, a hierarchy of the forms it engenders, notably of its ideological forms, which, moreover, cannot be considered or described in themselves, in an alleged objectivity—which only marks life's yielding or failure—as alleged totalities which they never are, but only in reference to this life outside of which they have no meaning in the strict sense, without which they would not exist. Once again the rationality of ideology lies in its genealogy. When the latter is omitted, when practice is left out, there is room only for the dumbfoundedness of theory abandoned to itself, what is called the curiosity of the gaze, the objectivity of the scientist.

The ideological conception of ideology finds its most naïve expression in the claim to explain what an individual is thinking in each instance on the basis of the dominant ideology, of the ideology of his age or that of the class to which he belongs. Philosophers themselves are not exceptions to this law. At most they are known to be able to invent concepts that are best suited to translating the ideological horizon which necessarily precedes their research and determines it, not only in its responses but in its very questions. A problematic concerned with the individual, with life or action, is not in any way explained by the fact that there exist living and acting individuals but by the prior ideological horizon that gives rise to a problematic such as this. In this way one sees ideology recover its own ground and claim to found it in its turn. It is no longer individuals and their practice that produce ideology, as Marx naïvely believed, but ideology that produces the former. As for the fact that the most sophisticated philosophical systems as well as the most familiar commonsensical conceptions are determined by the preexisting horizon of an ideology, this goes without saying. It is on the basis of the historical *a priori* of an epoch and of the epistemological field in which it unfolds, that a thought, even a thought of genius, is explained and takes shape. "Hume became possible."[33]

It is far off the mark to say that this ideological conception of ideology results from the methodological illusion alone, which consists in pointing out in the various works of the thinkers of an epoch a certain number of common themes in order to construct out of these what is called the *epistémè* of that epoch and in claiming then to deduce from it these same themes and, after them, these thinkers themselves. The presupposition holding that an ideology precedes the thoughts of a philosopher or of any individual, even any group of individuals, is itself ideological. For it makes an ideology into something it never is, the productive principle, the *naturans*, of a series of representations; it confers upon the ideal the power it never possesses—that is, precisely, a power—that of producing ideal objectivities, of presenting itself as the law of their construction, whereas, according to Marx, this law resides in life. This is to forget the genealogy, that is, at one and the same time to hypostatize ideology, thereby making it a prior condition for individual thoughts, the horizon to which these thoughts offer no more than a place where ideology is actualized. Marx sharply denounced this hypostasis of ideology and its alleged determination of individuals and of their thoughts: " . . . after their thoughts have been divorced from them themselves and from their empirical relations, it became possible to consider people as mere vehicles for these thoughts. . . ."[34]

The illusion peculiar to the ideological conception of ideology is now before us: whereas it is individuals who produce their thought in compliance with the specific mode of their practice and whereas ideology is only the whole of the thoughts produced in this way, it is claimed, on the contrary, that these thoughts are explained by ideology, which is only the sum or the résumé of these thoughts, and the individuals who are the producers of these thoughts are taken to be their mere receptacle, their "container." The hypostasis of ideology then appears to run strictly parallel to that of the classes: just as it is not because an individual belongs to the peasant class that he labors in the fields, plants seeds, harvests, cares for the animals, etc., but precisely because he does all this that he belongs to this class, likewise it is not because he belongs to this class and participates in its ideology that he thinks what he thinks but only because he does what he does. Here again, the analysis of the peasant class in France in the middle of the nineteenth century plays the role of an essential analysis. What characterizes the situation of these peasants is, as we have seen, the scattering of families over a wide number of small farms, the absence of any relations between them other than purely local ones, the absence of any political, cultural, or spiritual community, of any ideology in the sense of an objective and intersubjective ideal reality, of a set of representations or of ideas recorded in books, transmitted by teaching, circulated in newspapers, possessing in any form whatsoever an actual existence and as such capable of defining this horizon on the basis of which the thought of all those who are included within it could be explained. It is because one would seek in vain a cultural and moral community such as this that Marx said that peasants, despite the similarity of their way of life, do not form a class properly speaking.[35] *How then could an ideological horizon determine the thought of French peasants in the middle of the nineteenth century when it does not exist?*

And yet these peasants think more or less the same thing; the identity of their views is translated on the political level, for example, by the support they provided to Louis Bonaparte, thereby making his *coup d'état* possible. How, then, can this similarity of thoughts and "ideological reflexes" be explained if it does not involve simply putting into effect a preexisting ideology? The theory of genealogy then offers itself in its undeniable self-evidence: it is the activity of each individual that determines his thinking; the latter arises out of this very life, without the mediation of any objective ideological structure. It is because a number of individuals do the same thing and live in the same way that they also think in a similar manner and that all these thoughts seem to form, after the fact, what can be called a common ideology. No more than is a class, an ideology is not an historical *a priori*; no more than the former is the latter presented as an objective generality. And what the theory of genealogy also shows is that it is never a class which determines an ideology, but that the latter is formed directly by individuals who, starting from what in every instance is their practice, form this class and produce this ideology. And just as a class is not a mediation for determining the social existence of individuals, so too there is no mediation by ideology when these same individuals form their own ideas. This is what is categorically asserted by this essential text: "They [the individuals] entered into intercourse with one another as what they were, they proceeded 'from themselves', as they were, irrespective of their 'outlook on life'. This 'outlook on life'—even the warped one of the philosophers—could, of course, only be determined by their actual life."[36]

The genealogy is thus the internal tie, the direct procession of the idea starting from life, a procession which carries its intelligibility within itself and which posits the ideal content that it produces in the self-comprehension of this production. Is the latter not consciousness? If the genealogy is the self-bestowal of meaning, intentionality, must it not appear as a new formulation of idealism and, in its claim to fully explain the intelligibility of ideas by producing it, as its extreme form? But, for Marx, consciousness is no more than representation; the intelligibility it produces is only the light of objectivity and, as the 1843 manuscript has shown, what bathes in this ideal light is in no way explained by it. *The content of representation is not comprehensible starting from it and from its structure.* The genealogy is, precisely, not that of consciousness.

What is signified by this radical critique of *the reduction of the genealogy to the genesis of consciousness, that is to say, of idealism,* must be elucidated. To say that *consciousness produces its representations* does not mean simply, in the eyes of idealism, that it is the place in which the latter surge forth one after the other, consequently, that it is their common essence, namely the structure of representation as such. It is this structure of representation, that is, the structure and the essence of consciousness itself, which, in accordance with this idealism, determines the particular content of the representations it thus produces in a radical sense, not only because it gives them to itself in the form of representation, because it *is* this form, but also because it produces the content that it gives to itself in this form, which it itself is. It is necessarily as a transcendental deduction of the fundamental categories of thought that the genesis of consciousness finds its adequate philosophical expression at the same time as idealism its content, as this occurs in Kant. Doubtless, the Kantian genesis is indirect, for it is not the analysis of the pure structure of representation which produces the categories. These are instead presupposed inasmuch as they are found to be at work in the judgments of the understanding or as a list of them can be drawn up in accordance with logical tables. One is limited to showing—and the explicit motivation of the problematic, namely the refutation of empiricism, seems to content itself with this project—that these ideas are not mere matters of fact and, for example, the products of experience, but, on the contrary, pure principles and the, *a priori* conditions for experience itself.

And this is so because representation is possible only if it carries the diversity of what it represents back to the unity which is its own, which is the very condition of its possibility because, in Kantian language, the analytical unity of consciousness presupposes its synthetic unity. Causality, for example, is a principle and not simply an idea or an opinion because the causal connection of phenomena substitutes for their sheer diversity their unity in representation, which thus subsists as unitary representation and, as such, as the possibility of this representation.

The reason why the transcendental deduction of the categories is not really a deduction at all lies in the portion of facticity which it does not reduce, and in the fact that it continually presupposes what it claims to deduce. It founds causality transcendentally, but founding transcendentally means legitimizing, validating, producing as an *a priori* principle of experience that which first gives itself as a content of experience. This is precisely the presupposition of the Kantian deduction, the prior givenness of the idea of causality as such, its *existence* in the human mind. No more than in the case of causality, the analytical reading of the pure structure of representation does not display the other categories in itself; these are already given to the problematic even before it formulates the project of showing that these are not empirical concepts but principles. To say that the categories are not included in an analytical reading of the pure structure of representation means precisely that the fundamental concepts of consciousness are in no way explained by it, nor do they proceed from it; ideal representations have neither their origin nor the specificity of their content in the pure milieu of ideality as such, that is, precisely, in the structure of representation and of consciousness.

It is the idea of the genesis of consciousness, of the transcendental deduction of the categories *stricto sensu*, which delimits the question of the genealogy, gives it its sense and makes it possible. The question of the genealogy is formulated in this way: whence comes the specific content of the categories if not from the structure of pure representation as such? We know Marx's reply. It is life—let us understand by this, as he does, subjective praxis, original phenomenological life which constitutes the ground of the representations of consciousness, the origin of their content, while, as representations, they are, of course, only modalities of consciousness itself, ideal—that is, for Marx, irreal—determinations. Such is the immense philosophical import of the genealogy: to affirm that the origin of the fundamental categories of thought does not lie in thought itself, does not lie in either reason or consciousness. To situate this origin, on the contrary, in life means: the specific content of the categories belongs in itself to life; it is a determination, a moment of this life. How life "founds" the specific content of the categories is thus extremely clear: life founds it inasmuch *as it is itself* this content. Or again: the original categories are not ideas but real determinations and the very modalities of praxis.

Had anyone in the history of Western philosophy ever proposed the decisive ontological interpretation in accordance with which the categories of thought do not depend upon it and, before giving themselves to it in the form of representation, have first of all a real existence as the very modalities of subjective praxis and, in general, of life itself? Forty years before *The German Ideology*, two essential texts, *Mémoire sur la décomposition de la pensée* and *Essai sur les fondements de la psychologie* explicitly formulate this interpretation. Maine de Biran breaks in an exemplary manner with the idealist tradition of philosophical thought by affirming that causality is not an idea but action itself in the reality of its original subjective realization, which in its turn is for him nothing other than the body. This essential shift, whereby the categories are taken out of the sphere of consciousness in order to grasp their original existence as that of life, properly forms the thesis of the genealogy, which in this way possesses a rigorous ontological meaning residing in this very shift. At the same time, the concept of category is taken out of its deep-rooted ambiguity. According to the genealogical thesis, "category" has two senses: on the one hand, that of a real category, of a determination of life, and, on the other hand, that of an idea, of a determination of consciousness. As an idea, the category is the representation of the real category. It is in this sense that life founds the categories, inasmuch as its fundamental determinations and the modalities of its realization constitute real categories and, in the same stroke, the represented content in the case of ideal categories. The theory of the genealogy appears as the rigorous formulation of the relation between practice and theory, as a radical clarification of the "founding" of the second by the first.

With the decisive substitution of corporeal action for the ideal content of consciousness, the problematic is carried back to the same place where Marx's analysis will be situated. It may seem that in many respects the latter falls far short of the theoretical work done by Maine de Biran and with which Marx, moreover, was unacquainted. In Marx one finds no thematic development of the being of corporeal action, of manual labor; the status of the body, of the idealities of consciousness, the nature of the genealogy itself nowhere appear in his work as philosophical problems that are posited and dealt with explicitly. But, in the first place, Marx was fully aware of this omission and, far from presenting it as taking leave of first philosophy, he holds it to be what it effectively was in his life as a researcher, that is, as one task among all those whose urgency weighed upon him that it was impossible to carry to completion. When the introductory texts to *The German Ideology* suddenly delimit the principle of both history and the genealogy, namely the activity of living individuals, when the fact of taking the latter into consideration is presented as thereby eliminating the difficulties of speculation, Marx says: "The removal of these difficulties is governed by premises which certainly cannot be stated here, but which only the study of the actual life-process and the activity of the individuals of each epoch will make evident."[37] Elsewhere Marx explicitly cites the study of the body as belonging to these premises.[38]

The fact that the activity of individuals and their actual life-process, in their opposition to the ideal schemata under which speculation attempts to subsume them, constitute the essential and finally the sole object of Marx's problematic—this is what the problematic allows us to glimpse in its own way, *to the extent that it henceforth takes the economy as its theme*. For the consideration of the economy, which seems to preoccupy Marx's thought exclusively after *The German Ideology, directly results from the fundamental philosophical theses developed by this thought,* and therefore, despite the interpretation denounced above, it by no means signifies that philosophy is abandoned in favor of a scientific discipline. Marx's abandonment of philosophy is, as we have shown, the abandonment of Hegelian philosophy, of the autonomous thematization of the field circumscribing the ideality of consciousness, and this is accomplished to the benefit of reality, which is identified with praxis. It is the emergence of praxis which inspires the orientation of the problematic in the direction of the economy, which itself is originally nothing other than this thematization of praxis.

The genealogy brings us to understand finally what "abstraction" is for Marx. In his work ideas, categories, notions, etc. are continually said to be "abstract." But the concept of abstraction changes its sense from the 1843 manuscript— where its function and its content are determined by the critique of Hegelianism—to *The German Ideology*—where, with the critique of Hegelianism having been transformed into the positive theory of genealogy, it is the latter that henceforth defines the meaning of this concept—passing by way of *The Holy Family*, where the reality on the basis of which the concept of abstraction is produced and is understood is sensuous reality. So that it is only with regard to *The Holy Family* and to the 1844 texts that one can speak of the existence of an empiricist concept of abstraction in Marx. This is also why the rejection of this empiricist concept in no way means the rejection of the concept of abstraction in general but rather its rigorous and definitive elaboration by Marx during the years 1845–46. In what does the elaboration of the concept of abstraction within the theory of genealogy consist, inasmuch as this involves no more than carrying out what this framework implies? "The *abstraction*, the *category taken as such,* i.e. apart from men and their material activities. . . ."[39] What is abstract, therefore, is every ideal content considered in itself apart from the process of its production, to the extent that this process is that of life and not of consciousness, to the extent that it is a practical and not a theoretical process. This is why when Marx writes in *The Poverty of Philosophy* that "economic categories are only the theoretical expressions, the abstractions of the social relations of production,"[40] the tie linking abstraction and pure theory, taken independently from its foundation in practice, is evident. The latter, moreover, is clearly designated as the reality which is abstracted from in abstraction, and the empiricist concept of abstraction is definitively set aside. Abstraction is no longer the thought process that manipulates a content from outside, retaining certain determinations and setting aside others in order to constitute with the former set of determinations the comprehension of a concept; it is the break with the internal tie of the genealogy. This is why Stirner's work, that of the neo-

Hegelians and of classical philosophy in general is said to be abstract, because in analyzing representations in themselves this approach misses both their true meaning and their *raison d'être*. Their true meaning is that meaning which is no longer posited by consciousness in its autonomous theoretical activity which as such is rational, but the meaning they have for life, which thereby constitutes their actual motivation, their true *raison d'être*. Conceived of in light of the genealogy and defined on the basis of it, the "abstraction" of the categories marks their status, constitutes at one and the same time their radical critique and their legitimation. The legitimation of the categories consists in the practical process of individuals who produce their life and, at the same time, the categories in which they represent this process to themselves. The fact that the categories are abstracted from this process thus signifies, first of all, that they come from it and are grounded in it. The origin of the categories is the same thing as the reality to which they refer, and this reference is what allows them to have meaning. Marx says that in Stirner the categories have lost "the last vestige of connection with reality, and with it the last vestige of meaning."[41] The critique of the categories is precisely the affirmation that they lose all meaning when they cease to refer to reality. This means in the first place that the meaning of the categories is in no way reduced to their intrinsic ideal content, nor can it be defined by it. Let us consider two juridical categories, the category of privilege and that of equal rights. They have a direct, directly intelligible sense, which is none other than a concept, the concept of privilege and the concept of equality. But this analytical conceptual meaning does not provide us with the meaning of the categories in question; instead it conceals it inasmuch as it carries their meaning back to itself, back to pure ideas. To understand privilege and equal rights as juridical categories is to refer the former to the medieval mode of production and the latter to the capitalist mode of production, that is in each case, to the specific living process in which individuals produce their life. To reduce juridical propositions to the ideal analysis of a certain number of concepts, to consider the interconnection of these concepts in the light of their immanent meaning, to study these types of interconnections in themselves and the ensembles they constitute, to compose these systems, etc.—this is what is characteristic of ideology.

Does law belong to ideology? There is an ideological conception of law, and it is by this that one is generally taken in when one declares that law is an ideology, when, believing that one is defining one's object, one reduces it to what is called a code by a sort of juridical reduction consisting in putting out of the picture anything that is not law itself. Law is an ideology for Marx but in an entirely different sense, in a positive sense which the genealogy has given to it, as an ideal system no doubt, but as one that formulates on the level of ideality the actual regulations of the practical social process. The juridical categories can then no longer be constructed on the basis of fundamental juridical concepts, that is to say, once again, by an ideal analysis. They are determined by the real modalities of production and can be explained by them.[42]

How the analytical reading of the ideal content of a category, far from being able to give us its meaning, on the contrary conceals it—this is what Marx wanted to show with regard to an essential economic category, labor. Labor is apparently a simple category and, one might even say again here, a simple nature of political economy. Let us note, however, that considered in this simplicity and in its broadest generality as a concept under which could be subsumed all the work performed by men on earth, regardless of the epoch and of the differences involved, the category of labor is nonetheless abstracted from a reality out of which it draws its meaning. However vague this may be, it is nevertheless referential. The abstraction from which the simple category of "labor," understood in this way, proceeds has a Feuerbachian aspect to it; it retains a character that is common to various and sundry realities; it is, says Marx, "the mental product of a concrete totality of labors."[43] What is concealed under this apparent universal, however, is a specific mode of individual subjective life in which the individual works while remaining completely indifferent to the particular nature of the work he has to accomplish, a work for which he is no longer destined or prepared by his birth, education, or choice. ". . . this abstraction of labor as such is not merely the mental product of a concrete totality of labors. Indifference towards specific labors corresponds to a form of society in which individuals can with ease transfer from one labor to another, and where the specific kind is a matter of chance for them, hence of indifference."[44] Labor such as this is characteristic of the modern period, and this is what political economy is concerned with. Thus, the universality of labor can no longer delude us; this is no longer the universality of its conceptual essence, its abstraction with respect to all possible labors—if indeed it refers to a specific mode of labor, to that of a given period. Marx's critique of the categories still consists in denouncing as merely apparent the universality relating to the ideality of their specific mode of phenomenological presentation in order to elicit from it the singularity of a reality in relation to which the category is no more than a representation.

It follows that the critique of the categories, resembling in this their legitimation, is never located on their level; the movement that topples them from the theoretical pedestal that is momentarily their own is never, in the final analysis, their own movement but that of reality, which, inasmuch as it constitutes this movement, is, precisely, history. This text, in which the category of property finds at one and the same time its legitimation and its critique, brings this fact clearly to light: "Ancient 'property relations' were swallowed up by feudal property relations and these by 'bourgeois' property relations. Thus *history itself had practiced its criticism* upon past property relations."[45] The critique of theory is radical if neither the erasure of categories nor their replacement by other categories stems from the theory itself, from the self-movement of these categories. Thus, there is no history of the sciences, if, with Marx, we understand by this an autonomous history; instead, this history depends upon "entirely different conditions." These conditions are those of production, but as real production, as the production of life producing itself, producing its own conditions, as history. In order to state this essential dependence characteristic of science, Marx's language becomes more concise: ". . . science . . . is a product of the historical movement. . . ."[46]

It is not only the content of each of the fundamental concepts of a theory that finds its origin outside of the theory but also, for this very reason, its connection with all of the other concepts, its place in the theory. The order of the categories is no longer their own order, a logical order which can be determined on the basis of the categories alone and, precisely, by their analysis. *The order of the categories is an historical order.* Such is the thesis asserted in opposition to Proudhon. Whereas, for Proudhon, the succession of the categories in history, the order of their temporal manifestation is, precisely, only the manifestation of an ideal order which dominates this temporal succession and governs it, so that a period which may be considered as having embodied a principle—that of authority or of individuality, etc.—is in fact no more than the embodiment of this principle and is explained on the basis of this principle, so that it is not historical reality which founds the principle but the latter which makes history, Marx asserts, on the contrary, that the analysis of the categories and the ability to understand their succession implies a radical shift in the problematic and requires that the problematic take as its theme not the categories themselves but a reality that is defined at once by its heterogeneity with regard to this sphere of categorial ideality and, positively, by the praxis of individuals producing their life. This reality in its twofold definition—anticategorial and practical—is, precisely, history.[47]

In positing the historicity of the categories, Marx does not call their ideality into question; he affirms that they are founded by a reality of a different order. With the question of the perenniality or the historicity of the categories, what is at issue is not temporal determinations but an ontological partition. To hold that the categories lack autonomy signifies that they are powerless, that is, to be specific, that they are heterogeneous with respect to reality which, as praxis, is indeed the power of life, the sphere in which this power unfolds, history. This is why, when Marx reproaches bourgeois economists and Proudhon with having understood the laws of bourgeois production as "eternal laws which must always govern society,"[48] one must well grasp why these laws do not always govern society: because they never govern it. Because laws, categories, cannot govern anything at all, cannot regulate, order, direct any sort of real processes nor, *a fortiori,* bring them about. *Laws, laws of production, for example, produce nothing.* If the "natural laws" spoken of by bourgeois economists are a myth, this is by no means because they are conceived of as eternal and hence as determining a state of things that is always the same—bourgeois society—but rather because they are understood as determining this state of things, because the law, which is only the ideal representation of a real process, is mistakenly included in this process and interpreted as a real force acting within it precisely in order to direct it, to regulate it, or to produce it. It is truly as a stroke of genius that Husserl will write in the *Prolegomena to Pure Logic:* "In other fields, too, we familiarly employ mythic talk of natural laws as presiding powers in natural events—as if the rules of causal connection could themselves once more significantly function as causes, i.e. as terms in just such connections."[49] Ultimately, espistemology runs up against the insurmountable question of existence. Whenever it attempts to reduce existence, to include it within the system of ideal regulations that it constructs, it is but "the shadow of movement and the movement of shadows";[50] it is not the historicity of what is real that is lost, it is what is real itself.

The "absurd problem of eliminating history"[51] may seem to arise when one considers a given society in itself, abstracting from the historical movement from which it results. What one finds in this cross-section of reality, which gives it in the present, is not a linear progression but a series of typical "structures" which function autonomously and for which a theory must in each case be provided. Thus there will be a theory of the Asian mode of production, a theory of the modes of production of antiquity, of the Middle Ages, of capitalism and of socialism. What relation can the categories which constitute these various theories maintain with reality? Is the latter anything other than that which is produced in these different worlds as a product and which is governed by the laws of these worlds, by these different theories? Far from being produced by history, the categories present themselves once again here as its regulating principles. The illusion of an ideal determination of the real, an illusion which finds its modern expression in "structuralism," once again stands out clearly before us.

Marx provided the theory of the relation of theories to history. This theory is intelligible only if one recalls that, for Marx, history designates neither an objective series of events nor the homogeneous milieu in which economic and social formations would take their place. History is the movement of life; it is its concrete realization as need giving rise to action, as praxis. Far from containing them as within a formal horizon, history is internal to economic and social formations as that which produces them and never ceases to produce them. History is what Marx called the concrete. Theory is the analysis of this concrete reality. It seeks the concepts which enable us to understand it, and, in order to do so, it uncovers and isolates the simplest concepts, such as "labor, division of labor, need, exchange value," to reconstruct with these the concrete totality and then to proceed from this "to the level of the state, exchange between nations and the world market." "The latter," Marx immediately adds, "is obviously the scientifically correct method."[52] The development of the scientific method implies a twofold determination of the fundamental concepts it employs, namely the concepts of the concrete and the abstract. Generally speaking, the determinations inherent in the method are abstract, and they are so considered to the extent that they are categorial determinations, concepts. The interpretation of scientific determinations in general as abstract is an ontological interpretation which is primary and decisive; it belongs to the philosophical horizon of Marx's thinking and determines it; the concept of ideology rests upon this interpretation. Within the abstract determinations of science, a distinction is established, however, between those that could be termed abstract in the sense that they constitute simple and very general determinations, such as, for example, labor, the division of labor, etc., and those that will be termed concrete because they are richer than the preceding ones and result from the grouping together and the synthesis of a number of simple determinations, for example, financial capital, annuities, etc. Let us note that this definition of the concrete is Hegelian, and it is to it that Marx adheres when he writes in the same Introduction: "The concrete is concrete because it is the concentration of many determinations, hence unity of the diverse."[53] Only, this Hegelian definition of the concrete as the unity and as the result of many determinations is retained by Marx only on the level of theory. Whereas in Hegel it is being itself which, starting with primitive simple determinations, moves through the process of its successive determinations in such a way that the categorial determinations of being are at one and the same time its real determinations—so that the primitive abstract determinations express an initial ontological poverty and the final syntheses express the concreteness of being itself—Marx abruptly dissociates these two processes and affirms their heterogeneity. This is why the passage from the abstract to the concrete, in the very particular sense of a passage taking place entirely on the level of ideality, as a passage from an abstract which is ideal to a concrete which is itself ideal, can serve to define the movement of theory, since the latter indeed always consists in an interconnection of increasingly complex categorial determinations of the form S is p (S is p) is q, etc. If on the level of theory, then, the concrete categorial, that is to say, the richest categorial, is always a result, this is not at the same time the case, precisely, on the level of reality.

Here the illusion belonging to every theory that is incapable of situating itself, that is, of understanding itself on the basis of its own genealogy—the illusion of ideology itself—becomes intelligible. Because, within theoretical development, the concrete is always given as the result of this development, as the result of a thought process, as the concrete as it is thought, theory imagines that the concrete is just as it presents itself to theory, that it really is the result of a theoretical process, that the concrete is in itself as it is thought. "[The concrete] *appears in the process of thinking*, therefore, as a process of concentration, as a result, not as a point of departure, *even though it is the point of departure in reality*. . . . In this way Hegel fell into the illusion of conceiving the real as the product of thought. . . ."[54] The process by which the categorial determinations are themselves determined categorically, in a movement without end, is thus nothing other than the process by which *thought represents the real to itself*, and it is in no way the process of the real itself, the practical process which constantly produces society and all its formations, including the theoretical formations, including even the theoretical process in which the real process is represented. ". . . the method of rising from the abstract to the concrete is only the way in which thought appropriates the concrete, reproduces it as the concrete in the mind. But this is by no means the process by which the concrete itself comes into being."[55]

Thus is maintained the radical distinction between the concrete reality of praxis and its categorial determination in a theory. The latter rests upon the former and presupposes it. Of the concrete as it is *thought*, Marx says: "[it is] not in any way a product of the concept which thinks and generates itself *outside or above observation and conception; a product, rather, of the working-up of observation and conception into concepts*."[56] Marx would therefore concur with a thinker like Husserl in asserting the anteriority of perceptual data in relation to the work of its theoretical elaboration. And what if one were to say that it is in theory and through it that this anteriority is asserted? But the anteriority of perceptual data is wholly independent of theory and of its conceptualization; it consists in the phenomenological manifestation of the datum itself, and this original manifestation owes nothing to theory, which, on the contrary, presupposes it. Moreover, the forms of this elaboration, the theoretical forms, are dependent on the datum because they are determined by it, since, as has been shown, the categories are not autonomous idealities but receive their content from a heterogeneous reality and are themselves produced by it. This reality is life. It is because life *constitutes the content of this world, the content of history, the process of production, the consumption and the becoming of social formations that the categories of need, labor, causality, use-value, etc., are adequate to it, are adequate to this world which it is itself and which it unceasingly produces at the same time as it produces the categories with the help of which it thinks the world and thus thinks itself*. Thought is nothing but the representation of life by life itself, and, for Marx, the epistemological circle is completed.

Does not the necessary reference of theory to the reality of practice and of history call into question its claim to attain reality; does it not mark theory with an insurmountable relativism? Do we not see the spectre of historicism rising up before us? The critique of Proudhon, of bourgeois economists in general, abounds in warnings to this effect. Let us retain only this one: "Thus the categories are no more eternal than the relations they express. They are historical and transitory products."[57] Does not this relativization of theory, however, concern the theory of genealogy itself, for is not the affirmation that a certain historical state of society determines all ideal truth itself dependent on an historical state and condemned, as it is, to disappear? Here we encounter the well-known objection levelled at all relativism and which was given a rigorous formulation by Husserl in the *Prolegomena to Pure Logic*, the objection that the content of a theory—here, the relative character of truth—cannot enter into contradiction with the *a priori* conditions of any possible theory in general— namely the possibility and the actuality of an absolute truth—without this theory destroying itself. Whence the difficulty experienced by Marxism when it understands itself as an historicism and as a relativism. Whence the effort that is easily discernible in it to escape the contradiction inherent in this relativism by assuming it while claiming to go beyond it.

This is the case in Gramsci. "If the philosophy of praxis affirms theoretically that all truth which is believed to be eternal and absolute has had practical origins and represents a 'provisional' value . . . it is very difficult to make it understood 'practically' that such an interpretation also applies to the philosophy of praxis itself, without upsetting the convictions that are necessary for action. Moreover, this difficulty presents itself to every historicist philosophy."[58] Gramsci attempted to overcome this relativism by pretending to believe that it is the plurality of opinions, a plurality which itself results from that of the classes, which harms true being. One has then only to suppress class antagonisms for the conflict of ideologies to be replaced by a unitary thought. How can we fail to recognize, however, that the latter would be simply a collective ideology whose *de facto* universality has nothing to do with a *de jure* universality? It is significant, at any rate, to see that in order to navigate around the reef of relativism Marxism turned to Hegel and to the idea of absolute knowledge, that is, of a radical awareness—whether this is located at the end of history or at the time of the revolution—which allows the total sense of human development to be grasped once again. To return to Hegel was to follow the path in the opposite direction from that taken by Marx. For it is most noteworthy that Marx never ran up against relativism as an inevitable consequence of his own doctrine. All of his essential theses, and in particular that of the genealogy of ideas, are asserted to be truths as definitive as they are absolute. This is because the doctrine of the genealogy, far from making every truth relative, constitutes, on the contrary, a *foundation for truth in general*. To found truth is, in the first place, to recognize the place where it resides, to reject the claim of ideal truth to be self-sufficient, to constitute truth in itself and of itself, and instead to affirm its necessary reference to reality. This reality, it is true, is history. To found truth is, in the second place, to recognize in the historical reality which has just been acknowledged as its sphere of origin, a true origin, the principle of history itself, namely life in its fundamental determinations, which are need and labor. The foundation of truth does not only lead back to history, it founds history itself. In this second sense, the foundation of truth is nothing other than historical materialism such as we have presented it. Inasmuch as all theoretical truth is rooted not in factitious history but in what founds this history, it too escapes the universal condition of passing away; it is not the mere fact of passing but, rooted in this way in the principle of history and in determinations whose indefinite reiteration produces it and has never ceased to produce it, this truth has planted itself on the solid ground of permanence.

Just as the reality of history—the reality that produces it—is not carried away by history, neither is the representation of history, the thought of what is simple and of what is permanent. What is foreign to history, therefore, is not just the thought of life in its permanent and indefinitely reiterable determinations, the thought of that which produces history, but also that of the production of thought by life. The theory of the genealogy is thus the representation of a permanence lying within life itself and is permanent just as it is. In the thought of the permanent resides the possibility of all theory. Inasmuch as it is this thought, historical materialism is directed toward this possibility and is legitimized. The theory of all possible theories, it is precisely a theory of this sort. This is why its propositions are not only, as has been stated, apodictic propositions; in their most fundamental meaning they also allow the foundation of their apodicticity to appear. "Whatever the social form of production, laborers and means of production always remain factors of it. But in a state of separation from each other either of these factors can be such only potentially. For production to go on at all they must unite. The specific manner in which this union is accomplished distinguishes the different economic epochs of the structure of society from one another."[59]

It is not, however, the simple permanence of what remains throughout history which founds the universality of the theory of this history and makes its truth possible. Or rather, this permanence has to be understood. It is not the "always-being-there" in the midst of all that unceasingly flows by, the single fixed point in the moving immensity of the sea. What remains, the simple, cannot found truth except to the extent that in itself it is constituted as the most original essence of truth. It is praxis, inasmuch as it is subjective, which founds both history and the possibility of a theory of history. By leading back from the ideal truth of theory to the praxis of subjective life, the genealogy does not only shift the place of truth, it entirely changes its nature. It is no longer the representation of consciousness but instead the radical immanence of life which now constitutes the essence of truth. This is why Marx's problematic firmly turns its back on Hegelianism, as it turns its back on the Marxisms that directly stem from it. Neither theory as such nor universal knowledge, the self-awareness of history as a whole, can constitute the truth of this history, and this is so not because this self-awareness would remain problematical but for the more profound reason that neither consciousness as such, nor knowledge, nor theory can continue to claim to constitute truth. Truth resides in history itself—let us understand by this the reality which produces it. It is *the most original knowledge of life as identical to it and to its subjectivity* which founds truth and the possibility of all theories, as Engels, for once the faithful interpreter of Marx's most profound thinking, has us understand in a text written as a supplement to Book Three of *Capital* and which, in its apparent simplicity, at last allows the Simple to appear. In it one sees how, at the origin of the entire economic process as of that of the science of this process, a primary knowledge unfolds in an essential domain. This knowledge is that of the workers *as such,* of those who know what they are doing inasmuch as they are doing it and as this doing is itself a knowledge and the ground of all possible knowledge but, first of all, of the economic process, of exchange, etc.

> Hence the peasant of the Middle Ages knew fairly accurately the labor-time required for the manufacture of the articles obtained by him in barter. . . . The peasants, as well as the people from whom they bought, were themselves workers; the exchanged articles were each one's own products. What had they ex-

pended in making these products? Labor and labor alone . . . how then could they exchange these products of theirs for those of other laboring producers otherwise than in the ratio of the labor expended on them? Not only was the labor-time spent on these products the only suitable measure for the quantitative determination of the values to be exchanged: no other was at all possible. Or is it believed that the peasant and the artisan were so stupid as to give up the product of ten hours' labor of one person for that of a single hour's labor of another? . . . and the people of that time were certainly clever enough—both the cattle-breeder and their customers—not to give away the labor-time expended by them without an equivalent in barter.[60]

Against the backdrop of a radical phenomenology of individual life and of its daily practice, economics, the theory of economics, and its critique are possible.

Chapter 6

THE TRANSCENDENTAL GENESIS
OF THE ECONOMY

The essential possibility of exchange: real labor and abstract labor

To the question, What is the object of *Capital?* Marx himself replied in the Preface to Book One, which he wrote in London on July 25, 1867: "In this work I have to examine the capitalist mode of production, and the conditions of production and exchange corresponding to that mode."[1] One would be greatly mistaken, however, in thinking that Marx's problematic could be reduced to an economic analysis. If the capitalist system does indeed constitute the dominant and constant theme of the economic writings, that is to say, of the quasi-totality of his work after 1846, an attentive reading of the first chapters of *Capital* suffices to show that the aim of the inquiry is something altogether different from constructing a science in the ordinary sense of the word, that is, the acquisition and the systematic formulation of a certain amount of positive knowledge concerning a specific domain of being. For if this were the case, if the study of the capitalist system and its laws constituted the sole theme of his inquiry, Marx would be no more than the last representative of the English economic school; and whatever the importance of the modifications made in the theses of Smith and of Ricardo, this work would indeed amount to no more than "modifications," no more than theories, which might perhaps be "different" but which would be situated within the framework of one and the same interrogation and of, precisely, one and the same science. This is, moreover, an inauthentic science despite its abundant results, to the extent that, just as every science, it relies on the positive character of the knowledge it produces without first questioning the very possibility of this production, without questioning its own possibility.

Since Kant—but this was already the meaning of the work of Descartes and of Plato before him—we recognize as transcendental every investigation which, far from identifying with the spontaneous course of science, on the contrary, poses in the guise of a problem the essential possibility for this science to orientate itself toward its peculiar object and to attain this object. Even more essential than the search for an *a priori* condition for science is the work of bringing to

190

light that which constitutes the internal possibility of the very being which is grasped in its questioning. And this is so because, for Marx, the possibility of knowing, theory, rests upon reality. This is why, from Kant to Marx, the transcendental question shifts; it is no longer an interrogation concerning the essential possibility of science, in this case of political economy, but one that concerns first of all the reality which comes to be the object of this science, the "economy," now understood in its relation to praxis and to the fundamental modes of its actual realization. These modes henceforth form the theme of transcendental philosophy. When it is a question of the market economy—that is, precisely, of one of the essential modalities through which human praxis is realized and continues to be realized today—the question is thus the following: What makes this sort of economy possible? What is it that has allowed something like exchange to be produced in history and that, in an essential and radical manner, is capable of doing this?

The transcendental, and hence universal, significance of a question such as this may appear doubtful. Is not the market economy a transitory mode of social praxis? Is not the critique which Marx constantly levels at it intended to present it in this way? To the extent that it comes after the communal modes of primitive production, after the artisanal mode of medieval production and before the socialism that will follow it, does not the market economy obviously share in the facticity of history? Does it not as such escape the transcendental dimension of radical founding and of apodicticity? But it is not exchange as an historical phenomenon, its emergence in the distant past, its development and its generalization in capitalism, and its demonstrated or prophesied demise in the near future which constitute the ultimate object of Marx's reflection, but the possibility of exchange and, consequently, the possibility of a market economy in general. This is why *Capital* is not restricted to the study of a given economic system but is presented from the outset as a transcendental investigation. Exchange is no doubt a transitory phenomenon, and the system that rests upon it is destined to be a part of history, but the possibility of exchange is a pure essence, even if there had never been and never would be any actual exchange on the face of the earth. And the thought which thinks it elicits a transcendental truth or, yet again, an eternal truth; it goes beyond the factitious science of a factitious reality and escapes history: it is philosophy.

Here the profound unity of Marx's reflection becomes apparent to us, inasmuch as the economic problematic, finding its completion in *Capital*, links up with the problematic of history as it is presented in *The German Ideology*. For, just as historical materialism is not in itself a science—that is, precisely, history—but a reflection on the necessary conditions for all possible history, and as it is actually for this reason that it escapes history or, as we have said, that it is not an ideology, in the same way the economic analysis is not part of the history of economic doctrines and is not presented as one among these. And just as the concept of history is ambiguous, since by this is understood both history as science *(Historie)* and historical reality *(Geschichte)*, so too is this the case for the concept of economy, which designates at one and the same time political economy, that is, economics, and the economic reality itself, the actuality of a specific type of social praxis. The analogy that is formed in Marx's thought between history and the economy is then evident. The shift in the transcendental question concerns both of them and allows us to say in both cases that, in Marx, transcendental philosophy ceases to be a philosophy of transcendental consciousness in order to become a philosophy of reality. For the genesis which *The German Ideology* traces for us is that of the reality of history and not that of history as a science. Likewise, *Capital*, in its essential opening analyses, provides in its turn the transcendental genesis of the reality of exchange and of the social praxis which rests upon it and not simply that of the political economy. But when the genesis is no longer within the province of consciousness, is no longer the constitution by consciousness of its object as a scientific object but instead the genesis of reality starting from reality itself and from what it includes that is most essential, when knowledge itself finds its possibility in that of reality, then idealism is rejected once and for all.

The transcendental question of the *a priori* possibility of exchange can only come to light if exchange is itself perceived as a problem. However, it is by no means simply for us, for modern-day economists, that exchange is given as problematical but for as long as there have been men and for as long as they have found themselves in the situation of having to exchange their products. The question of the possibility of exchange is not a theoretical but a practical question. It is not resolved by the production of an adequate concept of exchange, even when this occurs within the context of a rigorous science of the market economy which itself is adequate, but by exchange as such, by men inasmuch as they have always, in any case for as long as commerce has existed, exchanged their products. The adequate concept of exchange—as a philosophical concept, however, not as a scientific concept, as a transcendental concept of the possibility of exchange—is, it is true, produced for the first time in *Capital*. But it is not produced as what makes exchange possible, as theoretical—and moreover contingent—consciousness of its practical possibility. It is precisely this practical possibility, but as a transcendental possibility, which Marx has in mind, and by no means the epistemological question of knowing how it was possible for him to form an adequate theoretical concept of this practical possibility. *Capital* is a philosophy of the economy, not a theory of political economy. And it is only as such, as a philosophy of the economy, that it constitutes as well the ground of a rational theory of political economy.

How is exchange possible? To begin with, why does it pose a problem? In exchange—whether it is a question of a primitive form of barter or of the circulation of commodities in a modern industrial society—the products that are to be exchanged and that as such become commodities are qualitatively different, both in their material nature and in their use-value. Actually, these two aspects are closely connected. The natural qualities of the commodities are necessarily taken into consideration when one considers the utility they are likely to offer for life. The natural properties of commodities "claim our attention only in so far as they affect the utility of those commodities, make them use-values."[2] Consequently, considered in themselves, in other words in their use-value, the products that are exchanged have nothing in common. On the one hand, we have salt, canvas, skins, and on the other, wheat, metal, or whatever. How can any equality be established among all these products? How can one determine the correct proportion in accordance with which they have to be and, consequently, can be exchanged? How does it happen that a certain quantity of commodity A can be deemed the equivalent of a certain quantity of commodity B, that $x\,cA = y\,cB$?

This question is at one and the same time that of the exchange-value of commodities. For it is precisely the exchange-value of a commodity that determines the proportional relation that it carries into exchange, namely the quantity of this commodity that must be supplied in order to obtain a given quantity of some other commodity. The problem of value and of determining it is the problem of classical economics and, moreover, its exclusive problem, since it knows no system other than that of exchange. We know the reply of political economy to its crucial question: the origin of value resides in labor; the value of a commodity is determined by the amount of labor required to produce it. Since determining the value of a commodity is identical to determining the conditions for its exchange, one will be able to exchange $x\,cA$ for $y\,cB$ once it appears that these different quantities of different commodities have required the same amount of labor.

Where political economy sees a solution, Marx, however, perceives no more than a problem. Labor, it is said, produces the substance of value and determines it quantitatively. Only, for Marx, labor *in itself as such* does not exist. Because the essence of praxis is a living, individual subjectivity, the exploration of the universe of labor necessarily leads to the recognition of a wide number of concrete, subjective, individual, specific, and qualitatively different labors. When, confronted with the variety of the products brought to the market, one moves back from these to the labor from which they result, what one finds is precisely not a unity capable of reducing this plurality of diverse objects to itself nor a standard capable of serving as a common unit of measurement. To the irreducible diversity of commodities considered in their material form, in other words, in their use-value, corresponds the irreducible diversity of the different sorts of labor that produced them. *Capital* speaks of "the equalisation of the most different kinds of labor."[3] To leave the objective world of commodities for that of labor is not to exclude the sphere of qualitative heterogeneity and of incommunicability, which is inconsistent with exchange, but to rediscover it in its original and irreducible form.

However, this difficulty must be given its radical meaning. Not only do the different "kinds" of labor—weaving, ploughing, metal extraction, etc.—differ from one another and, due to what in each case constitutes their specificity, refuse to submit to a common unit of measurement; but one and the "same" labor—let us understand by this labor of the same kind, activity of the same type—once it is performed by different individuals ceases, precisely, to be "the same." If, for example, it is a matter of unloading coal from a truck and of carrying the sacks to a nearby warehouse, the effort of one worker, his activity as it is lived subjectively, differs substantially from that of another. What is felt by one to be an "unbearable burden" will be experienced by the other as the positive release of his physical strength and as the expression of his vitality. Or again, what is boring to one person will be indifferent or agreeable to another. This is why the "time" of their activity is also not the same. One person will take support in the living present of corporeal actualization and will tend to lose himself in it; the other, from the start, will project himself toward the future time when the work will have ended. In other words, existences cannot be exchanged, they are not comparable, and real labor, its subjective temporality, possessing in each case a particular mode of a peculiar realization, cannot be exchanged either.

That a philosophy of monadic subjectivity, by recognizing the irreducibility of each individual and as a result of each of the modalities of his praxis, excludes at the same time, along with any unit of objective measurement, the possibility of making apparent between different individuals and their different kinds of labor some sort of "equality" and, consequently, the very possibility of exchange—this is categorically affirmed in the text of the *Critique of the Gotha Programme*, written in 1875. This is a decisive text because it considers from the same standpoint bourgeois society, that is, the market economy; communist society, that is, socialist society in its first phase, not as it is developed on its own bases but as it has emerged from capitalist society;[4] and finally, socialist society properly speaking, which is constructed on the basis of its own principles. This is a decisive text because it shows that the single standpoint from which Marx considers together the three essential forms of modern society rests upon a common ground, which no longer belongs to any of these forms and cannot be explained by them but which, on the contrary, explains them and accounts for the problem on the basis of which they have to decide just what they are. A ground such as this, namely monadic subjectivity as the fundamental structure of being, transforms into an insurmountable aporia the very possibility of any sort of equality between individuals, that is to say, between their different kinds of work as well, inasmuch as the latter are no longer defined in terms of an objective norm, a method or a process that can be observed in the world, but find their actuality, precisely, in the irreducible, unrepresentable, and undefinable subjectivity of the absolute monad. This aporia of equality is at the same time that of right, for there is no right other than an "equal right," as Marx says,[5] that is to say, that right exists when, for one and the same work, those who do it receive the same value, *whether this is an exchange-value or a use-value*. In stressing this indifference with respect to the nature of the value produced by the worker and which must be received by him as such, we wish clearly to indicate the vast scope of Marx's problematic here, the fact that it concerns not only the economy of exchange but also the communist regime in transition toward socialism and, even more so, this regime in its completed form, consequently, every possible type of economy. If we were to suppose that the mediation of the exchange-value were suppressed, by placing ourselves through a willful fiction outside of the capitalist regime and of the communist regime, the question of attributing to workers the same use-value for the same labor would remain unchanged if the concept of "the same labor" lost its meaning, if, as the realization of a praxis that was fundamentally subjective and monadic, labor was precisely never "the same."

This is the rigorous thesis formulated by Marx in the *Critique of the Gotha Programme*. With respect to society in its communist phase, Marx says that "the individual producer receives back . . . exactly what he gives to it."[6] What he gives to it is a certain labor and what he receives back from it—what alone becomes individual property in a system such as this—are the objects of personal consumption which correspond to this labor. These are not objects he himself has produced but objects which take exactly as much time to produce as the labor time he himself has contributed to society, which then correspond to the objects that he produced himself. This is why there is an equivalence between what he gives and what he receives. Of the individual means of consumption, Marx says: "But, as far as the distribution of the latter among individual producers is concerned, *the same principle prevails as in the exchange of commodity-equivalents:* a given amount of labor in one form is exchanged for an equal amount in another form."[7] *The principle upon which the communist regime is based is thus the right, the principle of exchange, the very principle of the market economy.* The sole difference that exists between communism and the market system is that the former undertakes actually to apply the principle which the latter countervenes in practice to the extent that it does not give the worker the true equivalent of his work. What differentiates communism from capitalism is thus not a question of principle, but quite the opposite: communism wishes only to realize the market principle. One must not simply say, therefore, that "Communist society . . . is thus . . . still stamped with the birth marks of the old society from whose womb it emerges," but that it fulfills this old society by fulfilling its principle. And Marx states: "Hence, equal right here is still—in principle—bourgeois right, although principle and practice are no longer at loggerheads."[8]

Because it is the radical development of the principle of the market economy instead of being a fallacious application like capitalism, communism is revealing in this regard; it is the pure form produced by the principle and in which the principle appears as it is in itself. What is remarkable is that, against all logic, Marx calls this principle of right and of equality a bourgeois principle. If in bourgeois—that is in capitalist—society, it finds simply its distorted image and so is fully realized only in communism, it is rather as a principle of communism that it should be recognized by the problematic. Only, Marx will make such a radical critique of this principle that it seems preferable in presenting a revolutionary program to direct this critique against the birthmarks of the old order rather than against the very essence of the regime one is going to institute. It is significant, in any case, that this critique comes about just when we arrive at the study of the communist order and of its foundation. The "progress" of this regime lies precisely in the fact that the principle of equal right is no longer belied by the facts. "In spite of this advance, this equal right is still constantly stigmatized by a bourgeois limitation. The right of the producers is proportional to the labor they supply; the equality consists in the fact that measurement is made with an equal standard, labor."[9]

Where, then, are the "bourgeois" limitations of this principle of equal right, in accordance with which each person receives exactly what he has produced? Not in bourgeois society but in a monadic distinction understood metaphysically as the structure of reality. The text we are discussing continues, "But one man is superior to another physically or mentally and so supplies more labor in the same time or can labor for a longer time." If under these conditions one and the same product, that is, one and the same objectively defined "labor," one and the same objective process, requires, due to the inequality of subjective capacities, a much greater effort from one individual than from another, it is unjust to give to the first the same value, whether exchange-value or use-value, as to the second, since the latter has worked harder or longer than the former. In other words, the labor that should serve as the criterion for determining what is due to the worker cannot be subjective labor, the effort actually accomplished, the particular intensity which it must have had in a given individual due to his aptitude, the time required to do what someone else might have done more quickly or more slowly. ". . . labor, to serve as a measure, must be defined by its duration or intensity, otherwise it ceases to be a standard of measurement."[10] Only, real labor never plays this role and is incapable of playing it: just as there is no way of measuring subjectivity, subjectivity itself cannot serve as a standard of measurement. It is the objective definition of a program, of a production, and this by means of a method which itself is defined objectively—it is the objective process which constitutes the standard by which right measures each individual praxis, and it is only in light of this norm, which is objective and valid for everyone, of this universal unit of measurement, that there is and can claim to be an equal right for all. Measuring every form of individual praxis in the light of a common norm, it necessarily fails to recognize their fundamental difference. Thus, right is prey to an inflexible dialectic which literally destroys it. To apply one and the same standard, for example, the same salary, to objectively identical but subjectively unequal labors is inequality itself; as Marx abruptly states, "This equal right is an unequal right for unequal labor." And again, in a no less essential declaration: "Right by its very nature can consist only in the application of an equal standard; but unequal individuals (and they would not be different individuals if they were not unequal). . . ."[11]

Communism claims to abolish privileges and, in order to do this, to eliminate classes, henceforth treating all individuals in the same way, as workers. The

elimination of classes is for it, precisely, the abolition of difference, the abolition of individual differences which are traceable to class differences. The
abolition of individual differences is, in its turn, nothing other than the abolition
of privileges, and the elimination of privileges is right as such. Only, the work
of right is contradictory and, as we have just seen, its concept self-destructs.
Individual differences are so far from being abolished by the work of right, they
are so far from being eliminated when one claims to eliminate them or not to
take account of them that, in this abstract destruction of themselves, they are,
on the contrary, maintained and are carried to the level of the absolute. As soon
as one places oneself in the communist universe of the right of labor and
considers all men as workers, one recognizes their fundamental inequality,
since their productive capacities, their strength, their agility, their intelligence,
etc.—in short, all the determinations they present as workers—are fundamentally unequal. Of the equal right that opens the communist horizon, Marx says:
"It recognizes no class differences, because everyone is only a worker like
everyone else; *but it tacitly recognizes unequal individual endowment and thus
productive capacities as natural privileges.*"[12] Actually, communism does not
only recognize the inequality of individuals against the background of the
difference in their productive capacities; it carries this in a sense to the extreme
when it defines the individual in terms of these capacities, that is, as a worker:
of a state of affairs it makes a right. In this way, either one gives every
individual his due—but then one is simply ratifying the inequality of different
talents, and right is precisely the right of inequality—or one claims to apply to
all individuals and to all labors, despite their fundamental inequality, the same
measurement and the same remuneration, and the inequality is no less obvious.
Marx concludes his analysis of equal right as the principle of communism in this
way: "*It is therefore a right of inequality, in its content, like every right.*"[13]

The fact that right, that of communism but also all right in general, is the
right of inequality, and that this is so because ultimately reality, as monadic
subjective reality, is irreducible to the universality of an objective measurement[14] is made even more obvious in what follows in this text. For it is not
only the actual praxis of an individual which escapes the definition of "labor"; it
is his entire nonprofessional life which is placed out of bounds when he is
reduced to the condition of a worker. Now, in this private life there are numerous circumstances that result in the needs of one person being greater than
those of another so that, here again, to give an equal share of social wealth to
these two workers is to wrong the one who has, for example, a family to support.
" . . . unequal individuals . . . are measurable only by an equal standard in so
far as they are brought under an equal point of view, are taken from one definite
side only, for instance, in the present case, are regarded only as workers and
nothing more is seen in them, everything else being ignored. Further, one
worker is married, another not; one has more children than another, and so on
and so forth. Thus, with an equal performance of labor, and hence an equal
share in the social consumption fund, one will in fact receive more than

another, one will be richer than another, and so on. To avoid all these defects, right instead of being equal would have to be unequal."[15]

The problematic of socialism can be understood only on the basis of this radical critique of equal right, and this is why it must be said that socialism, as Marx understood it, is not built on the idea of justice but on the clear awareness of the absurdity of this idea, an absurdity which finds its most obvious expression in the collapse of the concept of right. It is therefore not in opposition to capitalism, where the use of this concept remains purely theoretical, but rather in opposition to communism, which wants to realize it, that socialism must be thought of. Thinking of it in this way is nothing other than dismissing the idea of a possible equivalence between subjectivities, and this is why we are led back to each subjectivity and to the interiority proper to it. Labor can no longer be a mediation between need and the goods capable of satisfying it, not only because it is impossible to establish a socially defined equivalence between them, but because, as a moment of subjectivity, labor in itself cannot be a mediation. The critique of right is then nothing more than the critique of objectivity in a new form, a new affirmation of the radical immanence of life. The relation of the individual to being cannot be an external relation with something outside, a relation in which no equality is possible because it immediately throws us into the realm of heterogeneity, but a relation of subjectivity with itself. To begin with, labor is returned to what it actually is, neither a mediation nor an equivalent but a determination of life willed by it. " . . . after labor has become not only a means of life but life's prime want. . . ."[16] As a mode of life, work can be willed by it, can be its want, only in a society in which each person can perform the activity that is best suited to him. A society such as this is a society of abundance, or rather of overabundance. Moreover, in it alone can it happen that, devoting himself to the activity of his choice, each person nevertheless finds in the social wealth the possibility of satisfying all his other needs. The overabundance of social wealth is therefore what allows the activity that comes from me and expresses me to connect up with the satisfaction of all my other needs, what enables the immediate synthetic relation of praxis and enjoyment to be added onto their analytical relation, to the extent that praxis has itself become a need and the satisfaction of this need. This relation, which is no longer mediated by anything, this relation internal to subjectivity between its capacities and its needs, is subjectivity itself in its immanent temporality; it is the movement of life understood as its self-realization. It is precisely because, even though he himself was compelled to live through its initial and most terrible phase, he grasped capitalism as being a formidable development of the productive forces of society that Marx saw in it the condition for socialism, which is to be defined as *that place where an impossible justice becomes useless* since, as a result of overabundance, all the needs of the individual are satisfied even though he devotes himself to the activity that corresponds to his deepest wish. Marx characterizes in the following manner this socialist society, which he still calls "a higher phase of communist society," where exchange and right will have disappeared, where with the abolition of all mediation subjectivity will be restored to itself: "After labor has become not only a means of life but life's prime want; after the productive forces have also increased with the all-round development of the individual, and all the springs of co-operative wealth flow more abundantly—only then can the narrow horizon of bourgeois right be crossed in its entirety and society inscribe on its banners: 'From each according to his ability, to each according to his needs!' "[17]

The presuppositions upon which the socialist utopia is constructed are not themselves utopian. Because they constitute the internal structure of reality and express it, they are the presuppositions of every possible society and, in particular, of bourgeois society. With respect to the latter and to what founds it, namely exchange, the difficulty has become even more urgent. It is no longer a matter of simply opposing the question of its possibility to the factitious description of the market society and the different forms in which it appears in history, starting with primitive bartering. Inasmuch as the exchange of commodities, in accordance with the theory of value formulated by the English school and taken up again by Marx, is only that of the labor of different individuals, and inasmuch as the latter are, however—and this is Marx's personal and decisive contribution—subjectively, qualitatively different and as such irreducible to one another just as to any unit of measurement, the transcendental question of exchange is now formulated as follows: how is exchange possible starting from its own impossibility?

Here the implications of the theory of praxis, the final consequences of the critique directed at Hegel, become all the more obvious. For it is only when labor ceases to be interpreted as an objectification process that the problem of exchange is posed in apparently insoluble terms. If indeed labor is objectified in the product, if the being of the product is constituted by labor, then the question of exchange is resolved. What is before our eyes, what is there on the market with the product is, precisely, the work it contains, and the comparison of products is immediately possible or, rather, has already been effected, since merely perceiving them is identical to perceiving the labor inscribed in them. Because subjectivity is understood by Marx in its radical immanence, labor, then, is not displayed in its product—to be specific, it is not objectified. And it is for this reason that labor "in itself as such" does not exist, because since it never exists in the form of the product, it is never this unitary, objective reality which is the same for everyone. By rejecting the Hegelian concept of labor as objectification, this thesis denies its unity, its identity, its universality and renders all objective knowledge and all measurement of its being impossible and reduces it instead to the insurmountable plurality of different types of labor that are concrete and subjective; this is thereby, precisely, the thesis that raises the possibility of exchange to a transcendental question.

Capital approaches this question in its opening chapters. The problem that takes shape here is, as we see, by no means limited to capitalism. And this is not only because the market economy does not coincide with capitalism, which represents no more than its most advanced form, but, on a more essential level, because the possibility of exchange must be constructed on the basis of a reality which is heterogeneous to it and which as such escapes the sphere of the market economy itself. A reality such as this constitutes the ontological ground upon which *Capital* and, generally speaking, Marx's entire economic problematic is built.

The transcendental question of the possibility of exchange is formulated with inspired concision in the *Grundrisse*. This formulation goes as follows: (1) the affirmation of the radically subjective character of praxis and hence of labor and labor time: *"Labor time itself exists as such only subjectively, only in the form of activity"*; (2) the consequence of the subjective status of labor: the impossibility of exchanging one particular labor, that is, an individual and subjective labor, for another: *"This statement means, subjectively expressed, nothing more than that the worker's particular labor time cannot be directly exchanged for every other particular labor time"*; (3) the construction of the possibility of exchange starting from its very impossibility, that is, substituting for real labor, which cannot be exchanged, some other entity capable of representing it and of being exchanged in its place. Right after stating that a particular labor cannot be exchanged by the individual who performs it, Marx adds: " . . . its general exchangeability has first to be mediated . . . it has first to take on an objective form, *a form different from itself*, in order to attain this general exchangeability."[18] To take on a form different from itself, to become other is, properly speaking, to be alienated. Inasmuch as it is the condition of the possibility of exchange of labor and, consequently, of the exchange of commodities, alienation appears as the fundamental concept of the economy, of the market economy—capitalist and communist—in any case. Fundamental: as that which founds the economy and makes it possible. But we must see under what condition: alienation constitutes the principle of the transcendental genesis of the economy only to the extent that its concept has been stripped of its Hegelian signification. To be alienated does indeed mean to be objectified, but it is not real labor as such that is objectified. This is precisely because, according to Marx, real labor is incapable of being objectified and, consequently, of admitting measurement, because it is necessary to substitute for it an equivalent different from it, an equivalent that is presumed to be or alleged to be objective, ideal, and quantifiable, that will play this role and make a quasi-exchange possible. Because alienation understood in this way is certainly not the alienation of labor in the sense in which labor itself would be alienated, would become substantively other, would change in its very reality—this is, precisely, impossible—but instead signifies that something is substituted for real labor, that, to be more precise, an ideality is superimposed on the reality of labor without in any way changing the latter, and in this sense, it is indeed alienation that is in question here. An alienation such as this, by which an ideality is substituted for a reality, allowing this reality (which nevertheless subsists intact just where it is) to escape—this is what Marx calls abstraction. *Alienation, as identical to*

abstraction, is the originary founding act of the economy and, precisely, of its
transcendental genesis.

Like all great thinkers Marx wrote only a single book, at least as far as the
economy is concerned, whose structure, themes, and theses are to be discovered throughout its different stages. The opening theme of this work is
precisely the fundamental theme; it is the transcendental genesis of the economy, the theory of the abstraction starting from which the economy becomes
possible and, in the same stroke, *constitutes an object within the sphere of*
human experience. This abstraction is presented in a double form. First of all, it
is the abstraction by virtue of which a commodity is considered to be a product
of labor and nothing more. This consideration, which indeed makes it into a
commodity and marks the boundaries of the market economy, is an abstraction
because, by viewing what is offered on the market as simply a product of labor,
its material qualities, that is, its use-value as well, are lost from sight. "But the
exchange of commodities," says *Capital*, "is evidently an act characterized by a
total abstraction from use-value, and *every relation of exchange is even charac-*
terized by this abstraction."[19] What indeed remains once one has abstracted from
the material qualities and the usefulness of commodities is solely the fact that
they have been produced by labor. "If then we leave out of consideration the
use-value of commodities, they have only one common property left, that of
being products of labor."[20]

We must see then in what way the "product of labor" *considered as such* is an
abstraction: it is, precisely, not a real thing, resulting from the action of real
labor, but a pseudo-thing, stripped of all real determinations and reduced to the
pure meaning of having been produced by labor. This radical modification by
which every real property is abolished to the benefit of a pure meaning, Marx
calls a change, a metamorphosis.[21] This chemical or rather metaphysical
transubstantiation which changes the real object, fashioned by real labor, into a
mere meaning, makes of it a "residue." It is not an impoverished reality which
has lost some of its properties but, having lost them all and reality along with
them—and hence all possibility of being distinguishable from another reality—
it is no more than a shadow, a ghost. "Let us now consider the residue of each of
these products; it consists of the same unsubstantial reality in each."[22] This
unsubstantial reality, this irreality is, however, neither empty nor undetermined; it is precisely a meaning, that of being a "product of labor." A meaning
such as this is nothing other than value.[23]

But this abstraction, by virtue of which commodities stripped of their real
property are no longer anything but values, presupposes another abstraction
which founds it. Indeed, inasmuch as "value" means "a product of labor," the
values which compensate for one another and are exchanged for one another on
the market can do this only to the extent that the labor which they "crystallize"
is one and the same labor. But, as we have seen, the kinds of labor that produce
commodities are as varied as the commodities themselves and, no more than the
latter, do not allow comparison. *The original abstraction which constitutes the*

transcendental condition for the possibility of exchange is that by which the various labors of diverse individuals are reduced to one and the same labor. For it is only to the extent that the various real labors are carried back to one single and undifferentiated labor which serves as a standard for them all that the commodities produced by these real labors can themselves be reduced to "values" measured, as are these labors, by the yardstick of the uniform labor that has been substituted for them. "To measure the exchange-value of commodities by the labor-time they contain, the different kinds of labor have to be reduced to uniform, homogeneous, simple labor, in short to labor of uniform quality, whose only difference, therefore, is quantity."[24]

How is this reduction of all kinds of real labor to one and the same labor accomplished? "This reduction," Marx says, "appears to be an abstraction."[25] As in the case of the process which leads from the products of labor to their value, abstraction designates here the exclusion of all characteristics belonging to reality and their replacement by ideal determinations. Only, the reality from which the abstraction is then made is no longer the objective reality of commodities; it is the subjective reality of praxis. This is why the characteristics that are excluded in this abstraction are quite specific; they are the characteristics of subjectivity itself. If it appears that the determinations lost by the abstraction which is made here resemble those of commodities (for example, qualitative difference, specificity, etc.), this is inasmuch as the commodities themselves possessed these properties because they were secretly related to a subjectivity: as use-values they are first of all connected to the powers and the needs of life. We are acquainted with the characteristics of subjective praxis, with quality—but considered an original quality designating nothing other than the quality of the determinations of subjectivity, the distinctions separating these determinations themselves on the basis of their subjective realization, with, as a corollary, the radical distinction separating all the determinations and all the given properties inasmuch as they belong to different subjectivities: that is, individuality which designates the essential particularity of that which belongs to one and the same monadic sphere. Such are the characteristics which are abolished in the process of abstraction, which leads from real labor, as determined qualitatively and accomplished by individuals who, in each case, are different, to labor which, as the result of this process of abstraction, is, precisely, abstract or, rather, general labor, whose characteristics are, on the contrary, uniformity, homogeneity, and indifference with respect to quality, to any particularity of a specific type of labor and, what is more, of the individuals who perform it.[26]

Because the individuality of real praxis is its very essence, the negation of this ontological characteristic in general labor makes the latter the "opposite" of real labor. Marx says that "the particular individual labor contained in the commodity can only through alienation be represented as its opposite, impersonal, abstract, general—and only in this form social—labor. . . ." And further on, speaking of the contradiction characterizing the commodity, Marx once again states that it results from the fact that "the particular labor of an isolated individual can become socially effective only if it is expressed as its direct opposite, i.e., abstract universal labor."[27] The indifference of labor with respect to the particular individual who performs it goes so far that a reversal in perspective is produced and that labor, which in its real being is but a determination of individual subjective life, becomes, properly speaking, hypostatized due to this abstraction and therefore seems to deny the individuals themselves, who are reduced to the level of mere instruments of this labor. "Labor . . . does not seem, indeed, to be the labor of different persons, but on the contrary the different working individuals seem to be mere organs of this labor."[28]

The indifference of labor with respect to the individual who performs it cannot be understood as a consideration of an ethical nature; it is what constitutes it as labor in itself, as typical labor, as what has to be done in order to produce a given object, so that what has to be done in this way has also to be accomplished within a specific amount of time. "The labor-time of the individual is thus, in fact, the labor-time required by society to produce a particular use-value. . . ."[29] Naturally, this typical labor necessary for producing a specific object is dependent on the capacities of the individual, but of the individual in general and not of this or that particular individual. It is an average labor adapted to an average individual, an ideal norm defined in relation to a concept which itself is ideal. Even more than the capacities of the individual in general, this sort of norm depends on the technical means existing in a given society, on the development of productivity, etc.[30] We are better able to see that this average labor is constructed as a norm when it is, precisely, impossible to consider abstractly the qualities peculiar to certain individuals such as knowledge, agility, intense effort, etc. Then it will be a question of establishing a strict equivalence between labor that everyone can do, or "simple labor," and skilled labor, or "complicated labor," so that, for example, one hour of the latter counts for two or three hours of the former. How is this equivalence obtained if not, again here, by means of a reduction which is only a new form of the process of abstraction thanks to which a quantitative proportion is substituted for a qualitative difference?[31]

Establishing a norm for labor on an absolutely general level, namely simple labor to which skilled or complicated labor is reduced, defining for the production of each object a particular norm for labor, namely the (simple or skilled) labor-time required for the production of a given object, this, then, is what enables one to definitively overcome the qualitative plurality of the labor performed by different individuals: since the labor of each individual is no more than the exemplar of a type of labor, it is then, in the same stroke, alleged to be identical to the labor of other individuals obeying the same norm. The equality of different labors, the possibility of exchange, is founded. *Marx terms social the labor of each individual considered not in itself, in its peculiar subjective reality, but as it is reduced by abstraction to the ideal norm to which it corresponds, inasmuch, moreover, as this norm was itself constructed on the basis of this labor.*

Social labor is precisely equal labor, that which, having lost all of its real and, as such, particular properties is henceforth the same for all.[32]

Insofar as social labor is abstract labor, it finds its possibility in abstraction, which itself must be possible. For it is not enough to describe the substitution of social labor for real labor; one must also say how this substitution occurs. Real labor becomes social labor when it is measured, and the measure of real labor is the time it takes. It is solely because the labor that produces a commodity is measured by the time it takes that this product is itself capable of being measured and compared with another whose production will have required the same amount of time, or twice as much time, etc. How can the magnitude of the value of any particular article be measured? asks *Capital*, and the answer is: "by the quantity of the value-creating substance, the labor, contained in the article. The quantity of labor, however, is measured by its duration, and labor-time in its turn finds its standard in weeks, days, and hours."[33]

Why, then, is labor-time said to be abstract? Is not the time a man devotes to his labor in the day, in the year, in his life, something very concrete and very real and, in most cases, what is most real and most concrete in this life? Inasmuch, however, as "labor-time . . . finds its standard in weeks, days, and hours," this time is an objective time. Far from being identified with the immanent temporality of objective praxis, it is but the external milieu of its representation. What is measured in this milieu, in the homogeneous milieu of time that is spatialized, divided, and quantified according to the divisions and the quantifications of the space in terms of which it is itself measured—the trajectory of the sun in the sky, that of a shadow on the sundial which measures this time—is thus represented time, the objective double, the irreal copy of praxis. This is why labor-time is abstract, because it is precisely not the real time of real labor, the subjective duration of effort as it is lived, but the empty dial upon which one claims to lay this effort out in order to measure it. An empty claim: between sunrise and sunset the worker is at the factory, the laborer is in the field, but what are they doing there, how are they doing it, and what is the intensity of their effort? In this way the standard of measurement lies outside the reality it wants to measure, a reality which, in fact, escapes it.

Once he finds himself confronted with the fundamental problems and concepts of the economy, Marx, starting in 1844, makes the crucial distinction between objective time and the subjective temporality of real praxis, a distinction which will command the entire subsequent problematic. In order to make the illegitimate character of property manifest, Proudhon had shown that the latter could not result from simple *de facto* possession, from its consolidation and its legitimation through the passage of time. "Never . . . will you succeed in making length of time, which of itself creates nothing, changes nothing, modifies nothing, able to change the user into a proprietor."[34] This thesis was adhered to by Edgar Bauer in order to denounce the contradiction in which Proudhon had been trapped, for, if it is true that time creates nothing, how can it be made the source of economic value? "Herr Edgar's conclusion is: since

Proudhon said that mere time cannot change one legal principle into another, that by itself it cannot change or modify anything, he is inconsistent when he makes labor time the measure of the economic value of the product of labor."[35] It is at this point that we find, issuing from Marx's pen as he relates this discussion in *The Holy Family*, the decisive assertion that Bauer was able to formulate this objection against Proudhon only *"by identifying empty length of time with time filled with labor."*[36] In the text following this passage, it is to the real temporality of actual labor that is unequivocally attributed both the formation of economic value—an assertion to which we shall return—and the real production of a real object, which, precisely, is impossible outside of real duration: "And even as far as intellectual production is concerned, must I not . . . consider the time necessary for the production of an intellectual work when I determine its scope, its character and its plan? Otherwise I risk at least that the object that is in my idea will never become an object in reality, and can therefore acquire only the value of an imaginary object, i.e., an imaginary value."[37]

However, just when Marx makes the distinction, a stroke of genius for this epoch, between immanent subjective temporality and objective time, he has a presentiment, which is no less a stroke of genius, that the economy is itself established on the ground of this distinction, which although essential is not perceived, and that the economy then slips from real time into abstract time, which consists in substituting objective time for subjective temporality. This is precisely the alienation which constitutes both the economy and the transcendental condition of its possibility. "The criticism of political economy . . . converts *the importance of time for human labor into its importance for wages, for wage-labor."*[38] The radical critique that Marx undertakes here against Proudhon can thus be fully understood. Proudhon places labor at the center of his problematic, as the source of value in place of capital and landed property. The critique he directs in this way against political economy nevertheless remains prisoner to the latter, and this is so because labor is considered an economic concept, because for real labor is substituted its standard of measurement, its objective determination in objective time. Such is the "importance of time" not for "human labor"—let us understand by this real praxis—but "for wages, for wage-labor." It is in objective time, in fact, in its equal divisions that the different types of real labor become equal, measured wage-labors. Then arises the world of political economy which finally had duped Proudhon, and in which "the mere quantity of labor functions as a measure of value regardless of quality"; it results from this that "men are effaced by their labor; that the pendulum of the clock has become as accurate a measure of the relative activity of two workers as it is of the speed of two locomotives. Therefore, we should not say that one man's hour is worth another man's hour, but rather that one man during an hour is worth just as much as another man during an hour. *Time is everything, man is nothing; he is at most time's carcase.* Quality no longer matters. Quantity alone decides everything; hour for hour, day for day." In the name of justice, Proudhon wanted equality, equality of men and thus of different men's labor, but with "his smoothing-plane of 'equalization'," with time as the standard of measurement, he does no more than express a state of affairs, that of right, precisely, that of the market economy: "this equalising of labor is not by any means the work of M. Proudhon's eternal justice; it is purely and simply a fact of modern industry."[39]

Not just its fact: its possibility, if the measurement of labor by its objective duration is the concrete mode through which its quantitative determination, the determination of value, and, consequently, the condition of exchange are produced. The critique directed at Proudhon allows its transcendental meaning to appear behind its anthropological and ethical appearance. Marx returns to this in *Capital* when he favorably cites one of Adam Smith's precursors who said with regard to the exchange of commodities that it "in effect is no more than exchanging one man's labor in one thing for a time certain, for another man's labor in another thing for the same time."[40] And still in *Capital*, concerning labor-time: "The worker is here nothing more than personified labor-time. All individual distinctions are merged in those of 'full-timers' and 'half-timers'."[41]

We want to establish the possibility of abstract labor upon which the economy of exchange reposes. The objective temporal determination of labor grounds its quantitative determination and is identical with it. But, as has been frequently repeated, the real labor performed by different individuals is qualitatively different in each case, and the fact that the duration is identical does not, for all that, make them homogeneous. This is the reason why the reduction of diverse labors to a type of labor, to one and the same abstract labor, was posited. Far from being able to found this reduction, the objective temporal determination *of labor* presupposes it instead as its own condition. It is therefore a question of the constitution of abstract labor starting from qualitatively different labors, independently of their objective temporal measurement, and it is this abstraction of simple or complicated labor which can no longer be simply described but must itself be grasped in its possibility.

Such is the decisive progress realized by the analysis of *Capital* in its introductory stages, just when it appears to repeat purely and simply that of *The Critique of Political Economy*. It shows that the thematization of a single labor starting from qualitatively different labors is possible only to the extent that the latter reveal themselves to be substantively and ontologically identical, to the extent that they are but the diverse modalities of one and the same reality, namely the subjective force which itself constitutes the essence of all real praxis. Not only are the real labors of different individuals comparable among themselves as being for each person nothing other than the actualization of his very existence, involving his bodily powers, but in order to make this metaphysical truth apparent Marx places himself at the outset within the domain where this truth lies and is not afraid to make the leap into the monadic sphere. What, in fact, shows the identical essence of "qualitatively different kinds of labor" like tailoring and weaving is that they can be performed by the same individual. *It is in the individual that they are the same thing, namely this individual himself. Capital* abruptly poses the question of the possibility of exchange and of the market economy: "So far as they are values, the coat and the linen are things of a like substance, objective expressions of essentially identical labor. But tailoring and weaving are, qualitatively, different kinds of labor." Under the appearance of these relativist and historicizing considerations which were to nourish Marxism and, after it, the human sciences, the absolute character of the transcendental condition shines forth: "There are, however, states of society in which *one and the same man does tailoring and weaving alternately, in which case these two forms of labor are mere modifications of the labor of the same individual. . . .*"[42] The fact that a condition such as this is characteristic of no particular regime, for example, that of the family-centered economy, in which each person must do everything, but of every conceivable kind of economic regime, including that of the division of labor and of modern industry, is asserted by what directly follows in the text: "*just as* the coat which our tailor makes one day, and the trousers which he makes another day, imply only a variation in the labor of one and the same individual." This then is what all sorts of real labor have in common: they involve one and the same organic force, of which they are but the diverse actualizations. "Productive activity, if we leave out of sight its special form, viz., the useful character of the labor, is nothing but the expenditure of human labor-power. Tailoring and weaving, though qualitatively of different productive activities, are each a productive expenditure of human brains, nerves, and muscles, and in this sense are human labor. They are but two different modes of expending human labor-power. Of course, *this labor-power, which remains the same under all its modifications. . . .*"[43]

"Simple average labor," which serves as the measure of all labor, which is represented in the exchange-value of the product and out of which skilled labor is constructed, is nothing other than "the expenditure of simple labor-power . . . which, on an average, apart from any special development, exists in the organism of every ordinary individual."[44] Let us therefore recognize the essential distinction which serves as the ground for the problematic of *Capital* just when it seems to blur, the distinction between, on the one hand, primordial labor, namely the activity of organic subjectivity as it is capable of unfolding spontaneously and of being realized without preparation or training of any sort, and, on the other hand, simple labor, which is only the abstraction of primordial labor. In what does this abstraction consist? *In the case of primordial labor, which Marx terms labor-power, we are in the presence of the possibility of identical labor, which serves as the ground for all economic determinations: simple labor, for its part, is the representation of primordial labor; the abstraction that constitutes it resides in this representation.* This is why simple labor is abstract, because, bound to representation, held within its field of vision and rendered objective by it, it is, in the same stroke, separated from the original domain of real praxis. This is why this labor serves as a standard of measurement for the complex forms of labor and for the determination of value, because primordial labor is the essence common to all kinds of concrete labor and is their reality.

Because abstract labor is only the representation of real labor, the relation that is established between these two forms of labor can be determined rigorously: to be precise, there are not two forms of labor but a single labor, real labor, considered the actualization of labor-power, of organic subjectivity and, on the other hand, this same labor as it is opposed to itself in representation and as it henceforth takes on the form of irreality. Real labor produces the real object, the commodity in its materiality and as a use-value. Abstract labor, which is the pure representation of this real labor, is in its turn represented in the commodity as its exchange-value, which is thus nothing other than the objectification in the product of the prior objectification of real labor in abstract labor. *Capital* states, touching on the essence of the matter: *"If there are not, properly speaking, two sorts of labor in the commodity, nevertheless the same labor is opposed to itself therein depending on whether it is related to the use-value of the commodity, as to its object, or to the value of this commodity as to its pure objective expression."*[45]

The genesis of abstract labor, starting from real labor and in opposition to it, is presented by Marx as his great discovery and at the same time as the foundation for political economy. "At first sight a commodity presented itself to us as a complex of two things—use-value and exchange-value. Later on, we saw also that labor, too, possesses the same two-fold nature; for, so far as it finds expression in value, it does not possess the same characteristics that belong to it as a creator of use-values. I was the first to point out and to examine critically this two-fold nature of the labor contained in commodities. As this point is the pivot on which a clear comprehension of political economy turns, we must go into more detail."[46] A good many years later, in the Preface he wrote for what was to be called Book Two of *Capital*, Engels, asking himself about the importance of Marx's work on economics—"But what is there new in Marx's utterances on surplus-value?"—replies to his own question in these terms: he "was the first to ascertain *what* labor it was that produced value."[47] The thesis which asserts that labor produces value is the thesis of classical economics, but as long as one has not ascertained "what labor" produces value, an assertion such as this not only remains thoroughly vague, it is false. For by labor is quite naturally meant real labor, the labor of an individual as he performs it in accordance with his capabilities and his own rhythm. Now value is neither produced nor determined by labor such as this, which depends upon the particularities of each person; otherwise, one would have to say that "the lazier a man, or the clumsier a man, the more valuable his commodity, because the greater the time of labor required for finishing the commodity."[48] In this way, the problematic of abstract labor and all its determinations, notably that of socially necessary labor, is seen to be a necessary development, and it is demonstrated that abstract labor alone, and not real labor, is capable of producing and determining the value of commodities.[49] Political economy is reproached by Marx precisely for its inability to recognize labor as social labor.[50] This shortcoming becomes evident when, renouncing its attempt to establish the standard of value in precious metals, political economy turns instead toward labor. It is amidst general confusion that labor is cast in the role of a central concept, and Benjamin Franklin, one of the first—after Petty—to have reduced value to labor and, as such, the founder of classical political economy, confuses real labor with social labor.

The distinction between real labor and abstract labor, founding the latter on the basis of the former—a manner of founding which is none other than the transcendental genesis of the economy—on the contrary signifies for the economy the radical clarification of its fundamental concepts.

The radical clarification of the fundamental concepts of the economy and the delimitation of its status

What is clarified, first of all, is the concept of value in its relation to the definitive formulation of the being of labor. It is real labor that creates use-value; it is abstract labor that creates exchange-value.[51] Inasmuch as it is both use-value and exchange-value, the commodity refers to these two essentially different and heterogeneous forms of labor, relating in its materiality to real labor and in its economic value to social labor.[52] Because real labor differs ontologically from social labor, just as use-value differs substantially from exchange-value, *the relation of real labor to its product has nothing to do with the relation of abstract labor to value*. Here, in the rigor of phenomenological evidence, is revealed the source of the illusion according to which Marx is held to have retained in his economic analysis the conceptual underpinnings by means of which Hegel himself had sketched out, as early as 1803, the philosophical interpretation of the thesis of the English school. This concerns notably the interpretation of the concept of labor as objectification. *The conservation of this concept in Marx's subsequent work concerns abstract labor alone, more precisely, its relation to what is found to be created by it, namely exchange-value*. Exchange-value—and it alone—must be said to be the objectification of labor, which, precisely because it refers back to this value, is no more than— and can be no more than—abstract, general, ideal, irreal labor, as is strikingly demonstrated by this text in the *Grundrisse:* "The objectification of the general, social character of labor . . . is precisely what makes the product of labor time into exchange value; this is what gives the commodity the attributes of money." And a few lines further on, Marx says that "money is labor time in the form of a general object, or the objectification of general labor time, labor time as a general commodity."[53]

One may still have some doubt as to the legitimacy of using the concept of objectification to characterize the relation between labor and value. Understood in this way, objectification, at any rate, has already lost its Hegelian signification. For Hegel, labor is objectified in the sense in which mind is objectified, in the sense of a real power which itself accomplishes the act of objectification, which carries itself into the domain of objectivity and, above all, establishes objectivity as such. But social labor is not real and has no power. Moreover, it is not labor which is objectified but its "general, social character." Now, the "general, social character of labor," consequently abstract labor, is only a representation in the sense of a *cogitatum*, not in the sense of a power of representation. The "objectification" of social labor in exchange-value is thus only the representation of a representation. This is why, instead of speaking of the objectification of social labor, it is better to say, as Marx himself does most often, that social labor "is represented" in the value of the commodity.

It is true that Marx uses a similar expression in relation to real labor, of which it is said that it is presented in the product.[54] The reason is precisely that the relation of real labor to its product can no longer be subsumed under the Hegelian schema. Fundamentally different from the relation between social labor and value, the relation which unfolds on the level of irreality and which is only the representation by a representation—value—of an initial representation—abstract labor as the representation of real labor—the relation of the latter, of real praxis, to what it actually produces is by no means an objectification because, since it is of its essence subjective and incapable of being anything other than subjective, praxis, precisely, cannot objectify itself but can only transform the product it confronts in the internal tension of organic subjectivity. It is the result of labor that is objective, not the living labor itself which is and remains subjective, as this decisive text affirms: "*. . . labor time as subject corresponds as little to the general labor time which determines exchange values as the particular commodities and products correspond to it as object.*"[55] This is stated no less explicitly in another, equally essential passage which establishes in turn that the product—the commodity—is the result of real labor, of the temporal process of praxis and not this process itself: (1) "it [the commodity] is not labor time as labor time, but materialized labor time; labor time not in the form of motion, but at rest; *not in the form of the process, but of the result*"— that, distinct from the temporal process of real praxis, it nevertheless results from this process and not from abstract labor, which, as a mere representation, as an ideal determination, is, precisely, incapable of producing anything at all; (2) ". . . it [the commodity] is not the objectification of labor time in general, which exists only as a conception (*it is only a conception of labor* separated from its quality, subject merely to quantitative variations), but rather the specific *result* of a specific, of a naturally specified, kind of labor which differs quantitatively from other kinds. . . ."[56]

The radical clarification of the relation of labor to the commodity renders this decisive form of economic alienation intelligible; Marx called this alienation the making into a thing, or the reification, of social relations, namely their transformation into relations between things. The ambiguity of Marx's problematic is tied here to the fact that he denounces this reification at one and the same time (thereby contradicting himself) as a scandal and as an illusion: if it is an illusion, then the scandal is merely an apparent one. The illusion is that in their circulation commodities seem to be exchanged by virtue of their own inherent qualities. It is gold itself or iron which demands opposite itself a given quantity of tea or of cloth. "Exchange-value thus appears to be a social determination of use-values, a determination which is proper to them as things and in consequence of which they are able in definite proportions to take one another's place in the exchange process. . . ."[57] In fact, as we know, if commodities are exchanged in a definite proportion, this is not by virtue of their natural properties, as use-values, but because they represent equal labor-times. The relation of commodities, which seems to be a relation between things, is in reality a relation between the different kinds of labor that produced them and, consequently, between the individuals who performed this labor. It is in this way that the material relation connecting use-values presents only an appearance of another type of relation, the economic relation of exchange-values, which is only a social relation, that of the different kinds of labor which these values represent. The social relation is thus concealed within a relation between things. "Although it is thus correct to say"—as did Galiani—"that exchange-value is a relation between persons, it is however necessary to add that it is a relation hidden by a material veil."[58] To the extent that it substitutes the world of things for the world of persons, this disguise appears as a scandal. The 1844 text—"The devaluation of the human world grows in direct proportion to the increase in value of the world of things"[59]—seems to find an echo in this protest of *The Critique of Political Economy:* "Only the conventions of our everyday life make it appear commonplace and ordinary that social relations of production should assume the shape of things, so that the relations into which people enter in the course of their work appear as the relations of things to one another and of things to people."[60]

Whatever the importance of this disguise and of the illusions to which it gives rise—for example, those of the monetary system[61]—it should not be forgotten, however, that this is no more than an illusion, than *an erroneous way of representing things to oneself which changes nothing with regard to their real essence.* Now if an illusion such as this, which is purely theoretical, in fact defines the error from a scientific point of view, it cannot constitute a real alienation. Increasing the value of the world of things and devaluing the world of men is thus only an appearance, tied to our perception. And if it is stated that the task of science is precisely to correct this perception and to reestablish scientific truth in opposition to it and to the ideology of the classical economy which it produces, by eliminating the illusion this truth also eliminates alienation, and the world of exchange is justified.

The situation, in fact, is the following. The exchange of commodities is, it is true, only that of the different kinds of labor which produced them. Everyone knows this to be the case despite the appearance that commodities themselves circulate.[62] Science establishes the truth of this suspicion. An identity exists between the relation of commodities and that of different kinds of labor, and affirming this relation is merely a tautology.[63] But a tautology is neither an illusion nor a disguise; even less is it capable of constituting something like the

process of real alienation. The fact is, therefore, that illusion, disguise, alienation do not dwell within the relation between social labor and exchange-value, a
tautological relation, but are situated in advance of it, in a domain out of which
this relation proceeds, in a process which makes this relation possible. Alienation is not internal to the system of exchange, it belongs to its genealogy and is
identical with it. It is to the extent that different kinds of real labor and,
consequently, the relation between persons, have previously been alienated in
social labor, considered homogeneous and defined quantitatively, that they are
capable of being alienated in the equivalent of this labor, in the value of
commodities, and of taking on the aspect of a relation between things. " . . . *it is
a characteristic feature of labor which posits exchange-value* that it causes the
social relations of individuals to appear in the perverted form of a social relation
between things."[64] Reification is not originally the objectification of social labor
in commodities: social labor is already objective, it is an ideal meaning, "so
many hours of socially necessary labor," and the value of the commodity is
nothing other than this meaning. Reification secretly refers to the prior process
in which real labor was transformed into social labor. It does not constitute the
becoming of reality but the abstraction in which reality has been lost. It is only
inasmuch as reality has originally been lost that it can take on the form of a
thing. It is only because, in the mystification upon which the system of exchange is built, subjective praxis has become abstract social labor that the real
practical relations between persons can become the relations of this labor to
itself, the relations of commodities between themselves. *Capital* relates in a
concise manner how the substitution of the relation between products for that
between producers finds its condition in the abstraction of social labor. "The
equality of all sorts of human labor is expressed objectively by their products all
being equally values; the measure of the expenditure of labor-power by the
duration of that expenditure, takes the form of the quantity of value of the
products of labor; and finally, the mutual relations of the producers, within
which the social character of their labor affirms itself, take the form of a social
relation between the products."[65]

In determining social labor and value as abstractions, the transcendental
genesis of the economy rigorously defines the "economic" in its pure state.
What is established is, first of all, that far from opposing one another, as subject
and object or as reality and its representation, *economic labor and value are
ontologically identical and are situated on the same plane of existence, namely
that, precisely, of abstraction, of irreality, and of ideality*. It is the status of
abstract labor which determines that of value, but it is with respect to the latter
that the status of the "economic" is, first and foremost and most often, brought
to light in Marx's work. The ideality of value is itself made evident by the
opposition which is continually asserted between value and the material reality
of the product. " . . . the existence of the things *qua* commodities, and the
value-relation between the products of labor which stamp them as commodities,
have absolutely no connection with their physical properties."[66] It is because it

is opposed to the material content of the commodity that the value is termed a form. The form of value must then be clearly distinguished from the form of the product, which is only a determination of its reality and, as such, something material like it. The formal character of value as it is opposed to the material content of commodities or, again, to their "natural form" is, on the contrary, something ideal, as one sees in the case of prices or of money, which is precisely one of the forms in which the value form attains the pure expression of itself: "The price or money-form of commodities is, *like their form of value generally*, . . . a purely ideal or mental form."[67] "The value of the commodity," Marx again states, "is different from the commodity itself."[68] This opposition between the form of value and the content of the commodity is so thoroughgoing that it actually constitutes value as such: ". . . through just this separation from its substance, it collapses into itself and tends away from the sphere of simple exchange value. . . ."[69] Becoming value only by being separated from the substance of the commodity, value no longer carries anything material within itself; all natural determinations are foreign to it. "[Torn] free from the commodity," it appears as "a metaphysical, insubstantial quality," in Sismondi's words as they are quoted by Marx,[70] who himself declares in *Capital:* "The value of commodities is the very opposite of the coarse materiality of their substance, not an atom of matter enters into its composition."[71]

Now, the immateriality of value is not a simple property it would possess for one knows not what reason, a factitious determination that one must merely note. This is an operative characteristic, the principle of its action, its *raison d'être*. Because it is radically opposed to the substance of the commodity, the form of value is indifferent with regard to the latter and can, while remaining identical to itself, subsume under itself any content whatsoever. Concerning money, which represents the pure form of value, the *Grundrisse* comment on ". . . the indifference of value towards the particular form of use value which it assumes, and at the same time its metamorphosis into all these forms, which appear, however, merely as disguises."[72] But the metamorphosis of value into the numerous use-values in which it is successively embodied is nothing more than the circulation of commodities, than exchange: exchange has its condition in the indifference of value with respect to the substance of the product. The ontological heterogeneity separating the use-value and the exchange-value does not belong to a sphere of philosophical considerations that are obsolete, external to the properly economic or scientific analysis, in short, of no interest; rather, it defines the internal possibility of the market economy and is only a new way of formulating its transcendental genesis, as is expressed once again by this innocent statement: "Trade has robbed things, pieces of wealth, of their primitive character of usefulness. . . ."[73]

Inasmuch as value is opposed to the material properties of commodities, it possesses its own peculiar mode of existence, *"purely economic"* existence.[74] We know what this purely economic existence is: it is the ideal representation of a specific quantity of abstract labor; it is the ideal representation of an ideal reality. This is why, in the doubly ideal existence of value, there is not a single particle of matter, because "the value of commodities has a purely social reality; and . . . they acquire this reality only in so far as they are expressions or embodiments of one identical social substance, viz., human labor."[75] In this way the being of the "social thing," that is, the product transformed into value in the commodity, is fully elucidated: "the products of labor become commodities, social things whose qualities are at the same time perceptible and imperceptible by the senses."[76]

How are the thing which is perceptible by the senses, and insubstantial, "metaphysical," or, yet again, "social" value related to one another in order to constitute the commodity? How does an ideal or categorial relation refer in general to its material "basis"? By adding itself on to it by means of a synthetic relation which leaves it unaffected in its reality. This ideal relation, namely the representation of a specific quantity of abstract labor, alone makes the thing that it subsumes under itself become a social thing, alone makes it enter into the realm of the economy and participate in it. To the question: "How is use-value transformed into commodity?" is replied: ". . . the use value of the commodity is a given presupposition—the material basis in which a specific economic relation presents itself. It is only this specific relation which stamps the use value as a commodity."[77] Because the economic relation is purely ideal, the manner in which it determines reality is defined rigorously: a determination such as this is contingent, accidental; it could just as easily not occur, just as the universe of material things could exist without the things in it ever having to be counted. This is what Marx means when he repeats that the market economy is only an historical and transitory system, that it is certainly possible but that it could very well never have occurred, just as it is possible that within one family the various members sell their labor or its results to one another, although this is not the rule for all family life in general.[78]

The dissociation of economic properties and reality presents an absolutely general signification and invites us to establish an *essential difference between the material process and the economic process of production*. The real or material process of production is the transformation of nature into use-values. It is an activity of life stemming from need and directed toward making everything homogeneous with this need. This real process of production has existed since the dawn of history; it is the transcendental condition of its possibility and its reality, and this is why it is immanent to history and reappears in each of its stages. ". . . the labor process . . . is common to all forms of production."[79] This is why this real process is present in capitalism: "Capital becomes the process of production through the incorporation of labor into capital; initially however, it becomes the material process of production; the process of production in general, so that the process of the production of capital is not distinct from the material process of production as such."[80] Insofar as the process of production which is realized in capitalism is a material process, we can find in it the elements of every real process, namely, matter which is worked on, the instrument, and, finally, labor itself. "Originally, when we examined the development of value into capital, the labor process was simply included within capital, and, as regards its physical conditions, its material presence, capital appeared as the totality of the conditions of this process, and correspondingly sorted itself out into certain qualitatively different parts, *material of labor*, means of labor and living labor. On one side, capital was divided into these three elements in accordance with its material composition. . . ."[81] Marx categorically asserts this once again: "capital presupposes: 1) the production process in general, such as is common to all social conditions, that is, without historic character, *human*, if you like."[82]

If, however, the real process of production is present within capitalism, the latter is by no means reduced to the former; instead it differs from it in an essential way, to the extent that it superimposes on this initial process something quite different from it, an economic process. The real process produces real objects, use-values. *The economic process produces exchange-values, it produces value as such and for itself.* This is why the productivity of the second process has nothing to do with that of the first; it concerns neither the production of use-values nor the increase of this production. Its sole role lies in the production and increase of value; it is a process of realization.[83] This is also why the material differences present within the real process of production—the material of labor, the means of labor, and living labor—are effaced in the process of realization in favor of new differences which are properly economic and tied to the essence and to the teleology of this process. After speaking of the three elements of the real process, Marx adds: "But this material side—or, its character as use value and as real process—did not at all coincide with its formal side."[84] This non-coincidence is at the same time a recomposition, and it consists in the fact that the material determinations of the real process are, in capital, no more than fractions of the latter, quantitative determinations of value situated within the process of realization and subordinated to it. It is in this way that the means of labor becomes something quite different from a physical system organized for the manufacture of a certain number of objects: a certain portion of capital, a certain quantity of value, possessing its own peculiar characteristics, characteristics that belong to value and obey its laws, the great law of realization that defines capital ". . . as fixed capital."[85]

But what is true for the means of labor which has become fixed capital is also true of all the other material elements of the real process: raw materials, auxiliary materials, and, even more so, living labor have lost their primitive character and are now nothing more than economic elements, moments in the destiny of capital.[86] Then the economic reality appears in its formal purity, a reality composed solely of values and as such foreign to the materiality of the process and to its elements.[87] This presumes, precisely, that all the material elements of the process of production have been converted into economic elements, that for them has been substituted their value, and that the result of the process, which has become economic, is no longer the product but a new value, the sum of all the values involved in this process and superior to them.

The difference between the real process and the economic process, and the indifference of the latter with respect to the former, can easily be seen in the following examples. Let us assume that as a result of an increase in productivity, which constitutes a real determination of concrete labor, this labor produces in the same lapse of time a quantity of use-values double that previously produced. The social wealth, if by this we understand the actual material wealth, that which consists precisely in use-values, has doubled. But the economic wealth, namely the value produced by this same labor, has not changed, for it is measured by the labor-time, which, precisely, has remained the same. Inversely, "if some factor were to cause the productivity of all types of labor to fall in equal degree, thus requiring the same proportion of additional labor for the production of all commodities, then the value of all commodities would rise, the actual expression of their exchange-value remaining unchanged, and the real wealth of society would decrease, since the production of the same quantity of use-values would require a larger amount of labor-time."[88]

Marx stressed a number of times the paradoxical character of the relation between real wealth and economic wealth, namely its contingency, the fact that real wealth can diminish while economic wealth increases or, on the contrary, that real wealth can increase while economic wealth decreases. Such was the case at the time of the "misery of agricultural overproduction, recorded in French history," which showed that "the mere increase of products does not increase their value."[89] Now despite this contingency, this is not a mere accident but a rigorous eidetic law which governs the correlative development of economic wealth and real wealth and which determines their relation as an inverse relation. Marx formulates this law on two different occasions: "In general, the greater the productiveness of labor, the less is the labor-time required for the production of an article, the less is the amount of labor crystallised in that article, and the less is its value; and *vice versa*, the less the productiveness of labor, the greater is the labor-time required for the production of an article, and the greater is its value."[90] And again in *Wages, Price and Profit*: "The values of commodities are directly as the times of labor employed in their production, and are inversely as the productive powers of the labor employed."[91] At the moment when Marx's analysis reveals to us for the first time this blatant contradiction between real wealth, which is displayed through the number and the quality of the products, and on the other hand, their value, let us immediately make the decisive remark that this is not an economic contradiction, inherent in the economic world and belonging to it, finding therein its origin as well as, doubtless, its solution: it is, instead, a contradiction between the economy and something else, between the economy and reality, between the economy and life.

Superimposed on the eidetic law governing the contradictory relation between real wealth and economic wealth is an historical law which itself is also rooted in life and which expresses the spontaneous development of real praxis: precisely because real praxis continues to develop, its efficiency, what is called the productivity of labor, constantly increases. The determination of the eidetic relation between real wealth and economic wealth by the historical law of the development of praxis is then clear. It is not enough simply to say apodictically: "an increased quantity of material wealth may correspond to a simultaneous fall in the magnitude of its value";[92] one must add: historically this has been the case. This is why, describing the astounding progress of capitalist production due to the increase in productivity in the various branches of production, Book Three of *Capital* shows that "the same amount of value represents a progressively increasing mass of use-values and enjoyments."[93]

The implications of this historical-essential situation are numerous; their systematic development is nothing other than the analysis of the economy in its entirety. For the moment, we shall limit ourselves to tentative remarks which, nonetheless, all display the fundamental gap that separates the level of the economy from that of reality. The increase in the productivity of real labor continually results in the decrease in the value of its product. But this productivity is not the same everywhere. The person who continues to use traditional means sees the value of his product measured not by his own labor, by real labor, but by the labor that could have or should have been performed with the help of the most modern methods. The difference between real labor and economic labor assumes its full meaning when it is seen that only economic labor enters into account in economic production. We know the situation of the English weaver when the hand loom was replaced by the steam-powered loom. Working with the old loom, it thereafter took twice as much time to produce the same value, seventeen to eighteen hours a day instead of nine to ten hours![94] Here again, it is not a matter of a circumstantial difficulty but of the application of a law, namely the law of the antinomic relation between the economy and reality as it is both actualized and overdetermined in the historical movement of praxis. A law such as this does not simply result in the ruin of the "poor weaver"; it determines the entire economy. For example, it determines the fate of fixed capital, whose cycle of rotation is no longer predictable since it is no longer related to the wear on machinery but to the future invention and the installation of improved means which will thereby reduce the value of the products in equal proportion and will lead to abandoning the old machines. The essential law of capital, the tendency toward lower profits, will itself be overdetermined by the contradictory relation between the real process and the economic process.

Just when the immense role it will play in the internal determination of capitalism becomes apparent, this contradictory relation between economy and life must be carried back to its source and perceived therein. Its source is to be found in the very principle of their initial difference, the distinction between economic labor and real labor, against the backdrop of the abstraction of the former starting from the latter. At the same time as it founds exchange, this distinction explains the decisive division in the process of production, a division by virtue of which the real process will henceforth always be found to be accompanied by an economic process which will enter into conflict with it, so that two processes will then unfold conjointly but separately, each obeying its own principle and the results determined by it, so that the growth of economic wealth and of real wealth are thereafter distinct and even opposed to one another. A fundamental text in *Capital* unequivocally designates the initial distinction between real labor and economic labor as the principle of the distinction between the two processes. It is due to the abstract character of economic labor in relation to real labor that the actual properties of real labor, which, like it, are real—in particular, its productivity—no longer appear in abstract labor or in the process of realization that it determines. This is why this economic process, oblivious to the essential determinations of the real process, thereafter continues in monstrous indifference with regard to the real process and to reality: the break between the economy and life, the possibility of their conflictual development, which capitalism demonstrates, is thus founded. ". . . an increased quantity of material wealth may correspond to a simultaneous fall in the magnitude of its value. *This antagonistic movement has its origin in the two-fold character of labor*. . . . Useful labor becomes, therefore, a more or less abundant source of products, in proportion to the rise or fall of its productiveness. On the other hand, no change in this productiveness affects the labor represented by value. Since productive power is an attribute of the concrete useful forms of labor, *of course it can no longer have any bearing on that labor, so soon as we make abstraction from those concrete useful forms*. However then productive power may vary, the same labor, exercised during equal periods of time, always yields equal amounts of value."[95]

The dissociation opposing the real process to the economic process against the backdrop of their different and contradictory principles—real labor, abstract labor; real products, the value of the products—is at one and the same time the dissociation inherent in the commodity which splits it into its opposing elements, since the commodity is both a real product and an exchange-value and since in it the difference between these two terms is only the result of a duality of the principles of the two processes found in the market economy, real praxis on the one hand and its abstract, ideal representation as social labor on the other.[96] This duality can remain hidden under the appearance of the commodity to the extent that the latter contains both aspects within it—and we shall see that the "fetishism" of which Marx speaks is the result of being misled by this appearance and of confusing thoroughly the economic properties with the real properties that accompany them—the elements that merge together in the commodity are dissociated in the process of circulation, when exchange is nothing but this sort of process. Originally the exchange-value of commodities is, as we have seen, only a mediation which allows the exchange of products, and this continues to obey the teleology of life. Only, it then happens that the traders, in order to fix the proportion according to which two products will be exchanged, represent to themselves the amount of labor contained in each of these products and, in the same stroke, determine the exchange-value.[97] The exchange-value is indeed here a representation of labor, but it continues to be tied to the material substance of the product in the sense that the sole aim is to allow its use. Due to this explicit teleological subordination to use-value, exchange-value, despite its ideal character, has no existence independent of the former. In the circulation of commodities, on the contrary, when the figure M-C-M is substituted for the figure C-M-C, when it is no longer a matter of ceding one commodity in order to obtain another but of selling, of ceding a commodity in exchange for money, the exchange-value of the commodity becomes the goal of the process; or again, as Marx says, its formal existence becomes its content. "The exchange of material is the content of C-M-C, whereas the real content of the second circuit, M-C-M, is the commodity in the form in which it emerges from the first circuit."[98]

Every sale, C-M, it is true, is at the same time a purchase, M-C, for someone else. But nothing obliges the person who has sold something to buy; this is why "if the split between the sale and the purchase becomes too pronounced, the intimate connection between them, their oneness, asserts itself by producing— a crisis."[99] In any event, once he has sold and before buying the seller holds money in his hands in place of the commodity. *Then, the exchange-value is no longer bound to the material substance of the commodity but exists for itself:* "The golden chrysalis state forms an independent phase in the life of the commodity, in which it can remain for a shorter or a longer period."[100] Between the sale and the purchase, therefore, the formal existence of value—the ideal representation of abstract labor—exists for itself and this existence for-itself of the formal existence of exchange-value is money. "In money the medium of exchange becomes a thing, or, the exchange value of the thing achieves an independent existence apart from the thing."[101] The existence for-itself of the exchange-value in opposition to its existence as still synthetically bound to the substance of the commodity remains visible when money takes the form of gold. Unlike an ordinary commodity, gold is not a substance, a use-value that would possess a particular exchange-value; it is itself the exchange-value and the metal substance is only the support for this value.[102]

The existence for-itself of the exchange-value as it is realized in money, outside of the commodity, creates a new contradiction within the market economy. Or rather, this contradiction shifts: it is no longer based within the commodity itself, between its use-value and its exchange-value, but since the exchange-value has acquired an autonomous form, the contradiction is now found between the commodity itself and this form which has been separated from it, between the commodity and money, between the commodity and its price. The price, which was only the index of the product's exchange-value and which allowed it, precisely, to be exchanged, which thus remained within the sphere of commodities as a function enabling the exchange-value to be realized, takes on a new form in money, a form external and foreign to this sphere, a form by which all commodities will henceforth be compared. It is no longer a matter of knowing how one commodity will be exchanged for another; it is a matter of knowing if the commodity can be exchanged for money. The price, money, is the end; the commodity is only a means to obtain it, a means that has lost its value and that is, ultimately, without any significance if it cannot realize its aim. This is also why, as soon as money is offered for the commodity, as soon as the commodity can be sold, it has to be sold right away, for in this way it realizes the exchange-value for which it represents only a means or a predicate. [103]

The realization of exchange-value in a form external to the commodity creates a paradoxical situation. For the exchange-value is nothing but the exchange-ability of commodities. When the exchange-value becomes autonomous, it is therefore its own exchangeability which is separated from the commodity. "By existing outside the commodity as money, the exchangeability of the commodity has become something different from and alien to the commodity. . . ." [104] But when the exchangeability has become alien to the commodity, then the exchange of the commodity is contingent and depends upon external, chance circumstances. [105] To take the case of two commodities, leaving aside their qualitative differences, their exchange-value was the common element by which they were said to be equal, by which they became equivalent and could be exchanged. However, when this exchange-value becomes autonomous as money, it is no longer the internal element common to both commodities but represents, above and beyond them, a third thing which each of them confronts separately. [106] When the exchange-value is no longer the value *of the commodity* but, as money, a third thing separate from it, the identity between the commodity and its value, between the commodity and money, vanishes, and the two parts of exchange, purchase and sale, no longer balance one another. "Since these have now achieved a spatially and temporally separate and mutually indifferent form of existence, their immediate identity ceases. They may correspond or not; they may balance or not. . . ." [107]

Such is the paradox of the market economy: when exchange is its own value and its own aim, it is, precisely, no longer possible. There is really nothing mysterious about this, for it is the faithful expression of the becoming-for-itself of the exchange-value above and beyond the commodity. "The rise of exchange [commerce] as an independent function torn away from the exchangers corresponds to the rise of exchange value as an independent entity, as money, torn away from products." [108] This means that *there is no relation between use-values that are qualitatively defined and adapted to the needs of life and an autonomous ideal existence that claims to possess value and whose value is intrinsic*. Or, rather, the only relation that remains is the perverted relation characterizing the market economy, the inverse relation of use-value and exchange-value. When the exchange-value of the commodity exists outside it, this inverse relation becomes that between the commodity and money and it is expressed as follows: it is no longer money which represents the commodity; it is the commodity which represents money. This inversion exists whenever the commodity has a price, whenever its formal existence as the exchange-value is separated from the commodity. [109] The antagonistic distinction between the commodity and money is, in fact, only the result of the prior distinction between use-value and exchange-value. Consequently, the more the exchange-value frees itself, the more it becomes the aim of production, and, correlatively, the more the immediate exchange of products is eliminated in favor of the circulation of commodities,[110] the more the problems created by money increase along with the contradictions between money and commodities.[111] However, because money is only "exchange-value which has assumed an independent existence,"[112] because it is the exchange-value that creates money, it is useless to want to resolve monetary problems or contradictions on their own level or even to claim to eliminate money or to replace it with coupons representing labor, as long as the process of abstraction of exchange-value on the basis of use-value continues.[113] However, abstracting the exchange-value from the use-value is itself only the result of abstracting social labor from real praxis and the original alienation of praxis in social labor. With regard to the "universal alienation of commodities" in the pure form of their exchange-value, *Capital* says: "[Gold] became real money, by the general alienation of commodities, by actually changing places with their natural forms as useful objects, and thus becoming in reality the embodiment of their values. When they assume this money-shape, commodities strip off every trace of their natural use-value, and of the particular kind of labor to which they owe their creation, in order to transform themselves into the uniform socially recognized incarnation of homogeneous human labor."[114] Alone, the transcendental gaze which examines the genesis of the economy as the common genesis of social labor and of exchange-value holds within its field of vision the totality of economic and social characteristics along with the reason for their "contradiction."

The transcendental genesis of the economy allows us to understand in retrospect the famous text on money in the third *Economic and Philosophical Manuscript* of 1844. The reign of money is described more than analyzed here it would seem, and the concept of alienation that governs this romantic description inspired by Shakespeare bears within it all of the anthropological, even the ideological, defects of the young Marx. It must first of all be noted, however, that the term "alienation" has exactly the meaning it will possess in Chapter III of *Capital* and designates purely and simply the exchange of commodities, understood nonetheless as a universal and unlimited possibility, as the fact that anything at all can be exchanged for anything else. Money, which in the third manuscript is already said to be "the existing and active concept of value," is precisely the condition of this universal and monstrous possibility; this is why it "confounds and exchanges everything, it is the universal confusion and exchange of all things, an inverted world."[115] Echoing this text, the *Grundrisse* will in turn state: "The exchangeability of all products, activities and relations with a third, objective entity which can be re-exchanged for everything without distinction—that is, the development of exchange values (and of money relations) is identical with universal venality, corruption. Universal prostitution. . . ."[116] What characterizes the third manuscript, however, is that the things whose universal exchange is allowed by money, money in which all things are confused, are neither principally nor first of all the products of labor, commodities, but instead *the modalities of individual life itself, the determinations of subjectivity*. And it is for this reason alone, because it claims to act as the exchange of existences themselves, in what they have that is most intimate and most personal, that the world of money appears as an "inverted world." The confusion and the exchange that are realized in money are, in the text we are commenting on, "the confusion and the exchange of all natural and human qualities."[117] The first condition allowing money to realize the exchange of subjective determinations is that these be no longer defined or determined by subjectivity, of which they are the determinations, but, precisely, by money. "That which exists for me through the medium of money, that which I pay for, i.e. which money can buy, that am I, the possessor of the money. The stronger the power of my money, the stronger am I. The properties of money are my, the possessor's, properties and essential powers. *Therefore what I am and what I can do is by no means determined by my individuality*. I am ugly, but I can buy the most beautiful woman. Which means to say that I am not ugly. . . ."[118] It then appears that, finally, money is no longer the exchange of commodities, of things, but indeed the exchange of the determinations of subjectivity and of life itself. "It transforms loyalty into treason, love into hate, hate into love, virtue into vice, vice into virtue, servant into master, master into servant, nonsense into reason and reason into nonsense." It is then that the text's Shakespearean romanticism is given free reign: "Can it [money] not bind and loose all bonds? Is it therefore not the universal means of separation? It is the true agent of separation and the true cementing agent, it is the chemical power of society"; ". . . it is the power which brings together impossibilities and forces contradictions to embrace." "Shakespeare brings out two properties of money in particular: 1) It is the visible divinity, the transformation of all human and natural qualities into their opposites, the universal confusion and inversion of all things; it brings together impossibilities. 2) It is the universal whore, the universal pimp of men and peoples."

Marx opposes to this the original real situation in which each determination of subjectivity is what it is, and is such by reason of what this subjectivity is itself, a situation in which what each person is depends on him: "If we assume man to be man, and his relation to the world to be a human one, then love can be exchanged only for love, trust for trust and so on. If you wish to enjoy art you must be an artistically educated person; if you wish to exercise influence on other men you must be the sort of person who has a truly stimulating and encouraging effect on others. Each one of your relations to man—and to nature—must be a particular expression . . . of your real individual life."[119]

The exchange of subjective determinations which makes the exchange the "universal . . . inversion of things" and money, in Shakespeare's words, "the common whore of mankind" is, however, not something different from the simple exchange of commodities but its condition, if it is true that the exchange of commodities is only the exchange of different kinds of real labor, that is, precisely, the exchange of the subjective determinations of living praxis. Shakespearean romanticism is the transcendental truth of the market economy. The alienation of commodities appears to designate their transformation into one another, the fact that x cA is changed into y cB. "Alienation" here is only a throwback to the Hegelian terminology, a philosophical, pretentious, and uselessly complicated way of describing this very simple process. Nevertheless, inasmuch as the exchange of commodities is but that of the subjective determinations of praxis, it presupposes the alienation of these determinations, the transcendental process which, by substituting for the latter the objective quantitative determinations of alienated labor, founds this exchange and the market economy in general. Marx shows that alienation, understood in general as the alienation of life in the economy, is concentrated in the decisive event within which labor itself becomes a commodity. But the event in which labor becomes a commodity is no different from that in which commodities themselves are created. Labor becomes a commodity when abstract labor is formed, a process which founds the economy and which determines it as an abstract reality, which enables us to understand what this abstract reality is in its utter ontological insufficiency—precisely, an abstraction—and, in addition, what it is that constitutes its reality, the reality of economic reality.

Chapter 7

THE REALITY OF ECONOMIC REALITY

*The meta-economic ground of the economy. The dialectic of
use-value and exchange-value*

Inasmuch as economic reality is the becoming-other of reality, or, more
precisely, the substitution for reality of a reality of another order, of an ontological nature which is different from it and opposed to it—that is, an ideal
entity—it appears in the first place that, *considered in itself, reality is nothing
economic*. We must denounce and set right here the monumental error and the
completely mistaken interpretation with regard to Marx's thought, that is, the
well-known thesis upheld by "Marxism" according to which reality, at least the
reality which is to be found at the base of human societies as that which
englobes them and determines them, is precisely economic reality. Along with
this is also rejected the classic Marxist opposition between structure and superstructure, to the extent that the first is considered an economic structure capable of producing and determining the second, namely all of the systems of
representation. *Stricto sensu*, the "economic" is constituted by ideal representations, by abstract realities such as "labor," "value," "money," etc. Far from
being the principle of a genesis, it is its product, the product of the transcendental genesis of the economy as this has just been presented.

Marx's fundamental and repeated assertion is indeed that reality considered
in itself is by no means economic. Reality is the movement of life transforming
nature in order to satisfy its need; it is praxis. It is what Marx, after *The German
Ideology*, calls production; it is what *Capital* names the labor-process. But
regardless of the name given to this fundamental process, it is what, for Marx,
constitutes reality; this is why it is constantly described as "real" or again as
"material." Because it constitutes reality, a process such as this is omnipresent,
and this signifies: (1) that it founds and determines every form of society, every
historical formation, and can do so because it first of all founds society and
history as such, because it defines the transcendental condition of their possibility; (2) that it continually produces itself and never ceases to be produced: as
such the process of production is at one and the same time a process of
reproduction. "Whatever the form of the process of production in a society, it
must be a continuous process, must continue to go periodically through the
same phases. *A society can no more cease to produce than it can cease to*

224

consume. When viewed, therefore, as a connected whole, and as flowing on with incessant renewal, every social process of production is, at the same time, a process of reproduction. The conditions of production are also those of reproduction."[1] The reason for this is that because the process of production is continuous, so, too, are its elements, the relations they maintain among themselves inasmuch as, like raw materials for example, they are fused in the product or, like the instruments of labor, they maintain, on the contrary, their autonomy with respect to labor and, consequently, their own form: "These different ways in which means of production are consumed to form the product, some of them preserving their independent shape vis-à-vis the product, others changing or losing it entirely—this difference pertaining to the labor-process as such and therefore just as well to labor-processes aimed at satisfying merely one's own needs, e.g., the needs of the patriarchal family, without any exchange, without production of commodities."[2]

Capital describes as follows the elements which compose every labor-process, whatever it may be: "1, the personal activity of man, i.e., work itself, 2, the subject of that work, and 3, its instruments."[3] The three elements which compose the labor-process are not, however, of the same nature; the reality that they define can itself be divided along two essentially distinct lines. If "the word 'process' . . . expresses a development considered as it is situated within the totality of its real conditions,"[4] if the labor-process thus forms a whole, one cannot fail to distinguish within it, on the one hand, its means and its object and, on the other, labor "properly speaking."[5] The instrument and the object of labor belong to the materiality of beings, understood in the "Theses on Feuerbach" as objectivity; labor itself "properly speaking" is subjective. Talking about the elements of the labor-process that the capitalist will purchase on the market, *Capital* says, touching on the essence of the matter: ". . . all the necessary factors, the means of production, as well as its subjective factor, labor-power."[6] It is precisely because it is subjective that labor properly speaking is described in the text cited above as "the personal activity of man." Speaking of the production of real wealth, that is to say, precisely, of the real labor-process which is the object of political economy and the continuous element of history, the *Grundrisse* state no less categorically: "Political economy has to do with the specific social forms of wealth or rather of the production of wealth. The material of wealth, whether subjective, like labor, or objective, like objects for the satisfaction of natural or historical needs, initially appears as common to all epochs of production."[7] The ontological opposition, within material reality, between labor understood as the subjective essence of activity and, on the other hand, the instrument and the object of labor understood as its objective conditions is reaffirmed by another text in the *Grundrisse*, just when the relation of the first to the second is grasped not as a theoretical relation but as this practical activity itself and as constituted by it, in such a way that—and this reaffirms the decisive theses of the first part of *The German Ideology*—the "world" is originally nothing other than the object, that is, the result of this praxis: *"The real appropriation takes place not in the mental but in the real, active relation to these conditions—in their real positing as the conditions of his subjective activity.* It is thereby also clear that these conditions change. Only when tribes hunt upon it does a region of the earth become a hunting domain, only cultivation of the soil posits the land as the individual's extended body."[8]

The subjective character of labor results from the fact that it is the actualization of the labor-power, which in its turn is nothing other than the subjectivity of the individual, what in him is most alive, what defines him, what constitutes his personality. The labor-power of a man is quite simply what is alive in him as an individual. In reference to labor-power, *Capital* will state ". . . labor-power as it exists in the personality of the laborer."[9] It is precisely because labor-power is subjective, possessing a subjectivity defined by its radical immanence, that "this power exists only in him," and that when the laborer is forced to sell it, he is unable, precisely, to separate himself from it as from a commodity which is alienated and he must therefore, as we have seen, sell himself. This is why Marx also says of labor: "But could the laborer give it an independent objective existence, he would sell a commodity and not labor."[10] Because selling his labor-power, the laborer sells himself; he would be no more than a slave if the period during which he is allowed to sell this power were not limited. "What the working man sells is not directly his labor, but his laboring power. . . . If allowed to do so for any indefinite period whatever, slavery would be immediately restored."[11]

The subjective character of labor is also brought out by its opposition to the objective result of its process, which lies in the form that this labor has imparted to the substance. "The real use value is the form given to the substance. But this form itself is only static labor."[12] It is noteworthy that just when, as a vestige of Hegelianism, Marx terms objectified labor the objective modification stamped on beings, the actual act of labor is clearly understood in its opposition to the objectivity produced—or rather modified—in this way, as belonging to the form of a monadic subjectivity of which it is the actualization, the *living present*. This essential text, which must be taken literally, is written as follows: "The only thing distinct from objectified labor is non-objectified labor, labor which is still objectifying itself, labor *as subjectivity*. Or, objectified labor, i.e. labor which is present in space, can also be opposed, as past labor, to labor which is present in time. *If it is to be present in time, alive, then it can be present only as the living subjectivity in which it exists as capacity, as possibility; hence as worker.*"[13] In a language addressed to the general public, *Capital* will say the same thing.[14] The opposition between labor grasped in the present of its subjective realization and its result as an objective form of transformed nature will be thought of by Marx in terms of an opposition between living labor and dead labor, and this opposition will play a decisive role in the subsequent economic analysis.

Now, the following point must be firmly established if the economic analysis is to be intelligible: *none of the real or material elements of the labor-process which we have just examined in the light of the fundamental philosophy of praxis, none of its subjective or objective elements, consequently, is in itself an "economic" element.* Inasmuch as it is subjective, labor is only a moment of life. Labor, Marx says concisely, is "the existing not-value."[15] As we have seen, economists have fallen prey to an illusion, retroactively projecting economic determinations on the original reality and, essentially, on living praxis, and believing that one or another of the modalities of this praxis can, by itself, be an economic modality: "Or the modern economists have turned themselves into such sycophants of the bourgeois that they want to demonstrate to the latter that it is productive labor when somebody picks the lice out of his hair, or strokes his tail."[16] By productive activity, one is to understand, according to the economists' illusion, activity which produces *value*, "labor" in the economic sense. The *Grundrisse* tell us that only labor which produces value is productive.[17] This is why, in answer to the objection raised by Senior regarding living praxis and the condition proper to it—"But doesn't the pianist produce music?"— Marx replies: "He does indeed: his labor produces something; but that does not make it productive labor in the economic sense; no more than the labor of the madman who produces delusions is productive."[18]

The illusion of the economists who imagine that living activity as such is part of the economy can be seen in Adam Smith's conception of labor as sacrifice. It should be noted that a conception such as this, despite its moral appearance inherited from the past, is tied to a precise economic thesis, namely that labor never varies in value, that an hour's labor is always an hour's labor and that for this hour of labor one will always obtain the same value—whether this value is represented by many or few products; this depends solely on the productivity of this hour of labor. In other words, in order to obtain the equivalent of this value, a person must always give an hour of labor and, in Adam Smith's own words, "give up the identical portion of his tranquillity, his freedom, and his happiness."[19] Thus, "one must always pay the price," and labor is precisely the price one pays for everything one obtains. To consider labor in its relation to the value which it itself defines or which stands as its equivalent—the things it enables one to buy—is precisely no longer to consider labor in itself, in its subjective reality, and to be thoroughly mistaken about it. This is just what happens when labor is declared to be a sacrifice, when it is seen simply as the counterpart to the value of the product: one forgets what it is in itself, namely a determination of living praxis possessing its own end, its problems, its difficulties, and, above all, its internal positivity, its tonality, which is identical to the experience of the activity that is being performed as it overcomes the difficulties that it encounters, difficulties which are the corollary to its free exercise: "But Smith has no inkling whatever that this overcoming of obstacles is in itself a liberating activity—and that, further, the external aims become stripped of the semblance of merely external natural urgencies, and become posited as aims which the individual himself posits—hence as self-realization, objectification of the subject, hence real freedom, whose action is, precisely, labor."[20]

This is why labor cannot be opposed to rest as the negative to the positive, because the former is just as positive as the latter, because activity is an integral part of organic subjectivity as one of its essential potentialities and as its need, just as—and no doubt even more than—rest itself. " 'Tranquillity'," says Marx, "appears as the adequate state, as identical with 'freedom' and 'happiness'. It seems quite far from Smith's mind that the individual, 'in his normal state of health, strength, activity, skill, facility', also needs a normal portion of work, and of the suspension of tranquillity."[21] This certainly does not mean that work is easy, "that it becomes mere fun, mere amusement, as Fourier, with *grisette*-like naïveté, conceives it. Really free working, e.g. composing, is at the same time precisely the most damned seriousness, the most intense exertion."[22] But considered *as effort, work is no different from existence in its original condition*, prior to all economic determination. In fact, Smith's negative assessment of work is suitable only for "forced labor," that is, labor grasped within a certain economic system. "A. Smith, by the way, has only the slaves of capital in mind. For example, even the semi-artistic worker of the Middle Ages does not fit into his definition."[23] Smith, then, confuses the tonality proper to the activity as effort, the ontological tonality belonging to it by reason of its essence, with the more peculiar determinations characterizing this tonality when existence is placed within conditions which, like slavery, serfdom, or the wage system, give activity its "repugnant" character. The fact that this character attaches to practical existence in accordance with the play of economic determinations *but that this occurs on the basis of the fundamental tonality proper to this existence, that is, on the basis of its essence*, shows precisely that activity, which is a mode of life, is originally and in itself nothing of an economic nature. *Capital* will twice reaffirm the positivity and the original living specificity of labor as activity, beyond all of its economic determinations: "he [Smith] has a pressentiment that labor . . . counts only as expenditure of labor-power, but he treats this expenditure as the mere sacrifice of rest, freedom, and happiness, not as at the same time *the normal activity of living beings*. But then, he has the modern wage-laborer in his eye."[24]

Marx's notes on economics which were collected by Engels in Book Two of *Capital* give an absolutely general import to the critique of Adam Smith: the entirety of the real elements of the labor-process, both subjective and objective, labor itself on the one hand and the instruments of labor on the other, are clearly designated as noneconomic in the original and characteristic reality, as "personal" and "material," whereas the economic determinations they receive when they become "wage-labor" and "capital" in the market system and, more precisely, in the capitalist system, are designated no less clearly as heterogeneous, synthetic adjuncts and, as such, as masks concealing the primitive noneconomic reality. Here before our eyes stands one of Marx's decisive themes, namely that *the economy and, in particular, every economic system is nothing but the appearance and, precisely, the mask of reality*. "Adam Smith identifies the production of commodities in general with capitalist commodity production; the means of production are to him from the outset "capital", labor is from the outset wage-labor. . . . In short, *the various factors of the labor-process—both objective and personal—appear from the first with the masks characteristic of the period of capitalist production.*"[25] Not only subjective labor, consequently, but also its objective conditions, its instruments and materials are in themselves foreign to the economy. A published text of the lecture "Wage Labor and Capital" includes the remark "So say the economists" and continues: "A Negro is a Negro. He only becomes a slave in certain relations. A cotton-spinning jenny is a machine for spinning cotton. It becomes capital only in certain relations. Torn from these relationships it is no more capital than *gold* in itself is *money* or *sugar* the *price* of sugar."[26] The parallel established between the subjective and objective factors of the labor process, despite their essential difference, which will be asserted later, is due precisely to the fact that, considered in themselves, they are foreign to the economic determinations that they possess, for example, in the capitalist system. "The means of production do not become the material forms of productive capital, or productive capital, until labor-power, the personal form of existence of productive capital, is capable of being embodied in them. *Human labor-power is by nature no more capital than are the means of production*. They acquire this specific social character only under definite, historically developed conditions. . . ."[27]

No more than the subjective and objective elements of the process is the product itself to be considered economic: "3 bushels of rye are in themselves no value; rather, rye filling up a certain volume, measured by a standard of volume."[28] This is why the product enters the sphere of the economy only to the extent that it becomes other than itself and is expressed in this alienated form, namely in the economic form as such: "If a bushel of wheat has the price of 77s.7d., *then it is expressed as something else*, to which it is equal."[29] The original relation to things is not an economic relation; it is a practical, living relation, and in this relation the thing or the product receives its original, noneconomic determination; it is use-value not exchange-value. The noneconomic character of the product is asserted straightforwardly: ". . . the use value, i.e. the content, the natural particularity of the commodity has as such no standing as an economic form."[30] This is why economic exchange will have the nature of a formal metamorphosis external to real exchange, while the latter, the physical exchange of products, will itself remain foreign to the economic process.[31] Once the content of a product stands for itself, has value in and of itself, once, placed in relation with life, it enters into the cycle of consumption, the superstructure constituting the economic relation vanishes.[32] On the contrary, it is necessary to abstract from the reality of the product in order to find the economic "reality" and, when this abstracting is complete, in order to find the economic determination in the pure ideal form of money: "If we abstract from the material substance of the circulation of commodities, that is, from the exchange of the various use-values, and consider only the *economic forms produced by this process of circulation*, we find its result to be money. . . ."[33] It is precisely because, considered in itself, the product is not of an economic nature that its determination as value does not appear as long as the product is considered in isolation.[34] On the contrary, its value can be assessed only when it is placed in relation with another product and only inasmuch as this relation, which in its own economic reality is foreign to both of the commodities, is but the objectification of a reality of a different order.[35] In *Capital* the problem of value begins with the analysis of its relative form because the economic existence of use-value lies solely in a relation unconnected to their substantive reality. The noneconomic character of the real process of production and of the real product to which it leads is categorically asserted in this text from the *Grundrisse:* ". . . exchange value expresses the social form of value, *while use value no economic form of it whatever.* . . ."[36]

Confusing the economic form with reality, when they are not purely and simply held to be identical, is what Marx calls fetishism. "Furthermore this brings to completion the fetishism peculiar to bourgeois Political Economy, the fetishism which metamorphoses the *social, economic* character impressed on things in the process of social production into a *natural* character stemming from the material nature of those things."[37] Inasmuch as it confuses the material properties of things with the ideal determinations they take on as they represent a reality of a different order, fetishism is at one and the same time a materialism or, if one prefers, an idealism; the identity between materialism and idealism is reaffirmed here with regard to the economy and is once again rejected. "The crude materialism of the economists who regard as the natural properties of things what are the social relations of production among people, and qualities which things obtain because they are subsumed under these relations, is at the same time just as crude an idealism, even fetishism, since it imputes social relations to things as inherent characteristics, and thus mystifies them."[38]

The transcendental genesis of the economy has shown that, far from being identified with reality, economic reality is, on the contrary, abstract and is constituted as its ideal equivalent. *As "abstract," economic reality has no self-sufficient being, no ontological autonomy, and is unable to subsist by itself.* There is no economic structure. The lack of autarchy characterizing economic reality does not only signify that it presupposes something prior to itself, an "origin," something from which it has been abstracted, from which it derives. Instead, this derivation is never ended; this origin is not a temporal origin which once was active and since has disappeared. Rather, this origin remains within economic reality as that which bears it and gives it its being. The origin of economic reality is its ground. The transcendental genesis of the economy has the following radical meaning: *reality, which in itself is noneconomic, is the reality of economic reality.*

From this stems the twofold movement and the very sense of Marx's entire problematic. Abstracted from reality, founded on it and by it, economic reality unceasingly refers to it and is carried back to it. This is why the analysis of economic reality is not situated within it and does not consider it to be what it is on its own level, in its specificity; instead the analysis cuts through the economic element in order to move back to its source, to its true substance, to its real determining factors. And in every case it appears that these real determining factors of the economy are not themselves of an economic nature, but must instead be conceived of as noneconomic, as an extra-economic reality, to borrow Marx's expression. The resolution of each problem, each difficulty, in particular of each aporia belonging to classical political economy, will consist in this return to an origin, to a region of being different from that of the economic, although it serves to found the economic. Henceforth, the economic element, just as it cannot be the place where reality is to be found, is also incapable of being the place of truth, the place of ultimate explanation. Quite the opposite, the economic is presented as an appearance, as an enigma, and, finally, as a mystification. And the analysis that cuts through this appearance, resolves this enigma, and clears up this mystification is no longer an economic analysis, properly speaking, but rather a critique of political economy, a philosophy of the economy. The philosophy of the economy does not appear in Marx simply in the form of this questioning moving backwards toward the founding origin; it is realized in the inverse movement. Inasmuch as economic reality is grounded in the noneconomic reality of the labor-process, the latter must be shown to be the condition for the former. To display the lack of autarchy of economic reality is at one and the same time to show that the economy is radically determined by life.

This backwards reference of economic reality to reality is first formulated in the dialectic of exchange-value and use-value. The substitution of the first for the second has been understood as constituting the dimension proper to the economy, but it would be a mistake to believe that once this substitution has been made, we then find ourselves confronting an autonomous universe, that of the market economy, from which use-value is now excluded or, at any rate, in which it no longer plays any role. This was exactly the mistake Ricardo made.[39] The reference of the exchange-value to the use-value is instead categorically affirmed: "Value exists only in articles of utility, in objects: we leave out of consideration its purely symbolical representation by tokens."[40] The essential character of use-value in opposition to the inessential character of exchange-value is brought to light through an eidetic analysis: *use-value can exist without being an exchange-value, whereas exchange-value cannot exist unless it is first of all a use-value. Capital* formulates two interrelated assertions: "A thing can be a use-value, without having value." ". . . nothing can have value, without being an object of utility."[41]

To the fact that use-value is indifferent with respect to exchange-value, the transcendental genesis of the economy has now opposed, it is true, the fact that exchange-value is indifferent with respect to use-value.[42] But this indifference is by no means the counterpart to the first; it signifies instead the ontological heterogeneity of economic existence as an ideal, formal existence in relation to the substantive existence of use-value which designates reality; in no way does it signify the independence of the former with regard to the latter. This is why, even when the teleology of life is reversed in the teleology of commodities and when it is of no matter what is produced—provided only that money is produced—this elimination of use-value is only part of the illusion whereby capitalism represents things and its own activity to itself. The indifference of exchange-value with respect to use-value cannot break the tie that makes use-value the support and the ground of exchange-value. "Value is independent of the particular use-value by which it is borne, but it must be embodied in a use-value of some kind."[43] Indeed, even in exchange, where it unfolds and appears to activate the entire process, exchange-value displays its ultimate subordination to use-value. It is as exchange-value that the commodity is produced, and it can be useful to someone, be a use-value, only if in the process of exchange it is first torn away from its producer. This is Marx's great reproach, the fact that in the market economy the condition for appropriation lies in alienation.[44] Thus the use-value can be realized, can attain life, only inasmuch as it becomes exchange-value and is realized as such. But the reversal of the teleology of life in economic teleology is, in its turn, reversed. The realization of exchange-value itself poses a problem: it no doubt depends upon economic conditions but, above all, upon a fundamental condition which simply expresses its ultimate structure, the fact that it is only the formal existence of use-value and that its substance and its very possibility are to be found in use-value. Since exchange-values are what they are only if they are first use-values, they are exchanged, precisely, only if their usefulness has been recognized. ". . . they must show that they are use-values before they can be realized as values."[45] The economic form never ceases to presuppose what it has abolished. "The alienation of a commodity as a use-value is only possible to the person for whom it is a use-value, *i.e.*, an object satisfying particular needs."[46] This is the reason why the substantive diversity of use-values is continually apparent in the economic form of exchange; why exchange, which continually arises and is abolished in the gap between need and use-value, is precisely no more than a form. Whether this form appears or disappears, the content remains intact, and it is a living process; the relation between the product and life never ceases to exist.[47]

As we have seen, exchange-value is only the objectification of social labor, whereas use-value is the product of useful labor. The inevitable reference of exchange-value to use-value is at one and the same time that of abstract labor to real labor. The movement of commodities is governed by their destination, by the fact that they continue to pass into the hands of those for whom they are useful. This movement, which takes on the appearance of economic exchange and which constitutes it, is at the same time that through which abstract labor—by virtue of which commodities are exchanged—proves that it is in every case useful labor and that it is actually for this reason that there is an exchange. "Thus the use-values of commodities become use-values by a mutual exchange of places: they pass from the hands of those for whom they were means of exchange into the hands of those for whom they serve as consumer goods. *Only as a result of universal alienation of commodities does the labor contained in them become useful labor*. Commodities . . . in the course of their mutual relations as use-values. . . ."[48] How it is that the referral of the exchange-value back to the use-value is at one and the same time the referral of general labor back to useful labor, how the latter is clearly designated in this referral—is stated once more in the following text: ". . . the commodity as it comes into being is only materialized individual labor-time of a specific kind, and not universal labor-time. The commodity is thus not immediately exchange-value, but has still to become exchange-value. *To begin with, it can be materialization of universal labor-time only when it represents a particular useful application of labor-time, that is a use-value*."[49]

The foundational character of use-value in relation to exchange-value is obvious if one makes the trivial, yet decisive, remark that a commodity loses all value when its use-value is destroyed.[50] Once this is recognized, the whole of economic circulation is found to depend on use-value and on its specific properties: "if they [commodities] are not productively or individually consumed within a certain time, depending on what they are intended for, in other words, if they are not sold within a certain period, they spoil and lose with their use-value the property of being vehicles of exchange-value."[51] The fact that value is determined by use-value is shown not only on the level of circulation but, in a more essential way, within the process of production. Within this process raw materials are transformed, and the use-values tied to their original properties are thus abolished; their exchange-value should be abolished as well by virtue of the axiom repeated in *Capital*—"If therefore an article loses its utility, it also loses its value"[52]—and would be unable to be transferred to the product. If this is not the case, if the value of the instruments of labor is not destroyed, it is because their use-value is not destroyed either: it appears in a new form in the product. *The possibility belonging to the product by which it repeats the value of its conditions is inherent in the becoming of use-value and presupposes its conservation or its development*. From now on, we can perceive in the process of realization* an essential dependence with respect to the real process.[53] And this is not the case only for raw materials; the instruments of labor themselves can transfer their value to the product only to the extent that their use-value is preserved. *What will preserve this use-value will also preserve their value*, namely capital itself. Speaking of the conservation of the use-values of raw materials and of instruments, the *Grundrisse* state in a proposition whose essential character will soon be apparent: ". . . since every use value by its nature consists of transitory material, but since exchange value is present, exists, only in use value, therefore this maintenance = protection from decay and ruin, or negation of the transitory nature of the values owned by the capitalists; hence, this maintenance means to posit them as values-for-themselves, as indestructable wealth."[54]

The use-value not only determines the process of realization, of "valoriza-

---

*Process of realization is the standard English translation of *Verwertungsprozess*, which in French is rendered as *procès de valorisation*. The term *valorisation* includes both the notion of realization or completion and that of enhancement, of increase of value. This twofold sense should be kept in mind whenever this term appears in Henry's text.—TRANS.

tion"; it also makes this process at the same time a process of devalorization. The process of realization, no doubt, has certain specific laws which are economic laws; and the limits which it encounters that are external to it are in part, it is true, economic limits: the values that are produced must be able to be realized, that is, be convertible into money, which presumes that this money exists. But realizing the exchange-values of commodities presumes first of all, as we know, that the latter have a use, correspond to a need. With regard to the process of realization Marx says: "Its first barrier, then, is consumption itself—the need for it [the commodity]."[55] Need sets an absolute limit on the indefinite realization process of capital, not only because it is located outside this process but, for a more essential reason, because in itself it is limited, qualitatively determined, as has been stated; because, as a determination of life, need is determined by it: "Use value in itself does not have the boundlessness of value as such. Given objects can be consumed as objects of needs only up to a certain point. . . . But as soon as it ceases to be a use value, it ceases to be an object of circulation. . . ."[56] In this way life abruptly displays its strength in the face of the economic process. The object of need reaches us only on the condition that it enter into exchange and become value; it is then merely a question of producing this value in ever greater quantities. However, the exchange-value is only the value of the use-value, whose quantity is determined by this value itself: it is this use-value that decides under what conditions and in what quantities it can become value. "What is posited now is that the measure of its availability is given in its natural composition itself. In order to be transposed into the general form, the use value has to be present in a limited and specific quantity; *a quantity whose measure does not lie in the amount of labor objectified in it, but arises from its nature as use value, in particular, use value for others*."[57] No doubt economic production attempts to stimulate consumption by raising it to its own level, by imparting to it an infinite development: "Firstly quantitative expansion of existing consumption; secondly: creation of new needs by propagating existing ones in a wide circle; thirdly: production of new needs and discovery and creation of new use values."[58] This is what today is called the "consumer society." But this reasoning, which is called for by the process of realization, is not determined by it, by the exchange-value, by abstract labor; *it is the increase and the diversification of needs and of the objects suited to satisfying them; it finds its law in the exploitation of nature and of subjectivity:* "Hence exploration of all of nature. . . ."[59] But nature, just as subjectivity itself, is finite; both are foreign to value.

We have seen that the economy finds its pure form in money, and that money is constituted through a series of abstractions starting from reality. In the final analysis, money stands for itself, has value in and of itself, and its production is the goal of the entire process. Money's standing for itself is value's standing for itself. However, the pure economic element cannot maintain itself by itself; money has only an illusory autonomy. "Its independence is a mere semblance."[60] There are two reasons for this. Just as the exchange-value of each commodity is inseparable from its use-value, so money only appears to represent exchange-value in its pure state: of all commodities it is the one whose reference to use-value is the most obvious. For every commodity satisfies only one need, represents only one use-value. With money, on the contrary, one can obtain the totality of use-values, and money signifies wealth only because it adds to the formal concept of economic wealth, namely value as such, the material concept of real wealth, which is nothing other than all products useful to life. "But money satisfies any need since it can be immediately turned into the object of any need."[61]

The illusory character of the autonomy of the economic element when it has attained the pure form of money becomes obvious not only in the fact that money itself has value simply as the equivalent of the whole of the use-values existing at a given moment in a society. As money, and to the extent that it obeys its own dialectic, that is, the law of indefinite quantitative growth, it must continually be exchanged in use-values which enable it in the first place to maintain itself and then, precisely, to increase. The fact that money, exchange-value, rests on use-value now signifies that the money process cannot unfold without continually giving rise to a real process which is that of use-values, with regard to which money simply expresses the value. Whereas the process of use-values is directed exclusively at value, at its production, and its growth, this growth (to begin with even the simple maintenance of value) demands that it be continually sacrificed to the real elements of the process. The paradox of value which, just when it claims to stand for itself, cannot be separated from the substance of the commodities but must, on the contrary, be situated within this substance—this is the truth of capital. Capital is value standing for itself, possessing intrinsic worth, abandoned to itself and to the law of realization. As such it, precisely, cannot exist as money, that is, in the form of the economic element, but, on the contrary, must be embodied in the material reality of use-values. "Capital is by definition money, but not merely money in the simple form of gold and silver, nor merely as money in opposition to circulation, but in the form of all substances—commodities. To that degree, therefore, it does not, as capital, stand in opposition to use value, but exists apart from money precisely only in use values."[62] Existing only in use-values, capital becomes dependent on them; it subsists only inasmuch as they are preserved. Here, then, is capital under attack, obliged not only to invest itself in use-values but to take action to preserve and to renew them, in such a way that the principle of its action lies outside itself, in the particular nature of the use-values to which it is referred. "The greater or lesser perishability of the commodity in which value exists requires a slower or faster reproduction; i.e. repetition of the labor process. *The particular nature of use value, in which the value exists, or which now appears as itself a determinant of the form and of the action of capital;* as giving one capital a particular property as against another; as particularizing it."[63] In being referred in this way to a reality which determines it, capital has lost its indifference with respect to any determinate form of use-value; it is already in contradiction with itself.

Capital's backwards reference to use-value takes on its decisive meaning, however, only when the concept of use-value is thought in its fundamental ambiguity. For use-value does not designate first of all in Marx simply the product of useful labor, the natural element that is transformed and made adequate to living subjectivity. What is intended is purely and simply living subjectivity as such. The fundamental use-value is praxis as the possibility included within monadic subjectivity and as identical with it; the use of this "value" is its actualization in effective labor, and this actualization is its "consumption." *Capital* states: "The capitalist buys labor-power in order to use it; and labor-power in use is labor itself. The purchaser of labor-power consumes it by setting the seller of it to work."[64] It is only on the basis of this fundamental meaning of the concept of use-value that one then passes to its customary meaning: "In order that his labor may reappear in a commodity," the text continues, "he must, before all things, expend it on something useful, on something capable of satisfying a want of some sort. Hence, what the capitalist sets the laborer to produce, is a particular use-value, a specific article." The production of use-values capable of satisfying needs is in itself, as the use of labor-power, the fundamental use-value, *which differs from the other use-values in that, since it is radically subjective, it has not the objective existence they have and is instead identified with the life of the worker*. "The use value which the worker has to offer to the capitalist, which he has to offer to others in general, is not materialized in a product, does not exist apart from him at all, thus exists not really, but only in potentiality, as his capacity . . . this use value exists as the worker's specific, productive activity; it is his vitality itself, directed toward a specific purpose and hence expressing itself in a specific form."[65] It is this use-value which alone, finally, is of importance to capital; its essential reference to use-value is co-extensive with it. "As use value, labor exists only for capital, and is itself the use value of capital, i.e. the mediating activity by means of which it realizes [*verwertet*] itself."[66] And again: ". . . labor confronts capital not as a use value, but as the use value pure and simple."[67] It is because use-value ultimately designates living labor and subjectivity itself that its concept is the referential concept of capital, the fundamental concept of the economy.

Fundamental use-value: the critique of circulation and the "exchange" of capital and labor

The fact that capital refers to fundamental use-value is behind the entire economic analysis; in the first place, it determines the critique of circulation. The latter is based on the reversal of the living teleology of exchange, when the formula M-C-M is substituted for the form C-M-C. Now Marx shows, on the one hand, that M-C-M is actually M-C-M' (where M' designates the amount of money initially advanced plus an increase, or M + $\triangle$M) and that this process is meaningful only if the final amount of money is greater than the initial amount, only if it is a process of increasing value; on the other hand, Marx shows that this process is without end since each new quantity of money has the same need to increase as the preceding quantity. But what characterizes this boundless increase of value from an economic standpoint is that it is related to value itself; of itself as if by its own effort, capital never ceases to grow out of new surplus-value. This appearance, it is true, is due to the nature of circulation and is produced within it. Indeed, in circulation, value never ceases to possess worth through its various metamorphoses; money and commodities are merely forms it assumes and which are subordinate to it. This is why, to begin with, value is preserved in circulation because it is never a matter of anything else, because the purchase and sale of money, of commodities, of labor are never anything but the diverse moments and the diverse forms of its existence. "The first quality of capital is, then, this: that exchange value deriving from circulation and presupposing circulation preserves itself within it and by means of it; does not lose itself by entering into it; that circulation is not the movement of its disappearance, but rather the movement of its real self-positing [*Sichsetzen*] as exchange value, its self-realization as exchange value."⁶⁸

Inasmuch as circulation is but the existence of value which is preserved and continued throughout its different forms, everything that occurs within it—not simply these different qualitative forms, but also the quantitative differences of value—must be carried back to it; it is the value itself that increases. The surplus-value which is produced by it is but the development of its own substance, its autonomous and spontaneous proliferation: "In truth, however, value is here the active factor in a process, in which, while constantly assuming the form in turn of money and commodities, it at the same time changes in magnitude, differentiates itself by throwing surplus-value from itself; the original value, in other words, expands spontaneously. For the movement, in the course of which it adds surplus-value, is its own movement, its expansion, therefore, is automatic expansion. Because it is value, it has acquired the occult quality of being able to add value to itself. It brings forth living offspring. . . ."⁶⁹ The self-positing of value, that is, the economic element itself as such, which signifies at one and the same time its self-growth, is capital: "value therefore now becomes value in process, money in process, and, as such, capital."⁷⁰

The critique of capital, that is, of economic reality in its claim to substantiality and to autonomy, first takes the form of the critique of circulation because this is where value presents the appearance of self-realization, where M becomes M'. What this critique shows is precisely that circulation by itself is incapable of producing a new value, any sort of surplus-value. Incapable, by definition. For circulation is nothing but the exchange of commodities, and it has been shown that the *condition of the possibility of exchange is the equal value of the commodities exchanged*. Because the exchange concerns only commodities which have the same value, this value is preserved, identical to itself, in the exchange. A given exchanger originally had $x A$ commodities on hand; he now has $y B$ commodities, but the exchange assumes that $x A c = y B c$; he thus has, in the form $y B c$, *the same value* as that he had before in the form $x A$

commodities. This is the reason why commodities and money finally appear as forms of value, because it is precisely one and the same value which by turns takes these different forms and which remains identical throughout them. One cannot, therefore, wish that a surplus-value be produced in circulation: it is circulation which would immediately become impossible.

The powerlessness of circulation to produce by itself an increase of value is repeatedly asserted by Marx. *Capital* brings to light the identity of value throughout the different forms in which it is embodied by assuming the standpoint of the exchanger: whether it is a matter of the commodity that he has produced, of the money which is its equivalent, or of the commodity that he can buy with this money, what he holds in his hand is always, as the principle of all of these possible exchanges, the same value.[71] Nor can one take into account the trivial objection that an exchanger could sell his commodity for more than its value and thereby make a profit. It is Marx's constant thesis that the price of commodities is governed by their value and that, contrary to a widespread opinion, in a society products are only very rarely sold for a value greater than their real value; rather, the opposite is most often the case. However, if one were to leave the level of eidetic regulations in order to consider accidental and circumstantial exchanges, tied to the personality of the exchangers, the conclusion would still be the same. Let us assume, with Marx, that "A may be clever enough to get the advantage of B or C" and manages to exchange wine worth £40 for wheat worth £50. In his hands, it is true, a certain quantity of money has become a greater quantity of money. The total value in circulation, however, has not changed; it £90 after the exchange just as before it, and the exchange itself has produced nothing. "The value in circulation has not increased by one iota. . . ."[72]

One might then ask why circulation occurs if it is a mere tautology in which the same value is indefinitely repeated. The reason for this is, as we have seen, that the exchangers exchange their products not for their value, which by definition is identical, but for their use-values, that is, in relation to the needs they have. Here again the economic element can be preserved and circulation can take place only against the backdrop of the underlying reality of life.[73] The capitalist, nevertheless, differs entirely from the ordinary exchanger whom we have just discussed. On the one hand, the use-value of commodities is of absolutely no interest to him, for it is not use-value that can give him, like Condillac, the illusion of "gain." On the other hand, this gain is now real; it concerns the exchange-value, which, at the end of the circulation process, is presented with an increased quantity. It is precisely due to this surplus-value that the capitalist decides to place a certain value into circulation in order to take out a greater value. And this occurs in the following way: with a certain sum of money the capitalist buys the things necessary to manufacture a product, with the aim not of manufacturing it but of selling it and with this sale of acquiring a greater sum of money than that originally invested. After the question of value, that is, of economic reality and of its status, the second fundamental question raised by *Capital* is that of the origin of surplus-value. This question places us face-to-face with the *aporia of circulation:* no surplus-value can emerge from circulation and yet outside of circulation, that is, outside of "the mutual relations of commodity-owners," there is none. Consequently, the *quantitative* metamorphosis of value—and what results from it: surplus value— "must take place, both within the sphere of circulation and without it."[74] The resolution of this aporia gives us the ultimate signification of Marx's economic philosophy and enables us to understand what forms the reality of economic reality.

How can the realization, the increase of value—that is, the very possibility for capital to express itself in the form M-C-M′ as a form of circulation—emerge from circulation? In the second part, C-M′, of this form, namely the resale of the commodity, there is no change in value; the value simply passes from the commodity form to the money form. In the first part, M-C, by which the capitalist buys a commodity, the exchange is also between equivalents, the simple metamorphosis of value which this time passes from the money form to the commodity form. No increase in value is possible. Or this increase in value, which is impossible on the level of value itself and of its circulation, would have to come from the use-value of the particular commodity purchased by the capitalist. This would have to be an extraordinary commodity, a reality which, when put into effect, when used, would be able to produce value and, consequently, to provide its user with a greater exchange-value than that he gave to obtain it. A reality such as this does exist; it is the fundamental use-value which we have recognized as being that of the labor-power constituted by individual, organic subjectivity. Let the capitalist seize this power and he will be able to create value, and the process of realization that constitutes capitalism will itself be possible. The thesis of *Capital* is contained in the following proposition: "In order to be able to extract value from the consumption of a commodity, our friend, Moneybags, must be so lucky as to find, within the sphere of circulation, in the market, a commodity, whose use-value, whose actual consumption, therefore, is itself an embodiment of labor, and, consequently, a creation of value. The possessor of money does find on the market such a special commodity in capacity for labor or labor-power."[75]

When the enigma of increased value becomes the object of radical elucidation, this elucidation appears to consist in an abrupt shift in level, in moving from the level of exchange-value to that of use-value. This shift is identical to the shift from economic reality to monadic subjectivity, inasmuch as the use-value that is to be substituted for the exchange-value which the capitalist has just purchased from the worker is precisely nothing other than the actualization of his labor-power, the use and enjoyment of this labor, or what Marx called, by analogy with subjectivity, wherein use-values in general are realized, its "consumption." Speaking of the use-value that the worker offers to the capitalist, Marx says: "The use-value which the former [the purchaser] gets in exchange, manifests itself only in the actual usufruct, in the consumption of labor-power."[76] The use of individual labor-power is given unequivocally as creating not only the material reality of the objects produced in the real labor process but also the surplus-value which the capitalist will be able to realize by selling them: "The consumption of labor-power is at one and the same time the production of commodities and of surplus-value."[77] To refer the production of surplus-value to the actualization of the potentialities found in individual subjectivity is to leave the economic level of the circulation of commodities in order to inquire into an entirely different region of being, no longer that of economic objectivity but the secret region where, alone with itself, the body develops its powers in the silent interiority which marks its radical individualization. And because it is this effort alone, this *labor* performed in the secret laboratory of the body, which produces surplus-value, the comprehension of capital, *not of the existing capital which is presupposed in its structures and in its productions, but the comprehension of the production of capital itself* necessarily implies this conversion by which the scientific attitude which develops the theory of economic regulations becomes the transcendental attitude which grasps, under this apparent and noisy sequence of visible events, the genesis, no longer of value but of surplus-value, that is to say, precisely, of capital. In a programmatic definition of the very project of *Capital,* and right after declaring that it is the consumption of labor-power which produces surplus-value, Marx adds these truly essential lines: "The consumption of labor-power is completed, as is the case of every other commodity, outside the limits of the market or of the sphere of circulation. Accompanied by Mr. Moneybags and by the possessor of labor-power, we therefore *take leave for a time of this noisy sphere, where everything takes place on the surface and in view of all men, and follow them both into the hidden abode of production. . . . Here we shall see, not only how capital produces, but how capital is produced."*[78] "Accompanied by Mr. Moneybags and by the possessor of labor-power": it is not only on the level of theoretical analysis that there is a shift from the sphere of objective economic circulation to that of the subjective reality of the actualization of labor-power; this also occurs in practice as that which takes place on the level of the reality of capitalism providing its definition and constituting it.

We now understand how surplus-value can arise in circulation and at the same time not arise from it. Surplus-value stems from circulation to the extent that it results from the purchase of the worker's labor-power by the capitalist, a purchase which by definition belongs to the sphere of circulation, which, as Marx states, takes place "in its midst." However, as we shall see, this purchase in itself creates no value at all and, *a fortiori,* no surplus-value. It is for this reason that surplus-value, in reality, does not come from circulation and does not arise in it. Where does it come from? From the "consumption" of labor-power, from its actualization, which no longer takes place within the sphere of circulation but within that of production. It is the latter, *or rather it is, in it, the actualization of labor-power, it is living labor* and it alone, which creates surplus-value. Surplus-value, the realization and increase of value, is the transformation of money into capital. Summing up his analysis, Marx says with regard to the genesis of capital: "This metamorphosis, this conversion of money into capital, takes place both within the sphere of circulation and also outside it; within the circulation, because conditioned by the purchase of the labor-power in the market; outside the circulation, because what is done within it is only a stepping-stone to the production of surplus-value, *a process which is entirely confined to the sphere of production.*"[79]

Thus, there are two spheres, a sphere of objective appearance, where everything takes place "on the surface and in view of all men," and, on the other hand, the secret sphere of subjectivity, that of the actual production of surplus-value, where, before it produces, capital is itself produced. The sphere of circulation is apparent not as an economic determination opposed to another determination, but inasmuch as it is objective and as such neither contains nor exhibits that which, belonging to subjectivity and to it alone, nevertheless determines the entire system. The sphere of circulation is that of right, but the critique of right has already shown that there is no equal standard, no objective standard for what is subjective. With regard to the fundamental problem that concerns us, the problem of the capitalist's purchase and the worker's sale of his labor-power, what radically prevents the subjectivity of this labor-power, of its actualization in production, from complying with a fixed unit of objective measurement will be submitted to a twofold critique—on the one hand, to the critique of the pseudo-"exchange" which occurs between the worker and the capitalist and, on the other hand, to the critique of variable capital. The elucidation of the "exchange" of capital and of labor, however, runs up against an initial problem. Does not the crucial thesis by means of which Marx thinks he is able to resolve the aporia of circulation, namely the affirmation that only the use of labor-power is capable of producing surplus-value, contradict another thesis which is no less fundamental—because it is one of the major elements in the transcendental genesis of the economy—that value is created not by real labor but by abstract labor? For the use of labor-power is nothing other than real labor, and what it produces, surplus-value, is, according to a specific assertion made by Marx, ontologically of the same nature as value itself, surplus-value being simply a new value added onto a previously existing, yet itself created, value. This final point has first to be established. This text from the *Grundrisse*, which formulates briefly although in an especially enlightening way the critique of circulation, sets us on the right track. "The act of exchange is thus value-positing in so far as values are presupposed to it; it realizes the value-character of the subjects of exchange. But an act which posits a commodity as value, or, what is the same, which posits another commodity as its equivalent—or, again the same, which posits the equivalence of both commodities, obviously for its part adds nothing to value, as little as the sign $\pm$ increases or decreases the number coming after it."[80] It follows from this that circulation is itself incapable of increasing the value of the commodities that are exchanged in it, not primarily because, as circulation, it never involves anything other than the exchange of equivalent goods—this is the thesis expressed in *Capital*—but for the decisive, albeit implicit, reason that it only uncovers certain values, that it finds them, instead of being able to create value. Circulation is limited to realizing the value of commodities, a value which already exists in them before they enter into circulation. "The act of exchange is thus value-positing in so far as values are presupposed to it." This means that the values have already been produced, produced outside of circulation, by production. What is shown, therefore, is not the inability of circulation to produce surplus-value, but its more general inaptitude to produce value, to the extent that it presupposes the existence of the values it is content to compare and exchange, being itself this very exchange. Thus, exchange does not create the values that are exchanged; its role is limited, as the *Grundrisse* text clearly states, to placing them in contact with one another and observing their equality. Radically powerless with respect to surplus-value, circulation displays the same feature first of all with respect to value itself.

What we are then given to understand is that the origin of surplus-value, which lies outside circulation, is to begin with the origin of value and hence one and the same, and this is why value and surplus-value are of the same nature, the second being only, as has been stated, the addition of a new value. The ontological identity of value and surplus-value against the backdrop of the identity of their production is explicitly formulated by Marx: "If we now compare the two processes of producing value and of creating surplus-value, we see that the latter is nothing but the continuation of the former beyond a definite point. If on the one hand the process be not carried beyond the point where the value paid by the capitalist for the labor-power is replaced by an exact equivalent, it is simply a process of producing value; if, on the other hand, it be continued beyond that point, it becomes a process of creating surplus-value."[81] The difference between value and surplus-value will be clarified. Here, it is enough to observe that, against the backdrop of the ontological identity of their production and, consequently, of their nature as the pure result of this production, the modalities of value, precisely, cannot be connected to two principles that are as distinct and, what is more, as heterogeneous as reality and irreality. *Surplus-value cannot originate in living labor if value in general is the result of abstract labor.* Now, not only did Marx explicitly connect the production of surplus-value to the actualization of labor-power, to its effective *use*, but, in the same stroke, he was obliged to do the same thing in the case of value itself, as this text from the *Grundrisse* shows unequivocally in its critique of circulation, adding an essential remark: "Exchange as the positing of equivalents cannot therefore by its nature increase the sum of values, nor the value of the commodities exchanged. (The fact that it is different with the exchange with labor arises because *the use of labor is itself value-positing*, but is not directly connected with its exchange value.)"[82]

Engels' question: "What sort of labor creates value?" is thus posed once again and, with it, the question of the very sense of Marx's entire problematic is put to us anew and demands an ever more radical elucidation. It is a matter of determining whether the lack of autarchy of the economy is a provisional, and finally inexact, result—for, if abstract labor creates value, it also creates surplus-value. But abstract labor is an economic determination. The reference of surplus-value to abstract labor signifies, then, that it results from an economic determination, *that realization, the increase in value, and finally capital itself can be explained economically,* in short, that the economic determinations in their mutual interrelation form an autonomous totality. What is in question here, or rather what suddenly appears contradictory, is the transcendental genesis of the economy in its positing of the lack of autarchy of economic reality, since it has also, it seems, following not just Engels but Marx as well, referred value to abstract labor and not to real labor.

Or perhaps the transcendental genesis of the economy, on the contrary, does not enable us to overcome this contradiction, to consider it to be merely apparent? Indeed, what it has established—and this is a constant thesis in Marx—is that *there is only one labor,* the oneness of the process of production, which is *at once* the production of use-value and of exchange-value: "Just as commodities are, at the same time, use-values and values, so *the process of producing them must be a labor-process, and at the same time, a process of creating value.*"[83] The fact that one and the same labor creates use-value and exchange-value is reasserted in a text which is all the more remarkable in that it posits the unity of these two aspects of labor at the same time as it affirms their difference—their unity being what immediately overcomes their difference. This unity, moreover, is also affirmed in the case of the process of creating value as well as in that of creating surplus-value, thereby corroborating the ontological unity of value and surplus-value against the backdrop of the unity of abstract labor and useful labor: ". . . the difference between labor, considered on the one hand as producing utilities, and on the other hand, as creating value . . . resolves itself into a distinction between two aspects of the process of production. The process of production, considered on the one hand as *the unity of the labor-process and the process of creating value,* is the production of commodities; considered on the other hand as *the unity of the labor-process and the process of producing surplus-value,* it is the capitalist process of production, or capitalist production of commodities."[84] It is this unity of useful labor *stricto sensu* and of labor as value-creating which allows Marx, in *Capital,* to speak of the twofold utility of labor, the property of satisfying need and that of creating value.[85] This is why, just when the identity of labor and of surplus-labor is established in *Capital* with regard to the serf who works three days for himself and three days for his lord, the identity of this labor in relation to use-value and to exchange-value is also affirmed. "Both his voluntary labor for himself and his forced labor for his lord are equally labor; so far as this labor is considered with reference to the values, or to the useful articles created by it, there is no difference in his six days of labor."[86]

It is enough to keep in mind the sense of abstract labor in order to reply clearly to the question: "What sort of labor creates value?" If, properly speaking, there are not two types of labor,[87] as *Capital* affirms in significant passages already quoted; if abstract labor is no more than real labor "opposed to itself," that is to say, represented; if, more precisely, and as the problematic has established, abstract labor is only the representation of the common essence which is found in every form of real labor, namely the actualization in it of labor-power, then it is in reality labor-power which creates value; it is living labor and the actualization of life in organic subjectivity which is the source of value. Let us state this most clearly: it is not the representation of labor that can create any sort of value; only the actual labor that effectively produces an object can produce at the same time the value of this object, can *create value*. This is why the thesis that it is abstract labor that creates value is inexact if it is taken literally. It is the use of labor-power that creates value and this use has nothing abstract about it. Abstract labor is related to value only to the extent, precisely, that it represents the real essence of actual labor, to the extent that it *represents the source of value*. And this relation to the source of all value on the one hand and to value itself as such on the other, must be understood and has been understood. Living labor considered, indeed, not in its particular form as the labor of the potter, of the peasant, of the weaver or the spinner, but as the actualization of labor-power, creates value; whereas the determination of this value, which is a magnitude of some sort—consequently, its quantitative determination—is impossible because, as subjective, the actualization of labor-power is not a quantity and cannot be reduced to it. This is why—and this is the transcendental genesis of the economy, the construction of the possibility of exchange—one substitutes for the unquantifiable subjective actualization of the living bodily power a representation of this power which places it within the objective coordinates of the universe, coordinates which are measurable and which permit it to be measured: the day, the hour. On the other hand, as we have seen, this living labor is compared with ideal norms which are then substituted for it under the pretext of evaluating it and, in fact, in order to be able to do so. Abstract labor is the set of representations whose theory has been expounded and which are intended to measure that which, in itself, escapes measurement and to calculate that which does not allow itself to be subsumed under a formula. It is because abstract labor is the inevitable mediation by means of which to calculate the living labor-power that produces value that it appears finally as the substance of value: it is the only means, if not to produce value, at least to determine it. "This calculation by working days, and labor time as the only substance of value. . . ."[88] It is to be noted that wherever abstract labor seems to be presented as the substance or the source of value, it does no more than provide a measurement, an instrument invented by men to do this. "*To measure the exchange-value* of commodities by the labor-time they contain, the different kinds of labor have to be reduced to uniform, homogeneous, simple labor. . . ."[89] "The *magnitude* of this value *is measured* by the *amount* of labor expended."[90] The fact that the latter, abstract labor, is nothing other than the labor that creates use-values and exchange-value as well—or rather the quantifiable and quantified form that is substituted for it in order to determine on the basis of this the magnitude of the value produced, the fact that this substitution is that of the objective time of labor for the concrete subjective temporality of its immanent actualization, and that this substitution is intended only to enable making an account of living labor-power—all of this is contained in the following text:

> If we . . . compare the process of producing value with the labor-process, pure and simple, we find that the latter consists of the useful labor, the work, that produces use-values. Here we contemplate the labor as producing a particular article; we view it under its qualitative aspect alone, with regard to its end and aim. But viewed as a value-creating process, *the same labor-process presents itself under its quantitative aspect alone*. Here it is a question merely of the time occupied by the laborer in doing the work; of the period during which the labor-power is usefully expended. . . . They [the commodities] count merely as depositories of so much absorbed or materialized labor; that labor, whether previously embodied in the means of production, or incorporated in them for the first time during the process by the action of labor-power, *counts* in either case *only* according to its duration. . . . Moreover, only so much of the time spent in the production of any article is counted, as, under the given social conditions, is necessary.[91]

Thus it becomes apparent that the economic determination, far from being substituted for the real process, is merely the objective framework within which living labor has to be set so that, measured in terms of this framework, it can in turn measure the value it alone is capable of producing. "At the end of one hour's spinning, that act is represented by a definite quantity of yarn; in other words, a definite quantity of labor, namely that of one hour, has become embodied in the cotton. We say labor, i.e. *the expenditure of his vital force by the spinner*. . . ."[92]

Certain decisive texts unconditionally ascribe the creation of value to living labor. For example, the following text, which is all the more revealing in that, by distinguishing between labor-power—that is, subjectivity itself—and its actualization in effective labor, it ascribes to the first the capacity of being this power in act; this actual or potential creation of value is as such the condition and the ground of the entire economic process: ". . . *labor-power preserve[s] its property of producing value only so long as it is employed and materialized in the labor-process; yet this does not argue against the fact that it is potentially, as a power, an activity which creates value, and that as such it does not spring from the process of production, but rather antecedes it*."[93] Another text concerning the problem of preserving and creating value is no less explicit: "*The property therefore which labor-power in action, living labor, possesses of preserving value, at the same time that it adds it*. . . ."[94] A text in Book Three, belonging to a more complex problematic which will be presented later, speaks of ". . . *living value-creating labor-power*."[95]

Attributing the creation of value to living labor is the only way of making sense of the fundamental analysis of the relation between capital and labor. For this relation consists in the fact that the capitalist gives to the worker the exchange-value of his labor-power in order to receive in return its use-value. It is precisely with this, with living labor, that he will produce the value that constitutes the goal of his entire enterprise. Before we submit this to a profound examination, it is certainly appropriate to recall that the exchange of capital and labor obeys historical or, if one prefers, social conditions. Moreover, these conditions appear to make the exchange seem not really to be an exchange at all.[96] Why? Because, it seems, the exchangers, just when they are about to perform the exchange, are no longer on equal terms; one is already a worker and the other already a capitalist. The first is already a worker because, when he is separated from the objective conditions of his labor, he cannot, as we have seen, produce anything himself but must offer his labor-power to the one who possesses these conditions. The second is already a capitalist since the one who purchases this force is, as the possessor of the objective conditions of its realization, the possessor of this realization itself and of what it produces, of value. "The class relation between capitalist and wage-laborer therefore exists, is presupposed from the moment the two face each other. . . ."[97] As we see, the prior conditions which from the outset disturb the alleged equality of the exchange correspond to the break of the direct tie which formerly joined the worker to his instrument, a break which, finally, constitutes at one and the same time the definition of the two basic classes which are found in *Capital:* the proletariat is characterized by subjectivity reduced to itself, lacking the objective conditions for its realization, whereas capital, as a class, results from holding a monopoly on these conditions.[98]

However, the fact that the worker, who is separated from the means of realizing his labor-power, is forced to sell this labor-power to the capitalist, who does possess the means, no doubt shows the inequality of their social conditions at the time of the exchange, but it explains nothing about the inequality which has corrupted this exchange itself. What is more, by affirming a preexisting inequality, one loses sight of that *which will emerge out of the exchange;* the second inequality is confused with the first, the inequality which constitutes the principle of production with the social inequality resulting from it. For, in reality, the social classes do not precede capitalism in order to make it what it is; instead capitalism, on the contrary, determines the social classes, and this is because in the exchange between capitalism and labor, or as its direct result, an essential phenomenon will be produced, one that will act as the creative force, the *naturans,* for the entire system. As always, one is mistaken in hypostatizing classes, structures, objective ensembles in order to make them into explanatory principles, whereas they themselves have to be explained. The classes are not simply the historical, occasional cause of the exchange between capital and labor; they are actually the result of this exchange. Here again they must be grasped in terms of their genealogy, which Marx will now show *is identical to the transcendental genesis of surplus-value, that is, of capitalism itself.* It is in this way that economic determinations govern social determinations: against the backdrop of their own determination grasped as meta-economic.

With brilliant conciseness, a passage in the *Grundrisse*—the book Marx wrote for himself before writing *Capital* with other people in mind—posits the identity of the social genealogy and of the transcendental genesis of capitalism, and at the same time formulates the ultimate nature of this genesis. With respect to the alleged equality between the exchange of capital and of labor, it states: "In fact this equality is already disturbed because the worker's relation to the capitalist *as a use value, in the form specifically distinct from exchange value, in opposition to value posited as value. . . .*"[99] This, then, is what the exchange between capital and labor is reduced to, what the relation between the classes amounts to: to the fact that opposite an exchange-value, a use-value is posited. Now positing a use-value opposite an exchange-value is not itself an exchange, Marx says, because it takes into account only the value of the commodities exchanged and is by its nature indifferent to their use-value. This is the reason why, in the text we have just discussed, the relation between the capitalist and the worker is outside the category of exchange: "thus, he already stands in a . . . relation outside that of exchange, in which the nature of the use value, the particular use value of the commodity is, as such, irrelevant."[100] The collapse of the concept of exchange as the direct result of the fact that what is thematized in the "exchange" between capital and labor and what determines it is a use-value, is a constant assertion throughout Marx's analysis and his definition of capital. For money becomes capital only when it is exchanged, not for another value, but precisely for a use-value, for the use-value of labor-power, that is to say, for labor itself. It is for this reason, first of all, that the worker's money, for example, is not capital; its condition of value will serve to buy the necessary means of subsistence, that is, will be exchanged for other commodities of equivalent value according to the laws of circulation.[101] What will make capital of this money is, on the contrary, its exchange for labor considered in itself not as value—the equivalent of the sum of money—but as a use-value, for actual labor and, consequently, for living labor. ". . . the saved up money would itself have to become capital, i.e. buy labor, *relate to labor as use-value*." In order to participate in this pseudo-exchange constituted by the relation between capital and labor, and in order to define it, labor must then confront capital, that is, confront value, as use-value, that is, as not-value, as not-capital. "In order to become capital, it itself presupposes labor as not-capital." This means that capital cannot confront itself, that a value opposite a value cannot define the capitalist relation, which nevertheless seems to be a pure economic relation, and this is so because capital is capital only when placed opposite the fundamental use-value, labor. "But capital, too, cannot confront capital if capital does not confront labor." And again, in a thoroughly explicit manner: "As capital it can posit itself only by positing labor as not-capital, as pure use value,"[102] so that confronting industrial capital "labor must exist as pure use value."[103]

Placing the concept of exchange out of bounds in this way, the fact that for the homogeneity of the terms exchanged—a homogeneity which permits their equality—is substituted a glaring heterogeneity, the confrontation of two ontologically different realities is visible in many different ways. On the one hand, we find ideal economic determination, value, and on the other, use-value and, more precisely, the use-value of labor-power, that is, subjectivity itself and its actualization. This is first visible in the gap that opens up between the actualization of each of the terms in the exchange. With respect to the exchange-value of labor-power, it is determined straightaway. Moreover, and in this it resembles the values of all commodities, this value is fixed even before entering into circulation since it results from the amount of labor necessary for the production of the commodity. On the contrary, what is given to the capitalist by the worker in exchange for this already determined value, which is the exchange-value of his labor, is its use-value, which, as the unfolding of the potentialities of organic subjectivity, has its own immanent temporality, which passes away as it does, which thus occupies a certain duration.[104] In this way, for the determined value of labor-power is substituted the use of this power in the hands of the capitalist; that is, something whose product is still undetermined is neither measured nor taken into account in the exchange at the time of the exchange.

The heterogeneity of the terms of the exchange, which breaks apart the concept of exchange, is made apparent in another way as well. The value that the worker receives in exchange for the use of his labor-power enables him to buy what is necesssary for his subsistence. These goods are consumed, and in the same stroke their value disappears, so that the worker has nothing left, neither value nor use-value, and this is why he continually returns to the labor market. *What the capitalist gets out of this, on the contrary, does not vanish*, for it is the power that the worker has just given to him, no longer a limited or diminishing reality, even less something that disappears, but a power, a creative possibility capable of producing and of giving rise to a number of results. On the one hand, the disappearance of a use-value sacrificed to the maintenance of life and, on the other hand, the disposition of a productive activity which, as such, continues as power, origin, and source of new production—this is the figure describing the heterogeneity of the terms between which the exchange breaks apart.[105]

However, this is the time to make the essential remark that the heterogeneity of the terms of the exchange between capital and labor, which makes this exchange an illusory appearance, is not absolute and, quite the contrary, coincides with that which reestablishes the relation of homogeneity between these terms. Indeed, let us not forget the fundamental thesis which we have shown to be that of Marx, namely that it is the use-value of labor-power which creates value. Henceforth, for the exchange-value of the worker's labor-power the capitalist receives, along with this force, something which, as real, is certainly not of the same nature as economic value, but whose use has, precisely, as its result the production of economic value. The recourse to the living power of subjectivity which took us out of the economic circle of circulation—and which breaks this circle—does not prevent the circle from closing again, if indeed it is true that in exchange for a certain value the capitalist will finally obtain, through the use of the labor-power that he has secured and as its result, a value, one greater than the initial value.[106] An essential text in the *Grundrisse* establishes in succession: (1) that what the capitalist obtains from the worker in exchange for a certain value in the material form of the means of subsisting is his labor time, his living labor time, which functions not as exchange-value but as use-value, as the actualization of his subjective power—"The living labor time he gets in exchange is not the exchange value, but the use value of labor capacity"; (2) that the act of this living subjectivity is what produces value— "But the use value of the value the capitalist has acquired through exchange is itself the element of realization. . . ."[107]

Now, it is at the moment when the use-value received in exchange by the capitalist is understood as the power of realization, thus leading us back to value, that is, at the moment when the terms of the exchange permit the principle of a possible homogeneity to be glimpsed, namely their expression in terms of value—and this despite their radical heterogeneity—that this heterogeneity is once again manifested. For, considering things from the standpoint of value, there is a difference—and even, as has been shown, an ontological difference—between the value given to the worker, namely labor in the materialized form of the goods he will be able to buy with his wages, and, on the other hand, what he gives to the capitalist, namely no longer materialized labor but living labor, no longer a value but the element which creates, produces, and multiplies value. With regard to this new formulation of the inequality of the two terms in the exchange, Marx says in a text which is all the more noteworthy in that the connection between the critique of exchange and the thesis that it is living labor and living labor alone that creates value becomes evident here: ". . . because it is given in exchange as objectified labor, while its use value, by contrast, consists of living labor, i.e. of the positing of exchange value. The turn into its opposite arises from the fact that the use value of labor capacity, as value, is itself the value-creating force; the substance of value, and the value-increasing substance."[108] In this way, the dissimilarity of the terms in the exchange takes the form, in the relation to value or rather to the power that produces value, of an opposition between this value, itself understood, precisely, as a product, an effect, and this power grasped, on the contrary, as the generating power, the source and the cause of value. "He [the worker] sells himself as an effect. He is absorbed into the body of capital as a cause, as activity."[109] And it is this dissimilarity which is immediately given as the origin of the inequality which turns the exchange into its opposite at the same time as it overturns the entire ideology that political economy had based on exchange. "Thus," the text continues, "the exchange turns into its opposite, and the laws of private property—liberty, equality, property. . . ."

The fact that a fixed value, that of the means of subsistence, is exchanged by the capitalist for the very source and the creative power of value, for a power whose existence will, in his hands, lead to the creation of a new value—this by no means shows, however, in what way and for what reason the value resulting from this process is greater than the initial value given to the worker in the form of wages. Why, indeed, would the value produced not simply be equal to, or even less than, the value advanced initially? Now it is not by analyzing the value itself, whether the initial or the final value, that one will be able to reply to this question and to determine their relative magnitude, to note, for example, a surplus-value obtained at the end of the process. Just when the crucial phenomenon of realization constituting the essence of capitalism is about to be circumscribed, it appears that its principle cannot be sought, is by no means to be found on the economic level. And this must be understood in a radical sense. For it is no longer a matter of establishing that this level is not the only one and that, in order to be intelligible, it must be related to a reality of another order, namely, the living subjectivity that creates it. Up to now, the analysis of the relation between capital and labor has been limited to this—which is not to be underestimated—since it has shown that in exchange for the value paid to the worker, that is to say, for an economic determination, what the capitalist obtains is a real determination, the determination in terms of which Marx defines reality. Thus the inequality that corrupts the exchange has been unequivocally referred to the ontological heterogeneity of its terms, to the opposition between the economy and life. Yet, once again, the examination of these two terms, the initial value on the one hand and, on the other, the actualization of labor-power or rather that to which it directly leads, the value produced by it—this analysis by no means permits us to conclude that these two values are unequal, and the enigma of surplus-value remains intact. The reason is that in order to resolve this enigma, however strange it may seem, one must in fact leave the level of value, place the whole economic dimension out of bounds, and restrict oneself to the sphere of life and to it alone. It is no longer of value that one must speak, but of reality, of which value is a possible manifestation.

What is made manifest by the value paid to the worker is the amount of labor contained in the means of subsistence required by life for its continuance. Determined by the needs of life and by these alone, *the quantity of these goods has nothing to do with the quantity of labor required to produce them*. What is manifested by the value created at the end of the process through the actualization of the worker's labor-power is the use-values created by it, or more exactly, it is the quantity of labor that they "materialize," that is to say, precisely, the actualization of the labor-power during the time that it took to produce them. Now, just as the quantity of supplies needed by the worker is in no way connected to the quantity of labor necessary for their formation, to their value, neither is the quantity of use-values resulting from the actualization of labor-power during one day connected in a basic way to the problem of their value. No doubt it is the actualization of this power, it is the amount of labor expended by the worker that creates the value of the use-values produced, but this real production of use-values could very well occur—and it actually does occur in many instances, in the family "economy" for example—without the question of value ever arising. Let us therefore abstract from the question of value in order to consider only the realities that remain once this abstraction has been made. On one side, we have the use-values required to maintain the labor-power for, let us say, one day, and, on the other side, the actualization of this labor-power and the use-values that it produces during this same day. We are remaining within the living sphere which defines reality and it is on this level, irrespective of any economic consideration, that inequality arises: *it is the inequality between the use-values that labor-power is capable of producing and the use-values that are necessary for maintaining labor-power itself during the time of this production*. For example, a use-value produced over a half-day will be able to keep an individual alive and, consequently, enable him to work for a whole day. And, as a result, the time that he is actually producing will be only half that during which the use-value enables him to produce. Now, this essential relation between use-values, their capacity to maintain life and to permit production on the one hand and, on the other, the time of production proper to each, is entirely independent of all questions concerning value, although it founds them all. "First of all, a product which has cost only half a working day may suffice for me to live and work a whole day. Whether or not the product possesses this quality depends not on its value, i.e. the labor time bestowed on it, but rather on its use value. . . ."[110]

Therefore, if we go back to what is really produced in the exchange between capital and labor, we then see that in fact there is nothing economic in this exchange, no exchange-value enters into it originally; the exchange is not an exchange of value, and it is for this reason, in reality, that it is not an exchange. Rather we have, on one side, the use-value of individual labor-power and the use-values it is capable of producing in one day and, on the other side, the use-values required to maintain this labor-power during the same day. Now these use-values—those it needs, those it is capable of producing—are determined only by it, that is to say, by the nature of life, by its own needs and its own capabilities. ". . . the exchange which takes place in this regard between living labor and the product of labor is not an exchange between both as use values, but rather their relation lies on the one side in the use value of the product, on the other side in the conditions of the existence of living labor capacity."[111] It is precisely the relation between the use-value necessary for life and those it is capable of producing which establishes the original and decisive inequality, namely the vital fact that in actualizing its subjective potentialities life produces more use-values than it requires to maintain its existence. A fact such as this, which is completely foreign to the economy and which is meta- or extra-economic, also signifies that the individual, producing more than he consumes, does not need his entire labor time in order to produce the goods necessary for his existence and that, beyond this necessary labor time, he is therefore able either to rest or to perform surplus-labor, a labor producing use-values that exceed his consumption and that will remain at the end of the process as a surplus. Although it is part of a polemic against Proudhon, the following text is nevertheless the most important one written by Marx on the subject, since it reveals the principle and the secret of capitalism, just as, moreover, of any possible system. *"The only extra-economic fact in this is that the human being does not need his entire time for the production of the necessaries, that he has free time at his disposal above and beyond the labor time necessary for subsistence, and hence can also employ it for surplus labor."*[112]

This decisive property of life must no doubt be understood in the same way as all the properties of life, as a potentiality. This signifies, first of all, that it might not be actualized. It can be actualized, labor-power can be activated in order to produce more use-values than those necessary for subsistence, only if the latter have already been provided. Thus the individual is forced to consume before he produces: every life requires an initial credit. This necessity becomes precisely, at the dawn of the modern age, one of the historical conditions of capitalism, since it was when he was deprived of the means of subsistence to which he had been naturally bound that the peasant, driven off his land, had to pawn his labor. However, when the conditions for the actualization of labor-power are fulfilled, when vital needs are satisfied and the individual is able to work, the ways in which living subjectivity develops its fundamental property of producing more than it requires are most diverse. Fragile at first, when the means of subsistence are minimal and, correlatively, the production of labor-power is still limited, the historical manifestation of *life's property of contributing more than it has been given* finds in capitalism, which rests on it and which consciously pushes it to its furthest point, a spectacular accomplishment. With respect to the worker considered in his power to go beyond his needs, Marx says: ". . . his necessaries are small to the same degree that his labor power is in a primitive state. But wage labor as such enters only where the development of the productive force has already advanced so far that a significant amount of time has become free; this liberation is here already a historic product."[113] And it appears once again here that, in Marx, the philosophy of history is subordinated to a metaphysics of life, that in every case accidents are explained in terms of essence, that what occurs is never anything but the actualization of potentialities to be found within the metahistorical nature of existence and their progressive realization—in the case that concerns us here, the realization and the actualization of the most ultimate of life's possibilities, that of surpassing its own conditions, of being the power of growth which makes it precisely, in the face of everything confronting it in the world, life itself.

It is, in any event, to this fundamental possibility that we must refer if we are to understand what now occurs on the economic level as its simple consequence and as one illustration among other equally possible ones. When we recall the theory of value, namely the production of value through the use of labor-power, realization appears as the direct correlate and the ideal expression of the power of life. In the same stroke, the exchange between capital and labor becomes transparent from an economic standpoint. Expressed as values, the terms of this exchange allow their ideal quantitative inequality to appear as the simple consequence of their real inequality. We now have once again, on one side, the value of labor-power, that is, the amount of labor required to produce the goods that are indispensable to preserve this power, and, on the other side, to begin with, the use of this force that has been acquired by the capitalist, *a use that has no limits and no laws other than those belonging to the power of life itself.* "The value of the laboring power is determined by the quantity of labor necessary to maintain or reproduce it, but the use of that laboring power is only limited by the active energies and physical strength of the laborer."[114] Again we find the disparity distinguishing a value from a use-value; but the latter, the use of labor-power, is in its turn, in accordance with the law of value, value-creating. To say that this use is independent of the amount of labor required for the production of necessary goods therefore means that the amount of labor in which labor-power is actualized is independent of the amount of labor necessary for its preservation and its reproduction: "The quantity of labor by which the value of the workman's laboring power is limited forms by no means a limit to the quantity of labor which his laboring power is apt to perform."[115] In a lecture he gave, Marx was to employ numbers in order to allow the imagination to grasp this truth which belongs to another order, and this use of numbers was indeed justified since value is itself nothing but a figuration of this sort, the ideal figuration of living praxis. Let us imagine, then, a spinner who works six hours a day in order to produce the goods he needs, and let us ascribe to these a value of three shillings; nothing prevents him from working another six hours to produce an additional value of three shillings, and this is what he does in the hands of the capitalist. In this way, "over and above the six hours required to replace his wages, or the value of his laboring power, he will, therefore, have to work six other hours, which I shall call hours of surplus labor, which surplus labor will realize itself in a surplus value and a surplus produce."[116] If we now put ourselves in the place of the capitalist, we then have to say: "By advancing three shillings, the capitalist will, therefore, realize a value of six shillings, because, advancing a value in which six hours of labor are crystallized, he will receive in return a value in which twelve hours of labor are crystallized. . . . It is this sort of exchange between capital and labor upon which capitalistic production . . . is founded. . . ."[117] Just as whenever an ultimate principle of explanation is reached, and because this principle, as a principle, never ceases to produce its effects, we encounter the idea of an indefinite repetition of the system whose *naturans* has just been revealed. The wage system "must constantly result in reproducing the working man as a working man, and the capitalist as a capitalist."[118] However, the system's self-reproduction cannot be considered as an internal causality, or even a self-positing of the system itself, except inasmuch as the crucial phenomenon of individual praxis—which, with its specific life properties, is the principle of reiteration—itself continues to be overlooked.

The problem of the conservation of value

The problem of the increase of value is decisive, and yet it has helped to mask, not for Marx but instead for his commentators, another problem which in a sense is even more fundamental, that of the conservation of value. For, in the course of the process of production, value can grow in the form of a surplus-value only if it is first preserved, only if the values present at the start of this process in the elements employed are capable of reappearing at the end of the process in order to form together the value of the product. However, let us first see why, despite this self-evidence, the problem of the increase of value tends to mask that of its conservation. This is because it is introduced into the problematic of *Capital* in the form of a critique of circulation. To circulation is accorded the capacity to conserve value, since exchange is characterized by the fact that the same quantity of value is maintained. If there is no increase of value in the exchange, neither is there any possible decrease: the conservation of value is implied in circulation as its very definition. And this is also true, naturally, for exchanges surrounding the material process of production: a certain amount of money has been converted into raw materials, instruments of labor; the sum of the values of these elements reappears in the product, which can then be exchanged for an equivalent amount of money.[119] And it is in this way that value appears as a constant, identical to itself throughout all the phases in the process and indifferent to these phases, as to the use-values that determine them.[120] It is only when an unexplainable variation suddenly appears on the level of value itself and of its circulation, that is to say, of its indefinite tautological repetition, that Marx's problematic shifts to a different level, leaving behind that of the exchange-value, which, although capable of explaining its own conservation, cannot explain its growth. It is then that a reality of another order is taken into consideration, the use-value of labor-power, which alone is capable of producing a new value greater than its own value. Surplus-value, and it alone, is behind the substitution of the analysis of production for that of circulation, inspiring the backward questioning moving from the economic toward its own origin and toward life.

Presented in this form, the critique of circulation which plays an undeniably didactic role in the discussion in *Capital* runs the risk of provoking serious confusions, even outright errors. It is important, first of all, to distinguish between the maintenance of value on the one hand, and, on the other, what could be called the tautological repetition of value in exchange. It is clear that if a commodity has a certain value, this value is identical whether it is expressed in the form of this commodity or of a corresponding quantity of money. Exchange presupposes this identity and demonstrates it. If I exchange forty dollars' worth of tea for forty dollars and then for forty dollars' worth of coffee, the value I have in hand remains the same, it is "conserved." But here we are considering a specific exchange and the commodities exchanged in the instant in which they are exchanged. It is at the precise moment that this quantity of coffee is worth forty dollars that I can exchange it for a given quantity of tea which at this precise moment is also worth forty dollars. There can be no delay, for the coffee beans could split open, the tea mold, or the currency be devaluated. The entire problematic of value has shown its fundamental reference to use-value, which serves as its "support": if the properties of use-value are changed, its value disappears as well. And even on the plane which we can now call economic in appearance, on the plane of exchange-value considered in its relation to the abstract labor that it represents, the stability of this value is not to be taken for granted. Is it not, however, the objectification of a certain quantity of labor, that which was required for its production? Is not this quantity, which is fixed in the commodity, determined once and for all and the value as such "invariable"? But we know that the value of a commodity is not determined by the quantity of labor that it has cost but by that which would currently be necessary to produce it: should a modification in productivity occur, the value of the commodity will thereby diminish by the same amount. This condition may only intervene from time to time in determining the value of commodities intended for immediate consumption, but it is decisive for those that are destined for productive consumption, notably for the components of fixed capital. In modifying fixed capital, just as in modifying productivity, the entire scale of "invariable" values shifts and begins to slip, as if caught up in a vast current of actual production and carried along by its whirlpools. The stability of value, in reality, exists only within the relation between the commodity and its own value, and this is the case only for a given instant. It is for this reason that this stability is but a tautology. It expresses the fact that the exchange-value of a commodity can still take on an autonomous form over and against the commodity itself, as in the case of its price; and there is, of course, an identity between the value of the commodity and this value considered in itself as money. Indeed, this identity is the basis for exchange, since, before being exchanged for another, every commodity is in a way exchanged with itself and reveals its value in a pure form. It is precisely when the pure value of two commodities is identical that they can themselves be exchanged. But this basis for exchange is as yet simply ideal; it represents the eidetic possibility, not a real condition. In order that the exchange of two commodities take place, the needs of the exchangers must require the exchange. And even when it is a matter of the self-relation of a commodity's exchange-value, as in its price, we have seen that this relation can take on a contradictory form: in a period of crisis, this value, precisely, cannot be realized. This signifies once again that the tautological identity of the value that founds the exchange is a purely ideal condition and that ideality as such is never operative. *But the real conservation of value takes place outside the process of circulation; just as the production of value, its conservation refers to use-value and, moreover, to the specific use-value of labor-power.* As a result, it is not simply the process of realization which forces us to leave the sphere of circulation in order to enter into the secret laboratory of production; the simple conservation of value cannot itself be explained economically, and so we are forced to refer back to living subjectivity. What Marx will establish is that living subjectivity founds the entire process of value—its realization, of course, but first and foremost it conservation.

But, here again, if we want to avoid confusing matters, we must follow his analysis step by step. When the powerlessness of circulation has been revealed, both with respect to the simple conservation of value and to its creation, *the elucidation of the process of value is henceforth conducted within the process of production*. It is then quite remarkable to see that, in his effort to grasp the real origin of value, of its conservation or its growth, Marx radically challenges the distinction, which had been suggested by the critique of circulation, between the problem of value which is found to be quantitatively identical to itself at the end of the process, and the value which, on the contrary, appears there as an additional quantity, namely as surplus-value. The division, precisely, does not fall between value which remains quantitatively the same and surplus-value; besides, the value that remains the same is not the value that has been preserved. Let us consider a capital of one hundred thalers divided as follows in the production process: fifty thalers for cotton, forty for wages, and ten for instruments; to simplify we are also to suppose that the entire instrument of production is consumed in the course of production and, on the other hand, that the labor-power, covering a time of surplus-labor equal to the time of necessary labor, produces, in exchange for the forty thalers in wages, a value of eighty thalers.[121] In place of the one hundred thalers invested in this process, the capitalist receives one hundred and forty, and one could think that the problem is to found, on the one hand, the conservation of the value of the one hundred thalers and, on the other, the appearance of the new value of forty thalers, that is, of the surplus-value. Now, Marx's analysis rejects this dissociation of one hundred thalers on one side and forty thalers on the other, that is to say the representation of circulation as M-C-M′ where M′ represented M $+ \triangle$M, where the value is maintained identical to itself and, on the other hand, surplus-value: 100 + 40. This is, precisely, because circulation explains absolutely nothing about the phenomenon we have to analyze, for it entirely escapes the economic sphere and its laws and, consequently, is not subject to any sort of economic explanation.

Indeed, in this process we already know how to account for the production of the eighty thalers by means of the realization of labor-power. The latter produces during the first half of the day—the time of necessary labor—a value of forty thalers, which is equal to its own, to the value paid in wages; it is said to be *"reproduced."* During the second half of the day—the time of surplus-labor—labor-power produces a new value of forty thalers, which defines surplus-value, and this new value is *"produced"* stricto sensu. In this way the homogeneity of the production of value and of surplus-value is reaffirmed as a production whose sole origin and whose essence is to be found in living labor. But then a question arises: because the totality of the value produced by living labor, it also amounts, in our example, to eighty thalers. Now, one hundred thalers were initially put into the process, so does the process finally amount to a deficit of twenty thalers? There is, in fact, a third problem that has to be taken into consideration, that of the conservation of value, which concerns solely the value of the raw materials and of the instruments of labor. A definition such as this is not merely conventional; it is an integral part of the analysis and signifies that the problem of the conservation of the value of the objective conditions for the production process must be distinguished from that of the creation of value by labor-power: it is here then that we find the division imposed by Marx, no longer between maintaining a quantity of value identical to itself and, on the other hand, surplus-value, but between the production of value—which is the reproduction of the value paid in wages and production of surplus-value—and what can aptly be opposed to it here, the mere conservation of value, which is by no means a production of value and which is the conservation of the value of the raw materials and instruments—in our example, fifty thalers' worth of cotton and ten of instruments. Now this conservation of value is no less essential; it alone enables the process to lead to a final value of one hundred forty thalers and thus to an actual surplus-value. In what then does this conservation consist?

Although it is a matter of a simple conservation of value at the end of which this value is found to be identical to itself, this phenomenon has nothing to do with the tautological repetition of exchange. This is why, just as its production, the conservation of value is foreign to circulation and cannot be explained by it. This is why, just as its production, the conservation of value requires that in the problematic the economic level be replaced by that of reality and by the analysis of reality. The analysis in the *Grundrisse*, which here again plays the role of a guideline for the comprehension of Marx's thought, is situated straightaway within the reality of the process of production. The real process of production includes the objective conditions of labor and, confronting them, living labor. Each of these elements has its own value, and it is precisely the conservation of this value, at least that of the objective conditions of the process, which must be founded. But this question can be resolved only by abstracting from all of the economic determinations, from all of the values that enter into this process. However paradoxical this may seem, it is when the value of the elements included within and constituting the real process is set out of bounds that the value of its objective conditions can be, and effectively is, conserved. This is not a reduction performed by the mind which will permit an understanding of what occurs in the real process; this is a real reduction, namely the fact that all the elements in the process are carried back to their condition of use-value and are involved in the process solely under this aspect. It is precisely in this that the reality of the process lies, in the fact that the raw materials and the instruments are in it no longer values but rather use-values and offer themselves as such to the use made of them by labor-power, that is, to the action of living labor. "Now, in the realization process, the value components of capital—the one in the form of material, the other in the form of instrument—confront the worker, i.e. living labor . . . *not as values, but rather as simple moments of the production process; as use values for labor, as the objective conditions of its efficacy, or as its objective moments.*"[122] The use-values that have been worked over in this way are thus preserved, if need be in a modified form, by this action, and it is this action of living labor which, by preserving the use-values upon which it works, preserves in the same stroke the quantity of labor that was included in them, that is to say, their value. The conservation of values in the production process is nothing other than, and indeed is founded upon, the labor of the use-values whose value is thus preserved, founded upon the subjectivity of the worker and upon his living praxis. "The quantity of objectified labor is preserved in that its quality is preserved as use value for further labor, through the contact with living labor."[123] And again: "this natural animating power of labor—namely that, by using the material and instrument, it preserves them in one or another form, including the labor objectified in them, their exchange value. . . ."[124] Thus the economic process rests entirely upon the real process since it is the action of living subjectivity on use-value, that is to say, on unformed matter, which assumes and maintains this form, that is to say, the past labor objectified in it, in other words, its value. *"The preservation of the quality of previous labor in the simple production process—hence of its material as well—becomes, in the realization process, the preservation of the quantity of labor already objectified."*[125]

From the standpoint of value, that is, of capital, it must then be added that its conservation, the preservation of the quantity of labor materialized in the objective conditions of the real process, is realized through this process, whereas from the standpoint of living labor, it finds before it nothing but use-values, with which it works and to which it adds, by means of this work, a new quantity of labor, hence a new value. "For capital, this preservation is the preservation of the amount of objectified labor by the production process; for living labor itself, it is merely the preservation of the already present use value. Living labor adds a new amount of labor. . . ."[126] But here intervenes the radical distinction which Marx believed had to be made, no longer that between the preservation and the growth of value, but that between the production of value in general on the one hand and its simple conservation on the other. The text continues: ". . . however, it is not this quantitative addition which preserves the amount of already objectified labor, but rather its quality as living labor, the fact that it relates as labor to the use values in which the previous labor exists." Marx loses no time in drawing the conclusion that the wage, which expresses only the quantity of labor necessary for maintaining living labor-power, thereby fails to take into consideration not only the surplus-labor that this power may perform but also the specific quality by virtue of which living labor preserves the value of the use-values of labor, and this, due to the sole fact that labor is applied to them, that is, by reason of its very nature. "But living labor is not paid for this quality, which it possesses as living labor . . . rather, it is paid for the amount of labor contained in itself. . . . It does not receive payment for its specific quality of adding new amounts of labor to the amounts of labor already objectified, and at the same time preserving labor which is already objectified as objectified labor; *and this quality does not cost the worker anything either, since it is a natural property of his laboring capacity*."[127]

But why separate the production from the conservation of labor if both are the work of living labor? This inevitable question—inevitable even if it were never raised or perceived—implies an awareness of the ultimate level where Marx's meditation and his own specific theme are developed: living subjectivity and its actualization in living labor. And this question leads to a further elucidation of the essence of living labor. For, on the one hand, labor is a process which unfolds in accordance with the movement of its immanent temporality, in such a way that it depends on what is to be done and thus is determined in its duration. It is this concrete determination of labor, of a specific type of work, which is at the origin of the objective standard of measurement to which one tries to submit it and which allows it to be expressed in the form of a certain "quantity of labor" and thus of a value. This is the aspect through which living labor produces value before determining it as abstract labor. Moreover, when living labor is performed, and inasmuch as in this it makes use of certain use-values, manipulates them, modifies them, and shapes them in this or that way, it thereby maintains them in their capacity of use-value. This property has nothing to do with the duration of this or that particular work, or of labor in general as it adapts itself to the form of the object to be created and is determined by it; it belongs instead to labor itself inasmuch as it is applied to matter and, by thus retaining its form, thereby preserves its use. It is by revealing a general essence of labor—one which has nothing to do with "general labor," whose value is its objectification, but which designates the very fact of working and that in which it consists, the concrete essence of any and every sort of practice—that the *Grundrisse* reply to the question of how living labor preserves the labor that is already objectified in raw materials and in the instrument: "[this] . . . is a result *not of the quantity of labor*, but of its *quality* of being labor as such; and there is no special payment for this, its general quality, for the fact that *labor, as labor, is labor*. . . ."[128] It is because this specific quality, by virtue of which living labor preserves value, is independent of its duration, which itself is essential for the production of value, that one can say, as Marx does in the manuscripts constituting Book Three of *Capital*: "The mass of capital set in motion by the laborer, whose value he preserves by his labor and reproduces in his product, is quite different from the value which he adds to it."[129] And in this, one sees how a decisive property of the capitalist economy—namely that a certain kind of labor is, in itself and regardless of its duration or its quantity, capable of preserving more and more value and, finally, the enormous masses of value of fixed capital—has its origin and its possibility in the essence of a specific determination of individual subjectivity.

Employing a traditional terminology, Marx attempted to express this capacity of living labor to preserve the value of an object by preserving its use-value. Living labor is understood as an act that imprints a certain form upon a material substance, and objectified labor is this form as it subsists in matter and makes it suitable for a certain use, ready to offer itself to a new act of shaping which will be based on it in order to produce a new, more complex form starting from the previous form. However, this form which is imprinted upon the substance does not inhere in it because of its own properties, or because of the properties of the substance; *the form is not preserved in and of itself* but tends to become ineffective, "indifferent," says Marx, to the substance which it determines for a particular use, so that this use in its turn tends to be lost, along with the value that it carried. This process of deterioration and of becoming indifferent by which a form becomes external to its object and ceases to qualify it, characterizes objectified labor and makes of it dead labor. Over and above its conceptual formulation, the analysis of objectified labor which has just been made leads us to the *essential dialectic in Marx of dead labor and living labor*. For it is precisely living labor which, by integrating objectified labor within itself, by uniting with it, preserves it from death; it is the act of imprinting a form which meshes with the old form, prevents it from separating from the substance, where, once having become indifferent to its substance, it would then be lost along with the substance. "There is an indifference on the part of the substance [*Stoff*] towards the form, which develops out of merely objectified labor time . . . no immanent law of reproduction maintains this form. . . . However, when they are posited as conditions of living labor, they are themselves reanimated. Objectified labor ceases to exist in a dead state as an external, indifferent form on the substance, because it is itself again posited as a moment of living labor; as a relation of living labor to itself in an objective material, as the objectivity of living labor (as means and end [*Objekt*]), (the objective conditions of living labor)."[130]

Here a new and absolutely original sense of the concept of labor as objectification is revealed to us. To say that labor "is objectified" does not mean that its essence consists in the process through which it becomes an object— more precisely, in the form that is given to the object and which would be its objectification in the object—it does not mean that labor is real as objectified labor, in and through objectivity. Substantiality is no longer, as in Hegelianism, ascribed to exteriority, and it is false to claim that the theses of the *Economic and Philosophical Manuscripts*, notably those concerning labor, are to be found again in the *Grundrisse* just as they were in the former. This is to fail to see that, under the continuity of a terminology from which Marx, it is true, never managed to free himself totally, a radical mutation has taken place, a new philosophy has been born. Far from holding that labor, as simple subjective virtuality and as empty and, finally, illusory interiority, attains actuality only in the work accomplished by it, in objectified labor, it is, instead, objectified labor which is torn from the jaws of death only by the action of living subjectivity and only inasmuch as this action never ceases to be realized. It is no longer the instrument which confers being upon labor; it is living labor which wrests the former from rust and the dustbin. The *Grundrisse* text contrasts term by term with the text of the Iena manuscripts that Hegel wrote in 1803–1804, just as it does with Marx's own 1844 *Economic and Philosophical Manuscripts*. Just how far this opposition, which challenges the ultimate categories of Western thought, extends can be seen in the fact that, for Hegel, faced with the disappearance of subjectivity as it is lost in its own night,[131] the only being that remains is what is stable and permanent, and it is objective being which defines this permanence and constitutes its form. And time itself is but the unfolding of this objectivity. Before saying that in the world of culture, "if men die, institutions remain," we must recognize the original advent of this permanence in the living process of need: here, the thing that is made and the instrument are the primary figures and the condition for the subsistence of being. But, for Marx, the matter and form of the instrument subsist only when they are taken hold of in the act of praxis. Subjectivity is no longer the principle of what is swallowed up; instead it is what keeps all things from being swallowed up, and objectivity itself would be nothing without this grasp which prevents it from slipping away into nothingness, for the world is the world of praxis. It is true that men die, but this is because the power that maintains all things in being is itself perishable; it is life and its history is contingent. It is within this temporality of life and through it that all subsistence is finally maintained. This ultimate metaphysics holds that that which is most perishable and which can cease at every instant, living labor, extends its power over all that is; this metaphysics is not affirmed abstractly by Marx; instead it is grasped just where, before any conceptualization—that is, at the very heart of the production process—it appears precisely as the law of being. And it is, in truth, for this reason that a process such as this is made the theme of the problematic, not, let us repeat, because the economy would be substituted, with the advent of a positive age, for a metaphysics that lacked any object, but because this metaphysics stipulates the object for any inquiry that would deem itself essential. Within the process of production the fragile power of life shines forth as a glowing fire which shapes matter and breathes into it the form that preserves it and maintains it. "The transformation of the material by living labor . . . thus preserves the material in a definite form, and subjugates the transformation of the material to the purpose of labor. Labor is the living, form-giving fire; it is the transitoriness of things, their temporality, as their formation by living time."[132]

These decisive themes from the *Grundrisse* are also present in *Capital*, where are asserted in turn:

(1) The essence of production, namely *the determination of being not by the stable objectivity of the product, but by its integration in the process of living subjectivity* as a simple function and factor in this process—"whenever . . . a

product enters as a means of production into a new labor-process, it thereby loses its character of product, and serves as a mere objective factor of living labor."[133]

(2) The fallenness that characterizes being when it lies outside the grasp of living praxis, an abandonment to which labor itself is condemned when it assumes the instrumental form of objectified labor, so that, confronting that which is held far away from it in the death-like void of this distance, subjectivity appears as a genuine power of resurrection: "A machine which does not serve the purposes of labor . . . falls prey to the destructive influence of natural forces. Iron rusts and wood rots. Yarn with which we neither weave nor knit, is cotton wasted. *Living labor must seize upon these things and rouse them from their death-sleep, change them from mere possible use-values into real and effective ones*. Bathed in the fire of labor, appropriated as part and parcel of labor's organism, and, as it were, made alive for the performance of their functions in the process, they are in truth consumed. . . ."[134] And again: "In so far then as labor is such specific productive activity . . . it raises, by mere contact, the means of production from the dead, makes them living factors of the labor-process. . . ."[135]

(3) The fact that at the very contact of living labor and through this contact, this resurrection of dead labor objectified in the conditions of the process is precisely nothing other than the conservation of their use-value and, consequently, of their value—"If then, on the one hand, finished products are not only results, but also necessary conditions, of the labor-process, on the other hand, their assumption into that process, their contact with living labor, is the sole means by which they can be made to retain their character of use-values, and be utilized" [136]—and that it is first of all because it assures that the elements of the production process are maintained in being that the capitalist purchases living labor as the living ferment of these elements and the condition for this process: "By the purchase of labor-power, the capitalist incorporates labor, as a living ferment, with the lifeless constituents of the product."[137]

We have seen that Marx distinguished in an essential manner between two types of factors necessary for the completion of the labor-process, the objective factors and the subjective factor. However, by themselves the objective factors would be no more than inert terms, left to die; they become elements of production only if, poured into the crucible of production and consumed by it, turned as if into liquid by the fire of living labor, they are, due to living labor alone, given a new form which restores them to being. The objective factors and the subjective factors are thus by no means on the same level. The objective factors of production are unable to produce anything and do not produce anything. Of one and the same nature as praxis, production is the consequence of subjectivity and of it alone; the objective conditions of production become effective in production itself; living labor is the condition for the entire process and for its objective conditions which, like the world in general, belong to praxis.

The dialectic of dead labor and living labor—the fact that the second, by its embrace, keeps the first in being—constitutes the ultimate motive behind the critique of capitalism. At the original, ideal stage of man's presence on earth, of man as living on and as owner of the earth, there is an immediate unity of labor and of what is worked on and, above all, of that with which man works, unity of labor, instrument and material. In the dialectic of dead labor and living labor this unity receives a new sense, no longer that of a mere life phenomenon, not to say a biological phenomenon, analogous, for example, to the unity which makes the swelling of the mother's breast related to and complementary to the infant's hunger, making both participate as such in one and the same "life cycle." Over and beyond a mere complementarity or an objective connection, the living unity of subjective labor and its conditions signifies a necessary condition on the ontological level, the fact that these conditions come into being, understood as production, only, precisely, as they participate in this unity with production, in their tie to living labor which gives them life, inasmuch as living labor unites with them in the embrace of living fire. It is in this way that the separation of living labor and its conditions no longer exists in production, because these conditions have being and are productive only in and through living labor. Now, it is this fundamental unity of productive praxis that capitalism, paradoxically, breaks. "Within the production process, the separation of labor from its objective moments of existence—instruments and material—is suspended. The existence of capital and of wage labor rests on this separation."[138]

However, if the unity of subjective labor and its objective conditions has an ontological meaning, if it confers being upon the latter, how could this unity be broken; how is the capitalist able to damage it? This union "takes place . . . in the process of work itself, during production."[139] This capacity to unite with instruments and materials and to make of them, in this union, the *instruments of production*—this, Marx reminds us, is characteristic of living labor as such: "This is part of the material role which labor plays by its nature in the production process; of its use-value."[140] What then occurs is clear: far from breaking the unity of labor and the instrumental conditions of production, which are such only within this unity, capital seizes control of it and of what founds it, of labor as living labor, as use-value. "But as use value, labor belongs to the capitalist; it belongs to the worker merely as exchange value. *Its living quality of preserving objectified labor time* by using it as the objective condition of living labor in the production process is none of the worker's business."[141] The conclusion of this entire analysis forcefully repeats the denunciation of capital inasmuch as it claims to separate, and actually does separate, on the ideal level of economic and legal ownership that which, on the order of being, is united, namely the instrumental conditions of the production process, conditions that are presented in a striking manner as the material mode of existence of living labor, as the body for which living labor is the soul, awakening it from the dead: "This appropriation, by means of which living labor makes instrument and material in the production process into the body of its soul and thereby resurrects them from the dead, does indeed stand in antithesis to the fact that labor itself is objectless, is a reality only in the immediate vitality of the worker—and that the instrument and material, in capital, exist as beings-for-themselves [*für sich selbst seiende*]."[142]

The fact that living labor, which produces and reproduces value, preserves it as well, preserves the value of the means of production, to the extent that by maintaining the effectiveness of these means, it first preserves their use-value—this shows in a precise way how the process of realization, that is, capital itself, rests entirely on the production process and finds its own ground in the latter and in its founding essence, in living labor. "The process of the realization of capital proceeds by means of and within the simple production process, by putting living labor into its natural relation with its moments of material being."[143] The fact that the process of realization reposes entirely on the production process and, through this, on that which founds the latter in its turn, on living labor, lays bare the abstraction of economic reality as such and, along with this, the reality of that which founds it. Because the process of realization reposes entirely on the subjective essence of production, it is also determined by it, as will be shown by the problematic of variable capital and, in a general manner, by the radical reduction of capital to subjectivity.

Chapter 8

THE RADICAL REDUCTION OF CAPITAL
TO SUBJECTIVITY: $c = 0$

*The problematic of variable capital and the drift of the ideal
determinations of science*

The determination of economic reality by the real process of production
finds its expression in the concept of the organic composition of capital. Marx,
as we know, distinguishes between the technical composition of capital, which
is in fact the composition or decomposition of the production process into its
real elements; its composition in terms of value, namely the sum of the determinate and distinct values of which a given capital is formed; and, finally, its
organic composition, which is nothing other than its value-composition as it
results from and is determined by its technical composition.[1] However, the
determination of the organic composition by the technical composition, that of
capital by the real process of production, remains unclear as long as the elements that compose the latter have not themselves been made the object of a
radical elucidation. Thus, since every production process implies instruments
and raw materials, the difference which is established between the various
means of labor will be found on the economic level as well; this will be the
difference between fixed capital and circulating capital.[2] The difference between fixed capital and circulating capital is a difference in the mode of circulation of these values, a mode of circulation which itself depends on the nature of
the material elements of the process and on the use made of them within the
process. It is because the raw material is wholly consumed in the course of
production that its value passes entirely into the product and henceforth circulates with it—let us understand by this: circulates with the product considered
as a commodity, as being itself a value. It is because the instrument is "consumed" only at the end of a great number of processes that it gives up its value
gradually and thus accords only a minute part of this value to each product.[3]

However, like the raw material, the labor-power in action in the production
process is wholly consumed in it; its value, therefore, passes entirely into the
product, and this is why the value of labor-power constitutes, along with that of
the raw material circulating capital. What characterizes them is that, as values

incorporated into the product—whereas their material base has been wholly consumed—they will be converted into money, which will then have to be reconverted into labor-power and raw materials in order to replace the base that has disappeared.[4] No doubt, in each case, this reconversion obeys a different rhythm, and labor-power and raw materials each have a different circulation by reason of their specific reality.[5] Despite this difference in their mode of circulation, these two values, therefore, together constitute "circulating capital"; it is due to this common determination that they leave the production process at its end in order to pass entirely into the product, and it is in this way that they are both opposed to fixed capital.[6]

Inasmuch as the organic composition of capital is determined by its technical composition, it refers us back to the latter. Is the organic composition of capital, which has just been recognized and described, that is, its composition out of fixed elements and circulating elements, essential? This could be the case only if the real difference upon which it rests, the difference between elements that are partially or wholly consumed in the production process, were itself an essential difference. Now Marx gave another description of the organic composition of capital. In chapter XXV of *Capital* we read:

> The composition of capital is to be understood in a twofold sense. On the side of value, it is determined by the proportion in which it is divided into constant capital or value of the means of production, and variable capital or value of labor-power, the sum total of wages. On the side of material, as it functions in the process of production, all capital is divided into means of production and living labor-power. This latter composition is determined by the relation between the mass of the means of production employed, on the one hand, and the mass of labor necessary for their employment on the other. I call the former the value-composition, the latter the technical composition of capital. Between the two there is a strict correlation. To express this, I call the value-composition of capital, in so far as it is determined by its technical composition and mirrors the changes of the latter, the organic composition of capital.[7]

What is most noteworthy in this text, which is presented as an exhaustive clarification of the concept of the composition of capital and which allows the twofold stratification, revealed and adhered to throughout the entire analysis, to appear as the condition for this clarification—namely the level that seems to be the economic level as such or the level of value, of the determinations of this appearance by the real production process, the level, finally, of this process itself which is that of reality—is that it is no longer a question of the differentiation of capital into fixed and circulating capital. And this is the case because the real difference upon which this distinction rests and which it expresses, the difference in the manner of transmitting value to the product, depending on whether it is a question of the instrument of labor or, on the contrary, that of raw materials and labor-power, is itself placed out of bounds. Not that it disappears; the distinction between fixed capital and circulating capital still remains. But both are inessential distinctions, and this is why the introductory text of chapter XXV no longer mentions them. What arises in place of them, and is presented as the sole theme of analysis is the opposition between the variable part and the constant part of capital, and, on the other hand, what is given within the real production process as the ground of this opposition, namely the opposition between labor-power and its objective conditions.

Now, this modification of the concept of the value-composition of capital, namely the substitution of the opposition between variable capital and constant capital for that between fixed capital and circulating capital, does not startle the reader from one page to the next but constitutes the object of an explicit problematic. In addition, we find that the essential part of the critique addressed to Smith and Ricardo is concentrated and expressed here. Nor does this problematic enter into Marx's analysis by chance. If, as organic composition, the value-composition of capital reflects its technical composition, namely the real structure of the production process, then what plays a determining role in this process must in fact serve as a guide in determining the true concept of the organic composition of capital; the oppositions inherent in productive praxis must give rise to economic oppositions and account for them. Here again, we must recognize that economic determinations are not explained economically and that the principle of the internal structuring of capital, that is to say, precisely, its value-composition, is comprehensible neither in it nor in the system it develops. If, in fact, we consider the diverse values out of which a capital is formed, these can be grouped together and opposed to one another in various ways, according to the characteristics they present, according to the way in which they are transmitted to the product, their turnover time, etc., and nothing permits us to say, inasmuch as we restrict ourselves to these specific properties, that this or that grouping should prevail or this or that distinction be recognized as essential for the composition of the economic process as a whole. Does the organic composition find its adequate theoretical formulation in the opposition between fixed capital and circulating capital or in that between variable capital and constant capital? There is no reply to this question on the economic level.

However, if we leave the plane of economic analysis and consider the material realities into which values are converted in the movement by which capital is inevitably transformed into the process of production, then we see that a part of these values is transformed into the means of production and the other part into labor-power.[8] We see, or rather we know—the entire analysis of the real process of production has shown this—that, regardless of the way in which they transmit their value to the product, the means of production, raw materials, auxiliary materials, and instruments of labor do no more, precisely, than transmit their value to the product, and therefore cannot accord to it more value than they themselves possess, so that the value-composition of capital, its process of realization, and, finally, capital as such remain, in the phenomenon under consideration, unintelligible or rather non-existent. Capital's powerlessness to be capital, to grow in that part of itself which is converted into the means of production, results in this part of capital's being called the constant part of capital or constant capital. The entire analysis of the relation between capital and labor has shown, on the contrary, that, since the use-value of labor-power is capable of producing a value greater than its own, the value for which it is exchanged should be found again at the end of the activity of this power in the production process and in the production by it of a new value, in a form that is quantitatively superior to its initial form: it has varied in the course of this process; this variation is the realization of capital and indeed capital itself as such. To the extent that it accounts for the inner possibility of realization and, consequently, for capital, the determination of the organic composition of capital on the basis of its constant and variable parts is the adequate determination of its concept. In this way, we see that the terminology in which this conceptualization is expressed is the pure result of eidetic analysis.[9]

It has been shown, however, that labor-power's property of producing a value greater than its own is simply life's property of outstripping its own conditions. In the production process the analysis traced an essential line of demarcation between, on the one hand, living subjectivity as the power of creation and growth and, on the other hand, the objective elements, which are not only frozen in their objective state but which can, in reality, be maintained only through the activity of this subjectivity, which must never loosen its grasp on them if it is to keep them out of death's reach: the simple tautological reappearance of the same indeed implies the positive phenomenon of its preservation, which is nothing other than this continuous activity of life. In this way, the material reality of the production process appeared to be split into two elements that were not only different but ontologically heterogeneous: on the one hand, a subjective element which makes the entire process possible because, as living praxis, it is what produces and constitutes the production as such at the same time as it integrates into this production, by making them operative, the material that is worked upon and the instrument of labor; on the other hand, an objective element, namely this material and this instrument which have being only in and through praxis. *It is because the opposition between variable capital and constant capital does no more than express on the economic level the ultimate ontological distinction present at the heart of the production process and constituting its reality that it must, in its turn, be understood as the essential economic difference and that it constitutes the distinction internal to capital and the adequate concept of its organic composition.* In a text of admirable clarity and density, Marx formulates the fundamental reference of the entire economic analysis at once to its ontological ground and to its ultimate internal distinction: *"The same elements of capital which, from the point of view of the labor-process, present themselves respectively as the objective and subjective factors, as means of production and labor-power, present themselves, from the point of view of the process of creating surplus-value, as constant and variable capital."*[10]

How the definition of the organic composition of capital, as the opposition between variable capital and constant capital, originates in the ontological distinction internal to the production process is a question of sufficient importance for Marx to want to return to it in the manuscripts that have been collected as Book Two of *Capital*. What is affirmed once more to be essential here is that the enigma of variable capital, that is to say, the very possibility of capitalism, rests upon the subjectivity at work in the production process, upon the existence of a living power which, because it is capable of creating more use-value than its upkeep requires, produces in the same stroke a value greater than its own. Thus the capitalist, when he gives up a fixed value in order to secure this living power, receives for its use a value which reproduces the one that he has expended while producing a new value that is thus acquired without any equivalent. The definition of variable capital is therefore nothing but the repetition of the analysis of the exchange of capital and labor, and, ultimately, of the properties of organic subjectivity. In the following text are concentrated all of Marx's fundamental theses:

> The essential point in the definition of variable capital—and therefore for the conversion of any sum of values into capital—is that the capitalist exchanges a definite, given (and in this sense constant) magnitude of value for value-creating power, a magnitude of value for the production, self-expansion, of value. Whether the capitalist pays the laborer in money or in means of subsistence does not affect this basic definition . . . the creation of surplus-value—and consequently the capitalisation of the advanced sum of values—has its source neither in the money-form of wages nor in the form of wages paid in kind, nor in the capital laid out in the purchase of labor-power. It arises out of the exchange of value for value-creating power, out of the conversion of a constant into a variable magnitude.[11]

Let us insert a clarification here, for the concept of variable magnitude, and hence that of variable capital, may seem confused. According to the text quoted above, there is, on the one hand, a fixed value, that of wages, and, on the other, the variable magnitude which the capitalist obtains in exchange. But what the capitalist obtains is not variable; it is a new value—that of the product—greater than the value advanced initially but determined just as it is. One can speak of variable capital only to the extent that it is one and the same value that, advanced initially in the form of wages, is found to have increased quantitatively in the product. Now, this is an illusion, since the growth of value is not its own doing but results from this value's being replaced by a living power: the latter alone creates value and can produce a value greater than its own, than the value of wages. Thus, there is *stricto sensu* neither variable magnitude nor variable value but the substitution of a power for a fixed magnitude, and then of another magnitude which results from this power and which, at the end of its action, is presented as a magnitude similarly fixed and determined. It happens that the second is greater than the first, and it is only when one places oneself on the economic level of appearance that one thinks that it is a question of *one and the same value* and that this value has varied. As essential as it may be, and precisely to the extent that it is essential, the concept of variable capital exposes the irrational character of the fundamental determinations of the economy, namely the determinations that relate to realization, that is, to capital as such. And this irrational character of the fundamental economic determinations expresses in its turn nothing other than the *lack of autarchy* of economic reality, the fact that, unintelligible by itself, it is always founded upon a reality of another order by which it is determined and to which it refers. Thus the variation of value, when no value is capable of varying, is only the comparison of two unequal and distinct values. And Marx thought that the second, as it does not derive from the first but from a power foreign to all economic determination, has to be understood on the basis of this power, that the dynamism of labor-power in action is translated, once this value-creating action has occurred, into a value located in the product and whose magnitude, which is now fixed, is determined by the activity that created it. The following text from the manuscripts collected as Book Two of *Capital* clears up whatever might remain obscure in the concept of variable capital by reestablishing, under the appearance of a homogeneous variation of magnitude, the continuity of the real process of producing value and the manner in which the latter results from the former. "It follows from the nature of value, which is nothing but materialized labor, and from the nature of active labor-power, which is nothing but labor in process of materialization, that *labor-power continually creates value and surplus-value during the time it functions; that what on the part of labor-power appears as motion, as a creation of value,* appears on the part of its product in a state of rest, as created value. If the labor-power has performed its function capital no longer consists of labor-power on the one side and means of production on the other. The capital-value that was invested in labor-power is now value which (+ surplus-value) was added to the product."[12]

The radical reduction of variable capital to value-creating living subjectivity is made explicit in the same passage, thereby indicating that this power of realization remains internal to the production process whose essence it constitutes and that, consequently, it is not this power but only the value that it has produced which reappears at the end of the process in the form of a value greater than the initial value: *"The real substance of capital laid out in wages is labor itself, active, value-creating labor-power, living labor,* which the capitalist exchanges for dead, materialized labor and embodies in his capital, by which means, and by which alone, the value in his hands turns into self-expanding value. But this power of self-expansion is not sold by the capitalist. It is always only a constituent part of his productive capital . . . it is never a part of his commodity-capital, as for instance the finished product which he sells."[13]

When thought through rigorously, the concept of variable capital splits into two and is found to include two different, although complementary, meanings: on the one hand, the "substance," as Marx says, of variable capital is the power of living subjectivity; on the other hand, between the value that the capitalist has exchanged for this power and the value he receives after it has been put into motion, there is a difference of magnitude. *It is by considering these two values from the standpoint of their magnitude that one comes to see between them merely a difference, precisely, of magnitude, to identify them numerically, to believe that it is the same value which passes through different states or phases, which varies, and hence to speak of variable capital.* The latter can be maintained, and accorded the central role that Marx acknowledges for it in the economic problematic, only inasmuch as its fundamental meaning is never for one instant out of sight.

It is this meaning which leads us to dismiss the objection that the difference observed at the end of the production process between the value of its elements and that of the product, a difference which constitutes surplus-value, is not explained—or not, at any rate, explained solely—by variable capital, that is, by putting into motion a power creating a value greater than its own. Is not the value of constant capital, in fact, also capable of varying; can there not also be, and is there not frequently, a change in the price of raw materials or instruments? The price of cotton may well increase as a result of a poor harvest, for example; this change in value is, nonetheless, foreign to the production process in which cotton enters as a raw material, and regardless of the speculation affecting the price of raw materials, each raw material plays in a given production process simply the role of constant capital: in this process its value does not vary. The variation in the value of cotton intervenes in another process, that in which cotton is produced, and this variation in the value of cotton is ontologically homogeneous with that of all variable capital; it is labor-power which constitutes its ultimate possibility.[14] The same remark obviously concerns the instruments of labor. Even when this value has changed, fixed capital is no less constant capital for the reason that it functions as such in a specific production process.[15] Thus the analysis continues, in its rigorousness, to obey the teleology that secretly animates it: to say that neither the raw material nor the instrument can transfer to the product any more value than they themselves possess, that they are forms of constant capital, means at one and the same time that all surplus-value comes from living subjectivity and from it alone and that it alone produces value. Variable capital, capitalization, is explained only by living subjectivity and in it finds its sole foundation.

The opposition between variable capital and constant capital is the decisive economic opposition because it is not economic, because it distinguishes in a radical manner, in reality itself, between the living element and the dead element, between that which produces change and that which cannot even maintain itself in the tautology of what it is nor subsist by itself, between subjectivity and objectivity. Now, it happens that the economic analysis, conducted in light of this ultimate and, finally, metaphysical opposition (metaphysical, because it provides a definition of being, namely being as life and, as such and as capable of being such, as subjectivity, whereas the object has being only as it is kept within the action of subjectivity—and praxis itself is just this act of

keeping the object away from death and in being through the activity of subjectivity, which itself signifies life), to be precise, the distinction between variable
capital and constant capital, will itself be brought into question and, in the
same stroke, will in turn bring into question the fundamental opposition upon
which it rests. For, if it is true that capital is constituted organically by the
opposition of its variable and constant forms, and that this opposition must be
taken as a guideline for its analysis, then the phenomenon that will dominate its
evolution becomes visible—the increasing share in it taken by constant capital,
whereas the importance of variable capital will continue to diminish. In light of
the philosophical presupposition which placed the opposition between variable
capital and constant capital at the center of the economic analysis, the increase
of the second and the decrease of the first cannot, and are not intended to,
signify anything but the invasion of social life by the inessential and the decline
of the essential. This decline, it is true, announces that of capitalism. This is
because, in its very concept, capitalism is tied to value. And it is in fact the
decline of value and of the world to which this value gave rise that is under way,
as is shown in the law of the tendency toward reduced profit.

But what is important to us here is to note that at the very moment when Marx
believes that he can read the destiny of capitalism in its organic composition
understood as the opposition between constant capital and variable capital, at
the very moment when he perceives the increasing share taken by the former at
the expense of the latter, he never ceases to affirm their opposition, against the
backdrop of the ontological heterogeneity of the realities for which, as values,
they are but the ideal expression. Chapter VIII of *Capital*, entitled "Constant
Capital and Variable Capital," ends with these pathetic lines, for, in the final
analysis, they signify that if the share allotted to life never ceases to decrease in
the immensity of a dead world, it remains life nonetheless and continues to be
that which wrests the world away from sheer annihilation:

> . . . a change in the proportion of constant to variable capital does not affect the
> respective functions of these two kinds of capital. The technical conditions of the
> labor-process may be revolutionized to such an extent, that where formerly ten
> men using implements of small value worked up a relatively small quantity of raw
> material, one may now, with the aid of one expensive machine, work up one
> hundred times as much raw material. In the latter case we have an enormous
> increase in the constant capital, that is represented by the total value of the
> means of production used, and at the same time a great reduction in the variable
> capital, invested in labor-power. Such a revolution, however, alters only the
> quantitative relation between the constant and variable, or the proportions in
> which the total capital is split up into its constant and variable constituents; it has
> not in the least degree affected the essential difference between the two.[16]

Just when the role of this force is constantly diminishing in a production
process increasingly dominated by the plethora of mechanical means, consequently just when the share of variable capital itself continues to decrease in

favor of constant capital, Marx asserts the decisive character of variable capital—or rather of that which ultimately founds it, the power of living subjectivity—in an extraordinary analysis which governs the entire problematic of *Capital* and which should serve as a guide for any coherent interpretation that might be proposed. Let us consider a capital, C, in light of the essential opposition between constant capital *(c)* and variable capital *(v)*, and let us call the surplus-value s. We recall that c designates "the value of the means of production actually consumed in the process,"[17] and v the sum of money expended for the purchase of labor-power. At the start of the production process, this capital is expressed as $C = c + v$, for example, £500 = £410 + £90. When the process has ended, we find $C = (c + v) + s$, so that C has become C', or, to return to our example, £590 = £410 + 90 + 90. All the preceding analyses permit us to say, along with Marx, that as the value of constant capital simply reappears in the product, the value that is really created in the production process is not the total value of the product, $(c + v) + s$, £410 + 90 + 90 = £590, but $(v + s)$, or £90 + 90 = £180. The only way to make the value that is really created in the production process evident, that is, the value created by labor-power in action, is to set aside the value of constant capital or to assume that it is zero. Then, indeed, the production process will be reduced to what it has really produced, because production will be reduced to itself, to the efficacity of reality and to its pure essence: to living subjectivity. If it is posited that $c = 0$, then the initial capital, C, $= (0 + v) = v$; the capital resulting from the process, C', $= v + s$; and the difference between the two, $C' - C$, gives us the surplus-value, s. Then we have, in figures—the value of constant capital, £410, having been eliminated from all the preceding formulas—$C = 0 + 90 = 90$; $C' = 90 + 90 = 180$; $C' - C = 90$. We then see that *the total value produced in the production process*, £180, or the sum of the value reproduced (90) and of the surplus-value (90) *remains identical, whatever the value of constant capital may be, whether this be equal* to £410 or to zero. In other words, if one assumes a production process that is realized without raw materials, without auxiliary materials, and without instruments, one has to admit that it produces the same value as a process in which the means of production would represent an incommensurable value. This is why, once the value produced in the process is made apparent, the value of constant capital, however great it may be, has to be left out of consideration. Pure analysis requires that we "make abstraction from that portion of the value of the product, in which constant capital alone appears, and consequently must equate the constant capital to zero or make $c = 0$."[18]

Pure analysis: Marx's thought is an analytic thought, a thought which decomposes the Whole into its parts, which does not explain the parts by the Whole but, on the contrary, the Whole by its parts. In contrast to the entire structuralist approach, it is thus posited that the totality is not a principle of intelligibility, any more than it is a principle of reality, but an appearance, that which masks the real phenomenon. Thus, it is neither the total capital nor its global movement that enables us to perceive the principle of capitalism; instead, they hide it, and this is why, within this totality, it was appropriate to eliminate the largest part, constant capital, in order to perceive what is essential, the variation of value, variable capital, that which is capable of resolving the enigma of surplus-value. After recalling that "surplus-value is purely the result of a variation in the value of v, of that portion of the capital which is transformed into labor-power," Marx adds: "But the fact that it is v alone that varies, and the conditions of that variation, are obscured by the circumstance that in consequence of the increase in the variable component of the capital, there is also an increase in the sum total of the advanced capital. It was originally £500 and becomes £590."[19]

Let us add that this "pure analysis" is an essential analysis. For it is not simply a matter of decomposing the Whole into its parts; it is a matter of recognizing among these precisely which one determines all the others and the Whole along with them. How, then, does this recognition take place and, with it, the exclusion of all the elements that will be said to be inessential, all those that could be eliminated without affecting the possibility of the phenomenon considered, that is, without resulting in the cessation of the production of value? In positing $c = 0$, Marx says that the production of value takes place in the absence of all the values which are those of the means of production, consequently in the absence of these means. He does not say that it takes place despite everything, that it can still take place despite this absence, as in the event of catastrophe or in despair of other means of realization. He says that the production of value takes place completely, fully in the absence of constant capital and its material components. He says that constant capital and its material components are foreign to the production of value, that they in no way share in its nature, that this nature consists wholly in variable capital, which indeed is thus the essential element of capital or, better, its very essence.

However, just as constant capital, variable capital also refers to reality; it is the value of labor-power. It expresses the value of labor-power in the form of an ideal representation; precisely, it represents it, or as Marx rigorously states, it is the "index."[20] The double reference to the "material" reality of constant capital and of variable capital is then formulated as follows: whereas constant capital represents the objective element of the production process, variable capital represents its subjective element. When, in all the calculations which weigh down the text of *Capital*, the reader in amazement sees Marx posit this equation, c, constant capital, $= 0$, what this actually means is that *in order to grasp the essence of capital, its own nature and its possibility, all that is objective in the production process is to be struck out and what alone is to be retained is the subjective element reduced to itself* and understood in its purity, subjectivity alone as such. It is the common attitude that what economic reality involves is the objective world, determinations which are external to man and which force themselves upon him even more harshly than nature and its impassible laws. But this is an illusion, and Marx, who was able to recognize the ever-increasing importance in the production process of instruments and of constant capital, which expresses their value, was not afraid of reducing both the latter and the former to zero and to consider them to be null in the development of the economic process of the modern world. In the history of Western thought there are few philosophies of subjectivity, at least if this is understood in its pure concept not as the power to represent the world to oneself, that is to say, ultimately as objectivity itself, but as the essence, which is irreducible to the world and which exists in itself, of a life as it is someone's life and as that very thing which is life. At any rate, no philosophy has given to this pure concept of subjectivity such a consistently radical meaning, nor has any, by the reduction of all objectivity, satisfied its most extreme, if not to say wildest, exigencies.[21]

The presuppositions that guide the present interpretation of Marx's thought have made the irrational character of the concept of variable capital apparent, inasmuch as, taking its content literally, one would wish to see in it merely an economic concept, that of a value which varies. For an interpretation such as this it is decisive to see that the analysis provided in *Capital* explicitly concurs with our own conclusions. In the example given in chapter IX, where C = 410 (c) + 90 (v) becomes C' = 410 (c) + 90 (v) + 90 (s), the variable capital is thus constituted by the £90 given in wages; £90 spent on wages: this amount is fixed just as is the sum defining constant capital. Why is it called variable capital? And if it is fixed, in what way can it vary? The sum paid to the worker, in truth, does not vary; it indeed is fixed, but the capitalist has exchanged it for something that does vary and that is variation itself, that is, for life. "But £90 is a given and therefore a constant quantity; hence it appears absurd to treat it as a variable. . . . But in the process of production *the place of the £90 is taken by the labor-power in action,* dead labor is replaced by living labor, something stagnant by something flowing, a constant by a variable."[22] The heterogeneity of life and of the ideal discourse that claims to proclaim it, such is the contradiction of variable capital, that is to say, of its truth as well, since by destroying itself it allows, amidst the debris of the economic universe, the great current that carries them to appear. After the elimination of constant capital, which has been reduced to zero, and that of the £90 paid to the worker, that is, the elimination of variable capital itself, a final farewell is bid to numbers and to science. There is room for knowledge. Knowledge is always knowledge of the simplest thing; it is knowledge of life, whose innermost law is, however, that of the world and of its development.

The ultimate theses: the twofold aporia of "the value of labor" and of "the value of labor-power"

The problematic of variable capital paves the way for and makes possible the critique of wages, that is, of the "value of labor," the irrational character of the latter being simply a new manifestation of the irrational character of variable capital itself, considered as an economic determination. Inasmuch as variable

capital does vary, it admits of a double ideal equivalence; two different economic determinations can be made to correspond to it, and this is its paradox.
On the one hand, there is a specific and fixed sum of money, that, precisely,
which is spent on wages and which figures as such in the capitalist's accounts. It
is precisely in this form that variable capital is presented as a part of circulating
capital in the eyes of the economist just as it is in the eyes of the capitalist, as a
part of the sum advanced by the latter at the start of the labor process, alongside
the sum invested in the materials of production. On the other hand, there is a
final value of variable capital, that which it attains at the end, or so it seems, of
its variations and which, in reality, is nothing other than the new value produced by labor-power for which it was exchanged, at its initial value, in the
form of wages. If it is true that the final value of variable capital does not
coincide with its initial value and is actually greater than it, this results from the
fact that the value of labor-power, the quantity of labor materialized in it, that is
to say, the amount necessary for its subsistence, is indeed less than the quantity
of labor that it is capable of producing, less, consequently, than the value
produced by its actualization. The connection between the problematic of wages
and the problematic of variable capital can be read not only in the very order of
the chapters in *Capital*; it is also contained in this essential text of Book Three:

> A very essential distinction is thus to be made in regard to variable capital laid
> out in wages. Its value as the sum of wages, i.e. as a certain amount of mate-
> rialized labor, is to be distinguished from its value as a mere index of the mass of
> living labor which it sets in motion. The latter is always greater than the labor
> which it [variable capital] incorporates, and is, therefore, represented by a
> greater value than that of the variable capital [laid out]. This greater value is
> determined, on the one hand, by the number of laborers set in motion by the
> variable capital and, on the other, by the quantity of surplus-labor performed by
> them, [so that] variable capital is not only the index of the labor embodied in it.
> When the rate of surplus-value is known it is also an index of the amount of labor
> set in motion over and above that embodied in itself, i.e., of surplus-labor.[23]

The irrational character of the "value of labor" is thus not only that of every
economic determination inasmuch as, by defining a reality, it seems to belong to
it and to possess the same nature. In this sense, as Marx remarks, it is just as
absurd to speak of the value or of the price of sugar as of the value of labor.[24]
The irrationality peculiar to the value of labor consists in the fact that this
magnitude, not content to be as such ontologically heterogeneous with respect to
the reality it claims to define, transgresses the very laws of ideality and, first of
all, the laws of identity. Indeed, what does the concept of the value of labor
accomplish if not to confuse the initial value and the final value of variable
capital and to attempt, thanks to this confusion, to reduce surreptitiously the
first to the second? Marx's entire problematic attempts, on the contrary, to
dissociate radically these two values and, with respect to the question of wages,
this dissociation now assumes the following form.

Insofar as it designates the initial value of variable capital and inasmuch as its magnitude is identical to the quantity of money laid out for wages, the "value of labor" is, in reality, nothing other than the value of labor-power. It is the use of this power, for a day, a week, a month—by no means the labor or the product of this labor—which the capitalist purchases from the worker. Such is the first result of the analysis of wages, the radical dissociation of the value of labor—with regard to which it will be shown that this value does not exist—from the value of labor-power. If a dissociation such as this required a considerable theoretical labor, this is because it had to be established over and against an illusion, one which is all the more tenacious as it is not simply the illusion of the capitalist but of the worker as well. Since the latter receives his wages only after having done his work, at the end of the week for example, he believes that he is paid for this work and that the wage is precisely its price.[25] Consequently, if we assume, to return to the most constant hypothesis of *Capital*, that the worker has reproduced the value of his labor-power during the first half of his workday and that he then produced a new value, surplus-value, which is taken by the capitalist, one sees how this essential phenomenon manages to be hidden under the appearance that the worker has been paid the "value of his work," that is, the whole of his day. "Although one part only of the workman's daily labor is paid, while the other part is unpaid . . . it seems as if the aggregate labor was paid labor."[26] This illusion is what characterizes wage labor in contrast to serfdom, where the distinction between paid labor and unpaid labor is obvious, and to slavery, where labor seems to be entirely unpaid. An illusion such as this is at once the cause and the effect of the theoretical confusion between the value of labor-power and the value of labor, and of the assimilation of the first to the second.

Confusing the value of labor-power and the value of labor is thus the error of the economists as well. However, to the extent that it thematizes the "value of labor," economics runs up against the problem of its determination in the form of an *aporia*. For, in accordance with its thesis, if it is labor that determines value, how can the value of labor itself be determined? Marx will shatter the *aporia* with a blunt assertion. "Labor is the substance, and the immanent measure of value, but has itself no value."[27] It is here that the concept of the "value of labor" allows its fundamental irrationality to appear, an irrationality which no longer consists either in the fact of identifying two different magnitudes, or in the claim to overcome the ontological heterogeneity of the ideal economic determination of reality. A heterogeneity of this nature surely remains the unseen basis for the assertion that labor has no value. But it is not in the same sense as sugar that labor is said to have no value. Sugar, precisely, has a value; this proposition is irrational only insofar as it is interpreted analytically. But it is true that sugar receives a value as a synthetic addition to its material being. And once the theory of this synthesis, of this ideal or categorical determination of reality, has been formulated, a foundation is provided for the economic existence of sugar or of any material reality, that of a tool, for example. Now, the theory of this determination has indeed been supplied; it is the theory of value, which, it has been shown, is only the objectification of abstract labor, that is, the representation of the real labor which has produced an object possessing value. In this way the theory of the origin of value takes its place alongside the foundational philosophies of understanding, that is, of the categorial determination of reality, and entrusts to the latter, that is, to representation, the task of accomplishing this determination, with the restriction that, through a decisive mutation, the categorial operation of determination is now understood as a secondary operation in relation to a more primordial action belonging to a different order, in relation to praxis. For *it is only insofar as labor has produced an object that this production can be represented in a representation which is, precisely, that of value; the production of value or the categorial economic determination of reality is thus merely the representation of the original production of being as praxis*.

Now, this economic determination of reality which concerns sugar or tools— along with every possible material reality in general inasmuch as it is tied to its source, to the source of being understood as production—precisely, no longer concerns praxis itself. Such is the profound meaning of the assertion that labor has no value. For this is no longer identical to the case of sugar which, although, in its reality, it is of a different nature than any ideal determination, is nevertheless capable of possessing this sort of determination, and not just in an arbitrary manner but insofar as its being is understood on the basis of its source, as the effect of praxis, insofar as it is capable of being represented as such. For this is what it means for sugar "to have a value": to be the product of labor. Now, not only has labor no value, insofar as in itself it is foreign to the ideality of economic determination, but, in contrast to sugar, it is not capable of receiving a value. This is, first of all, the apodictic meaning of Marx's thesis. To say that labor has no value means: it cannot have value. Just as labor does not derive from any labor, so production is not the product of any production. If, then, value is the representation of this derivation and of this production, it cannot affect labor, which is not produced. In this way is affirmed, in itself and in its numerous implications, the original character of praxis which, since the "Theses on Feuerbach," constitutes the underlying presupposition of Marx's entire thought. This original character has still to be correctly understood. It by no means signifies that praxis, deriving from nothing, produced by nothing, would produce itself. As has been established, the concept of praxis has nothing to do with the Hegelian concept of being as production to the extent that the latter signifies the self-production of being. No doubt the Hegelian concept of being is overdetermined by the incorrect concept of production as objectification. By rejecting the latter, however, Marx rejects in the same stroke self-production and self-positing. This is why the concept of being as production is, in Marx, identical to the concept of life, that is, the concept of an existence which is radically passive in relation to itself and whose essence is, as a result, to experience.[28] This is also why this existence, as feeling and experiencing of self, is a Self. It is due to this passive givenness of the individual to himself that his existence as praxis has no value, is the result of no labor, of no production, of no action, and, *in particular, of no action that would be his own*.

The existence of the individual as praxis is labor-power. We are then in the presence of an aporia which is found in the thought of Marx himself. In order to escape the aporia of classical economics, which claimed to be based on the "value of labor," Marx substituted for the latter the value of labor-power. But now we are saying that the concept of the value of labor-power is as irrational as that of the value of labor. On the one hand, in fact, *labor-power and labor are ontologically homogeneous and, what is more, they are substantively identical*, the second being only the actualization of the first, the subjective effectuation of the subjective potentialities of organic subjectivity. This is why, on the other hand, *their situation with respect to value is the same*, and the fundamental texts of Marx which we have quoted concerning the origin of value ascribe the power of creating value to labor-power more often and more clearly than to labor itself. To recall just one example, which will suffice in this regard: "The place of the value of the labor-power that obtains within the advanced capital is taken in the actually functioning productive capital by living value-creating labor-power itself."[29] Henceforth, is not Marx's problematic found to be in exactly the same situation as classical economics, and faced with the same aporia? *Like labor, and for just the same reasons—because like labor it creates value—labor-power is incapable of receiving a value*.

In a more general form, it is indeed the same difficulty as that in which Proudhon was caught when he claimed to determine the value of commodities by the value of the labor required to produce them, thereby confusing the determination of value by the quantity of labor with its determination by the alleged value of this same labor. But if a value could be determined by a value, then labor would lose its metaphysical and ontological privilege as value-creating, and the value of any other commodity could, in this case, serve just as well as a standard for measuring value as the value of labor itself. But it is this determination of a value by a value that is impossible. "The value of labor," Marx writes, countering Proudhon, "can no more serve as a measure of value than the value of any other commodity."[30] One value, in fact, could determine another value only if it were itself determined, only if the problem of determining value were already solved in its own case. Labor, for example, could determine *by its value* the value of the object that it produces only if its own value were determined, which, in its turn, could be determined only by the value of another labor, and so on, indefinitely. "It is moving in a vicious circle, it is to determine relative value by a relative value which itself needs to be determined."[31]

It is true that this aporia of classical economics had been resolved. Proudhon did no more than recopy the thesis of "A. Smith and others, who fall into the same error regarding value as determined by labor, and value as determined by the price of labor (wages). . . ."[32] And Ricardo's decisive progress in this regard was precisely to have understood that "it is not the value of labor which is the measure of value, but the quantity of labor bestowed on the commodity."[33] Here, unequivocally and through a stroke of genius, the meta-economical character of the foundation of the economy is glimpsed, the fact that the creative power of value and of economic determinations in general, namely labor, is not itself a value but a principle of another order. Here, before Marx, opens up the possibility of a fundamental problematic that is no longer economics but an investigation into the conditions of its possibility, a philosophy of the economy.

The question of wages, however, incontestably ascribes a value to this foundation of the economy and secretly places this ground back within the economy. It matters little, in the final analysis, that it is a question of labor-power rather than of labor itself; once subjectivity is qualified by an economic determination, it is incapable of founding economics. In this way, science—here, economics—claims to replace philosophy, to reduce to itself the principle of value by making of this very principle an economic determination, and in so doing only succeeds in giving rise to an aporia. The economic definition of labor-power in terms of its value does not simply make it incapable of determining another value; it is its own value that remains undetermined. As soon as it is raised, the question of the value of labor-power, like that of labor itself, is a dead end.

Let us therefore ask: when, how, and why does the question of the value of labor-power enter into Marx's problematic? It then appears that this occurs, precisely, not within the field of his own problematic but within that of classical economics. The latter, like all ideology in general, it is true, is neither gratuitous nor aberrant. *The question of the value of labor and of determining it is only the consequence on the level of theory of the emergence of labor as commodity in the market universe of the modern world*. Along with the general definition of reality as economic reality (the doctrines which profess a definition such as this, in particular Marxism, are only a form of bourgeois ideology), the alienation of life in the economy implies the systematic effort to confer upon each modality of existence an equivalent or a substitute on the economic level. And it is in this way that labor has value. The dead-end question of the value of labor or of labor-power is the necessary sequel to the great shift which occurs at the end of the eighteenth and at the dawn of the nineteenth century and which marked the entrance of the human world into the world of the economy and the reduction of the former to the latter. It is when a shift such as this has occurred, when human praxis becomes an economic existence, that the value of labor is a question for the theoretical discipline which thematizes this new existence. Only, it happens that a question such as this remains without an answer, and it is by following the effort of bourgeois economics to answer this question, which it does raise, in order to determine the value of labor that, faced with the impossibility of arriving at this determination, Marx substitutes for the concept of the value of labor that of the value of labor-power. Or, rather, this substitution is that made by bourgeois economics itself in an effort to resolve the aporia within which it is enclosed.

This is what Marx says. In its effort to determine the value or the price of labor, classical economics first had recourse to the law of supply and demand, but it was quickly forced to recognize that what Adam Smith said with regard to commodities in general, namely that they "are sold for just what they are worth," is true of that particular commodity which is labor, and that the fluctuations of prices on the labor market, if they do in fact depend on variations in supply and demand, can by no means fix the value of labor itself: instead, they assume it and are themselves merely variations in value, as can be most clearly seen when supply and demand are balanced. What then appears is something that they no longer determine, since their effects on it cancel one another out, something whose positive character has to be sought elsewhere. And this something is, precisely, the value of labor. This is also apparent if one considers a period of several years. In the series of increases and reductions, one then sees an average price emerge, around which the others are grouped. Classical economics, which moves in this way from "the accidental prices of labor to the value of labor,"[34] finds itself confronting this value, confronting the problem of this value. We know how it claims to resolve this particular problem by submitting it to its own general principles, by applying the law of value in general to the value of labor: just as that of any other commodity, the value of labor will be determined by the quantity of labor necessary to produce it. What is the quantity of labor necessary for the production of this commodity called labor? It is that which is necessary for the production of the goods which the worker needs to live. But the value of these goods—the quantity of labor required to produce them—is no longer the value of labor; it is that of labor-power. *It is therefore classical economics itself which shifts from the consideration of the value of labor to that of the value of labor-power, which substitutes the second for the first and does so in order to resolve its own problem.*

However, Marx says that, by doing this, classical economics entirely changes levels, does not resolve its problem but completely modifies the terms of the problem, in short, that the entire problematic undergoes a decisive modification. This text is frequently quoted:

> In this way Political Economy expected to penetrate athwart the accidental prices of labor, to the value of labor. As with other commodities, this value was determined by the cost of production. But what is the cost of production—of the laborer, i.e., the cost of producing or reproducing the laborer himself? This question unconsciously substituted itself in Political Economy for the original one; for the search after the cost of production of labor as such turned in a circle and never left the spot. What economists therefore call value of labor, is in fact the value of labor-power, as it exists in the personality of the laborer, which is as different from its function, labor, as a machine is from the work it performs. Occupied with the difference between the market-price of labor and its so-called value, with the relation of this value to the rate of profit, and to the values of the

commodities produced by means of labor, etc., they never discovered that the course of the analysis had led to the resolution of this value of labor itself into the value of labor-power.[35]

Just what is decisive in this substitution of the value of labor-power for the value of labor, we believe we already know: it dispels the appearance that the worker is paid for the totality of his labor—an appearance that constitutes the very form of wages—whereas he is only paid for that part of the day's work during which he reproduces the value of the goods required for his subsistence, the other part and the value it produces having been taken over by the capitalist.[36] However, if the characteristic distinction of the value of labor-power in its opposition to the alleged value of labor ends the paradox of surplus-value, it in no way eliminates that which concerns us now, *the paradox according to which the principle which serves as a ground for value would itself be capable of receiving a value*. This paradox is at one and the same time that of the determination of labor as commodity, the paradox of the market economy in general and of its claim to integrate subjectivity into its own field by treating it as an element in this field, to be determined within it and starting from it. Now, it is this second paradox, which forms the basis of the market economy, that Marx unequivocally denounced when, speaking of the twofold usefulness of labor (the first being the satisfaction of need, something it has in common with all commodities), he contrasts the second aspect to the first, *that of creating value, which distinguishes it from all other commodities and, as the value-creating element, excludes it from the possibility of having any value*.[37] This impossibility for the founding principle of value to receive a value, its irreducibility, as the ground of the economy, to the latter, this is what constitutes its "irrationality." "The irrationality," states Book Two of *Capital*, "consists in the fact that labor itself as a value-creating element cannot have any value, nor can therefore any definite amount of labor have any value expressed in its price, in its equivalence to a definite quantity of money."[38]

Now, we have shown that the impossibility for labor to be defined in its own being by the economic determination that it itself creates concerns labor-power for the same reason, labor-power which is not only ontologically identical to labor but itself constitutes the essence of which labor is but the actualization. This is why, when Marx in chapter XIX in order to escape the aporia of the value of labor, suddenly concerns himself with opposing, on the contrary, labor and labor-power, one cannot fail to be struck by the ridiculousness of this opposition: ". . . labor-power, as it exists in the personality of the laborer, which is as different from its function, labor, as a machine is from the work it performs." But the "function" of labor-power itself exists only in the personality of the laborer and after having sold his labor-power, the worker does not thereby sever himself from its actualization in effective labor: he will perform this labor in the factory. Let us recall this essential text on the relation of the worker to his labor: "But could the laborer give it [his labor] an independent objective existence, he would sell a commodity and not labor."[39] As regards the comparison between the relation of labor-power to labor and that of a machine to its operations, its platitude and its uselessness cannot make us forget that it is totally inadequate besides, if it is true that the entire problematic of variable capital rests on the radical opposition, within the production process, between its subjective and objective elements: the relation that exists between the latter in no way helps us to understand the relation existing between the former.

Let us therefore pose the rigorous question: *is it indeed to labor-power, that is, to subjectivity, that value is attributed when one speaks of the value of labor-power?* By no means: the value at issue is that of the products necessary to maintain this power, the value not of subjectivity but of a certain number of objective realities such as bread, wine, wood, oil, housing, clothes, shoes, books, etc. *Such is the decisive mutation that takes place when the problematic of classical economics unconsciously substitutes the value of labor-power for that of labor itself, not the substitution of labor-power for labor, of one subjective element for another which, in reality is consubstantial and identical to it, but the substitution for the value-creating subjective element, one which itself cannot have value, of a set of objective elements whose value is determined according to the general laws of value, starting from the subjective principle of value, from the quantity of labor necessary for their production.*

But then, if the substitution of the value of labor-power for the value of labor is nothing other than that of an objectivity for a subjectivity, its meaning is revealed to us along with the unity of Marx's entire economic problematic. What gives this problematic its fundamental philosophical importance is, as we have seen, that it in no way constitutes one economic theory opposed to another, for example, to that of the English school, but a transcendental reflection on the condition of the possibility of the economy in general and of the market economy in particular. With respect to the market economy and to the concept that serves as its foundation—namely, value—it has been shown that the origin of value in human praxis cannot be transformed into a rigorous determination, nor, for example, can it make exchange possible, unless for the subjectivity of praxis is substituted the quantifiable objective equivalents on the basis of which value will itself be able to be quantified. It is this substitution for the unnamable subjectivity of praxis that the theory of wages performs in its turn. In paying for labor, let us say for the productive activity of the worker, it is indeed a matter of acknowledging that it possesses a value and of assigning one to it. But this is not possible. So a detour is made: what is paid is not this activity but the whole set of things, products and goods which are required by the activity in order that it be realized. And the value of these goods is determinable, or rather has already been determined. By the labor that was necessary for their production? *But this labor is itself subjective,* and this is why one substituted for it, as units of measurement, the objective divisions of an objective time and, as what was to be measured by these, the ideal standards of complex, simple, etc. labor, which themselves have been substituted for the real substance of praxis. In this way the circle is closed; the transcendental genesis of the economy is realized. The market economy rests on a relation between praxis and value. When value is to be determined on the basis of praxis, an objective quantity of "abstract labor" is substituted for praxis. When the value of praxis itself is to be determined—and by making labor a commodity the market economy cannot escape this aberrant project—for praxis is now substituted the value of the objective goods necessary to set it in motion. The substitution of the value of labor-power for the value of labor is simply the way in which the economy is substituted for life.

In identifying labor and labor-power for ontological reasons, against the backdrop of subjectivity which unites them, are we not abolishing the difference separating the value of the first from that of the second, a difference which affords a place for surplus-value? Is not the theory of surplus-value and, consequently, the very sense of Marx's problematic thereby lost? Or does not this problematic instead reach a full awareness of its fundamental theses and of their unity? What we have shown is that the value of labor-power is no less irrational than the value of labor, that *neither one nor the other designates the value of praxis itself*—it has none—but designates instead what is substituted for it, that is to say, in the first case, the value of the goods necessary for its realization, and, in the second, the value of its products. The difference between the "value" of labor-power and the "value" of labor is therefore nothing other than the difference between the quantity of labor necessary to maintain life for a certain time and the quantity of labor that this life can produce during this same time, the difference between the power of life and its conditions. In this way we are carried back to Marx's fundamental intuition, and this is an obvious way, if the following remark is made. It is said—and Marx concedes this point to classical economics—that the value of labor-power is determined, just as the value of every commodity, by the quantity of labor necessary for its production. "Like all others [commodities] it has a value. How is that value determined? . . . by the labor-time necessary for . . . [its] production."[40] But the "production" of labor-power is only that of the goods it needs. It is true that this production of necessary goods gives them their value. But the quantity of labor necessary for the production of these goods depends first of all on the amount of goods to be produced. Before it is determined by the laws of the economy, the value of necessary goods depends on life and on its needs. Thus it is indeed the difference between what living praxis needs in order to continue to function and what it is capable of producing that founds the difference between the "value of labor-power" and the "value of labor," a difference by which surplus-value is measured.

One then sees how the problematic of wages repeats that of variable capital and receives its illumination from the latter. For the alleged value of labor-power is nothing other than the initial value of variable capital, the alleged value of labor, its final value. And what the problematic of variable capital has taught us is that, despite what appears to be the case and the mathematical evidence provided, *the difference between these two values does not depend on them, on their priorly existing and previously defined magnitudes, of which it would be precisely the simple numerical difference*. It depends instead on labor-power, that is, on life and on its own nature: the first value is the index of its needs and of the action it undertakes to satisfy them, the second that of the action it accomplishes over and above the former and which has made the history of men possible.

In this way, the value of labor-power differs completely from the value of another commodity. In the case of any given commodity, its value is produced by the act that produces the commodity itself, so that it receives its value passively from this act and finds itself to be determined economically as it is determined materially by the act. In the case of labor-power, it preexists the definition of its value, and this is so because labor-power is not produced, because the living individual is not the result of any production but a primary given and the prior condition for Marx's entire problematic. This is also why the value it receives, the value the economy confers upon it when it is placed within the economic universe, is not its own but that of the various commodities, the objects which it needs to a greater or lesser extent and which are defined by it. *This distinction and this specificity of labor-power, the fact that the value it receives is not its own, is not produced in the act which would produce it as labor-power, the fact that the problematic of value—that is, economics—is forced to shift from the consideration of this prior reality, the reality of the individual which is presupposed, to that of the "means of subsistence"*—all of this is contained in the following text, which, by the essential disjunction of a "but" which must not fail to be heard, forever separates labor-power—inasmuch as it is considered as a value, inasmuch as it has become a commodity—from its primary and, so to speak, absolute reality, that which is presupposed by all the rest. "*So far as it has value*, it [labor-power] *represents* no more than a definite quantity of the average labor of society incorporated in it. [*But*] *labor-power exists only as a capacity or power of the living individual*. Its production consequently presupposes his existence. *Given the individual*, the production of labor-power consists in his reproduction of himself or his maintenance. For his maintenance he requires a given quantity of the means of subsistence. *Therefore the labor-time requisite for the production of labor-power reduces itself to that necessary for the production of those means of subsistence; in other words, the value of labor-power is the value of the means of subsistence necessary for the maintenance of the laborer.*"[41] It is because labor-power is a living power which is presupposed or already given that not only does it not allow itself to be defined passively by a value which is not its own, but, precisely as a power and as a productive force, it is capable of producing objects upon which this productive force confers a value which then merges with them. To resolve the origin of variable capital—the fact that the value of labor-power, which is but an index, or the value of "necessary goods" does not coincide with its final value, that is, indeed, with the value it is capable of producing—is not only to relate it to life's fundamental property of outstripping its own conditions but also to show the radical heterogeneity of life in relation to the economy, and how it is placed within the economy only by obstructing the interplay of its ideal determinations. The "irrationality" of the value of labor—and of the value of labor-power as well—carries us back to the fundamental presupposition of Marx's thought.

Conclusion

SOCIALISM

To the extent that it refers exclusively to the praxis of the individual, the subjective theory of value establishes the fate of capitalism and enables us to understand what socialism was intended to be for Marx. The ultimate contradiction of capitalism is henceforth to be understood and should be described in the following way: *Capitalism is the system of value, its development and its maintenance (money being the eternal value); value is produced exclusively by living labor; the fate of capital is thus the fate of this labor, of the subjective praxis of the individual. Inasmuch as the real process of production includes within it the accomplishment of this praxis, it is at the same time a process of value-formation, a process of the realization and increase of value.* Out of this stems the first moment of Marx's problematic, the analysis of capital in its actual existence, that is, the analysis of the process of its formation, which in turn leads back to the real process of production, revealing in this process the element that produces value, namely this subjective praxis. The economic analysis is thus nothing more than the analysis of the real components in the process; the value-composition of capital, just as the organic composition, refers to its technical composition and is explained entirely in terms of the latter.

If one were now to posit a material process of production from which living labor would be excluded, this process would no longer be a process of realization, of an increase in value; no system of value can—or ever could—result from it, and capitalism is, henceforth, impossible. The transition from capitalism to socialism is nothing other than that from a production process in which living labor has the greatest share to a process in which this share continually diminishes, tending ultimately toward zero. It is for this reason that in opposition to the decisive hypothesis of *Capital*, $c = 0$, can be posited, if one wants to grasp the eidetic cleavage between capitalism and socialism, this other, no less *essential* hypothesis—if by essential is understood that which is capable of exposing an essence—cv (variable capital) $= 0$. In concrete terms, this involves an entirely automatic system of production, in which the products, in spite of their quantity and their quality, have no value. The dissociation within social wealth of real wealth and of economic wealth is presented here in a pure form: an indefinite quantity of use-values which no longer possess any exchange-value. And this is indeed the unsurpassable theoretical limit of the market economy and, *a fortiori*, of capitalism. Marx analyzed on two different occasions this movement in which living labor is progressively eliminated from the production process. Once on the level of the effects of this process, on the economic level: this is in *Capital*. However, to the extent that this is indeed an analysis, the "immanent" law of the tendency toward a lower rate of profit is unequivocally referred to its real *naturans*, to the real process. It is in the *Grundrisse* that this process becomes in its turn an explicit object of investigation. Then unfolds before us the event which will determine modern history, even if that history is still to come, even if today we are only able to glimpse it: *the dissociation, within reality, of the production process and the labor process*.

A dissociation such as this is no doubt present in capitalism and, well before it, in the elementary forms of human production, for example, in agriculture.[1] If one examines the process which ends in the production of grain and which covers a certain number of months, it is clear that it does not coincide with the actual human labor which is its own condition: this labor ceases during the long periods necessary for the seed to germinate in the earth, for the crop to ripen in the sun, and so on. And the same thing will be true, much later, in industry, where the time it takes to manufacture a product goes far beyond the labor-time due to the inevitable interruptions in labor-time—whether this is the result of the material conditions of this manufacture or of living praxis itself (the time required for meals, for rest, for sleep, etc.). Now, it is most noteworthy that a dissociation such as this between production-time and labor-time—and consequently between production and labor—was taken into consideration by Marx in the way in which it was. Because this is a matter not of a banal, and moreover "contingent," fact which would have to be taken into account as one factor among others, but rather of the very principle of his analysis. If living labor, and it alone, produces value, then the delimitation of subjective accomplishments is at one and the same time the grasp of its creative principle, its *naturans*, within the production process. This is why, once the distinction between production-time and labor-time becomes evident, it is indeed the presupposition of Marx's thought that is in question: "The question is constituted by the unequal duration required by different products, although the same amount of labor time . . . is employed upon them. The fixed capital here allegedly acts quite by itself, *without human labor*, like e.g. the seed entrusted to the earth's womb. . . . *The question to be posed in pure form*." We already know the reply; it is that labor and its duration, and not that of production, constitute the principle of value. "*Value, hence also surplus value, is not = to the time which the production phase lasts, but rather to the labor time, objectified and living, employed during this production phase*. The living labor time alone—and, indeed, in the proportion in which it is employed relative to objective labor time—can create surplus value, because [it creates] surplus labor time." This is why, Marx adds, "It has therefore been correctly asserted that in this regard agriculture for instance is less productive [productivity is concerned here with the production of values] than other industries."[2] So if natural conditions separate the production process from the labor process, the latter remains the sole foundation of self-realization. *"The point to remember here* is only that capital creates no surplus value as long as it employs no living labor."[3] And it is then evident what the tendency of capital would be insofar as it constitutes its own end: to reduce, to the extent that this is possible, the production process to the labor process, that is, to a process which would be through and through a process of self-realization. "Hence the tendency of capitalist production to reduce the excess of the production time over the labor-time as much as possible."[4]

When the relation of the production process to the labor process obeys a tendency—the tendency of capital to increase indefinitely—and is determined by it, it is specific to capitalism. But then it becomes contradictory. For if capitalism strives to reduce production to labor, since the latter alone is the source of value, it also does the opposite. It is not labor, it is surplus-labor that is the ground of self-realization, and this is what has to increase. But as there are limits to the workday—here again, it is life which imposes its laws on the economy—an increase in surplus-labor amounts to a reduction in necessary labor, to increasing productivity constantly, to improving and developing indefinitely the technical and instrumental apparatus of production. Far from being reduced to living labor, production seems to be defined by its objective elements and, more and more, to conform to them. It is therefore necessary to restate again here the long history of modern industry. We know how, with the development of mechanization, the social powers of production—the skill and the cooperation among the individuals at work, their know-how and intelligence—cease to be subjective powers, the powers and accomplishments of these individuals, in order to be placed, on the contrary, over and against them, in the form of the "automatic system of machinery," which belongs to capital and which tends to constitute the essential part of the production process in relation to which individuals are no more than scattered auxiliary elements, mediocre and soon to be useless. ". . . (system of machinery: the automatic one is merely its most complete, most adequate form, and alone transforms machinery into a system), set in motion by an automaton, a moving power that moves itself; this automaton consisting of numerous mechanical and intellectual organs, so that the workers themselves are cast merely as its conscious linkages."[5] There then occurs the decisive transformation of the instrument of labor, which loses its "direct means" and which ceases precisely to be an instrument *of labor*, the means by which praxis carries out its activity working on and shaping the object. "In the machine . . . the use value, i.e. the material quality of the means of labor, is transformed. . . . In no way does the machine appear as the individual worker's means of labor. *Its distinguishing characteristic is not in the least, as with the means of labor, to transmit the worker's activity to the object.*"[6] The transformation of the nature and of the role of the instrument, now become machine, therefore also signifies, in the same stroke and as a consequence of this, the decisive transformation by virtue of which *the activity ceases to be that of the individual, a modality of living praxis and its realization, in order to become, on the contrary and paradoxically, the activity of the machine, an objective process.* The text we have been commenting on continues, ". . . *this activity, rather, is posited in such a way that it merely transmits the machine's work, the machine's action,* on to the raw material—supervises it and guards against interruptions. Not as with the instrument, which the worker animates and makes into his organ with his skill and strength, and whose handling therefore depends on his virtuosity. Rather, it is the machine which possesses skill and strength in place of the worker, is itself the virtuoso, with a soul of its own in the mechanical laws acting through it. . . ."[7]

We must be careful not to reduce the content of this text to the anthropological and axiological meanings it conveys, even if what directly follows seems to reinforce this appearance. Returning to a theme found frequently in Marx, it is deplored that science, which ceases to belong to men, is instead transferred and lodged in the body of the machines. "The science . . . does not exist in the worker's consciousness, but rather acts upon him through the machine as an alien power, as the power of the machine itself."[8] And again, we read that "in machinery, knowledge appears as alien, external to [the worker]."[9] But when the knowledge-bearing activity ceases to be that of the individual and is instead absorbed into that of the objective operation of the mechanical system, *it is the essence of production which has changed: no longer defined by subjective praxis, the production process has ceased to be a labor process.* "*The production process has ceased to be a labor process* in the sense of a process dominated by labor as its governing unity. Labor appears, rather, merely as a conscious organ, scattered among the individual living workers at numerous points of the mechanical system; subsumed under the total process of the machinery itself, as itself only a link of the system, whose unity exists not in the living workers, but rather in the living (active) machinery, which confronts his individual, insignificant doings as a mighty organism. In machinery, objectified labor confronts living labor within the labor process itself as the power which rules it; a power which, as the appropriation of living labor, is the form of capital."[10]

It is then that the contradiction inherent in capitalism manifests itself. As a "formal power," capital had living labor as its content; it lived off of it, feeding on it like a vampire, drawing from it the new value by which it increased. But when under the very effect of capital as it tends to reduce necessary labor, living labor finds itself gradually excluded from the production process, which takes on an objective form, it is the very source of value, along with its subjective realization, which is dried up. "Capital itself is the moving contradiction, [in] that it presses to reduce labor time to a minimum, while it posits labor time, on the other side, as sole measure and source of wealth. . . . On the one side, then, it calls to life all the powers of science and of nature, as of social combination and of social intercourse, in order to make the creation of wealth independent . . . of the labor time employed on it. On the other side, it wants to use labor time as the measuring rod for the giant social forces thereby created, and to confine them within the limits required to maintain the already created value as value."[11] In this way, the self-destruction of capital is at one and the same time the historical movement in which living labor, posited as the foundation of value, is itself eliminated from the production process, the movement in which therefore the production process and the labor process constantly diverge.

Is socialism, then, anything other than the consequence of this contradiction, or, if we place ourselves on the theoretical level, an awareness of it? What is prescribed by the theoreticians of socialism is the suppression of the market economy and of capitalism as well, but only to the extent that it has brought the market economy to the point at which it has become contradictory. This prescription, however, is only an observation and directly results from this contradiction. If the wealth of a society is no longer to be conceived as an economic wealth, if the value of a product is no longer to be defined by its exchange-value, this is because the latter is no more than a theoretical account of the living labor necessary for the production of this product; this is, finally, because living labor has, precisely, disappeared or tends to disappear from this production. We are not in a position to condemn the market economy; we are witnessing its end. And it is in the collapse of the universe of economic wealth that real wealth appears in its purest form, which is defined by use-values. Once again here, it is a fact that use-values proliferate when their exchange-value tends toward zero. The progression of real wealth at the expense of economic wealth is only the correlate of the decisive mutation that affects the production process, substituting within this process mechanical manufacture for living labor. [12]

Capitalism, certainly, does not merge totally with the market economy; it presupposes not only value but surplus-value as well. It is only with surplus-value that money becomes capital, for it alone makes the split within the production process, which stands in opposition to itself in the form of an ideal system of equivalence, lead as well to the constant imbalance between production and consumption. But surplus-labor is not condemned in the final analysis—we mean is not condemned by history—due to the economic disturbances it creates, but because *it itself disappears along with the living labor of which it is only a part*. The exploitation of man becomes useless when it is no longer he who produces or when his role in production is revealed to be ridiculously minor. Capitalism is in decline when the economic definition of wealth has become antiquated; its fall presupposes that of the market economy and follows after it. Marx presented in an essential text this "passage" from capitalism to socialism. "The theft of alien labor time, on which the present wealth [this refers to economic wealth] is based, appears a miserable foundation in face of this new one, created by large-scale industry itself. *As soon as labor in the direct form has ceased to be the great well-spring of wealth* [this refers to real wealth], *labor time ceases and must cease to be its measure, and hence exchange value* [*must cease to be the measure*] *of use value. The surplus labor of the mass has ceased to be the condition for the development of general wealth. . . .*"[13]

The decisive mutation which shakes the foundation of the market and capitalist economy is therefore the mutation affecting the production process itself, its "productive forces," and the concept of these forces must finally be brought clearly to light. It is too often said that the productive forces in a society are the determining factor on the basis of which everything—"social relations," ideology, etc.—can ultimately be explained. We have shown that in this external résumé Marx's thought has already been lost. For it consists precisely in the analysis of productive forces, in dividing them up into an objective element and living praxis. The entire economic analysis rests on this division. The decisive mutation of the concept of productive forces—and of what results from it: the passage from capitalism to socialism—signifies that henceforth this division will take place in another way. Now, this is, and we must understand it in this way, a change which modifies the very course of human history. As long as the determining element in production is subjective activity, *production coincides with the life of individuals*, its essence is their life process, and, conversely, what these individuals themselves are is what they do to produce the goods necessary for their maintenance, that is, their "material" production. The subjective definition of production has a twofold meaning, contains a twofold reduction, the reduction of production to the mode of individual life, to the conditions of men's existence, and the reduction of this life to what men do in this production, to this production itself. Such is the explicit content of one of the fundamental texts with which *The German Ideology* begins: "The way in which men produce their means of subsistence depends first of all on the nature of the means of subsistence they actually find in existence and have to reproduce. This mode of production must not be considered simply as being the reproduction of the physical existence of the individuals. *Rather it is a definite form of activity of these individuals, a definite form of expressing their life, a definite mode of life on their part. As individuals express their life, so they are. What they are, therefore, coincides with their production* [*Was sie sind, fällt also zusammen mit ihrer Produktion*]. . . ."[14]

It is therefore this subjective essence of the productive forces that will be eliminated when these forces are constituted, not only in what they are but also in what they do, as a set of elements foreign to praxis, as an objective process. Let us recall Marx's assertions: "It belongs to the concept of capital that the increased productive force of labor is posited rather *as the increase of a force* [Kraft] *outside itself, and as labor's own debilitation* [Entkräftung]."[15] "Thus, the specific mode of working here appears directly as becoming transferred from the worker to capital in the form of the machine. . . ."[16] "The incease of the productive force of labor and the greatest possible negation of necessary labor is the necessary tendency of capital. . . . The transformation of the means of labor into machinery is the realization of this tendency. In machinery, objectified labor materially confronts living labor as a ruling power. . . ."[17] The fact that this transformation, in which we can easily recognize the dialectic of living labor and dead labor—this is grasped, it is true, not as an element in a system but as its very development and as the very movement of history—is indeed the transformation by which the productive force ceases to be described in terms of subjectivity, finding instead its reality, its "force," in the objective instrumental machinery of production and in what Marx calls "objectified labor"—all this is formulated in a categorical manner: "In machinery, objectified labor itself appears not only in the form of product or of the product employed as means of labor, *but in the form of the force of production itself*."[18] It is only in light of these essential texts of the *Grundrisse* that the texts in *Capital* can be understood in a rigorous manner; the latter, under the appearance of what are once again anthropological considerations, to the extent that they seem to deplore the gradual exclusion of individual capacities and of the individual himself from the production process, actually simply reaffirm the ontological mutation of the productive forces. For it must indeed be understood that the "collective labor force," the "social productive forces"—in short the "productive forces" as they exist at the end of the evolution they undergo as a result of capitalism—can no longer designate, precisely, individual activities inasmuch as these are social in their very reality, inasmuch as human labor is always co-labor. Because productive forces are now the forces of the machine, they are no longer praxis, no longer "forces" in the sense of potentialities and realizations of organic subjectivity and, in general, of life. *They are no longer "labor-power" in the sense of* Capital, *the proof being that they no longer create any value*.

The "productive forces of capital," it is true, continue to produce value, although this production is shown to be more and more difficult. The fact is that the concept of "the productive force of capital" remains unclear and, finally, is unusable. Within the generic concept of the productive forces must be distinguished, on the one hand, the objective "forces" of capital, the "social," "collective" forces of labor, which are not "labor," the "labor forces," which are neither social nor collective—the social and the collective are and can only be modalities of life—all of which designate simply a coherent, instrumental totality and its objective functioning. On the other hand, we find the individual forces which are part of life, which may be social and collective, have been and are no longer, to the extent that workers are now scattered throughout various points of the mechanical system and relate to it, not to one another. These individual forces and these alone produce the value that is produced by the "productive forces of capital." The latter, among which the individual forces continue to be present, produce use-values. The regret occasioned by the decline of the role of the individual in capitalist production is not the nostalgic expression of an out-of-date humanism; instead it conveys a matter-of-fact observation concerning the progressively increasing gap between the subjective forces which create economic wealth and the objective forces which produce the ever greater mass of use-values. Without this distinction within the concept of wealth in its correlation with the ontological distinction inherent in the notion of productive forces, we could understand not a single word of this passage from *Capital*: "In manufacture, in order to make the *collective laborer, and through him capital, rich in social productive power*, each laborer must be made poor in *individual productive powers*."[19] Nor could we understand the statement, con-

cerning the productive forces in their relation to the division of labor in manufactures, that "it increases the *social productive power of labor* . . . *for the benefit
of the capitalist* instead of for that of the laborer. . . ."[20]

What happens, then, when the productive forces are no longer constituted in
their very essence by subjectivity and become objective? As we know, the
market economy, and capitalism along with it, is thereby struck to the quick.
And is the philosophy of praxis not affected in the same way? Does not the
decline of capitalism signify at the same time the decline of Marx's thought?
What indeed remains of the interpretation of being as production *and as subjectivity* when production, identifying itself with the mechanical instrumental apparatus, is no longer anything but the operation of this apparatus and, as such, a
third-person objective process? Is not the individual eliminated from the problematic along with the praxis by which he is defined, eliminated, that is, from
the concept of being as production? Marx has said what becomes of the individual in this "passage" from capitalism to socialism, that is, in the objective
development of the productive forces which it expresses, a development which,
by eliminating its subjective source, destroys exchange-value: "With that, production based on exchange value breaks down, and the direct, material production process is stripped of the form of penury and antithesis. *The free
development of individualities,* and hence not the reduction of necessary labor
time so as to posit surplus labor, but rather the general reduction of the necessary labor of society to a minimum, *which then corresponds to the artistic,
scientific etc. development of the individuals* in the time set free, and with the
means created, for all of them."[21] The decline of the subjective concept of
productive forces indeed marks a turning point in the history of humanity; it
expresses the fact that the union between the individual and production, the
definition of his life in terms of the material tasks which assure his subsistence,
"labor" in the sense it has had for thousands of years, cease to exist. But what
then arises is the "free development of individualities." Individual activity, life,
praxis are in no way abolished but are fulfilled. Individual activity is no longer
determined by material production—this means: it no longer merges with it,
and, for this reason as well, it no longer has as its parallel an economic
universe. Two things that have constantly been related to the point of merging
with one another and of being taken one for the other begin to dissociate
themselves and to follow hereafter their own respective paths: production,
handed over to technology, has become a natural process; life can finally be
what it is, experiencing itself and finding its end in reality as such: in itself. The
philosophy of the radical development of the individual and of the total individual is thus not just a leftover from the humanist anthropology of youth; it is
instead, at the end of the economic analysis, the result of this analysis and, at
the same time, a prophecy. The subjective definition of production is indeed
given in *The German Ideology* as belonging to that "premise" which is posited as
"the first premise of all human history";[22] and this is how we have understood it
in our investigations, as the transcendental condition of history as well as of

society. This was because such a definition of history remained dependent both
on the current state of civilization and on its millennial past, for which it is
adequate. The history which follows—which will follow—the market economy
will, to no lesser extent, be the history of individuals, the history of their life: in
a sense, it will be so for the first time. It will no longer be their history by being
the history of their life, but because this history of their life will be "intended,"
in accordance with the innermost and most personal potentialities of living
subjectivity. It will no longer be the history of "material" needs but of their
"spiritual" needs.

How can a spiritual life be "free"? Is it not always and necessarily dependent
on productive forces? *It seems that this is not so.* When Marxism raised the
problem of the individual's freedom, which incontestably belongs to the constant teleology of Marx's thought, he was able to resolve it only by continuing to
repeat his erroneous premises. Since, in his opinion, the productive forces
determine individual existence, the only way to free the latter is to organize
productive forces and social structures in such a way that their conditioning of
the individual—something they have always done and continue to do—will be
accomplished in accordance with the way this existence ought to be. The causal
determination of subjectivity is not ended; it is itself to be determined. And the
freedom of the individual will simply be this twofold determination and akin to a
ruse of reason, the use of determinism in behalf of a moral end. The fact is that
in every case the objectivity of the productive forces is posited, and their
activity continues to resemble a natural process. In the market economy, however, the productive forces do not determine the individual in the manner of an
external relation; they *are* the powers of this individual and subjectivity itself.
In socialism the relation between the productive forces and subjectivity has
become an extrinsic relation, one, moreover, that is destined to disappear; the
individual is not subjected to the activity of the productive forces, which have
become amenable to his will. He escapes their hold on him. As Marx finally
understands it, the freedom of the individual means two things: (1) individual
activity is foreign to the productive forces; his subjectivity no longer coincides
with their process, now an objective process, and is no longer affected by these
forces. The activity of the individual is developed in accordance with the pure
prescriptions of the life within him; it is, as Marx repeats throughout his entire
work, a "manifestation of his life." (2) The thought of the individual is governed
by his activity and by his life; as such it is now independent of the productive
forces. The idea that these forces determine "ideology" is without any substance. As we see, productive forces can be taken into account, in Marx, only
on the basis of the analysis of their technical composition and of the distinction
within them between objective and subjective elements. In the absence of such
a distinction, the discourse which claims to follow Marx oscillates between
confusion and absurdity. Particularly absurd is the assertion of the objectivity of
the productive forces when this claims to concern past or present history. And
when in some far distant future these forces are to become objective, they will,

precisely, have no influence on men's lives and will no longer give rise to any ideology.

The interpretation of socialism as the becoming and the realization in individual existence of its own inherent teleology eliminates once and for all the aberrant meanings that have traditionally clouded the concept of socialism in Marxism as in common thought. According to these, socialism is supposed to designate a mutation in the "history of humanity," the inauguration of a new state which could be characterized, precisely, as "social." This must be understood in the sense of a revolution situated within being itself. Reality would be changed; no longer defined by the anarchic plurality of separate individuals engaged in competition, it would instead be constituted in the form of a general reality, and this in a substantive manner. Just as production is no longer individual but now social, consisting in setting in motion an immense collective force, in the same way, the life of individuals should be raised above their insignificant particularity and their activity meld together into an activity in which all participate and which is, precisely, the activity of all, into "social praxis." When, stimulated by capital itself, production, which has now become social, unfolding its unlimited powers, itself traces out the horizon of its future, it is then the honor of each and every one no longer to ascribe to his own activity the ridiculously minor aims of individuality but rather the aims of history and to unite with this great movement. As men who no longer live of themselves nor for themselves alone but who, however modest their own role might be and whatever the part they may have in the enterprise or the common adventure, define themselves only in terms of the latter, in terms of history and revolution, politicians are indeed the forerunners of this state in which everyone lives an expanded life, a life which is no longer his own but that of the universal reality in which he is able to participate and which is realized through him. Everything, then, becomes collective—production which brings about this new world, but also, as a result, life itself, relations, thought, objects. This is the age of groups and of teams, of the community in all its forms. The individual is in the people like a fish in water, and his substance lies only in the social substance.

However, the metaphysics of the universal is that of Hegel, and we have shown that it falls to pieces in Marx's problematic. As early as the 1843 manuscript, the effort to repeat the political definition of individual life as universal life, using the Feuerbachian concept of species-being and situating it on the level of civil society, enters into contradiction with the introduction of elements that will guide the subsequent development of Marx's thought. The irreducible character of individual activity immediately ruled out the ontological claims of objective universality. In the works that followed—and precisely in the context of socialism—it is true that certain obscure points gave rise to serious misinterpretations, the most important of which being no doubt this definition of socialism by the "social." This is the case notably of a series of texts in which the market economy is condemned for having established the "social" only in the form of a mediation, namely that of exchange-value. This concerns, as we remember, the process in which the real and, in each case, particular labor of different individuals is replaced by general and social labor, which is held to be the common standard, which represents all the various sorts of labor equally and represents itself in the exchange-value. "Labor which manifests itself in exchange-value appears to be the labor of an isolated individual. It becomes social labor by assuming the form of its direct opposite, of abstract universal labor."[23] And again: ". . . on the basis of commodity production, labor becomes social labor only as a result of the universal alienation of individual kinds of labor."[24] Analyses such as these are not marginal. They describe nothing less than the constitution of the market economy in its very possibility, what we have called its transcendental genesis. We have seen that it is the representation in all the various sorts of labor of one and the same labor which bestows a value upon their products and allows their exchange. Inasmuch, however, as the social appears in the market economy only in the form of general and abstract labor opposed to the real labor of individuals, that is, to their actual existence, what ought to constitute the tie between all these existences and their substance, that is, precisely, the social, proves to be alien to immediate life. The domain of the social lies beyond life, in irreality, in a fantastic universe by which existence will constantly be affected.

Only, when the question of socialism is no longer in Marx's work the explicit object of analysis—which it almost never is—but instead is referred to in remarks or significant observations, his thought inevitably reveals the most original presupposition of the market economy. It then appears that the different sorts of labor in which the alienation process originates, the process which founds social labor and exchange-value, are themselves not only, as has been stated, the real labor of individuals, but *private* forms of labor. ". . . only particular commodities, the particular use-values embodying the labor of private individuals, confront one another in the exchange process."[25] It is because the labor that will be taken into account in exchange, and in reality exchanged therein, is first and foremost private labor, labor presented as such at the start of the economic process, that it can take on a social form only by ridding itself of its original nature, only by alienating itself. It is for this reason that *the "social" will appear not as a given on the level of immediate life, but rather as the result of this process of alienation, in an abstract and irreal form*. *"The point of departure is not the labor of individuals considered as social labor, but on the contrary the particular kinds of labor of private individuals, i.e., labor which proves that it is universal social labor only by the supersession of its original character in the exchange process. Universal social labor is consequently not a ready-made prerequisite. . . ."*[26]

The "solution" of socialism—of what seems to be Marx's socialism—then stands before us. It consists in the opposite presupposition to that of the market economy, in the presupposition whereby individual labor, which itself certainly constitutes the essence and the condition of all possible production, constitutes as well—and straightaway—a social labor. What is presupposed here is, as we see, the *actual becoming of the social substance*, the fact that it henceforth merges with the life of men instead of being lost somewhere beyond it in the irreality of abstraction—*as if the tie that unites individuals could be separated from each one of them*. This is precisely the paradox of the market economy. The presupposition of socialism is not, however, a simple presupposition in the sense of an ethical postulate. Instead it is, to borrow the language of *The German Ideology*, a "real premise," and Marx has no difficulty in showing that it has been realized in history and, in a certain sense, continues to exert its effect in each moment of history. This is what, in fact, occurs in the family—provided we exclude the family of the Manchester workers—where the labor of each individual is straightaway a "social" labor, which therefore has no need to have a parallel on the ideal plane in order to acquire a property it already possesses on the plane of reality. And the product of this labor, consequently, has no economic value and is not exchanged but takes its place naturally within the whole set of use-values placed at the disposal of all of the members of this family in accordance with the needs of each one. "These different articles are, as regards the family, so many products of its labor, but as between themselves, they are not commodities. The different kinds of labor . . . which result in the various products, are in themselves, and such as they are, direct social functions. . . ."²⁷ Far from being simply imaginary, a social and noneconomic organization of production and consumption is actually realized in what constitutes the basic unit of every more complex organization. Thus, it is not surprising to find this type of organization in certain historical forms of society, to begin with in those that remain close to the family-based structure. It is in this way that, in the "rural patriarchal system of production," the social character of the various sorts of labor was inseparable from them and did not lie in their exchange "as equal . . . expressions of the same universal labor-time."²⁸ In the same way, in tasks during the Middle Ages, "it was the distinct labor of the individual in its original form, the particular features of his labor and not its universal aspect that formed the social ties at that time."²⁹ In primitive communal existence, finally, "the social character of labor is evidently not effected by the labor of the individual assuming the abstract form of universal labor or his product assuming the form of a universal equivalent. *The communal system on which this mode of production is based prevents the labor of an individual from becoming private labor and his product the private product of a separate individual*."³⁰

The solution proposed by socialism thus takes the form of the community. What characterizes the latter, in the first place, is the *transparency of social relations*. By this must be understood intersubjective relations inasmuch as their substance is composed, precisely, of the life of the individuals of whom these are the relations, inasmuch as these relations, which are directly lived by the individuals, are also, for this reason, known to them and, as we have stated, are transparent in their eyes. When all contribute to a certain action and share in its product, consume it together, nothing unclear clouds this process, which itself is not separated from them; the reality of this process is their very life, as they experience it and live it. When the process becomes more complex, and even though it may be fraught with inequality or glaring injustices, these continue, precisely, to offer themselves to the light of analysis, to be "evident," and this in a necessary manner. Indeed, as long as individual relations are constituted and defined by the life of the individuals who enter into relation, then these relations are inevitably for each individual what his own life is, what he does and what he has experienced, what he cannot be mistaken about. Such is the case of the relations of "personal dependence" which we find in the Middle Ages. These are relations of inequality, certainly, because they are established between "serfs and lords, vassals and suzerains, laymen and clergy." These are relations which, because they are those of production and of labor, are at the same time the "social relations" which permeate and structure the society as a whole. "Personal dependence here characterizes the social relations of production just as much as it does the other spheres of life organized on the basis of that production." These relations are nevertheless transparent in their very inequality, and this is because, constituted by the very life of the individuals, their relations are clear to them.

> But for the very reason that personal dependence forms the ground-work of society, there is no necessity for labor and its products to assume a fantastic form different from their reality. They take the shape, in the transactions of society, of services in kind and payments in kind. Here the particular and natural form of labor, and not, as in a society based on production of commodities, its general abstract form is the immediate social form of labor. Compulsory labor is just as properly measured by time as commodity-producing labor, but *every serf knows that what he expends in the service of his lord, is a definite quantity of his own personal labor-power*. The tithe to be rendered to the priest is more matter of fact that his blessing. No matter, then, what we may think of the parts played by the different classes of people themselves in this society, *the social relations between individuals in the performance of their labor, appear at all events as their own mutual personal relations*, and are most disguised under the shape of social relations between the products of labor.[31]

It is remarkable to see in this text from *Capital*, which returns to and furthers the analyses made in the *Critique of Political Economy*, that the community is conceived of in opposition to the market economy. This opposition sheds light on both terms. And what the market society is reproached with is indeed having disguised social relations, having made them something other than the living relations of individuals, coming from them and directed to them, relations constituted by their own lives. And this, as we know, is because since these relations are to begin with the relations that individuals enter into in the production of their existence, when the work accomplished in realizing this production is private labor and the products are commodities,[32] then the tie that is established between individuals is merely that of these products. "Since the producers do not come into social contact with each other until they exchange their products, the specific social character of each producer's labor does not show itself except in the act of exchange."[33] The relations of these producers among themselves, then, are "not. . . direct social relations between individuals at work but . . . social relations between things,"[34] namely the value-relations that exist between commodities. *The social relation continues to exist, but its ontological status has changed: it is no longer an immanent relation, internal to existence and defined by it as a subjective relation between subjectivities; it is an ideal relation between realities which themselves are ideal, abstract, and foreign to the individual, a relation between values which are realized in accordance with their pure form.* The community no longer resides in life, but in money. "Money thereby directly and simultaneously becomes the real community [*Gemeinwesen*] . . . but . . . in money, the community [*Gemeinwesen*] is at the same time a mere abstraction, a mere external, accidental thing for the individual. . . ."[35] Archaic social forms, despite their limitations, awaken Marx's nostalgia only insofar as they oppose the reality of an individual tie to the ideal forms of the market economy. "The community of antiquity presupposes a quite different relation to, and on the part of, the individual. . . ."[36] This same opposition is revealed in *Capital*, where, still in contrast to peoples engaged in commerce, the same praise is bestowed upon the means of production in "ancient Asia" and in antiquity in general: "Those ancient social organisms of production are, as compared with bourgeois society, extremely simple and transparent."[37]

Thus, in the study of past historical forms of socialism, we find one of Marx's central themes. The demand for transparency (the context of the above-quoted analyses shows that transparency is nothing other than the phenomenological milieu immanent to individual life) is at one and the same time the rejection of all transcendence, the refusal to allow the social relation to be constituted beyond this life, in the phantasmagorical universe of economic determinations and of things. As was already the case in *The German Ideology*, it is in each and every case a matter of refusing to accept "the transformation . . . of personal powers . . . into material powers," and of making it happen that the community in which men have been united up to now ceases to "[take] on an independent existence in relation to them."[38] It is this rejection of all transcendence, in its correlation with the assertion of the positive character of life, which explains why the parallel established between the critique of the market economy and that of religion is maintained in the text from *Capital* which we have just been commenting on. "The religious world is but the reflection of the real world. And for a society based upon the production of commodities, in which the producers in general enter into social relations with one another by treating their products as commodities and values, whereby they reduce their individual private labor to the standard of homogeneous human labor—for such a society, Christianity with its *cultus* of abstract man, more especially in its bourgeois developments,

Protestantism, Deism, etc., is the most fitting form of religion."[39] As surprising as this definition of Christianity in terms of the concept and the *cultus* of abstract man may be—this is, in Marx, a final echo of the castoffs from his "young-Hegelian" days—it alone authorizes, by the rejection of the exteriority implied in this concept, the correlative rejection of the market economy; this, in its turn, is accompanied by the unveiling of the sphere in which, in living individual subjectivity, all reality and the living community of men are constituted.

How can there be a community which restores social relations to life and to the individual himself? This has already been stated: on the condition that individual labor be immediately a social labor. In the *Grundrisse* a project announcing an historical task refers to the dissolution of the mode of production and of the form of society founded on exchange-value, following which individual labor will be genuinely posited in a social form. The *Grundrisse* add a number of important clarifications concerning the presupposition that individual labor is social labor, inasmuch as this defines the very presupposition on which socialism is based. It is shown that only a *labor which in itself is general* can avoid the mediation of exchange and of exchange-value: "On the basis of exchange values, labor is posited as general only through exchange. But on this foundation it would be posited as such before exchange; i.e. the exchange of products would in no way be the medium by which the participation of the individual in the general production is mediated."[40] But is not labor subjective and, as such, particular and not general? Speaking of labor as existing "only subjectively, only in the form of activity," Marx adds: "[it] is by no means general, self-equivalent labor-time. . . ."[41] Only through a mediation can we be led from individual, subjective labor to general labor. In socialism this mediation is immediate: it consists in the fact that the activity which is singular in itself and which is lived in this way is nevertheless posited and grasped in its very realization as part of the collective activity, within which, moreover, it is always situated. It is in this way that an individual labor is nonetheless "general," not at all in the form of an ideal double, but in its reality, to the extent that, once again, this is not understood as "private" and related explicitly and in legalistic terms to a specific individual, but as a personal and active participation in the activity of all and as co-constituting this activity. "Mediation must, of course, take place. In the first case, which proceeds from the independent production of individuals—no matter how much these independent productions determine and modify each other *post festum* through their interrelations—mediation takes place through the exchange of commodities, through the exchange value and through money; all these are expressions of one and the same relation. In the second case, the presupposition is itself mediated; i.e. a communal production, communality, is presupposed as the basis of production. The labor of the individual is posited from the outset as social labor."[42] Like this labor, its product too is social and no longer private. What is more, because the whole set of products is the correlate of a collective production, no specific product can be related to the labor of an individual, no specific product can then be attributed to this labor, but rather a share in the collective product of this social production. The text continues: "Thus, whatever the particular material form of the product he [the individual] creates or helps to create, what he has bought with his labor is not a specific and particular product, but rather a specific share of the communal production."[43] Earlier in the same passage, we read: "The communal character of production would make the product into a communal, general product from the outset. The exchange which originally takes place in production—which would not be an exchange of exchange values but of activities, determined by communal needs and communal purposes— would from the outset include the participation of the individual in the communal world of products."

This is the crux of communal socialism—of what Marx called communism. If we can understand how it is that a labor which, in itself, is individual is nevertheless inscribed within a collective production as a real part of this production, then "the participation of the individual in the communal world of products" is nothing other than his consumption, and this consumption remains individual in its very essence. The participation of the individual no longer signifies here that a reality which in itself is singular is fused with a totality that goes beyond it, but, on the contrary, that this totality—a totality of goods—is divided into a number of shares which are to be attributed to different individuals. It is the principle of this distribution that cannot be avoided. The latter no longer resides in the fact that products are commodities and that they are obtained in exchange for a certain amount of money. What is exchanged in socialism, Marx tells us, is from the outset the individual activities of workers, and this occurs in the very act by which these activities are posited as constituting one and the same social production, with regard to which the various branches and, ultimately, the diverse types of labor they imply, are complementary and are intended to form a global wealth that will be adequate for the whole of human needs. *In the market economy, however, the exchange of products considered as commodities, that is to say, in relation to their value, is nothing other than the exchange of the labor of different individuals which this value represents.* What is more, this exchange of individual labor—just as in a "socialist economy"—is what occurs first. It is solely because, at the start of the process, the particular activity of each individual at work counts straightaway as social labor that the product has value, namely the representation of this part of *social labor* which it contains. It is thus completely false to oppose, as Marx does, the market economy, in which the exchange would involve—*post festum*—only values and the socialist economy, in which it would concern directly the particular activities of individuals working in light of collective goals. It was Marx's analysis which taught us that the exchange of commodities was in no way primary but instead represented a secondary phenomenon, which referred in its fundamental possibility to this act of positing at the very outset individual labor as social labor, that is, to the substitution of real labor by abstract labor. In this substitution, in which an ideality replaces subjectivity, resides the alienation that constitutes the market economy.

Is an alienation such as this absent from the socialist economy? By no means. When the share of social and "collective" wealth received by each worker is to be established, it is his own labor, his individual labor, that is taken into account. Counting labor, when subjective praxis escapes all measurement, means substituting for it a system of objective and ideal equivalents; it is counting labor-*time*. Just what is meant by positing directly individual labor as social labor has to be clarified. Either this means that real praxis is inscribed within a collective production—but then we must recognize that this is always the case, in the market economy just as in the socialist economy—or else this indicates the quantitative and qualitative standard under which praxis is sub-sumed in order to be defined and so to receive remuneration, that is, the substitution of a general, social labor for individual labor—and then we must recognize that this substitution exists in a socialist economy just as in a market economy. Marx wanted us to see what the division of social wealth might be. "Let us now picture to ourselves, by way of change, a community of free individuals, carrying on their work with the means of production in common, in which the labor-power of all the different individuals is consciously applied *as* the combined labor-power of the community. (. . .) The total product of our community is a *social* product. One portion serves as a fresh means of produc-tion and remains social. But another portion is consumed by the members as means of subsistence. (. . .) We will assume, but merely for the sake of a parallel with the production of commodities, that the share of each individual producer in the means of subsistence is determined by his *labor-time*. Labor-time would, in that case, play a double part. Its apportionment in accordance with a definite social plan maintains the proper proportion between the different kinds of work to be done and the various wants of the community. On the other hand, it also serves as a measure of the portion of the common labor borne by each individual, and of his share in the part of the total product destined for individual consumption."[44]

In exchange for a certain *labor-time* the worker receives a certain amount of money in the market economy and in the socialist economy "labor vouchers"— money or vouchers with which he can obtain a certain number of products. The question is then as follows: *are labor vouchers anything different from money?* In a text in Book Two of *Capital*, describing the constant element found in all production regardless of the social form involved (in this case the brief or extended duration of a specific production depending on the material nature of its components), Marx observes that "under socialized as well as capitalist production, the laborers in branches of business with shorter working periods will as before withdraw products only for a short time without giving any prod-ucts in return; while branches of business with long working periods continually withdraw products for a longer time before they return anything."[45] This raises the problem of what is "withdrawn" by the workers from the social wealth. The text continues: "The producers may, for all it matters, receive paper vouchers entitling them to withdraw from the social supplies of consumer goods a quantity corresponding to their labor-time. These vouchers are not money. They do not circulate." Vouchers given in exchange for certain products do circulate. When Marx says that these vouchers do not circulate, he has in mind not circulation *stricto sensu*, the exchange of equivalents, but capitalist circulation, in which money is exchanged for the instruments of labor and for labor itself, increases as a result of surplus-value, and becomes capital. "In the case of socialized production the money-capital is eliminated," Marx states just before the text quoted above. Let us recall that the critique Marx directs to the market economy is twofold. It is first a critique of capitalism, exposing the origin of surplus-value, that is, surplus-labor. But the alienation that is now in question is no longer capitalist alienation; it is the alienation peculiar to the market economy as such, and, despite certain Marxist theses,[46] this alienation subsists in the socialist system as well, that is, in fact, in communism. As soon as praxis is taken into account socially, as soon as it is represented figuratively, whether this be in a labor voucher or in money, that which constitutes it substantively as in each case peculiar to a specific individual and as identical to his existence, is excluded from consideration; the substitution of an ideal equivalent for life has then occurred. Capitalism conceals this fundamental alienation under another, communism displays it in its pure state. This is precisely the content of the *Critique of the Gotha Programme*. The decisive problematic of equal right has shown the impossibility in principle of producing an economic formulation that would be adequate to life.

It is thus of no use to assert that production is social from the outset, if the individual must inevitably be taken into account on the level of consumption just as on that of production, if the share of the social wealth that each person is allotted results from, and must result from, his labor. Far from being able to be defined by the social character of the production process and by the social development of this process in modern industry, by the socialization of the means of production, by the social or collective character of their management, socialism has only an extrinsic relation to these determinations, determinations with which it is too often identified. And this is true for three reasons: because in Marx's eyes these determinations constitute as yet only the historical precondition for socialism; because far from being founded on its internal principle and hence resulting from it, they are foreign to it; because, for these two reasons, the world that they unfold is not a socialist world.

Thus, instead of surreptitiously confusing them, socialism and communism must be opposed to one another, as Marx does in the *Critique of the Gotha Programme*. Inasmuch as it is based upon the socialization of the production process and accepts the consequences of this:—socializing the means of production, management, etc.—communism, as we have seen, cannot avoid the problems of the individual, the problem of consumption and of "labor." If it tries to reject the alienation that constitutes capitalism, the exploitation of man in surplus-labor,[47] it does not for all this abolish, as we have just recalled, the fundamental alienation of the market economy, the fact that real praxis becomes other in "social labor." Now, it is this final alienation that socialism has in view, and this is what Marx wanted to eliminate. *He could not do this by substituting the universality of a social essence for the activity of the individual if alienation consists precisely in a substitution such as this, if this activity is, on the contrary, what must be restored to itself and liberated.* This is the unequivocal content of the *Critique of the Gotha Programme.* The society of overabundance is not defined by the sum total of social goods that it places at the disposal of all but, decisively and at the same time explicitly, by the fact that in a society such as this the praxis of the individual no longer obeys anything but the individual himself and the specific potentialities of the life that is in him.

A situation such as this results from the evolution of the productive forces— not merely their linear development and their growth, as if by becoming increasingly "powerful" they were to offer an ever greater wealth for social consumption. *It is the structural modification of their internal ontological constitution which alone makes possible and explains what Marx means by a society of overabundance.* It is only when the objective element formed by the instrumental and technological apparatus increases within these powers to the point of merging with them and of defining them that living praxis is henceforth foreign to them, is finally "free" and is *stricto sensu* an activity *of the individual.* Then in fact is realized—will be realized—the absolutely new historical situation in which men's lives are no longer confused, as they have been for ages, with their "material" life, that is, with the production of the goods required to fulfill their needs. Then their new need will emerge, the need of their own activity itself as such and as a living activity, as the *activity of their life.*

When the concept of socialism emerges from the mists in which it has been lost in Marxist ideology and jargon, the socialization of the means of production and its usual results—scarcity on the material level, bureaucracy, and police— can assuredly no longer constitute its content. What is opposed to these nowadays, that is, workers' self-management, is no less external to Marx's fundamental project: the former seeks to make individual activity compatible with production, the latter presupposes their gradual divergence and ultimately their absolute separation. This separation, no doubt, defines only an ideal limit, and as long as production implies at least the partial maintenance of living labor, the question of preserving a "human" form for this labor will inevitably arise. This preoccupation is a constant one for Marx, at any rate. It not only governs the entire critique of the condition of the worker in capitalism but is also evident, in a positive sense, in a good many aspects of his doctrine, for example, in the theory of education. One can only prescribe that education, "in the case of every child over a given age, combine productive labor with instruction and gymnastics, not only as one of the methods of adding to the efficiency of production, but as the only method of producing fully developed human be-ings,"[48] if the immanence of individual activity in relation to production, "labor," remains within the framework of the problematic. The preponderant influence of Owen's ideas concerning these developments does not permit us to think of them as the pure product of Marx's thought. This thought, rather, is fully expressed only in the peculiar reversal that is evident in the above-cited text. For it is no longer for the sake of production that the individual, even the adolescent, has to participate in it; rather he does so only in order to realize the practical potentialities of his own subjectivity, whether this actualization is part of a social production or not. Socialism in any case reposes on essential ques-tions. If the exclusion of living labor outside of social production is part of its concept, then the topics that concern this production and its prescriptions—socialization, self-management, etc.—play only a secondary role, have only an extrinsic significance. Only the following can be said to be socialist: (1) a society of overabundance (2) in which living praxis is no longer concerned with production. The connection which unites these two fundamental meanings of the concept of socialism is, moreover, obvious if "overabundance" finally desig-nates nothing other than the "liberty" of praxis.

Within the concept of socialism there is a second, no less essential connec-tion, that which unites socialism to capitalism and makes it derive from the latter. The project or the claim to "pass directly from the Middle Ages to the twenty-first century" or to "move directly to socialism without passing through capitalism" can have no place in Marx's problematic, nor claim to be based upon it, if the mutual exclusion of subjectivity and production, in which social-ism finds its concept, is the result of capitalism and its contradiction. The essential connection between overabundance and freedom which defines social-ism is precisely no more than the historical form which has developed out of the contradiction inherent in capitalism of production and subjectivity.

Because the economic analysis is rooted in the ultimate structure of being and is determined by it, it draws from this origin the principle and the secret of its widespread influence and the strange power it still has on us today. For this reason, too, it cannot merely be placed in a survey of economic doctrines. This is fundamentally because the thought of Marx dominates history. Whether subjectivity forms the essence of production, or whether, in a socialist universe to come, it is withdrawn from production and restored to itself, subjectivity constitutes in any event the basis and the single theme of the conceptual development. Marx's thought places us before the profound question: What is life?

Notes

Introduction: The Theory of Marx's Texts

1. Frederick Engels, Preface to the *Communist Manifesto*, trans. Samuel Moore, in *The Revolutions of 1848*, ed. David Fernbach (Harmondsworth/Baltimore: Penguin Books Inc.), 1973, p. 65.

2. Karl Marx, *Oeuvres complètes*, I (Paris: Gallimard, La Pléiade), 1963, p. 1463; our italics.

3. Frederick Engels, *Ludwig Feuerbach and the End of Classical German Philosophy*, in Karl Marx and Frederick Engels, *Selected Works* (London: Lawrence and Wishart), 1968, p. 604.

4. In D. Riazanov, *Karl Marx, homme, penseur et révolutionnaire* (Paris: Anthropos), 1968, p. 78.

5. Herbert Marcuse, *Reason and Revolution* (Boston: Beacon Press), 1960, p. 258.

6. E. Mandel, *La formation de la pensée économique de Karl Marx* (Paris: Maspero), 1967, p. 154.

7. Riazanov, Paper on the literary heritage of Marx and Engels, presented on November 20, 1923, before the Moscow Socialist Academy, in *Karl Marx*, pp. 198–99.

8. Frederick Engels, Preface to the *Communist Manifesto*, p. 66.

9. *Socialisme et science positive* (Paris: Giard et Brière), 1897, p. 162.

10. Riazanov, Paper on the literary heritage of Marx and Engels, p. 195.

11. "L'Idéologie allemande et les thèses sur Feuerbach," in *L'homme et la société*, special issue, 150th anniversary of Karl Marx, January–March, 1968 (Paris: Anthropos).

12. Louis Althusser, *For Marx*, trans. Ben Brewster (London: Verso Edition), 1979, pp. 83–84.

13. Ibid., p. 156.

14. Ibid., p. 32; Althusser's italics.

15. Ibid., p. 38.

16. Ibid.

17. Ibid., p. 104.

18. ". . . to explain this *paradoxical dialectic* whose most extraordinary episode this is, the *Manuscripts* that Marx never published . . ." (ibid., p. 160; Althusser's italics); ". . . a text which *he never published*" (ibid., p. 36; Althusser's italics).

19. *A Contribution to the Critique of Political Economy*, trans. S. W. Ryazanskaya, ed. Maurice Dobbs (New York: International Publishers), 1970, p. 22. Our italics. We know, moreover, that for more than a year Marx and Engels did everything that they could to have their work published.

20. Althusser, *For Marx*, p. 223.

21. Ibid., p. 229.

22. Marx's letter to his father dated November 10, 1837, is revealing in this respect.

23. *The German Ideology* (Moscow: Progress Publishers), 1976, 3d ed., p. 253.

24. Cf. Althusser, *For Marx*, pp. 227–29.

25. Cf. Martin Heidegger, *Kant and the Problem of Metaphysics*, trans. James S. Churchill (Bloomington: Indiana University Press), 1962, p. 207.

Chapter 1: The Critique of Political Essence

1. *Critique of Hegel's Doctrine of the State,* in *Early Writings,* trans. Rodney Livingston and Gregor Benton (New York: Vintage Books), 1975, p. 61; Marx, Engels, *Werke,* I (Berlin: Dietz), 1961, p. 205. (Henceforth cited, in accordance with the French text, as D, I, with page reference following).

2. Ibid., p. 62; D, I, p. 206.

3. Ibid., p. 63; D, I, p. 207.

4. Ibid., p. 62; D, I, p. 206.

5. Ibid., p. 63; D, I, p. 208.

6. Ibid., p. 62; D, I, p. 206.

7. Ibid., p. 61; D, I, p. 206.

8. Ibid., p. 62; D, I, p. 206; our italics.

9. Ibid., p. 69; D, I, p. 212.

10. Ibid., p. 67; D, I, p. 211.

11. Ibid., p. 109; D, I, p. 250.

12. Ibid.

13. Ibid., p. 151; D, I, p. 288.

14. Hegel states: "The will is the unity of both these moments. It is particularity reflected into itself and so brought back to universality, i.e. it is individuality." *Hegel's Philosophy of Right,* trans. T. M. Knox (Oxford: Clarendon Press), 1952, p. 23. All references to the *Philosophy of Right* will quote from this translation.

15. Ibid., § 279, p. 181.

16. Ibid., § 279, pp. 181–82.

17. Cf. *Critique of Hegel's Doctrine of the State,* p. 93; D, I, p. 236: ". . . the subject here is the pure self-determination of the will, the simple concept itself; it is the essence of the will, which functions as a mystical determining force; it is no real, individual . . . willing . . ."; and later Marx speaks of "an action of the Idea devoid of all content" (ibid.)

18. *Hegel's Philosophy of Right,* § 279, p. 182.

19. *Critique of Hegel's Doctrine of the State,* p. 84; D, I, p. 228.

20. Ibid., p. 83; D, I, p. 227.

21. We already catch a glimpse of this thesis, however, when we see Marx "demand . . . a constitution that had the property and principle of advancing in step with *consciousness;* i.e. advancing in step with *real human beings*—which is very possible when 'man' has become the principle of the constitution" (ibid., p. 75; D, I, p. 218; our italics).

22. Ibid., p. 87; D, I, p. 231.

23. Ibid., p. 88; D, I, p. 231.

24. Ibid., p. 87; D, I, pp. 230–31.

25. Ibid., p. 72; D, I, p. 215.

26. Ibid., p. 80; D, I, p. 225.

27. Ibid., our italics; D, I, p. 224.

28. Ibid., p. 87; D, I, p. 231.

29. Ibid., p. 88; D, I, p. 224.

30. Ibid., pp. 124–25, translation modified; D, I, p. 264.

31. Ibid., p. 125, translation modified; D, I, p. 264.

32. Ibid., translation modified.

33. Ibid., p. 126; D, I, p. 265.

34. Ibid., translation modified.

35. *Economic and Philosophical Manuscripts,* in *Early Writings,* p. 389.

36. *Critique of Hegel's Doctrine of the State,* p. 155; D, I, p. 293.

37. Ibid., p. 156; D, I, p. 293.

38. Ibid., p. 98; D, I, p. 241.

39. Ibid., p. 175; D, I, p. 311.

40. Ibid., p. 88; D, I, p. 231.

41. Ibid.

42. Ibid., p. 89; D, I, pp. 232–33.

43. Ibid., pp. 88–89; D, I, p. 232.

44. Ibid., p. 88; D, I, p. 231.

45. Ibid.; D, I, p. 232.

46. Ibid., p. 89; D, I, p. 233.

47. Ibid., pp. 90–91; D, I, p. 234.

48. Ibid., p. 90; D, I, p. 233.

49. This was frequently pointed out by Jean Hyppolite.

50. Ibid., p. 131; D, I, p. 270.

51. Ibid.

52. Ibid., p. 141; D, I, p. 279.

53. Ibid., p. 142, translation modified; D, I, p. 280.

54. Ibid., pp. 142–43; D, I, p. 280.

55. Ibid., p. 143, translation modified; D, I, pp. 280–81.

56. Ibid.; D, I, p. 281.

57. Ibid.

58. Ibid., p. 142, translation modified; D, I, pp. 279–80.

59. Ibid., p. 144, translation modified; D, I, p. 282.

60. Ibid., p. 145; D, I, p. 283.

61. Ibid., p. 147; D, I, p. 284.

62. Ibid., translation modified; D, I, p. 285.

63. Ibid., p. 127; D, I, p. 266.

64. Ibid.

65. Ibid., p. 112; D, I, pp. 252–53.

66. Ibid., p. 113; D, I, p. 254.

67. Ibid., p. 112; D, I, p. 253.

68. Ibid.

69. Ibid., p. 115; D, I, p. 255.

70. Ibid., p. 114; D, I, p. 254.

71. Cf. ibid., p. 167; D, I, p. 303.

72. Ibid., p. 169; D, I, p. 306.

73. Ibid.

74. Ibid., p. 168; D, I, p. 305.

75. Ibid., p. 166; D, I, p. 303.

76. Ibid., p. 169; D, I, p. 306.

77. Ibid., p. 171; D, I, p. 308.

78. Ibid., p. 169; D, I, p. 306.

79. Ibid., p. 174; D, I, p. 310.

80. Ibid., p. 167; D, I, p. 304; in French in the original text.

81. Ibid.

82. Ibid., p. 173; D, I, p. 310.

83. Ibid., p. 174; D, I, p. 310.

84. Ibid.

85. Ibid.

86. Ibid., p. 175; D, I, p. 311.

87. Ludwig Feuerbach, *The Essence of Christianity*, trans. George Elliot (New York: Harper & Row), 1957, p. 35.

88. Ibid.

89. Ibid., p. 91.

90. *Critique of Hegel's Doctrine of the State*, p. 185; D, I, p. 321.
91. Ibid., p. 186; D, I, p. 322; our italics.
92. Ibid., p. 187; D, I, p. 322; our italics.
93. Ibid.
94. Cf. ibid.
95. Ibid., p. 87; D, I, p. 230.
96. Ibid., p. 77; D, I, p. 222.
97. Ibid., pp. 77–78; D, I, p. 222.
98. Ibid., p. 188; D, I, p. 323.
99. Ibid., p. 79; D, I, p. 223.
100. Ibid., p. 148; D, I, p. 285.
101. Ibid., p. 190; D, I, p. 326.
102. Ibid., pp. 189–90; D, I, p. 325.
103. Feuerbach, *The Essence of Christianity*, p. 23.
104. Although elsewhere Feuerbach, who was already deep in self-contradictions, tried to ascribe an existence to the species itself as such.
105. Feuerbach, *The Essence of Christianity*, p. 184.
106. Ibid., p. 158.
107. *Critique of Hegel's Doctrine of the State*, p. 84; D, I, p. 228.

Chapter 2: The Humanism of the Young Marx

1. "Compared with Hegel," Marx will later say, "Feuerbach is extremely poor" (Marx to J. B. Schweitzer, London, January 24, 1865, in *The Poverty of Philosophy*, [New York: International Publishers], 1963, p. 194).
2. Cf. *Economic and Philosophical Manuscripts* in *Early Writings*, p. 347.
3. Feuerbach, *The Essence of Christianity*, p. 2.
4. "Only by uniting man with nature can we conquer the supranaturalistic egoism of Christianity" (ibid., p. 270).
5. " . . . sex is the cord which connects the individuality with the species" (ibid., p. 170).
6. "Man and woman together are the existence of the race" (ibid., p. 167).
7. "Hence the man who does not deny his manhood is conscious that he is only a part of being, which needs another part for the making up of the whole of true humanity" (ibid.).
8. Ibid., p. 81.
9. Ibid.
10. Ibid., p. 82.
11. Ibid.
12. Ibid., pp. 82–83; our italics.
13. Ibid., pp. 85–86; italics correspond to those of the French translation of Feuerbach.
14. Hegel, *Phenomenology of Mind*, trans. J. B. Baillie (New York: Harper Colophon Books), 1967, p. 81.
15. *Economic and Philosophical Manuscripts*, pp. 385–86.
16. Ibid., p. 386.
17. Ibid., p. 328; our italics.
18. Ibid., p. 329.
19. Cf. ibid.
20. Ibid., pp. 328–29.
21. Ibid., p. 329; Marx's italics.
22. Ibid.

23. Ibid.
24. Ibid.
25. Ibid., p. 349.
26. Ibid.
27. Marx, Engels, *Historich-Kritische Gesamtausgabe Werke* (MEGA) (Berlin: Dietz Verlag), 1975, I, 3, p. 547.
28. *Economic and Philosophical Manuscripts*, p. 352.
29. Ibid., note.
30. Ibid., pp. 350–51.
31. Ibid., p. 350; Marx's italics.
32. Ibid., pp. 349–50; Marx's italics.
33. *A Contribution to the Critique of Hegel's Philosophy of Right. Introduction*, in *Early Writings*, p. 244; D, I, pp. 350–51.
34. *On the Jewish Question*, in *Early Writings*, p. 216; D, I, pp. 350–51.
35. *A Contribution to the Critique of Hegel's Philosophy of Right*, pp. 244–45; D, I, p. 379.
36. Ibid., p. 251; D, I, p. 385.
37. Ibid., p. 252; D, I, p. 386.
38. Ibid.
39. Ibid., p. 251; D, I, p. 386.
40. Ibid., p. 246; D, I, p. 381.
41. Cf. ibid., pp. 253–55; D, I, pp. 387–88.
42. Ibid., p. 253; D, I, p. 387.
43. Cf. ibid., p. 254; D, I, p. 388.
44. Ibid., pp. 255–56; D, I, p. 390.
45. Ibid., p. 257; D, I, p. 391; our italics.
46. Ibid., p. 251; D, I, p. 385.
47. Ibid., p. 256; D, I, p. 390.
48. Ibid., p. 257; D, I, p. 391.
49. This is notably the erroneous interpretation offered by Kojève in his *Introduction à la lecture de Hegel* (Paris: Gallimard), 1947, p. 472, note; pp. 483–85, note.
50. As we know, Cartesian physics was constituted in opposition to the Aristotelian conception of nature as a living power. If German dialectic, as its germ is found in alchemy, can claim an origin in ancient thought, one must look in the direction more of Aristotle than of Plato. But as regards the problem which occupies us here, alchemy cannot simply be reduced to a distant echo of Aristotelianism for the sole reason that alchemy establishes and conceives of a real and total transformation of things rather than the mere completion of their own essence.
51. We refer the reader who is interested in these problems to our work, *The Essence of Manifestation*, (The Hague: Nijhoff), in particular § 70.
52. "It is," says Cottier, "from Luther's translation of the letter to the Philippians that Hegel borrowed the term *Entäusserung* out of which he forged the substantive but which he also often uses in the form of the verb" (*L'Athéisme du jeune Marx* [Paris: Vrin], 1950, p. 28).
53. On all of this, cf. Enrico de Negri, *La teologia di Lutero, Rivelazione e Dialettica* (Firenze: La Nuova Italia Editoria), 1967, p. 315. We should also like to mention the German translation of this work: *Offenbarung und Dialektik Luthers Realtheologie* (Darmstadt: Wissenschafliche Buchgesellschaft), 1973, XV, p. 229.
54. The exact sentence by which Engels' book, *Ludwig Feuerbach and the End of Classical German Philosophy*, is concluded is the following: "The German working-class movement is the inheritor of German classical philosophy" (London: Lawrence and Wishart), 1968, p. 632.

55. Karl Marx, *The Class Struggles in France: 1848–1850*, trans. Paul Jackson, in *Surveys from Exile*, ed. with an Introduction by David Fernbach (New York: Vintage Books), 1974, p. 90.

56. On the question cf. G. Cottier, *Du romantisme au Marxisme* (Alsatia, 1961), p. 40.

57. It is remarkable that the major example given by Schelling of this irony of God is precisely that of Christ on the cross.

58. *The Eighteenth Brumaire of Louis Bonaparte*, trans. Ben Fowkes, in Fernbach, *Surveys from Exile*, p. 237; our italics.

59. *The Class Struggles in France*, p. 35.

60. Ibid., p. 43; Marx's italics. Here one finds another idea which belongs to this dialectic of opposites, namely that in the process which devours them, these opposites become less and less numerous, clumping together to form larger and larger, ever more compact masses, so that all of this finally ends in the gigantic confrontation of two opposites which confront one another alone, the bourgeoisie (or capitalism) and the proletariat.

61. *The Communist Manifesto*, p. 75.

62. *The Eighteenth Brumaire of Louis Bonaparte*, p. 189. Marx returned to this idea in *The Communist Manifesto*: "The weapons with which the bourgeoisie felled feudalism to the ground are now turned against the bourgeoisie itself" (p. 327). And once again: "The bourgeoisie itself, therefore, supplies the proletariat with its own elements of political and general education; in other words, it furnishes the proletariat with weapons for fighting the bourgeoisie" (ibid., p. 331).

63. Cf. *The Eighteenth Brumaire of Louis Bonaparte*, pp. 181, 186.

64. Ibid., p. 236.

65. W. Jankélévitch, *L'Odyssée de la conscience dans la dernière philosophie de Schelling* (Paris: Alcan), 1932, p. 196.

66. In this way the existence of evil is justified not only because evil itself is presented as something possible which, as such, has to be fully realized, but also for the more profound reason that it is perhaps nothing other than this summons of the possible, this exigency to try and to do everything, nothing other than temptation. The vertigo experienced when we confront the possible also expresses the metaphysical law of being and of its deepest volition, and this under the appearance of evil and even if it is lived as sin.

67. *The Critique of Hegel's Philosophy of Right*, p. 247; D, I, p. 382.

68. Ibid., p. 257; D, I, p. 391.

69. *The Eighteenth Brumaire of Louis Bonaparte*, p. 236.

70. Ibid., p. 170.

71. In Riazanov, *Karl Marx, homme, penseur et révolutionnaire*, p. 52.

72. Cf. *Contribution to the Critique of Hegel's Philosophy of Right*, pp. 247–48; D, I, p. 382.

73. *The Eighteenth Brumaire of Louis Bonaparte*, p. 146.

74. *Oeuvres*, I (La Pléiade), p. 995. It is interesting to note that this sentence does not appear in the German text and that Marx added it on to the French translation. In this final concession to rhetoric can be recognized the swan song of the dialectic. (Trans. note: The corresponding text in the English translation, *Capital*, 1, Part IV, Section 9, p. 490, does not include this addition.)

Chapter 3: The Reduction of Totalities

1. *The Poverty of Philosophy* (New York: International Publishers), 1963, p. 91; our italics. The text which is quoted by Marx and which he includes as part of his own argument is taken from a work by Thomas Cooper, *Lectures on the Elements of Political Economy* (Columbia, 1826).

2. Ibid.; Marx's italics.

3. Ibid., p. 96.

4. Ibid., p. 92; our italics.

5. Ibid., p. 95.

6. *The German Ideology*, p. 221.

7. Cf. ibid., p. 229.

8. Ibid.

9. Cf. ibid., p. 502, and also the critique of the "true socialists" who imagine that if individuals are unhappy or corrupt, the fault lies with society (ibid., p. 491).

10. *Grundrisse, Foundations of the Critique of Political Economy*, trans. Martin Nicolaus (New York: Vintage Books), 1973, p. 94.

11. *The Holy Family, or Critique of Critical Criticism*, trans. Richard Dixon and Clemens Dutt (Moscow: Progress Publishers), 1975, p. 110.

12. Ibid., p. 101.

13. Ibid., p. 93. And again: "For Herr Bauer, as for Hegel, truth is an automaton that proves itself. Man must follow it. As Hegel, the result of real development is nothing but the truth proven, i.e., brought to consciousness" (ibid.).

14. Ibid.

15. *The German Ideology*, p. 37.

16. Ibid., p. 43.

17. Ibid., p. 36.

18. Cf. ibid., pp. 47–48.

19. Ibid., p. 47; our italics.

20. *Capital*, 1, pp. 183–84. Cf. also *A Contribution to the Critique of Political Economy*, p. 36, and *Capital* 1, pp. 177, 184.

21. *Capital*, 1, p. 169.

22. A. Gramsci, *Opere complete* (Turino: Einaudi), 1952, II, p. 217.

23. *Capital*, 2, p. 344.

24. *The Communist Manifesto*, p. 67.

25. Martin Heidegger, *Sein und Zeit* (Halle: Niemeyer), 1941, p. 329; *Being and Time*, trans. John Macquarrie and Edward Robinson (New York: Harper & Row), 1962, pp. 431–32.

26. Ibid.

27. Cf. *The German Ideology*, p. 45, where Marx speaks of history in terms of the activity of a whole succession of generations.

28. *The Poverty of Philosophy*, pp. 98, 100.

29. *Grundrisse*, p. 265.

30. *The German Ideology*, p. 85; Marx's italics.

31. Marx, as we know, did not invent this concept of class. We find it not only in Hegel but also in contemporary French historians and in the book by Lorenz von Stein, *Socialisme et communisme de la France contemporaine*, published in 1842, which Marx read during this period.

32. *The German Ideology*, p. 85; Marx's italics.

33. Ibid., p. 380.

34. Ibid.; our italics.

35. Ibid., p. 462.

36. *The Eighteenth Brumaire of Louis Bonaparte*, p. 239.

37. Ibid.

38. Another "example," in the sense of Husserlian exemplification, whose role is to display the "essence" of a phenomenon, would be supplied by the description that Marx gives of vagabondage at the end of the fifteenth century and during the whole of the sixteenth century. We know that this concerns peasants who were expropriated from their

land by the great feudal lords and condemned to wander "with neither home nor hearth" until the day when industrial development was to provide them with a job. This mass of "beggars, robbers, vagabonds" itself already forms a class as well as constituting the origin of the modern industrial proletariat. The utter isolation of these individuals who have been stripped of all their possessions and of their roots is a constitutive characteristic of their "class," and this is so as an individual characteristic. Because the latter is found, according to Marx, in each proletarian in modern industry, because these beggars are the "fathers of the present working class" (*Capital*, 1, p. 734), the proletariat will possess, due to the very nature of its origin, that tragic aspect in which the tragedy is always and inevitably that of the individual. This is why the descriptions of the industrial proletariat that one finds in *Capital* will always place the individual at the center of the analysis, as its proper theme.

39. Marx explicitly ascribed to the power of representation belonging to thought the transformation of real social determinations into ideal conditions, the hypostasis of the latter in the form of "relations" which are themselves ideal and which possess a necessity that has become that of ideality. Speaking of the conditions under which men live and of the forms of relations which inevitably accompany them, Marx says that "*the personal and social relations thereby given, had to take the form—insofar as they were expressed in thoughts—of ideal conditions and necessary relations . . .*" (*The German Ideology*, p. 198; our italics). In this way arises the objectivist illusion that holds social conditions to be "objective" conditions and, finally, structures which are presented, on the one hand, as the regulating principles of all empirical determinations reduced to the role and the condition of "elements" and, on the other hand, as the sole themes of theoretical investigation, as the "objects" of science. Marx questioned the alleged objectivity of these determinations, an objectivity resulting from their separation from individual life understood—and this will be the essential theme of his thought—as activity. A note in the margin of the manuscript of *The German Ideology* states: "So-called objective historiography consists precisely in treating the historical relations separately from activity. Reactionary character" (p. 63).

40. *The Eighteenth Brumaire of Louis Bonaparte*, p. 239.
41. *The Class Struggles in France*, p. 91.
42. *The German Ideology*, p. 87.
43. Ibid., p. 86.
44. Ibid., pp. 85–86.
45. *Capital*, 1, p. 10.
46. *Capital*, 2, p. 351.
47. Ibid., pp. 375–76; our italics.
48. *The German Ideology*, pp. 262–63.
49. Marx distinguished between personal determinations, those that come out of the movement of life and out of the will proper to it, and social determinations that result within this life from its subordination to a type of labor, that is, to the social conditions of existence. He explicitly cited personal determinations as being essential and social determinations as accidental. Both, however, belong to subjectivity; what must be understood is how a determination belonging to life is nevertheless lived as an "outside" constraint. On all of this, cf. ibid., pp. 86–87, and the French text of the present work, vol. I, pp. 243–48.
50. *The Poverty of Philosophy, Appendix*, "Marx to P. V. Annenkov," p. 189; "social relations" italicized by Marx. Cf. also "Wage Labour and Capital" in Karl Marx and Frederick Engels, *Selected Works* (London: Lawrence and Wishart), 1968, p. 81.
51. *The German Ideology*, p. 91; our italics.
52. Ibid., p. 62.
53. Ibid., p. 85.

54. Cf. ibid., p. 62.

55. "Marx to P. V. Annenkov," p. 181.

56. *The German Ideology*, p. 463; our italics.

57. Cf. ibid., p. 50.

58. Cf. ibid., p. 72.

59. Cf. ibid.

60. Cf. ibid., p. 73.

61. Cf. ibid., pp. 50–51, 82, 84, 464–65.

62. Cf. *The Poverty of Philosophy*, pp. 127–28.

63. *Capital*, 1, p. 360; our italics.

64. Ibid.

65. Ibid., p. 361.

66. Ibid., p. 363.

67. Ibid.

68. *The German Ideology*, p. 86.

69. *Capital*, 1, p. 264.

70. Ibid., p. 361.

71. Ibid.

72. Cf. ibid.

73. Ibid., pp. 361–62.

74. Ibid., p. 361.

75. Ibid., p. 423.

76. Ibid., p. 361. The full comprehension of this text can be attained only at the end of our analysis, when the problematic of the forces of production will have clearly and definitively separated the subjective from the objective element in them; cf. our conclusion to the present work.

77. *Capital*, 1, p. 364.

78. *The German Ideology*, p. 51.

79. *The Poverty of Philosophy*, p. 138.

80. Ibid.

81. Marx's economic analysis will be based upon this decisive thesis. In fact, if the machine itself worked, it would produce value and capital, which possessed the machine could grow of itself.

82. ". . . the absurd fable of Menenius Agrippa which makes man a mere fragment of his own being" (*Capital*, 1, p. 360).

83. Cf. also *The German Ideology*, p. 418.

Chapter 4: The Determination of Reality

1. Cf., for example, *L'essence du christianisme*, trad. J.-P. Osier (Paris: Maspero), 1968, p. 108. (In the Preface to the second edition; this text belongs to the opening paragraphs omitted in the English translation.)

2. Ibid.

3. Ludwig Feuerbach, *Provisional Theses for the Reform of Philosophy*, §32, in *Kleinere Schriften II (1839–1846)*, vol. 9 of *Gesammelte Werke*, ed. Werner Schuffenhauer (Berlin: Akademie-Verlag), 1970.

4. Feuerbach, *The Essence of Christianity*, pp. XXXIV–XXXV.

5. Ibid., p. 63.

6. Ibid., p. 198.

7. Ibid., p. 63.

8. Ibid., p. 54.

9. Ibid., p. 62.

10. Ibid., p. 48.

11. This confusion persists throughout Feuerbach's work; it is found, for example, in this passage from *Provisional Theses*, §43: "A being without affection is, however, nothing other than a being *without sensation, without matter*" (p. 253; italics in original).

12. *Economic and Philosophical Manuscripts*. p. 389.

13. Ibid., p. 399; "self-externalizing sensuousness" is italicized by Marx.

14. Ibid., p. 389.

15. Ibid.

16. Ibid., p. 390.

17. Ibid., p. 389.

18. Ibid., p. 390.

19. Feuerbach, *The Essence of Christianity*, pp. 4–5.

20. Ludwig Feuerbach, *Principles of the Philosophy of the Future*, trans. Manfred H. Vogel, Library of Liberal Arts (Indianapolis and New York: Bobbs-Merrill), 1966, p. 9.

21. Feuerbach, *The Essence of Christianity*, p. 5.

22. *Economic and Philosophical Manuscripts*, p. 390; our italics.

23. Ibid., p. 391; our italics.

24. Ibid., p. 375.

25. Ibid.

26. Ibid.

27. Ibid., p. 353.

28. Ibid.

29. Ibid.

30. Ibid., p. 352.

31. Ibid., p. 353.

32. Ibid., p. 352.

33. Ibid.; our italics.

34. We have already seen this, for example, in relation to the will, cf. *supra*, chapter 1, pp. 22–23.

35. Feuerbach, *Principles of the Philosophy of the Future*, p. 44.

36. Hegel, *The Encyclopedia*, § 244; quoted by Marx in the *Economic and Philosophical Manuscripts*, p. 397.

37. *Economic and Philosophical Manuscripts*, p. 398.

38. Ibid., p. 386.

39. Ibid., p. 387.

40. Ibid., p. 388.

41. Ibid., p. 389.

42. Ibid., pp. 391–92; Marx's italics.

43. Ibid., p. 392.

44. Ibid., p. 393.

45. Ibid., p. 392.

46. Ibid., p. 393.

47. Ibid.

48. Ibid., p. 392.

49. Ibid.

50. Ibid., p. 394.

51. Ibid., p. 391; our italics.

52. Ibid., p. 387.

53. Ibid., pp. 399–400.

54. On this, cf. our general interpretation of Hegelian ontology in *The Essence of Manifestation*, II, Appendix.

55. Hegel, *Encyclopedia*, § 384; our italics. Quoted by Marx in the *Economic and Philosophical Manuscripts*, p. 400.

56. *Economic and Philosophical Manuscripts*, p. 391.

57. Ibid., p. 353; our italics.

58. Ibid.; our italics.

59. Ibid., p. 352; Marx's italics.

60. Ibid., p. 391.

61. Ibid., p. 353; our italics.

62. Ibid., p. 355.

63. Ibid.

64. Ibid., pp. 352–53.

65. Ibid., p. 355.

66. Feuerbach, *The Essence of Christianity*, p. 5; our italics.

67. *"The abstract hostility between sense and intellect* is inevitable so long as the human sense [*Sinn*] for nature, the human significance [*Sinn*] of nature and hence the natural sense of man, has not yet been produced by man's own labor" (*Economic and Philosophical Manuscripts*, p. 364; our italics).

68. Ibid., p. 399.

69. Ibid., pp. 355–56.

70. Ibid., p. 352; our italics.

71. Feuerbach, *The Essence of Christianity*, p. 5.

72. *The German Ideology*, p. 45.

73. Ibid., p. 616.

74. The sixth thesis states: "Feuerbach resolves the religious essence into the human essence. But the human essence is no abstraction inherent in each single individual. In its reality it is the ensemble of social relations."

75. Cf. the article quoted in *L'homme et la société*, Jan.–March 1968, pp. 18–35, and in particular p. 34: "The scientific character of Marx's text consists in the fact of thinking of structures in terms of individuals and vice versa. . . ."

76. In this is revealed to us the fundamental meaning of the concept of theory *which designates both the intuition of the sensuous world and the categorial determination of this world, its "theory" stricto sensu.* That this is indeed the Feuerbachian concept of theory which the "Theses on Feuerbach" will challenge is explicitly affirmed in this text of *The Essence of Christianity* (p. 187): ". . . the essential object of theory—*theory in its most original and general sense, namely that of objective intuition and experience, of the intellect, of science . . .*" (our italics; translation modified). This Feuerbachian definition of theory—upon which our entire analysis is based—suffices to show the perfectly illusory character of recent interpretations which try to present Marx's thought as an attempt to substitute "theory," precisely, for the immediate and naïve experience of sensuous perception, this substitution being understood, moreover, as "ideology" which has been repressed in the name of "science." An interpretation such as this can arise only out of the complete ignorance of the philosophical and conceptual framework of Marx's thought in 1845.

77. Our italics.

78. According to Marx, the neo-Hegelians, in their apparent opposition to Hegel, simply represent the scattered pieces of the system in decomposition: "Their polemics against Hegel and against one another are confined to this—each takes one aspect of the Hegelian system and turns this against the whole system as well as against the aspects chosen by the others" (*The German Ideology*, p. 35).

79. Hegel, *The Philosophy of Right*, § 142, p. 105.

80. Ibid., § 280, p. 184.

81. Ibid., § 9, p. 24.

82. Hegel, *Phenomenology of Mind*, trans. J. B. Baillie (New York: Harper & Row), 1967, p. 429.

83. Ibid., pp. 516–17.

84. Hegel, *System of Ethical Life and First Philosophy of Spirit*, trans. H. S. Harris and T. M. Knox (Albany: State University of New York Press), 1979.

85. Ibid., p. 211.

86. Hegel, *The Philosophy of Right*, Preface, pp. 12–13.

87. Hegel, *First Philosophy of Spirit*, p. 211.

88. Cf. Hegel, *System der Sittlichkeit*, p. 432; *Jenenser Realphilosophie*, II, pp. 197–98; *Wissenschaft der Logik*, II, p. 398; these references are given by G. Planty-Bonjour in his Introduction to Hegel's *First Philosophy of Mind* (Paris: Presses universitaires de France), 1969, p. 37, note 2.

89. Cf. Hegel, *First Philosophy of Spirit*, p. 246.

90. Ibid., p. 247.

91. Ibid., p. 243.

92. Hegel, *Phenomenology of Mind*, p. 517.

93. Ibid., p. 516.

94. Hegel, *The Philosophy of Right*, § 21, p. 30; our italics.

95. They also run up against the same aporias. With respect to this, cf. our study "The Hegelian concept of Manifestation" in *The Essence of Manifestation*.

96. *Economic and Philosophical Manuscripts*, p. 329; our italics.

97. Ibid., p. 396.

98. *The German Ideology*, p. 46.

99. An exception to this can be found, however, in Maine de Biran, with whom Marx was not acquainted. By elucidating in a radical fashion the essence of action, not on the level of thought as did his German contemporaries, but on that of the body, by thus proposing for the first time in the history of Western culture a problematic of real, individual, and concrete action, a problematic of "praxis," the thought of Maine de Biran is of critical importance for any serious interpretation of Marx and, in general, of "material labor."

100. Thus one is led to doubt the assertion made by G. Planty-Bonjour in his Introduction to Hegel's *First Philosophy of Mind*, p. 33: "To tie the actualization of mind to the sphere of labor is a conception radically foreign to idealism." It was Adam Smith, of course, who proposed the theme of labor to the reflection of the young Hegel, but the fundamental concept of self-objectification supplied Hegelian idealism with the schema that would enable it not only to give an immediate philosophical interpretation to labor but also to integrate the essence of labor in the inner structure of being, and, what is more, to interpret this structure as identical with labor itself. In this way is explained in particular the intervention of the term "labor" in the Preface to *The Phenomenology of Mind*, the definition of the essence of man as labor, the determining function recognized in the latter in the process of culture formation, etc. Georges Cottier has well shown the affinity between the Hegelian-Marxist interpretation of labor and the idealist concept of action as self-production and self-objectification. But this interpretation is found in Marx himself only in the 1844 *Economic and Philosophical Manuscripts;* it is with this interpretation that the "Theses on Feuerbach" make a deliberate break.

101. In a certain sense Marx's affirmation is most questionable: never was idealism developed in opposition to materialism, never was the concept of action elaborated by it as an antithesis to that of intuition. *The fact is that here Marx is retracing not the history of philosophy but simply that of his own thought.* The text of the first thesis is all the more enlightening for this reason.

102. This is the reproach one would be tempted to address to the interpretation proposed by G. Cottier in *L'Athéisme du jeune Marx*, despite its remarkable character, if it were not that it is deliberately confined to the study of those texts written before 1845.

103. The term "activity of the senses" is found several times in Feuerbach (for example, *The Essence of Christianity*, p. XXXIV, Preface to the second edition); it

defines, in addition, the reality of action by the fact that the latter refers to sensuous objects and is therefore particular as are these objects. This action is explicitly understood as objectification: "What is it to make, to create, to produce, but to make that which in the first instance is only subjective . . . into something objective, perceptible . . ." (ibid., p. 109).

104. *The German Ideology*, p. 41.
105. Ibid., pp. 47–48.
106. Ibid., p. 44.
107. Ibid., p. 46.
108. Ibid.
109. Ibid., p. 47.
110. Ibid., p. 46.
111. Cf. ibid., pp. 46–47. And also the text of the eighth thesis: "All social life is essentially practical."
112. With regard to this, Feuerbachian anthropology is not the antithesis but the ridiculous subproduct.
113. Let us recall that Husserl defended this thesis in his *Prolegemena to Pure Logic* in order to safeguard the autonomy and the rational consistency of logic in the face of the psychological reduction that threatened it at the end of the last century. It nonetheless remains that the Husserlian problematic is wholly located within a theoretical perspective and thereby misses the most original essence of being as it was conceived of by Marx.
114. Cf., for example, this passage from the article on the freedom of the press published in May 1842 in the *Rheinische Zeitung*, in which Marx speaks of "these liberal Germans who imagine they serve freedom by placing it in the starry heaven of the imagination, instead of leaving it on the solid ground of reality. These reasoners of the imagination, these sentimental enthusiasts, who abhor any contact of their ideal with vulgar reality and see in this contact a profanation, are men to whom the rest of us Germans owe the fact that in part, up until today, freedom has remained on the level of the imagination and of sentimentality" (D, I, p. 68). To what extent this Hegelian critique of abstract freedom belongs to the philosophical horizon of the neo-Hegelians before becoming a commonplace of Marxism can also be seen in this letter to Marx, dated March 1843, in which Ruge declares, concerning the freedom of German philosophers, ". . . one tolerated their boldness of declaring *in abstracto* that man is free . . . this liberty said to be scientific or in principle which resigns itself to remaining unrealized . . ." (Costes, V, p. 192).
115. The reason why normativity cannot be reduced to the rationalist concept of fundamental apodicticity is that it is not directed toward the privileged mode of theoretical actuality but toward that which escapes it, that which is an abyss for it.
116. Our italics.

Chapter 5: The Place of Ideology

1. Immanuel Kant, *Critique of Pure Reason*, trans. F. Max Müller (New York: Doubleday, Anchor Books), 1966, note, pp. 265–66.
2. *The German Ideology*, p. 42.
3. *The Communist Manifesto*, in *The Revolutions of 1848*, p. 85.
4. *The German Ideology*, p. 42.
5. In *Early Writings*, p. 426.
6. *The German Ideology*, p. 36.
7. Stirner, *L'Unique et sa propriété*, trans. H. Lasvignes (Paris: Editions de la Revue blanche), 1900, p. 21; our italics.

8. Sartre, *L'existentialisme est un humanisme*, (Paris: Nagel), 1946, p. 31.

9. Stirner, p. 85; our italics.

10. Ibid., p. 116.

11. *The German Ideology*, p. 314.

12. Ibid., p. 304.

13. Ibid., p. 313.

14. This is Feuerbach's concept of representation when he declares that God is the representation of man or the dream the representation of reality. The relation that is established between these terms is, as we have seen, the following: what is represented is the same thing as that which it represents, but this thing then exists in the dimension of irreality.

15. *The German Ideology*, p. 42.

16. Ibid., p. 42. The term "mental production" employed by Marx here shows that it is absurd to wish to consider theoretical activity as a "practice" and to christen it, for example, "theoretical practice." This is to destroy Marx's entire problematic concerning the foundation of ideology, only to slip back into ideology.

17. *Ludwig Feuerbach and the End of Classical German Philosophy*, in Karl Marx and Frederick Engels, *Selected Works*, p. 607.

18. *The German Ideology*, p. 42.

19. Ibid., p. 268; our italics.

20. Ibid., p. 349; our italics.

21. Ibid., p. 304.

22. Ibid., p. 281.

23. Ibid., pp. 280–81. Is there any need to emphasize once again the complete reversal of the Hegelian problematic that occurs here? The universal is no longer the substance which the individual comes to resemble at the end of his labor and of his history; it is a determination and a feature of his own life, and one that results from it, from his practice.

24. Cf. ibid., pp. 280–81.

25. Cf. ibid., pp. 67–68, and also ibid., pp. 41–42.

26. Ibid., p. 42; our italics.

27. *The Poverty of Philosophy*, p. 109; our italics. Is it by chance that this decisive proposition appears word-for-word in the famous letter that Marx wrote to Annenkov during the same period, Dec. 28, 1846? Cf. ibid., p. 189.

28. *The German Ideology*, p. 359.

29. Ibid., p. 174.

30. Ibid., p. 173.

31. Ibid., pp. 174–75.

32. Ibid., p. 29.

33. Michel Foucault, *Les Mots et les choses* (Paris: Gallimard), 1966, p. 74. Cf. also: "However, if we examine classical thought at the level of that which made it possible archeologically, we see that the dissociation of the sign and resemblance at the beginning of the seventeenth century brought to light the following new figures: probability, analysis, combinations, systems and universal language, not as successive themes . . . but as a single network of necessities. *And this is what made possible those individuals whom we call Hobbes, or Berkeley, or Hume, or Condillac*" (ibid., p. 77; our italics).

34. *The German Ideology*, p. 299; our italics.

35. Cf. *supra*, p. 103.

36. *The German Ideology*, p. 463.

37. Ibid., p. 43.

38. Ibid., pp. 44, 47, notes.

39. Letter to Annenkov, December 28, 1846, in *The Poverty of Philosophy*, p. 189; Marx's italics.

40. Ibid., p. 109.

41. *The German Ideology*, p. 476.

42. *The German Ideology*, p. 346: "Our Sancho first of all transforms the struggle over privilege and equal right into a struggle over the mere "concepts" privileged and equal. In this way he saves himself the trouble of having to know anything about the medieval mode of production, the political expression of which was privilege, and the modern mode of production, of which right as such, equal right, is the expression, or about the relation of these two modes of production to the legal relations which correspond to them."

43. *Grundrisse*, p. 104.

44. Ibid.

45. Letter to J. B. Schweitzer, January 24, 1865, in *The Poverty of Philosophy*, p. 196; our italics.

46. Ibid., p. 126.

47. Ibid., pp. 114–16.

48. Ibid., p. 121.

49. Edmund Husserl, *Logical Investigations*, I, trans. J. N. Findlay (London: Routledge & Kegan Paul), 1970, p. 102.

50. *The Poverty of Philosophy*, p. 116.

51. Ibid., p. 122.

52. *Grundrisse*, pp. 100–101.

53. Ibid., p. 101.

54. Ibid.; our italics.

55. Ibid.

56. Ibid.; our italics.

57. Letter to Annenkov, December 28, 1846, in *The Poverty of Philosophy*, p. 189.

58. Gramsci, *Opere complete*, II, p. 95.

59. *Capital*, 2, p. 34.

60. *Capital*, 3, pp. 897–99.

Chapter 6: The Transcendental Genesis of the Economy

1. *Capital*, 1, p. 8.

2. Ibid., p. 37.

3. Ibid., p. 73.

4. *Critique of the Gotha Programme*, in Karl Marx and Frederick Engels, *Selected Works* (London: Lawrence and Wishart), 1968, p. 323.

5. Ibid., p. 324.

6. Ibid., p. 323.

7. Ibid., p. 324; our italics.

8. Ibid., pp. 323–24.

9. Ibid., p. 324.

10. Ibid.

11. Ibid.

12. Ibid.; our italics.

13. Ibid.; Marx's italics.

14. It will not fail to be objected that one finds in Hegel, that is to say, precisely in a philosophy based on the premise of objective universality, a critique of the concept of equality. Cf., in particular, *Philosophy of Right* § 49. But Hegel's critique is radically different from that of Marx; it signifies that the equality we usually demand is still only the abstract concept of equality to which is opposed the still unequal development of individuals. This is because, for Hegel, equality must be realized and it will be an Idea only through this realization, which is not an ideal end but the actual history of individu-

als and of humanity. It is toward the unity of a common spiritual substance which their own reality gives them and, at the same time, toward equality that all individuals are directed. For Marx, on the contrary, and this is due to the monadic presupposition of his thought, it is equality as such, not its mere concept, which can be criticized or, better, which is absurd.

15. *Critique of the Gotha Programme*, p. 324.

16. Ibid.

17. Ibid., pp. 324–25.

18. *Grundrisse*, p. 171; our italics.

19. *Capital*, 1, p. 37 (translation modified to include the final clause, which is not found in the English translation); our italics. Cf. also *The Critique of Political Economy*, p. 28.

20. *Capital*, 1, p. 38.

21. Ibid.

22. Ibid.

23. Cf. ibid.

24. *The Critique of Political Economy*, p. 30.

25. Ibid.

26. Cf. ibid., p. 29.

27. Ibid., p. 69.

28. Ibid., p. 30.

29. Ibid., p. 32.

30. Cf. ibid., pp. 30–31.

31. Cf. ibid., p. 31.

32. Cf. ibid., p. 32.

33. *Capital*, 1, p. 38.

34. Quoted by Marx in *The Holy Family*, p. 58.

35. Ibid.

36. Ibid.; "empty" and "filled" are italicized by Marx.

37. Ibid., p. 59.

38. Ibid.; our italics.

39. *The Poverty of Philosophy*, pp. 53–54; our italics.

40. Quoted by Marx in *Capital*, 1, p. 47.

41. Ibid., p. 243.

42. Ibid., p. 43; our italics.

43. Ibid., p. 44; our italics.

44. Ibid.

45. *Le Capital (Oeuvres, La Pléiade*, I), 1963, p. 574; also note 1, p. 1636. This sentence was added by Marx to the French edition and is not found in the English translation, cf. *Capital*, 1, p. 46.

46. *Capital*, 1, p. 41.

47. *Capital*, 2, pp. 14–15.

48. *Wages, Price and Profit*, in *Selected Works*, p. 205.

49. "We see then that that which determines the magnitude of the value of any article is the amount of labor socially necessary, or the labor-time socially necessary for its production" (*Capital*, 1, p. 39).

50. Ibid., p. 80, note 2.

51. Cf. *The Critique of Political Economy*, p. 36.

52. Cf. ibid., pp. 68–69.

53. *Grundrisse*, p. 168.

54. Cf. *Capital*, 1, p. 80, note 1.

55. *Grundrisse*, p. 171; our italics.

56. Ibid., p. 143; our italics.
57. *The Critique of Political Economy*, p. 34.
58. Ibid.
59. *Economic and Philosophical Manuscripts*, p. 323.
60. *The Critique of Political Economy*, p. 34.
61. Cf. ibid., p. 35.
62. Cf. ibid., pp. 34–35.
63. Cf. ibid., p. 35.
64. Ibid., p. 34; our italics.
65. *Capital*, 1, p. 72.
66. Ibid.
67. Ibid., p. 95; our italics.
68. *Grundrisse*, p. 140.
69. Ibid., p. 268.
70. Ibid., p. 759.
71. *Capital*, 1, p. 47.
72. *Grundrisse*, p. 856.
73. Ibid., p. 860.
74. Ibid., p. 141; our italics. Cf. also ibid., pp. 856, 860.
75. *Capital*, 1, p. 47.
76. Ibid., p. 72.
77. *Grundrisse*, p. 881.
78. "Just as a Manchester family of factory workers, where the children stand in the exchange relation towards their parents and pay them room and board, does not represent the traditional economic organization of the family, so is the system of modern private exchange not the spontaneous economy of societies" (*Grundrisse*, p. 882).
79. Ibid., p. 304.
80. Ibid.
81. Ibid., p. 691; Marx's italics.
82. Ibid., p. 320; Marx's italics.
83. Cf. ibid., pp. 629–30.
84. Ibid., p. 691.
85. Ibid., p. 692.
86. Cf. ibid.
87. Cf. ibid., p. 312.
88. *The Critique of Political Economy*, p. 41.
89. *Grundrisse*, p. 757.
90. *Capital*, 1, p. 40.
91. *Wages, Price and Profit*, in *Selected Works*, p. 207.
92. *Capital*, 1, p. 46.
93. *Capital*, 3, p. 219.
94. Cf. *Wages, Price and Profit*, pp. 205–206, and *Capital*, 1, p. 39.
95. *Capital*, 1, p. 46; our italics.
96. Ibid., p. 114.
97. *Grundrisse*, p. 149.
98. *The Critique of Political Economy*, p. 123.
99. *Capital*, 1, p. 114.
100. *The Critique of Political Economy*, p. 91.
101. *Grundrisse*, pp. 199–200. Cf. also ibid., pp. 149, 150–51.
102. *The Critique of Political Economy*, p. 89.
103. Cf. *Grundrisse*, p. 198, and also *Capital*, 1, pp. 113, 130, 132.
104. *Grundrisse*, p. 148.

105. Cf. ibid., p. 147.
106. Cf. ibid., p. 151.
107. Ibid., p. 148.
108. Ibid., p. 149.
109. Cf. ibid., p. 198.
110. "The circulation of commodities differs from the direct exchange of products (barter), not only in form but in substance" *Capital*, 1, p. 112.
111. Cf. *Grundrisse*, pp. 146–47.
112. *Critique of Political Economy*, p. 131.
113. Cf. *Grundrisse*, p. 145.
114. *Capital*, 1, p. 109.
115. *Economic and Philosophical Manuscripts*, p. 379.
116. *Grundrisse*, p. 163.
117. *Economic and Philosophical Manuscripts*, p. 379.
118. Ibid., p. 377; our italics, except for *am* and *can do*, which are italicized by Marx.
119. Ibid., pp. 377–79.

Chapter 7: The Reality of Economic Reality

1. *Capital*, 1, p. 566; our italics.
2. *Capital*, 2, p. 202.
3. *Capital*, 1, p. 178.
4. Note to the French translation of *Capital*, explaining the sense of the German expression *Arbeits-Prozess*, Karl Marx, *Oeuvres*, I (La Pléiade), 1963, p. 728.
5. Cf. *Capital*, 1, p. 181.
6. Ibid., p. 184.
7. *Grundrisse*, p. 852.
8. Ibid., p. 493.
9. *Capital*, 1, p. 538.
10. Ibid., pp. 535–36.
11. *Wages, Price and Profit*, p. 209; cf. also: "Such a sale, if it comprised his lifetime, for example, would make him at once the lifelong slave of his employer" (ibid.).
12. *Grundrisse*, p. 780.
13. Ibid., p. 272; our italics; "subjectivity," "living subject," and "worker" are italicized by Marx.
14. Cf. *Capital*, 1, pp. 180, 189.
15. *Grundrisse*, p. 296. On the ultimate meaning of this essential proposition, cf. *supra*, pp. 277–78.
16. Ibid., p. 273.
17. Cf. ibid., p. 305; cf. *supra*, p. 217.
18. Ibid., p. 305.
19. Ibid., pp. 610–11.
20. Ibid., p. 611.
21. Ibid.
22. Ibid.
23. Ibid., p. 612.
24. *Capital*, 1, pp. 46–47, note; our italics.
25. *Capital*, 2, p. 388; our italics.
26. "Wage Labour and Capital," p. 81; Marx's italics.
27. *Capital*, 2, p. 35; our italics.
28. *Grundrisse*, p. 206.
29. Ibid.; our italics.

30. Ibid., p. 267, note.
31. Cf. ibid., p. 536.
32. Cf. ibid., p. 301.
33. *Capital*, 1, p. 146.
34. "It [the commodity] never assumes this value when isolated" (*Capital*, 1, p. 60).
35. Cf. *Grundrisse*, p. 795.
36. Ibid., p. 872.
37. *Capital*, 2, p. 225; our italics.
38. *Grundrisse*, p. 687. One of the essential aims of Marx's analysis, and this is the case here, is to distinguish rigorously between the real properties and the economic properties of the "reality" he is discussing. Cf., for example, the entire analysis of "fixed capital" which represents the value of the instruments of labor, the "fixed" character of this value having nothing to do with the "fixed" nature of the instrument itself, whether machine, warehouse, factory, etc.
39. Cf. *Grundrisse*, pp. 646–47.
40. *Capital*, 1, p. 202.
41. Ibid., p. 40; cf. *The Critique of Political Economy*, p. 28.
42. Cf. *supra*, pp. 212–13, and *Grundrisse*, p. 856.
43. *Capital*, 1, p. 188.
44. Cf. ibid., p. 85, and *The Critique of Political Economy*, pp. 42–43.
45. Ibid., p. 85.
46. *The Critique of Political Economy*, p. 43.
47. Cf. ibid., pp. 42–43; *Capital*, 1, p. 147.
48. *The Critique of Political Economy*, p. 42; our italics.
49. Ibid., p. 43; our italics.
50. Cf. *Grundrisse*, p. 404.
51. *Capital*, 2, p. 127.
52. *Capital*, 1, p. 202.
53. Cf. ibid.
54. *Grundrisse*, pp. 455–56.
55. Ibid., p. 404.
56. Ibid., p. 405.
57. Ibid., p. 406. Thus, one must admit, along with Marx, that capital finds its limit in "alien consumption" and that "the indifference of value as such towards use value is thereby brought into . . . [a] false position" (ibid., p. 407).
58. Ibid., p. 408.
59. Ibid., p. 409.
60. Ibid., p. 234.
61. *The Critique of Political Economy*, p. 124.
62. *Grundrisse*, p. 271.
63. Ibid., p. 646; "particular nature of use value" and "determinant . . . form" are italicized by Marx.
64. *Capital*, 1, p. 177.
65. *Grundrisse*, p. 267.
66. Ibid., p. 305.
67. Ibid., p. 295; our italics.
68. Ibid., pp. 259–60; cf. also *Capital*, 1, p. 153.
69. Ibid., pp. 153–54.
70. Ibid., p.154. Marx cites Sismondi's definition of capital: "portion fructifiante de la richesse accumulée . . . valeur permanente, multipliante," *Nouveaux principes de l'économie politique*, I, pp. 88–89; in French in the English translation, ibid., p. 155.
71. Cf. *Capital*, 1, pp. 158, 159, 160.

72. Ibid., p. 163.

73. Cf. Condillac, "Le commerce et le gouvernement" (1776), in *Mélanges d'économie politique* (Paris, 1847), p. 267, quoted by Marx, *Capital*, 1, p. 159. It is only because he confuses use-value with exchange-value that Condillac can believe that the advantage resulting from the usefulness of the product signifies its superior exchange-value.

74. *Capital*, 1, p. 166.

75. Ibid., p. 167.

76. Ibid., p. 175.

77. Ibid.

78. Ibid., pp. 175–76; our italics.

79. Ibid., pp. 194–95; our italics.

80. *Grundrisse*, p. 631.

81. *Capital*, 1, p. 195; cf. also: ". . . surplus-value . . . like the portion of value which replaces the variable capital advanced in wages, is a value newly created by the laborer during the process of production . . ." (*Capital*, 2, p. 387).

82. *Grundrisse*, p. 632; "value-positing" italicized by Marx; "the use value of labor is itself," our italics.

83. *Capital*, 1, p. 186; our italics.

84. Ibid., p. 197; our italics.

85. Cf. *Le Capital* in *Oeuvres*, I (La Pléiade), p. 1037; this text does not appear as such in the English translation of *Capital*, cf., 1, pp. 540–41.

86. *Capital*, 2, pp. 385–86.

87. Cf. *Le Capital* in *Oeuvres*, I (La Pléiade), p. 574; this text does not appear in the English translation of *Capital*, for as is explained in a note, ibid., p. 1636, this sentence was added by Marx for the French translation.

88. *Grundrisse*, p. 772.

89. *The Critique of Political Economy*, p. 30; our italics.

90. *Capital*, 2, p. 386; our italics.

91. *Capital*, 1, p. 195; our italics.

92. Ibid., p.192; our italics.

93. *Capital*, 3, p. 381; our italics.

94. *Capital*, 1, p. 206; our italics.

95. *Capital*, 3, p. 29; our italics.

96. Cf. *Grundrisse*, p. 274.

97. *Capital*, 2, p. 29.

98. Ibid., pp. 30–31.

99. *Grundrisse*, p. 284; our italics.

100. Ibid.

101. Cf. ibid., p. 288.

102. Ibid.

103. Ibid.

104. Cf. *Capital*, 1, p. 174.

105. Cf. "Wage Labour and Capital," pp. 82–83.

106. Cf. ibid., p. 82.

107. *Grundrisse*, p. 673.

108. Ibid., p. 674.

109. Ibid.

110. Ibid., p. 576.

111. Ibid.; our italics.

112. Ibid., p. 641; our italics.

113. Ibid., p. 641.

114. *Wages, Price and Profit*, p. 212.

115. Ibid.
116. Ibid.
117. Ibid.
118. Ibid.
119. Cf. *Grundrisse*, p. 312.
120. Cf. ibid., pp. 312–13.
121. Cf. ibid., p. 343.
122. Ibid., p. 363; our italics.
123. Ibid.
124. Ibid., p. 358; our italics.
125. Ibid., p. 363; our italics.
126. Ibid.
127. Ibid., pp. 363–64; our italics.
128. Ibid., p. 359; Marx's italics.
129. *Capital*, 3, p. 245.
130. *Grundrisse*, p. 360.
131. "Ego is the night of disappearance," *Realphilosophie*, Iena, Hegel, *Sämtliche Werke*, ed. Lasson, II, p. 185.
132. *Grundrisse*, pp. 360–61.
133. *Capital*, 1, p. 182; translation modified. (Last phrase in German text reads: "Sie funktioniren nur noch als gegenständliche Faktoren der Lebendigen Arbeit.")
134. Ibid., p. 183; our italics.
135. Ibid., p. 200. The analysis in the *Grundrisse* is obviously taken up again here; cf. *Grundrisse*, pp. 363–64.
136. *Capital*, 1, p. 183.
137. Ibid., p. 185.
138. *Grundrisse*, p. 364.
139. Ibid.
140. Ibid.
141. Ibid.; our italics.
142. Ibid.
143. Ibid.

Chapter 8: The Radical Reduction of Capital to Subjectivity

1. Cf. *Capital*, 3, pp. 145–46.
2. Cf. *Capital*, 2, p. 161.
3. Cf. ibid., p. 163.
4. Cf. ibid., pp. 164–65.
5. Cf. ibid., p. 188.
6. Ibid., pp. 163–64.
7. *Capital*, 1, p. 612.
8. Cf. ibid., p. 209.
9. Cf. ibid.: "That part of capital then, which is represented by the means of production, by the raw material, auxiliary material and the instruments of labor, does not, in the process of production, undergo any quantitative alteration of value. I therefore call it the constant part of capital, or, more shortly, constant capital. On the other hand, that part of capital, represented by labor-power, does, in the process of production, undergo an alteration of value. It both reproduces the equivalent of its own value, and also produces an excess, a surplus-value, which may itself vary, may be more or less according to circumstances. This part of capital is continually being transformed from a constant into a variable magnitude. I therefore call it the variable part of capital, or, variable capital."

10. Ibid.; our italics.

11. *Capital*, 2, pp. 219–20.

12. Ibid., p. 222; our italics.

13. Ibid., p. 221; our italics.

14. *Capital*, 1, p. 210.

15. Ibid.

16. Ibid., pp. 210–11.

17. Ibid., p. 213.

18. Ibid., p. 214. It must be noted that this rather extraordinary idea of positing constant capital $c = 0$ was suggested to Marx by Smith himself, as this text from Book Two shows: "with Adam Smith the entire value of the social product resolves itself into revenue, into $v + s$, so that the constant capital-value is set down as zero" (*Capital*, 2, p. 475). But Marx's stroke of genius was to give a radical meaning to this point of view, which, by reducing constant capital to zero, allows the variable capital to be isolated, whereas in Smith the situation is reversed. Because Smith confuses variable capital with wages, he reduces it to a fixed value whose variation is then incomprehensible and, in the same stroke, reduces it to circulating capital so that the specificity of variable capital is lost twice over. We see here how one and the same thesis ($c = 0$) can lead to diametrically opposed consequences; in one case it can completely cloud the essence of the phenomenon studied (surplus-value) and in the other case can lead to its clarification.

19. *Capital*, 1, p. 214.

20. *Capital*, 3, p. 145.

21. Let us note that setting constant capital aside is precisely the only method that permits calculating the real rate of surplus-value at the same time as it defines the scientific concept of surplus-value. Cf. ibid., pp. 215–16.

22. Ibid., p. 214; our italics.

23. Ibid., p. 147.

24. Cf. *Capital*, 1, pp. 538–39.

25. Cf. *Wages, Price and Profit*, p. 213.

26. Ibid.

27. Ibid., p. 537. As early as the first chapter of *Capital*, Marx stated: "Human labor-power in motion, or human labor, creates value, but is not itself value" (ibid., p. 51).

28. It is indeed this passivity of living praxis that Marx has in mind when he speaks of a "natural power."

29. *Capital*, 3, p. 29.

30. *The Poverty of Philosophy*, p. 55.

31. Ibid.

32. *Grundrisse*, p. 551.

33. A statement of Ricardo quoted by Marx in the *Grundrisse*, p. 561.

34. *Capital*, 1, p. 538.

35. Ibid.

36. Ibid., pp. 539–40.

37. Cf. ibid., pp. 540–41.

38. *Capital*, 2, p. 28.

39. *Capital*, 1, pp. 535–36.

40. Ibid., p. 170.

41. Ibid., p. 171; our italics. The constant presupposition of the living individual, which makes him the irreducible prior condition, the condition for every economic determination, is also evident in this singular declaration concerning the primary relation between the individual and the market economy, his entrance into this economy: "In order to be sold as a commodity in the market, labor must at all events exist before it is sold" (ibid., p. 535).

Conclusion: Socialism

1. Cf. *Grundrisse*, p. 603.
2. Ibid., pp. 668–69; our italics.
3. Ibid., p. 670; our italics.
4. *Capital*, 2, p. 124.
5. *Grundrisse*, p. 692.
6. Ibid.; our italics.
7. Ibid., pp. 692–93; our italics.
8. Ibid., p. 693.
9. Ibid., p. 695.
10. Ibid., p. 693; our italics.
11. Ibid., p. 706.
12. Cf. ibid.
13. Ibid., p. 705.
14. *The German Ideology*, p. 37; our italics. This identification which is made between production and the very existence of individuals, the nature of their life, is a constant in Marx's work. As an example, let us quote the following passage in *Capital*, in which this identification is asserted in reference to production and hence in reference to the peasant population: "Long before the period of Modern Industry, co-operation and the concentration of the instruments of labor in the hands of a few, gave rise, in numerous countries where these methods were applied in agriculture, to great, sudden and forcible revolutions *in the modes of production, and consequentially, in the conditions of existence, and the means of employment of the rural populations*" (*Capital*, 1, p. 430; our italics).
15. *Grundrisse*, p. 702.
16. Ibid., p. 704.
17. Ibid., p. 693.
18. Ibid., p. 694; our italics.
19. *Capital*, 1, p. 361; our italics.
20. Ibid., p. 364; our italics.
21. *Grundrisse*, pp. 705–706; our italics.
22. *The German Ideology*, p. 37.
23. *The Critique of Political Economy*, p. 34.
24. Ibid., p. 85; cf. ibid., p. 32.
25. Ibid., p. 45.
26. Ibid.; our italics.
27. *Capital*, 1, p. 78.
28. *The Critique of Political Economy*, p. 33.
29. Ibid.; our italics.
30. Ibid., pp. 33–34; our italics. It is because the social character of labor, in the sense of a real character, is understood by Marx as an original character that he conceives private labor and private property, on the contrary, as the historical effect and the result of the dissolution of the primitive mode of production: "A careful study of Asiatic, particularly Indian, forms of communal property would indicate that the disintegration of different forms of primitive communal ownership gives rise to diverse forms of property" (ibid., p. 33). Likewise, in the *Grundrisse* we find: "The system of production founded on private exchange is, to begin with, the historic dissolution of this naturally arisen communism" (p. 882).
31. *Capital*, 1, p. 77; our italics. Is there any need to point out that this text by itself provides clear confirmation of the theory of classes which we have proposed in these investigations, an interpretation which is also valid for social relations in the market

economy because, instead of changing anything about the fact that the relations of production are constituted by the very praxis of the individuals at work, an economy such as this, or capitalism, reposes, on the contrary, on this fact and is limited to "disguising" it?

32. " . . . articles of utility become commodities, only because they are products of the labor of private individuals . . ." (ibid., p. 77).

33. Ibid., p. 73.

34. Ibid.

35. *Grundrisse*, pp. 225–26.

36. Ibid., p. 226.

37. *Capital*, 1, p. 79. What follows this passage—"But they are founded . . . on the immature development of man individually, who has not yet severed the umbilical cord that unites him with his fellowmen in a primitive tribal community . . ."—is of the greatest interest: it confirms the critique of the Hegelian concept of the political man as defined by the collectivity and as realized in it, and shows incontestably that Marx's thought continues to be governed by the radical presupposition of a philosophy of individual development, at the very moment when he encounters historical socialism.

38. *The German Ideology*, p. 86.

39. *Capital*, 1, p. 79.

40. *Grundrisse*, p. 171.

41. Ibid.

42. Ibid., pp. 171–72.

43. Ibid., p. 172.

44. *Capital*, 1, pp. 78–79.

45. *Capital*, 2, p. 358.

46. It is therefore impossible to agree with Mandel's statement that Marx "categorically refused to identify the necessity for an accounting in terms of labor-time (which applies to every human society, except perhaps to the most advanced form of communist society) and the indirect expression of this accounting in the form of exchange-value. And he explicitly affirmed that, when the private ownership of the means of production is replaced by that of the associated producers, the market production will cease, giving way to a direct accounting in terms of work-hours." So that "one cannot assert that for Marx all living social labor would necessarily take the form of abstract value-creating labor" (*La formation de la pensée économique de Karl Marx*, pp. 48–49). What this author fails to see is that the indirect account of labor in the form of exchange-value presupposes its direct account, which is, as such, constitutive of abstract labor and which presupposes it. In *Capital* the problematic of abstract labor is part of the analysis of the market economy, not of that of capitalism.

47. Must it be recalled that in a communist system surplus-labor does not disappear totally? "Only by suppressing the capitalist form of production could the length of the working-day be reduced to the necessary labor-time. But even in that case the latter would extend its limits. . . . because a part of what is now surplus-labor, would then count as necessary labor; I mean the labor of forming a fund for reserve and accumulation" (*Capital*, 1, p. 530).

48. Ibid., p. 484; on the theory of education in its connection with the problematic of the division of labor and of individual subjectivity, cf. *supra*, pp. 109–17.